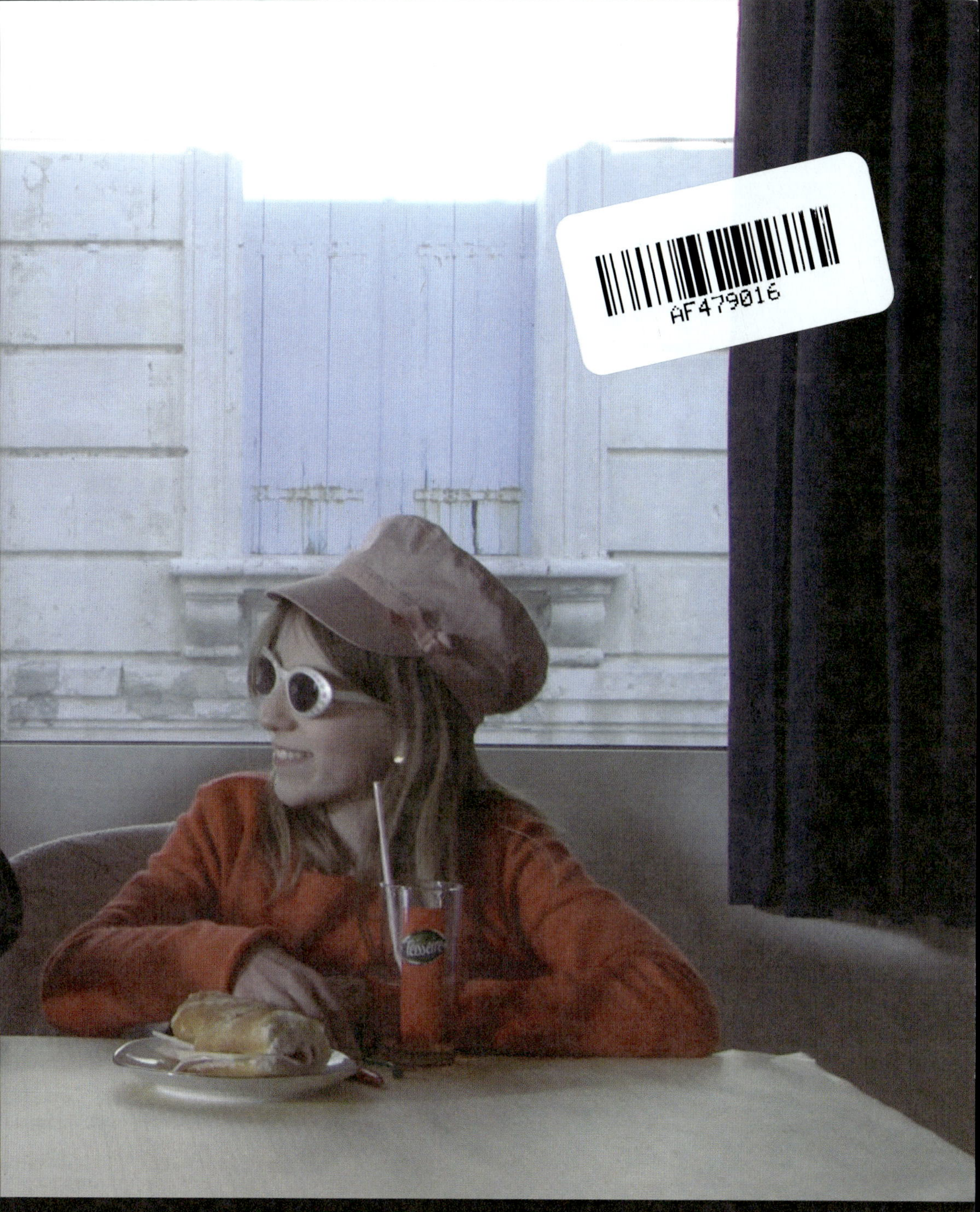

MY NAME IS HMMM....

a film by Agnès Troublé aka agnès b.
with Lou-Lélia Demerliac and Douglas Gordon

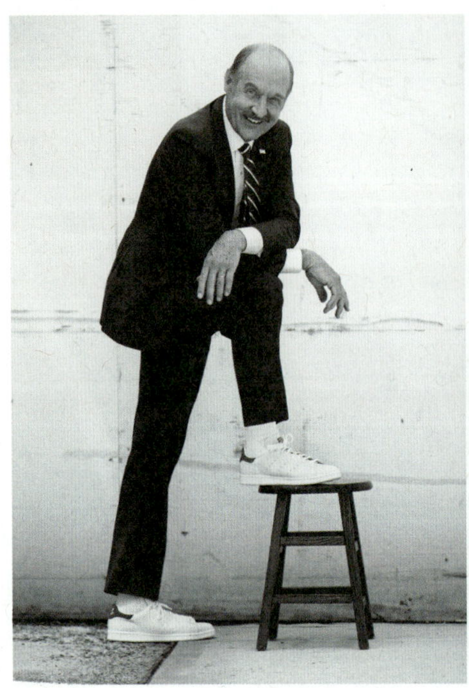

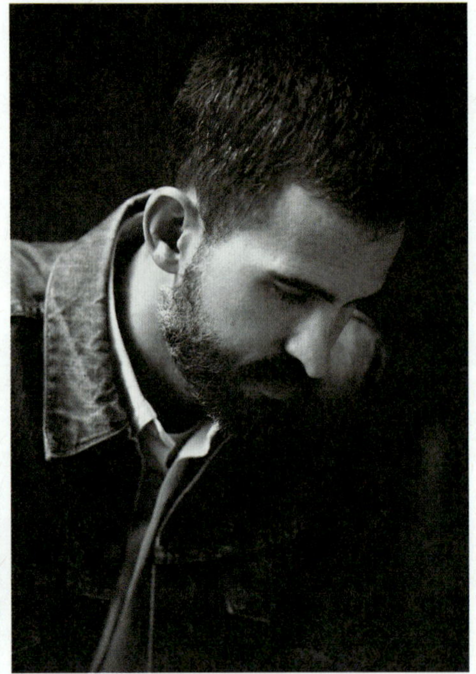

THE
STAN SMITH

EST. / 1973

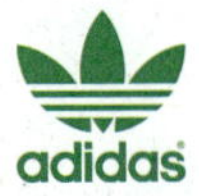

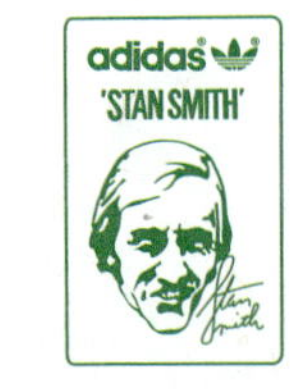

#STANSMITH

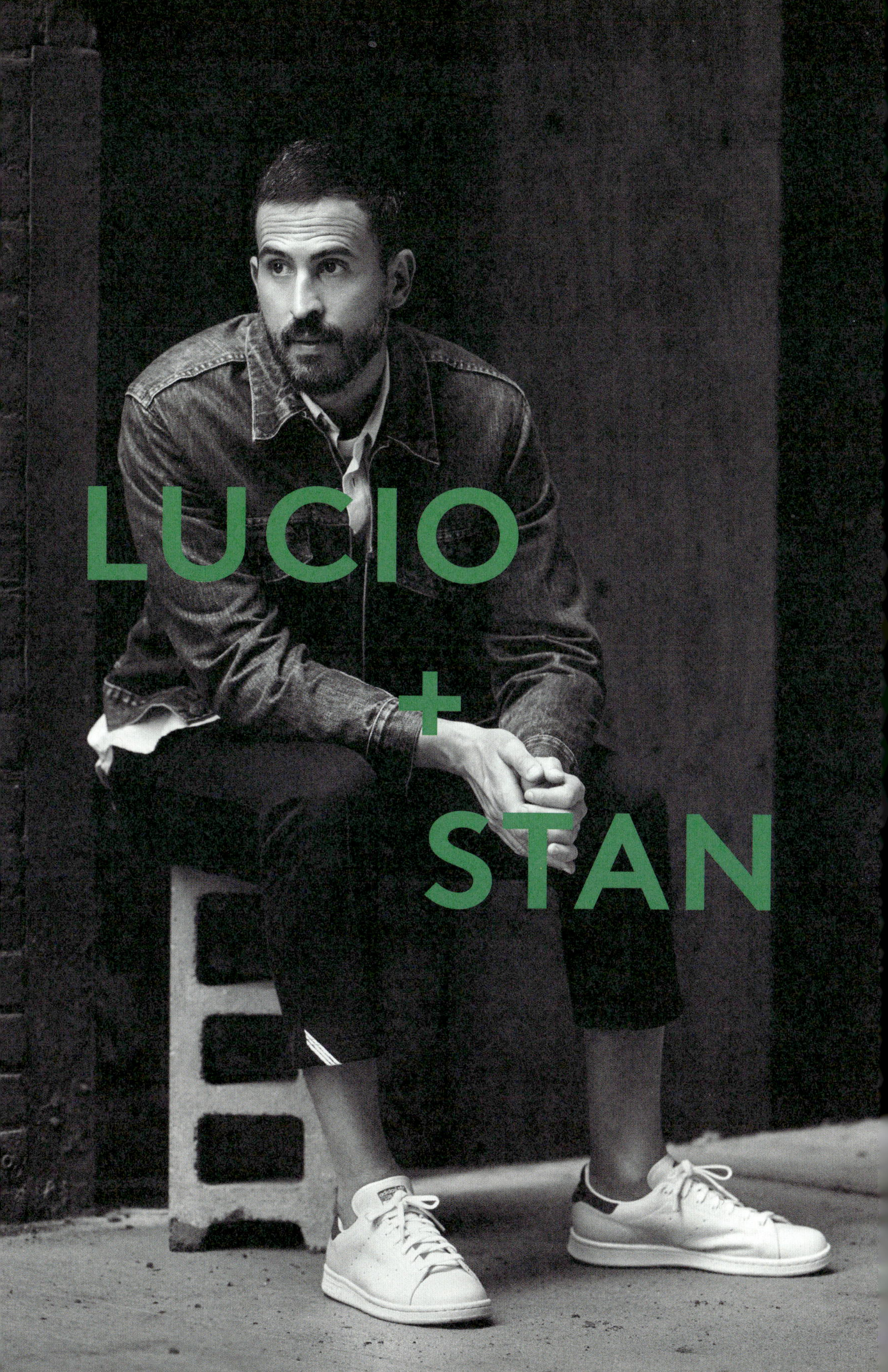

LUCIO
+
STAN

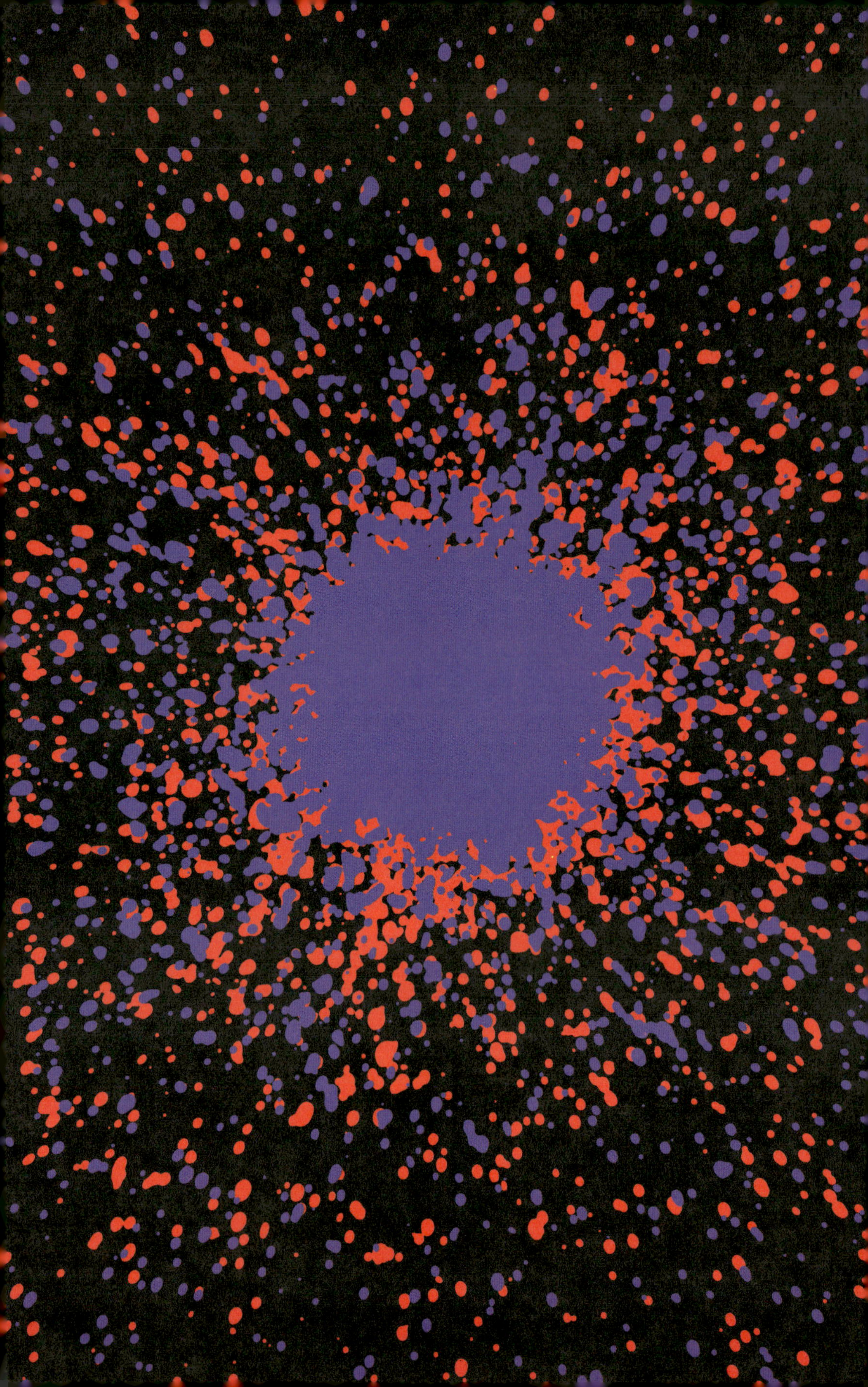

Lesser Yellowlegs

New York
Randall's Island Park
May 9–12, 2014
friezenewyork.com

Tickets on sale
February 2014

FRIEZE
ART
FAIR

'Frieze Art Fair
electrifies New York'
The Wall Street Journal

'Ground-breaking'
Financial Times

Media Partner
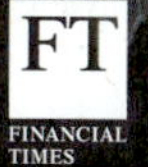
FT
FINANCIAL
TIMES

Main sponsor
Deutsche Bank
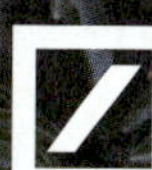

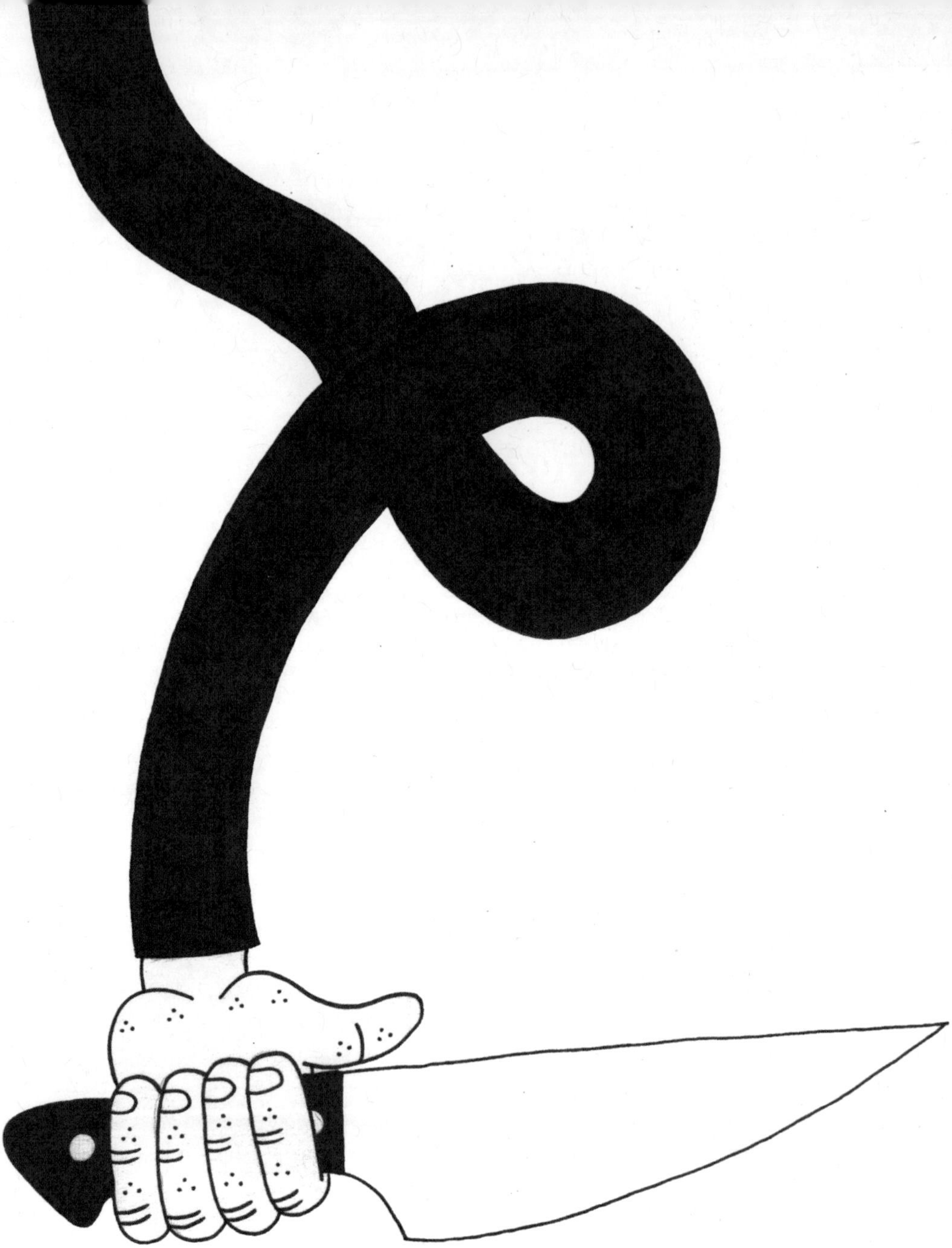

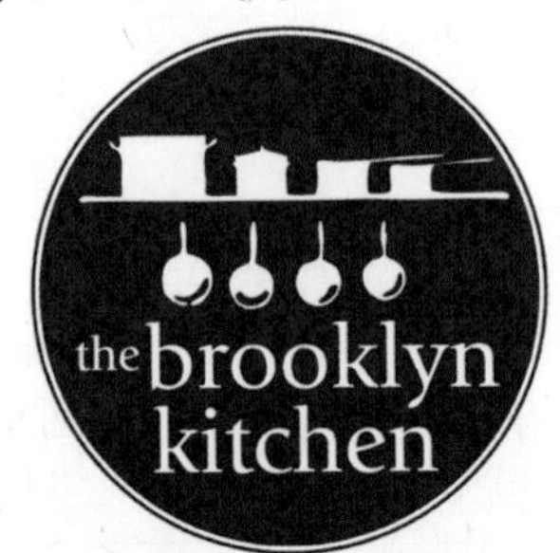
EAT REAL FOOD

WILLIAMSBURG
100 FROST ST.

BROOKLYN, NY 11211

the brooklyn kitchen

HELL'S KITCHEN
600 11TH AVE

NEW YORK, NY 10036

THEBROOKLYNKITCHEN.COM

Contents

APOLOGY

Editor-in-Chief / Art Director: Jesse Pearson
Design Director: Stacy Wakefield-Forte
Web Development: animalstyle.biz
Ad Sales: Gabe Rosner

Copy Editor / Proofreader: Sam Frank
Occasional Illustrated Explosions: Tara Sinn

Insight, advice, and camaraderie were gratefully received, as always, from Pickle.

Cover photograph made by Roe Ethridge for *Apology* while discussing with this magazine's editor the filial responsibilities of college football fandom and the triumphs and tribulations of Bama and FSU in 2013.

ISBN 978-0-9859326-2-6

Printed in Canada by The Prolific Group on FSC-certified paper with soy-based inks. All papers used are acid free. The interior paper contains FSC-certified, 100% post-consumer fiber. 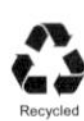

Distributed throughout North America, the United Kingdom, Asia, and Europe by D.A.P. / Artbook.com

We welcome submissions but cannot promise replies or the return of materials. Find our electronic and physical addresses at apologymagazine.com.

Apology also accepts telepathic feedback sent via the unified field.

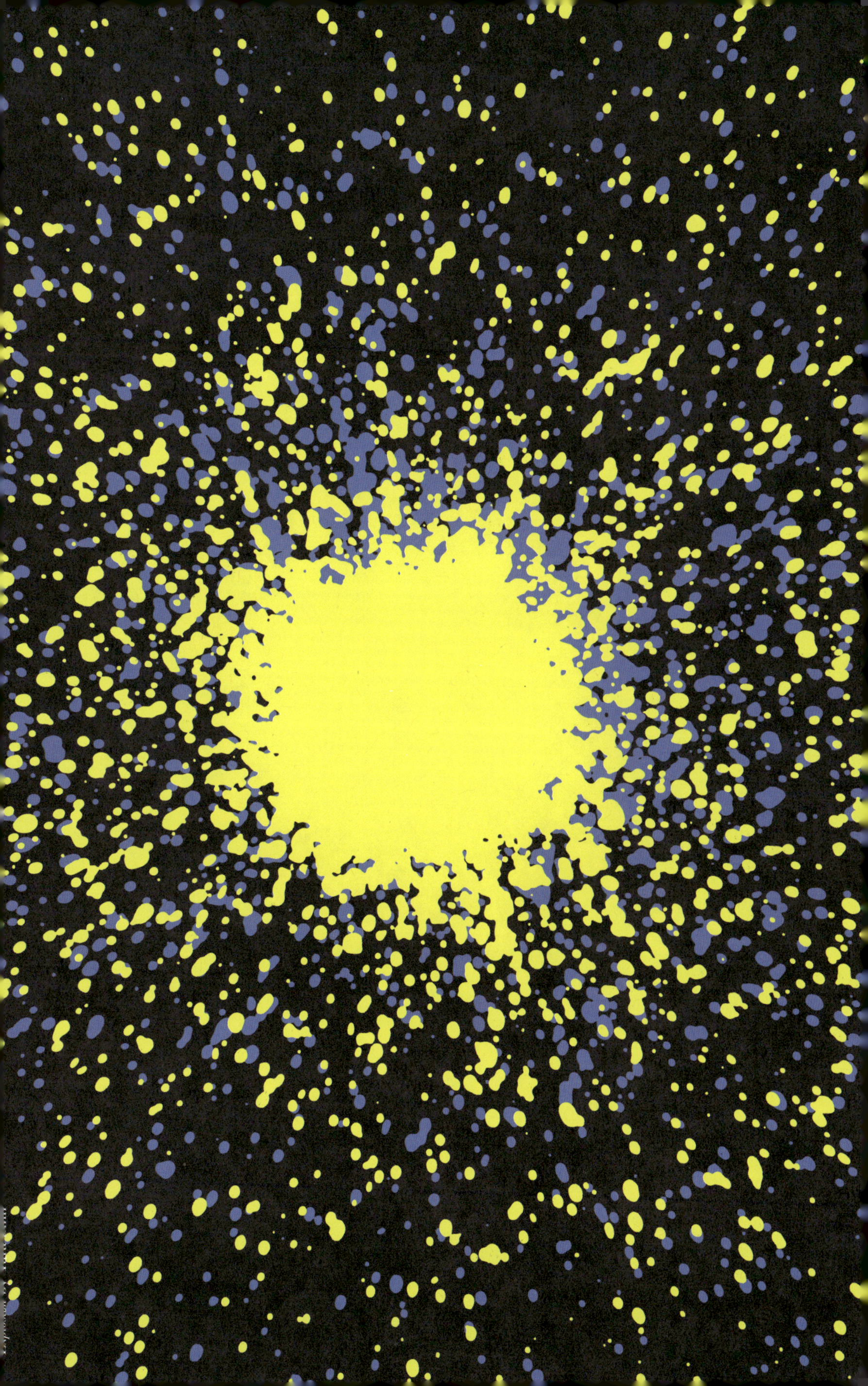

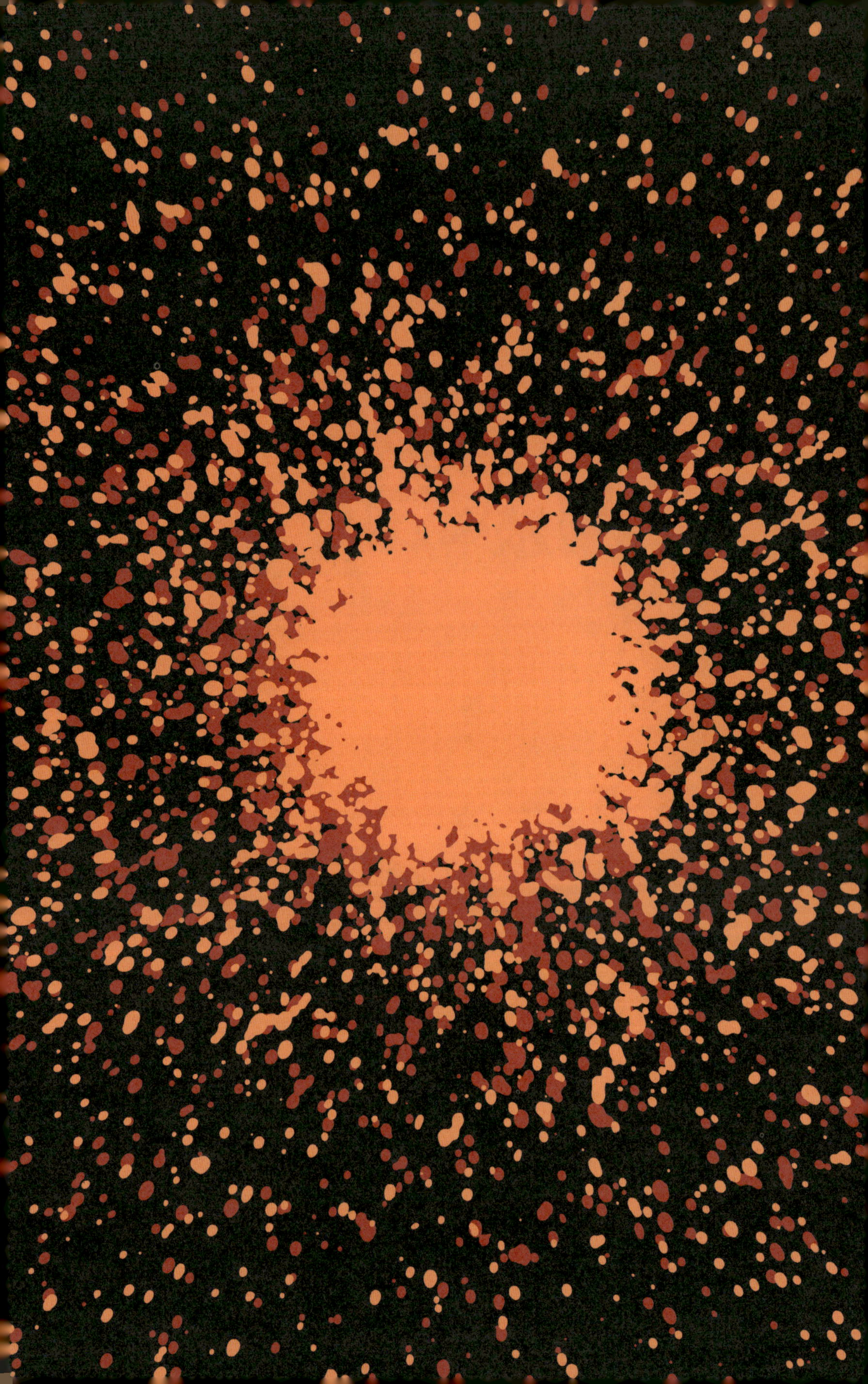

Percussion, salt and honey,
A quivering in the thighs;
He shakes me all over again,
Eros who cannot be thrown,
Who stalks on all fours
Like a beast.

—Sappho

Welcome to the third issue of *Apology*!

11 NEW PHOTOS BY DANIEL ARNOLD

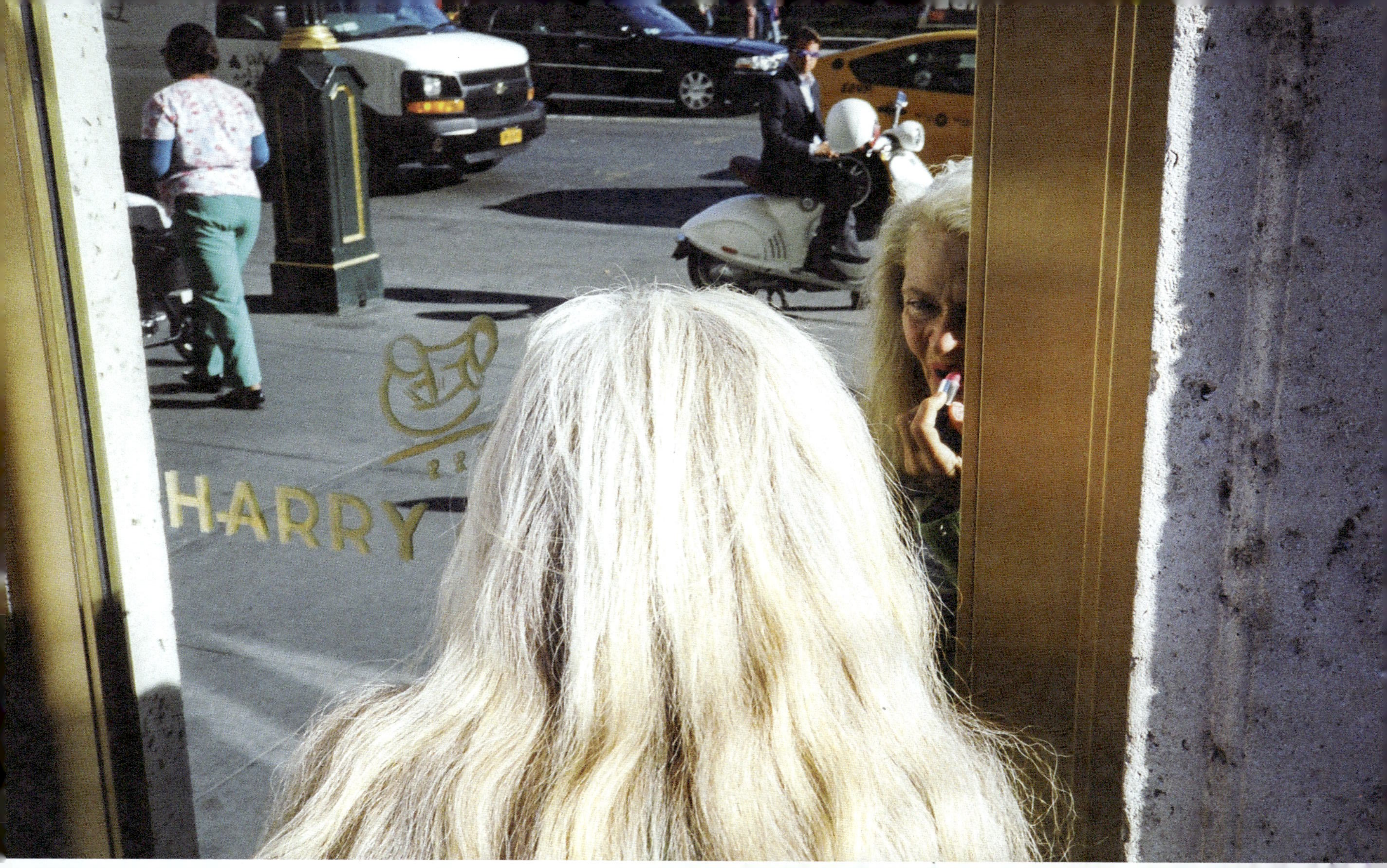
HARRY

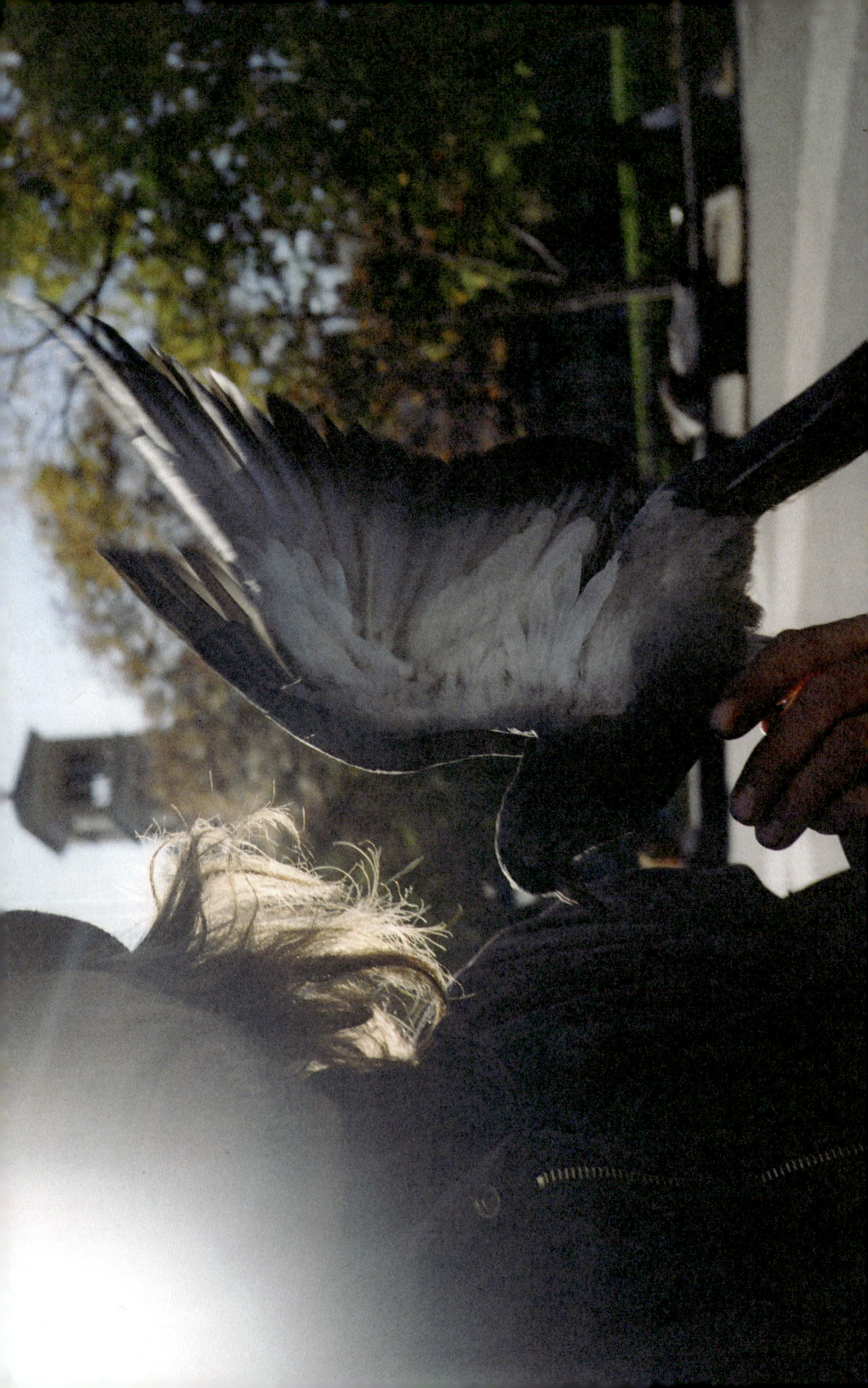

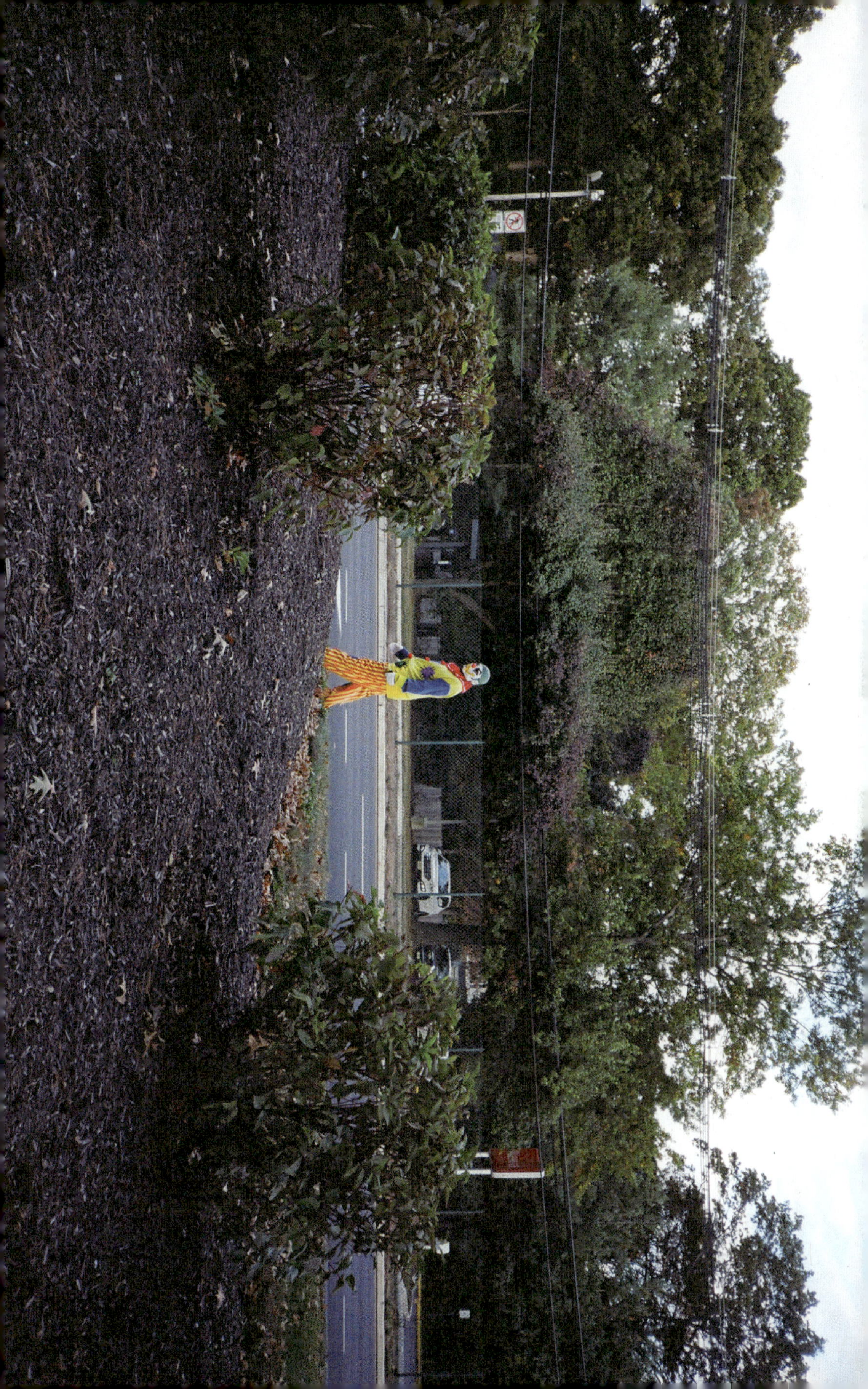

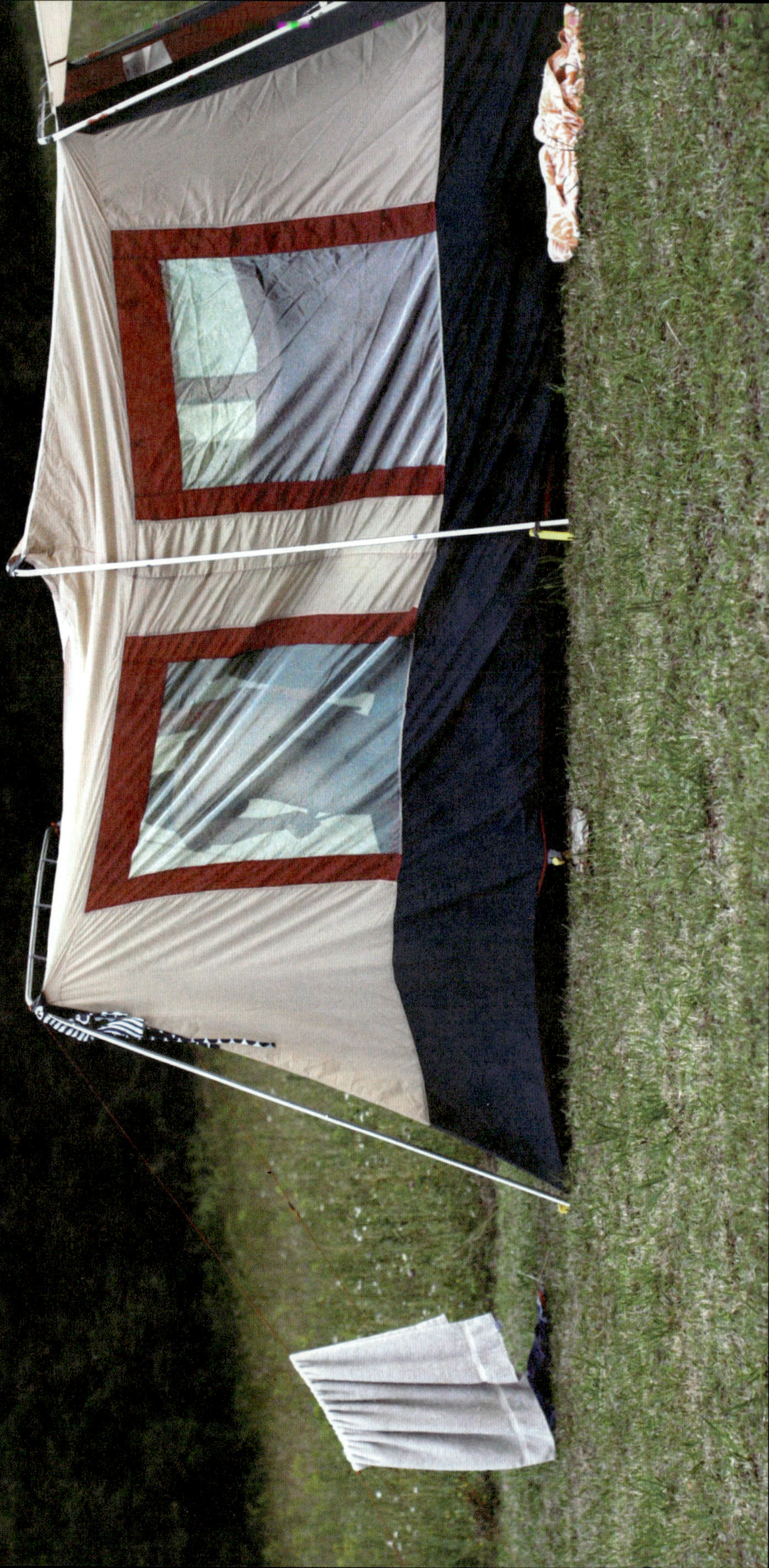

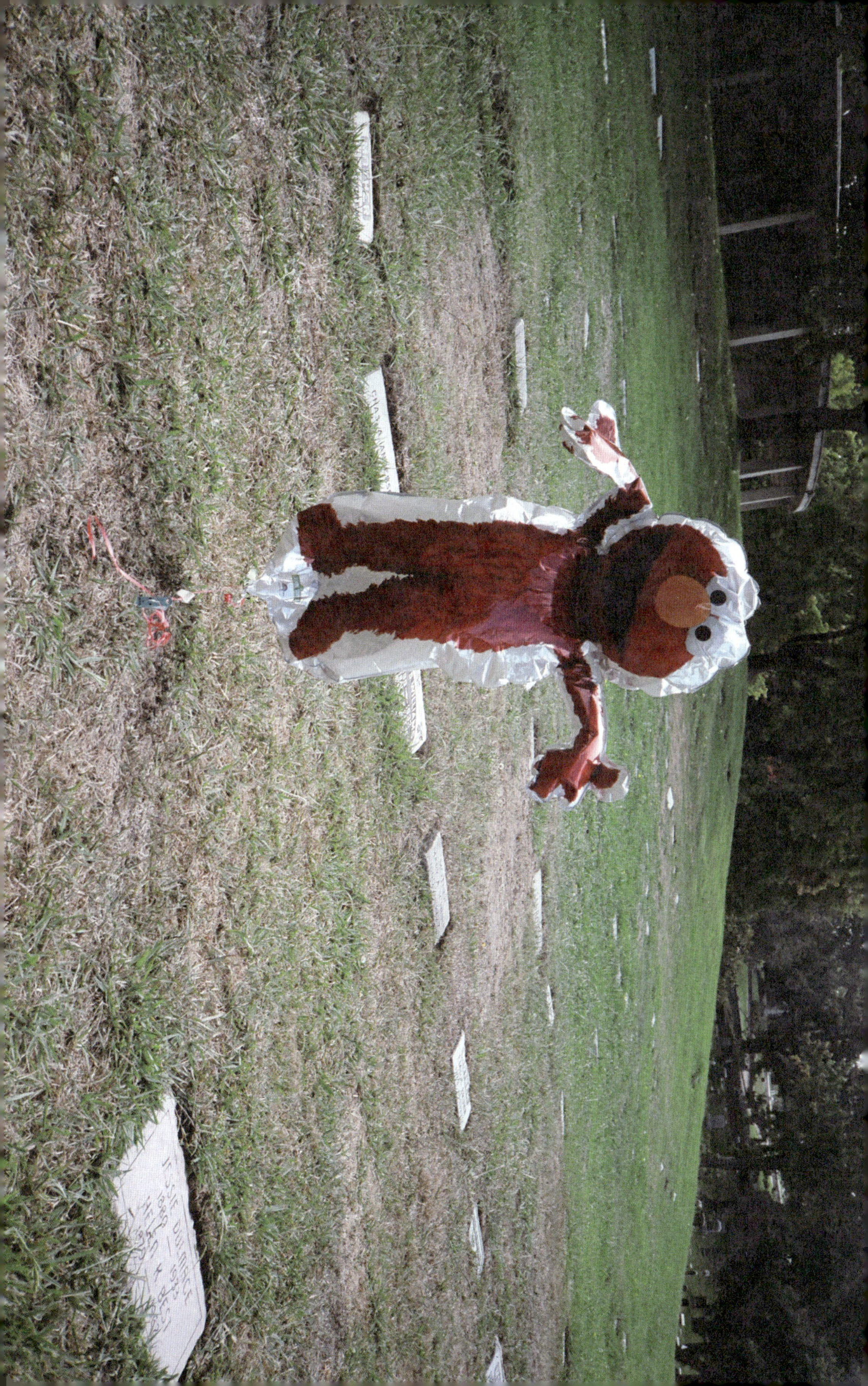

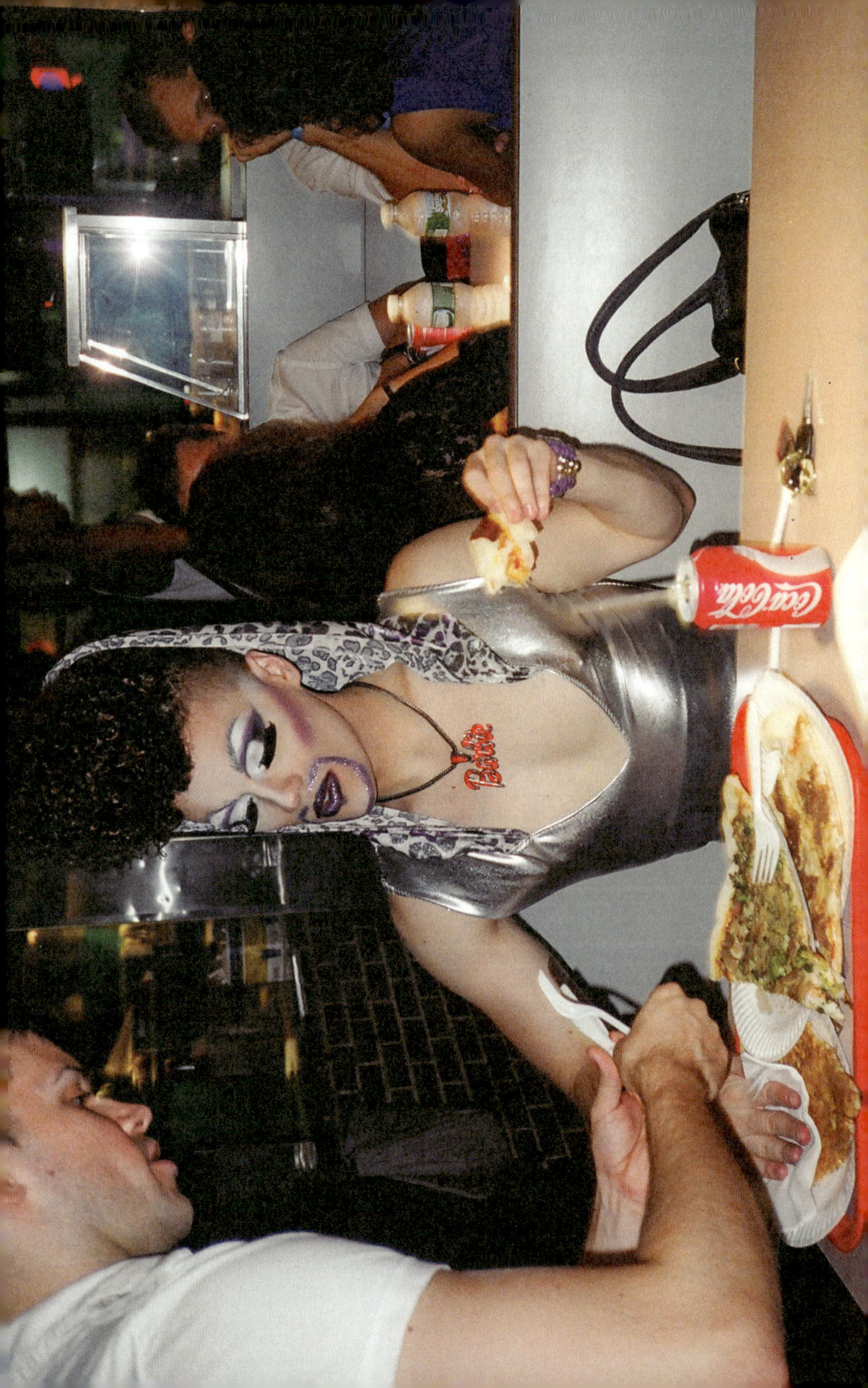

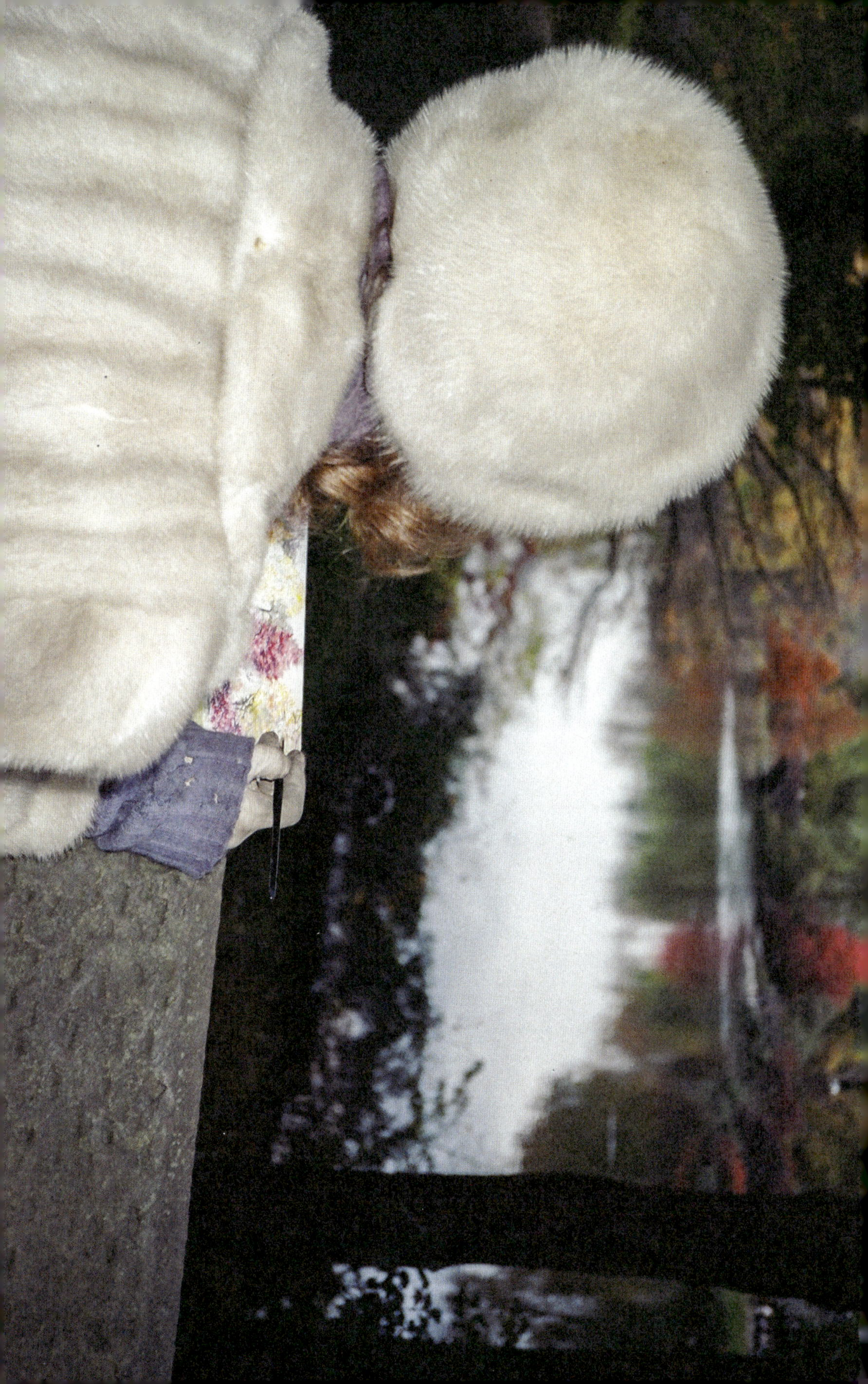

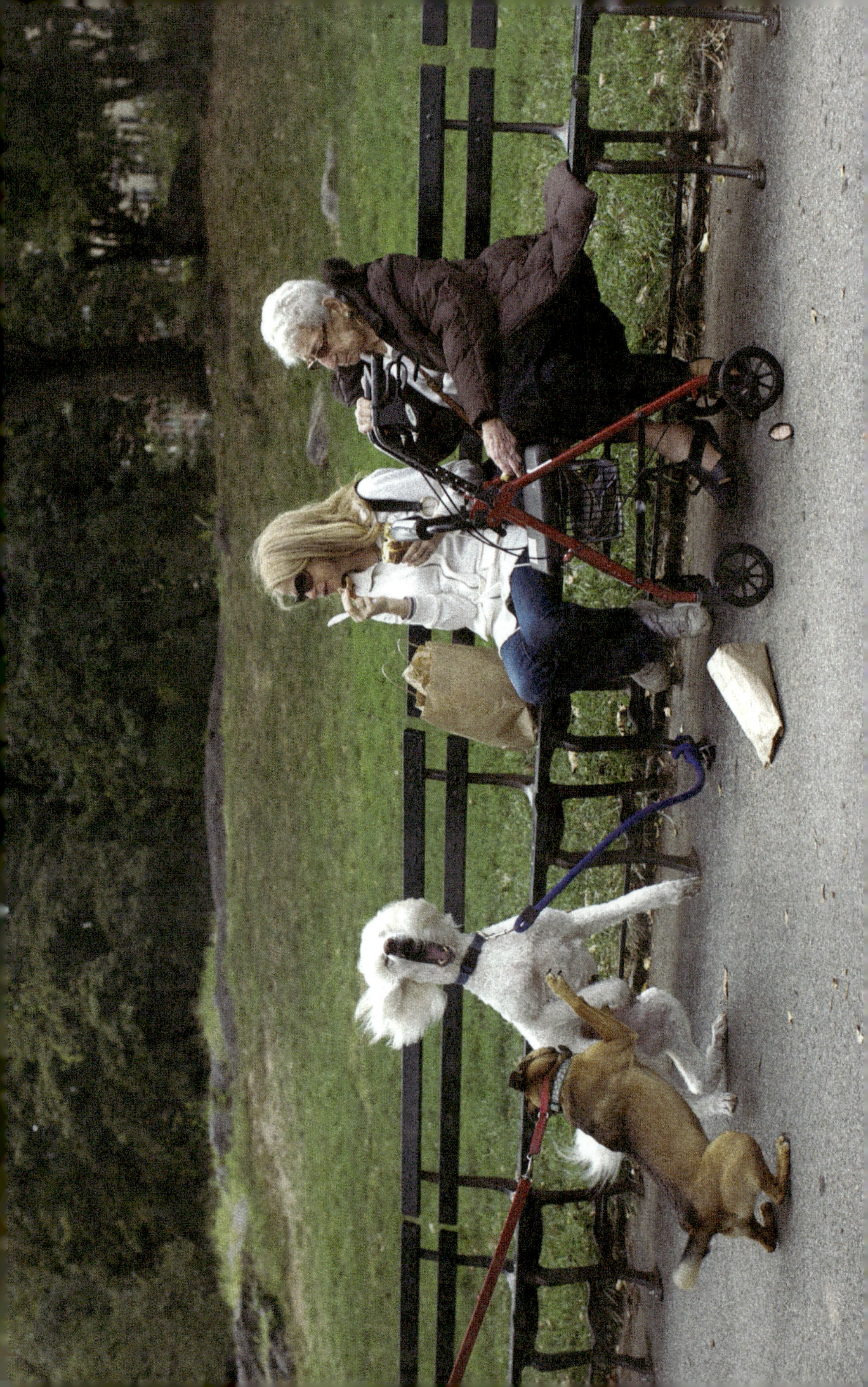

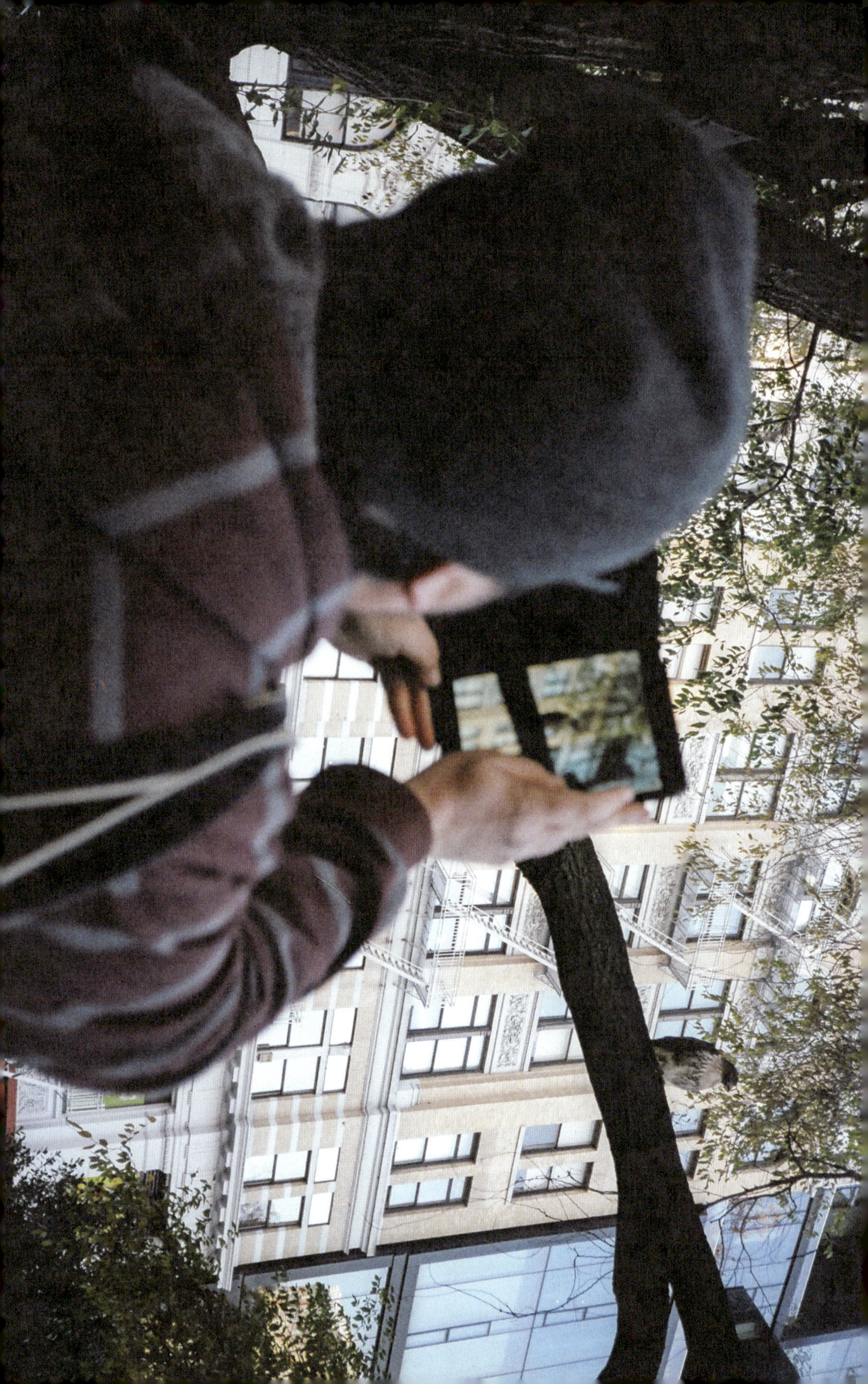

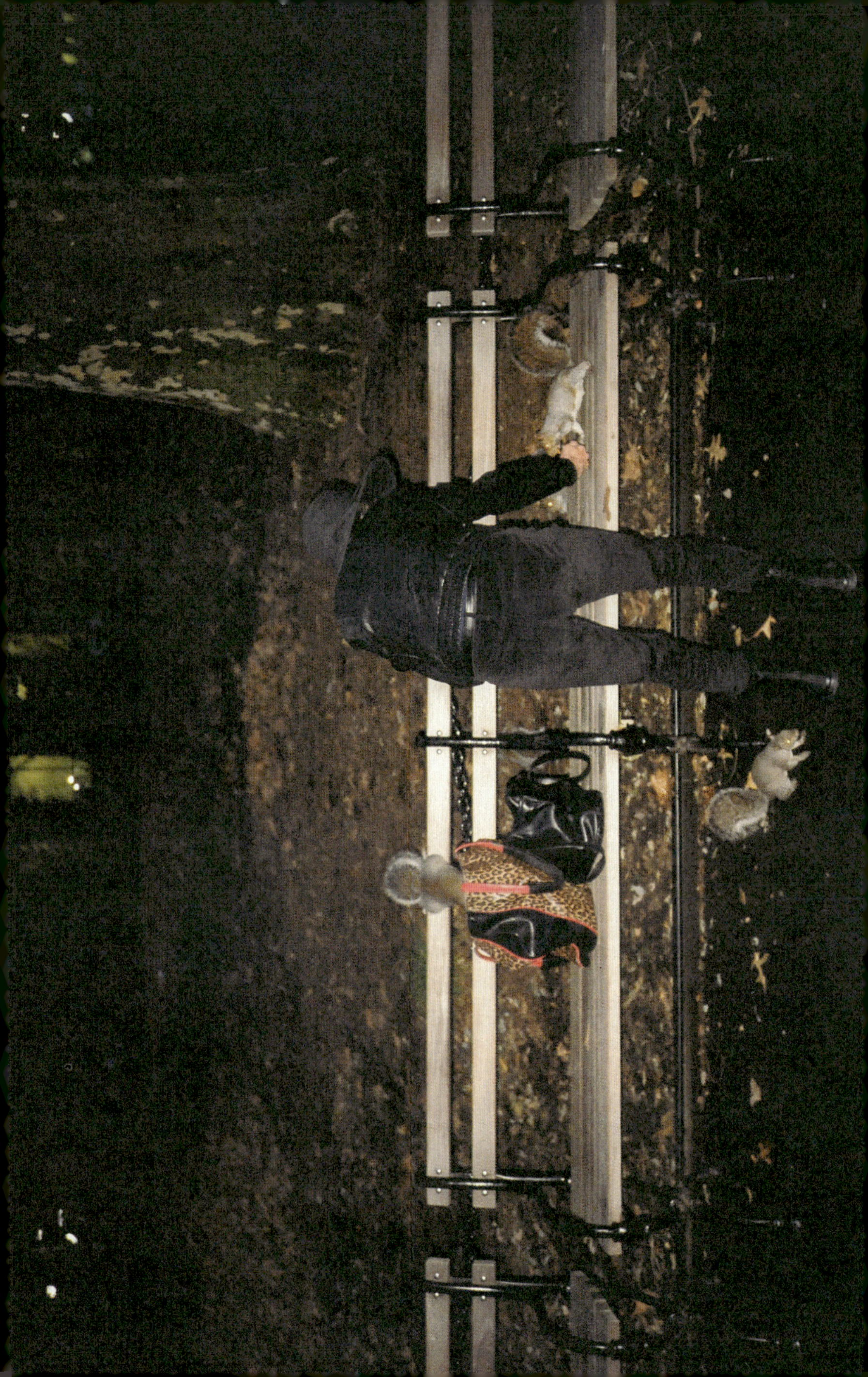

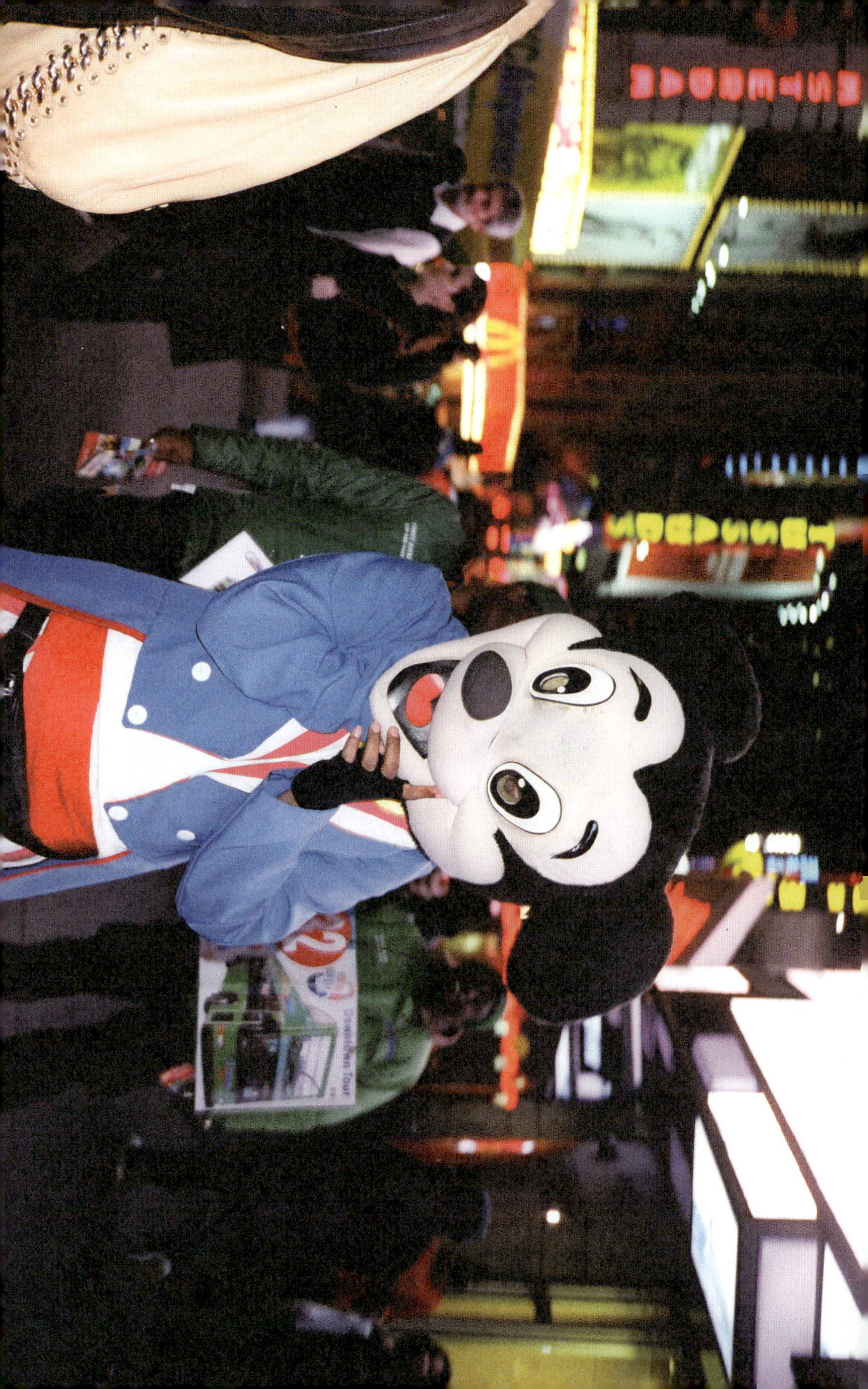

Nine Poems by

LEOPOLDINE CORE

VACATION

We're peeing on
God's rosebush
but God pees too
If God doesn't pee
what good
is he

BIRDS COME HERE

to shit
well
just one
hawk

ELF

You're like a milkmaid
who transitioned
There are these
little buds
left

ONE NIGHT

you were stumbling into bed
with a bowl of yogurt
to watch Mary Tyler Moore
drunk
and you hit your head on the wall

you were so delicate
you got black eyes
real bad ones
red yellow
blue

you didn't know then
or maybe you knew
you'd be the rat king

you

HAPPINESS

wait you actually feel terrible
when your anus is inside out
& dragging behind you
& birds are pecking out your eyes
& little men
& big men
are stabbing you with forks

ICE CREAM

is baby food
you get whacked
with a large
cold
tit
and see stars

YEAH

What do you do when you wanna fuck a bad artist?
I think you do it once.

MEATY

You know he was a fag.
You say that about everyone.
Well it's important.

AND HE IS JUST LIKE ME

I was not praying.
I was reading my poems to myself when God entered.
He was like so many people
who come near me.
He was an old man in a wheelchair
He had a rifle over his knees
And in the same breath he was a
young woman
young like me and watching.

You think I'm ridiculous, I said.

No. I think you're cunning. I'm crazy about you.

But why? I asked.

It's your thoughts. Your intolerance to heat. Your body complains loudly
wherever it goes.

But why would you love that? I asked.

I don't know, God said. It's what I have
to love.

Then he pointed to a picture of me
in his wallet
There you are suffering, he said. I love your frailty. It's like lace.

And this gave me a dirty feeling
And I looked into the pair of eggs
and the old man peeled away
like a mood
Then God was just an alien with no genitals at all
I love your fragile veins, it said
that's the feel of them
guitar strings
I love that you are dying it said with panting nostrils
right now
you are dying
and it gets me
off.

subscribe to Apology?

PRO	CON
Beauty	?
Learning	
Arousal	
Amusement	
Self-worth	
Will get me laid	
Is "cool"	
smells good	
It's just $	

APOLOGYMAGAZINE.COM

A Nature Poem
by Will Oldham

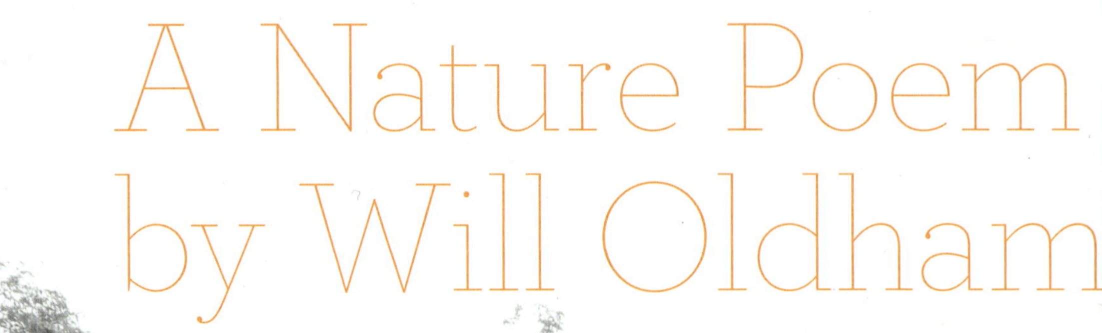

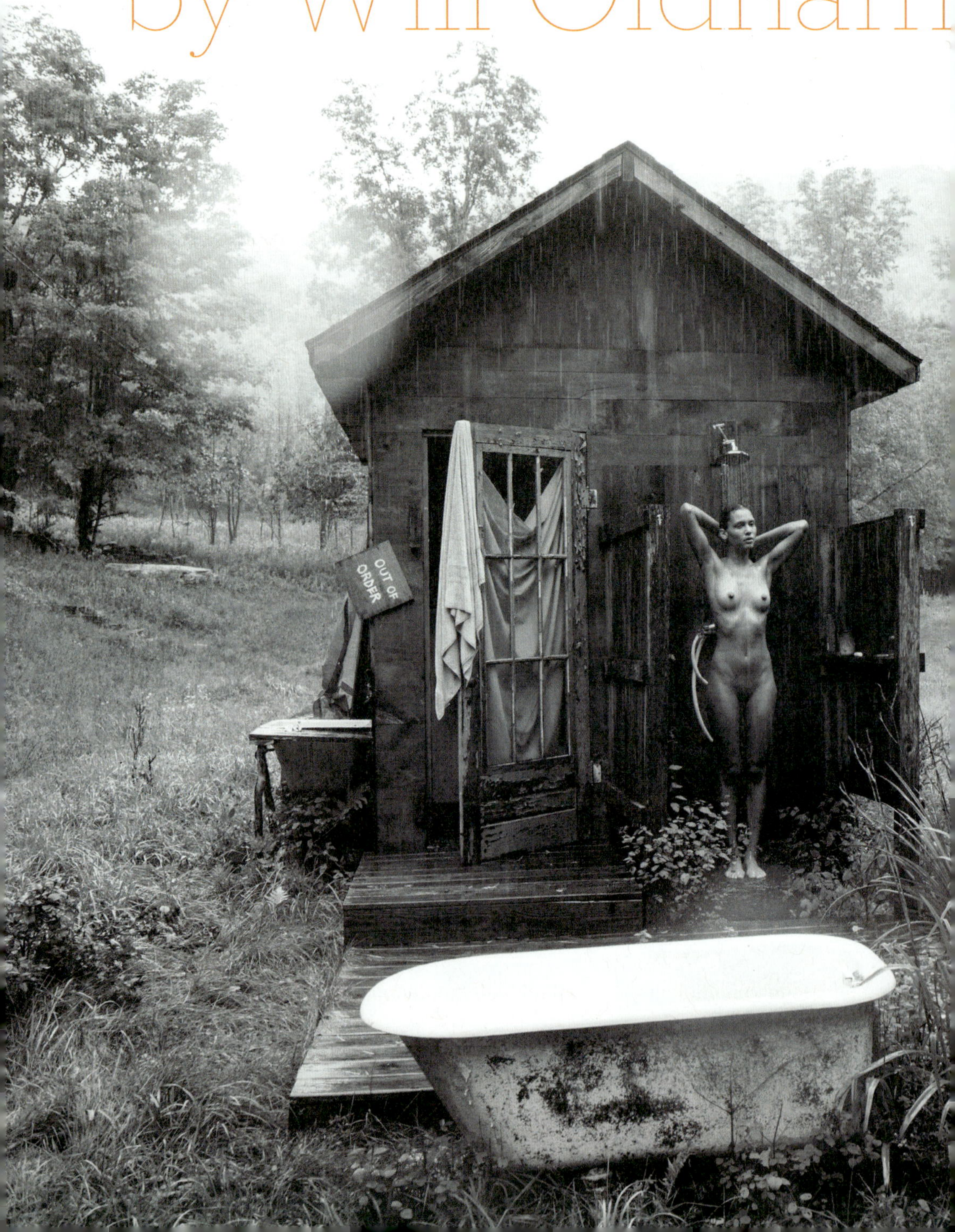

Fond of the earth's gray hairs,
And supportive of her malignancies
Especially when her malignancies are my own kinds
fighting among ourselves over who has the parasite's right.

Fond of holding things as they come to life
and of being fortunate enough to hold things
as they leave life behind. Not to kill!
Just to witness.

I like to look at living things among each other
And try to figure out how each thing
Is a variable equal to a rate of time passing

A whisker is one,
An ulna another,
a ring
Tree bark
Rockets.
A memory of a sung song.
And also the act of singing

Slow-moving time is the most fun of all.

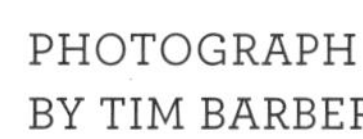

PHOTOGRAPH
BY TIM BARBER

Thank you Justin Davis
and David Berman.

THE THREE LITTLE PIGS

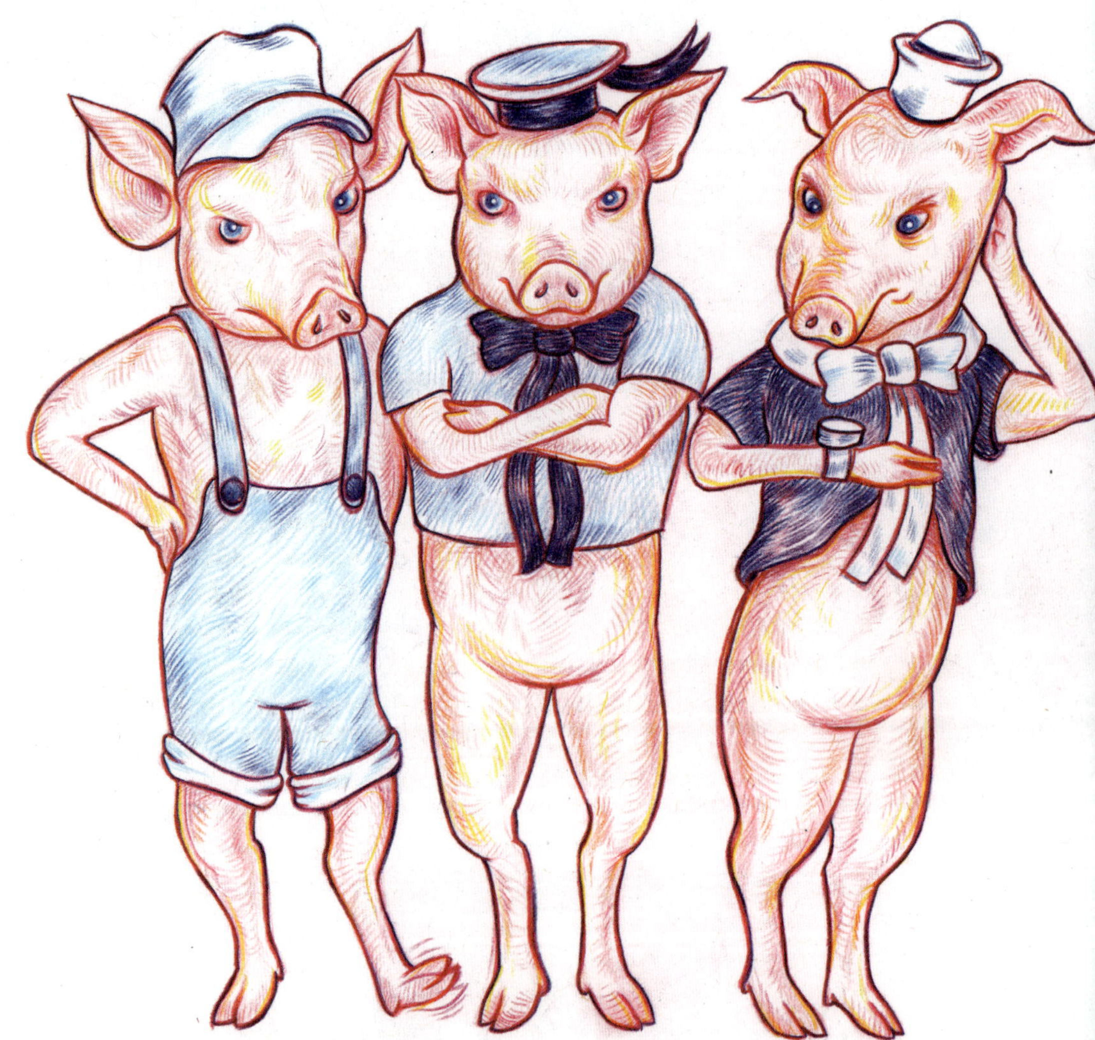

(WITH BACKSTORY)

By Scott Bradfield
Impatient Pigs *by Aiyana Udesen*

Once upon a time there were three little pigs.

They all had parents who had known one another in college. The college was located on a sunny hill in the Alps, and once there had been an avalanche that almost destroyed the college. But then the avalanche didn't quite happen since the sun came out—the sun having been created by the Big Bang many billions of years ago.

One little pig built his house out of straw. The straw came from a shop in Bromley that had opened shortly after World War II. Long before WWII occurred, there had been another war called World War I. Sadly, many men died in WWI. Those who lived through the war hoped it would never happen again.

The second little pig built his house out of wood. Wood comes from trees, which are often found in forests. The pigs used to live in the forest but eventually they wised up and moved into town. The town was built on an old Indian burial ground, but they never had any ghosts, not like in the famous Hollywood movie *Poltergeist*.

The third little pig built his house out of bricks. These bricks had been baked in a kiln by a master brick-maker named Ron Johnson. Ron was named after his father, who was named after *his* father. But his great-grandfather's name was Steve.

Eventually, the Big Bad Wolf came along, and since he hadn't eaten the day before, and the day before that he'd just had a sandwich, he determined to eat the three little pigs, since he had seen them at the market several years previously, and they had looked highly edible. But then he had bought a sandwich instead of eating them, and had regretted it ever since.

The Big Bad Wolf went to the first pig's house, but first he stopped by the laundrette and picked up his clothes, and picked up some toiletries at the pound shop, since the Big Bad Wolf was notoriously cheap with a quid. When he was a child, his dad had been overgenerous with money and the family had always been broke. Eventually his dad had gone to the poorhouse, leaving the Big Bad Wolf with lots of unresolved personal issues.

"Open your door!" the Big Bad Wolf said to the first little pig. "Even though I can see that your door was manufactured by the straw-maker, who doesn't make very sound doors since he never got into a decent profession, unlike his sister Hilda the dressmaker! If you don't open the door, I'll huff and I'll puff and—due to the extraordinarily powerful nature of my lungs, which is the result of having exercised a lot as a pup, especially in organized sports at school—I'll blow your house down!"

By this point, of course, all three of the little pigs had grown old and died. 🐾

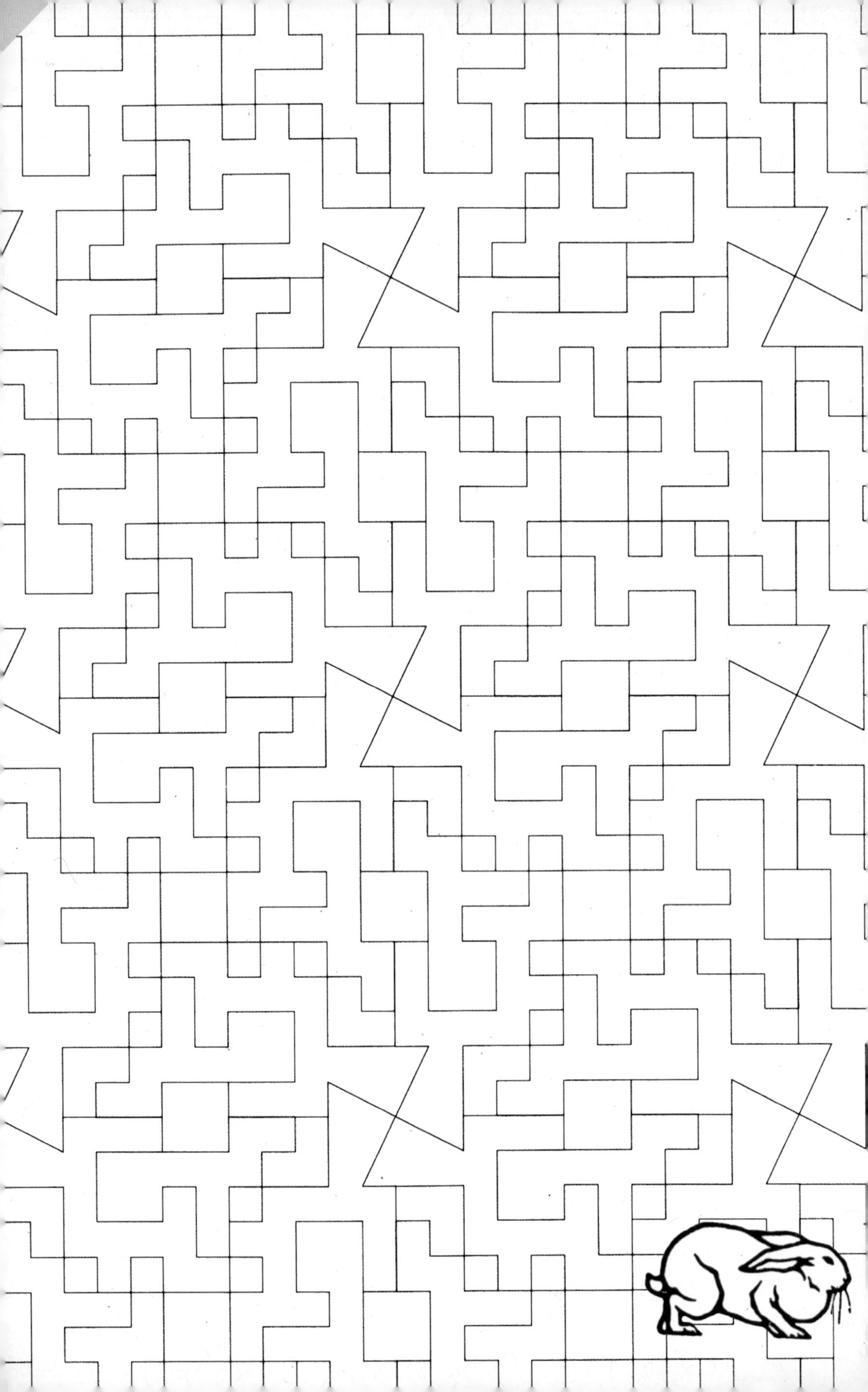

VARIABLES

By Steven Featherstone
Rabbit Plane *by Red Kuriak*

PRIMARY VARIABLES

1. Two unique sets of integers, hereafter referred to as Couple X and Couple Y, are traveling in a vehicle on a dark, rain-slick road in the province of Ontario, Canada.
2. The female integers form a subset of identical twins, equal in value.
3. The male integers form an unrelated subset that exists only in relation to the female integers.
4. A white rabbit hops unseen from the darkness onto the rain-slick road—directly in the path of the oncoming vehicle.
5. The female fraction of Couple Y emits a piercing scream.
6. The male fraction of Couple X applies the brake with sufficient force to transfer the vehicle's kinetic energy to its rear axle. The vehicle's rear tires lose traction with the rain-slick road, allowing the vehicle's front tires to pull the vehicle clockwise toward a ditch.
7. The vehicle's rear passenger tires regain traction, pulling the vehicle out of the skid.
8. The vehicle's front passenger tire crushes the rabbit.
9. Eleven meters from the point of impact the vehicle stops. Couple X and Couple Y exit the vehicle.
10. Couple X commit to an argument concerning the lateness of the hour.
11. Couple Y commit to an argument concerning the exact sequence of Variables #4 through #8 and the effect of the steadily falling rain.
12. The female integers redirect the attention of both sets to the status of the rabbit.
13. The two sets split into subsets as described in Variables #2 and #3. The subset of female integers waits in the car while the subset of male integers searches the roadside for large rocks.
14. The male integers euthanize the rabbit with two large rocks.
15. The subsets return to their original state, as observed in Variable #1.

COROLLARY VARIABLES

1.1 A full moon periodically reveals itself between scudding storm clouds in the dark sky. The reflected light of a full moon in the Northern Hemisphere, expressed in lux units, is 9—more than a city street at night (7 lux) but far less than typical home lighting (100 lux). This is sufficient brightness to illuminate ground features as small as a white rabbit, for example, as pointed out many times by the female fraction of Couple Y in her analysis of the situation.

2.1   The female integers share genetic material and, some hypothesize, share unspoken thoughts, although the latter is impossible to prove.

3.1   The male integers belong to this equation only through their unique relationships to the female integers. However, each male believes he shares a common and unspoken "bond" with the other male as a result of their many experiences, both positive and negative in value, with the female integers.

5.1   The male fraction of Couple X, startled and distracted by the female fraction of Couple Y's scream, believes this Variable to be the root mean cause of all Primary Variables that follow it.

6.1   The male fraction of Couple X drives because it has been determined through peer review that he is the most skilled driver, although he does not always operate vehicles in all situations involving transport of Couple X and Couple Y. Perhaps he drives on this particular night due to the unfavorable driving conditions, or because the female fraction of Couple X, to whom the vehicle is registered, is wearing high-heeled shoes that render her less capable of operating the vehicle's foot pedals. Whatever the reason, the male fraction of Couple X will often wish that he did not drive that night. Indeed, he will regret agreeing to attend a party hosted by a person he does not even like.

6.2   The male fraction of Couple Y feels equal to, if not greater than, the value of the male fraction of Couple X when it comes to driving, especially after the male fraction of Couple X locks the brakes in Variable #6, something he never would have done under those conditions, at night on a country road in the rain, although he remains silent on the subject.

8.1   Only the male fraction of Couple Y feels the slight "thump," transmitted through the vehicle's chassis, as the vehicle's front passenger tire crushes the rabbit.

12.1   In the near perfect dark, the rabbit is visible only as a quivering white spot at the road's edge. According to the female integers, the rabbit's struggle for life and the male integers' failure to act decisively prove that the male integers lack basic human empathy. According to the male integers, they lack only supernatural powers sufficient to revive a dead rabbit, and the female integers should stop being so irrational.

13.1   Being pragmatic integers, the male subset decides that the course of action with the best chance for a neutral outcome would be to euthanize the rabbit, regardless of whether or not its quiverings are merely involuntary nerve reflexes.

13.2   Over espresso at a café in Toronto six months from now, the female subset will recall sitting in the car that night, feeling rainwater trickling down their necks, listening to the slap-slap of the windshield wipers, watching the male subset stumble blindly along the roadside in search of large rocks, their faces lit by the dull red glow of the vehicle's taillights, and will refer to it as the precise moment in which they decided to nullify the unique set of combinations that were once Couple X and Couple Y.

14.1   For many years afterward, through the course of many unique set combinations, sometimes during distracted moments of wakefulness, and often during sleep, the unrelated male subset will independently recall this night, will even dream about it. In their minds they will see the quivering white spot glowing in the perfect darkness of their separate thoughts, and each will believe that he was not the one, that his rock was slightly smaller than the other's rock, his aim more crooked, his intent merciful, his value—neutral. ❧

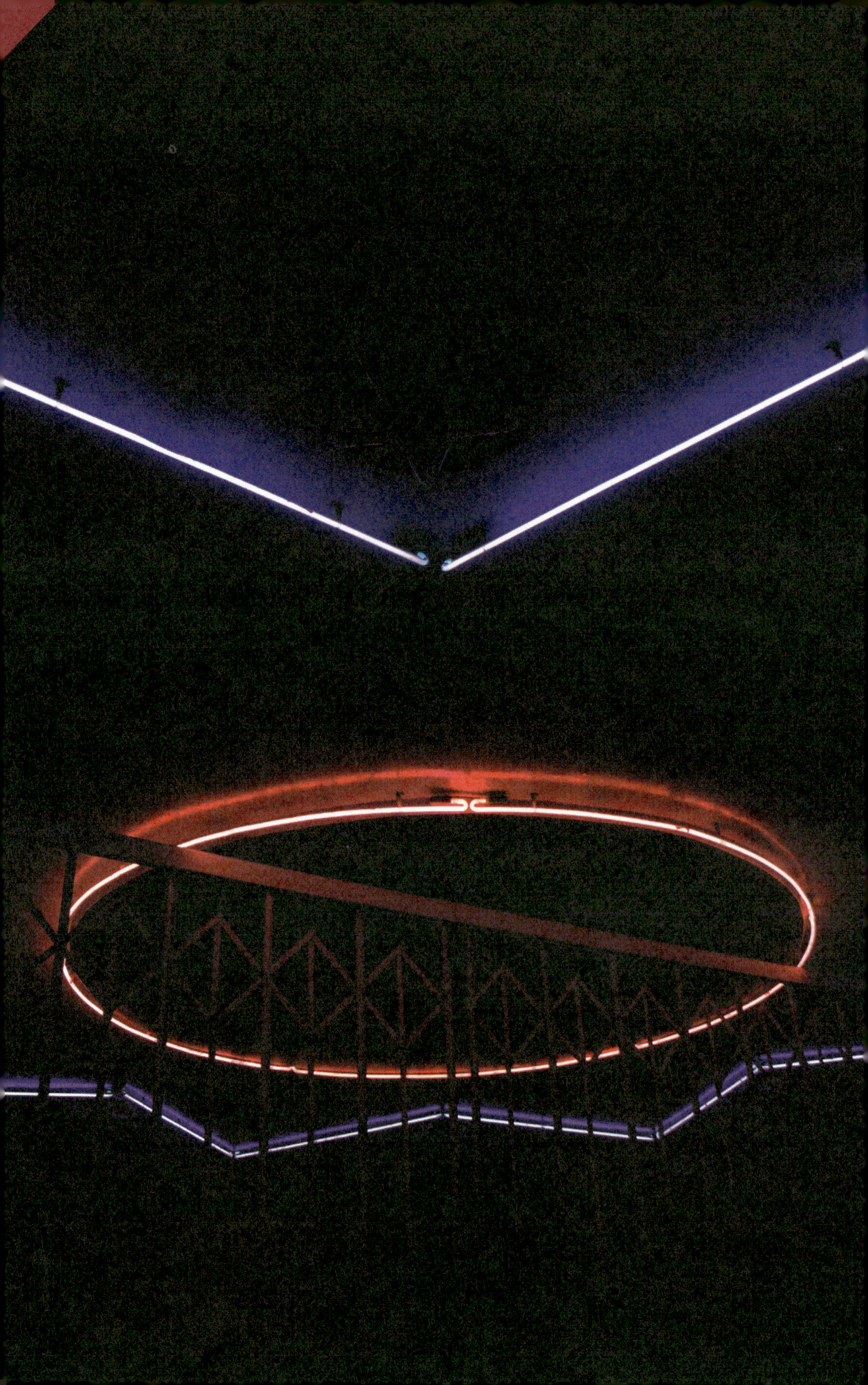

LOVE HOTEL

By Tamara Faith Berger
Photographs by Luisa Pelipetz

IN SEOUL AT twenty-three I lived large. I acquired envelopes stuffed full of money teaching ESL slander part-time.

Steam carried the smells of blistering meat through the screen doors of restaurant storefronts.

Women sold beer with their ponytails.

Girls, plucked and powdered, walked like stags through the city, their high heels pinned down by too-long pant legs.

In Seoul a ubiquitous female maintenance alarmed me.

I lived in a Love Hotel. Kelly, a brassy American girl who'd known my friend's boyfriend in Montreal, picked me up at the airport and took me to a four-story brick building with a pink neon sign. I got the last room at the end of a second-floor hallway.

Lock it from the inside, Kelly said. I'll see you in the morning. It's overwhelming, I know.

My room was windowless with a squat double bed. There was a kettle and a bar fridge in one wallpapered corner. I turned the air conditioner to high.

In the coffin-size bathroom, I took off my shirt and my bra and I looked at myself. Half-dressed and jet-lagged, lit by one bulb from a plug, I raised my arms like a centerfold. I was hairy and curvy but my body was okay. The air crackled. Every surface was hot.

At six in the morning, I left the damp room. There was no front desk at this hotel. The neon sign still flashed outside: a semicircle holding three flames. The storefronts were covered with corrugated metal. Brown juice pooled under garbage bags. Pieces of lettuce stuck to the sewer grates. I found a fluorescent twenty-four-hour where I bought two bowls of ramen and a pack of cigarettes.

Soon I spent my mornings teaching English conversation to men in suits in office towers. We were served paper cups of tea by candy dolls my age. I worked afternoons with housewives in the high-rise suburbs. We ate chewy rice sweets. The plastic floors gleamed. I taught at a one-room institute for girls in their twenties who were learning to be travel agents. Everyone was curious. We were all careful and polite.

I was cured by the chaos of night. Kelly plucked my eyebrows and braided my hair. We wore lingerie dresses with horse-heeled shoes. We met lesbian filmmakers and philosophy majors, Russian pimps and army brats, an Iranian teacher running away from the law and silent, stodgy Nigerian dealers. We ate street-hot egg sandwiches at four in the morning. Cabs whipped us back to our Love Hotel. I didn't sleep. I just passed out.

I heard long distance that my parents were having trouble. My mother's voice on the phone was the opposite of frantic. I didn't know if she was telling me a story or something that had already happened. She was using words like *separation* and *time*. She explained on repeat that my father was upset.

Let me talk to him, I said.

I hadn't seen my parents for six months.

He can't talk or else he'll cry, my mother said.

I've heard that your parents' relationship fills to the drenching point of your brain. Parents are your only understanding of *how do I do love?* It's not a matter of wanting to create a new system or revolt from some dysfunctional one—father strikes and mother strikes are lodged deep inside. In Seoul I asked this guy I met in a bar to whack my head onto the cement. I've never been in a fight, I said. I want to feel the feeling of my head on cement. I'll whack your head on cement, the guy said. This guy turned out to be a Canadian poet. We were drunk and I remember us running through an alley when he tripped me then swung me by the arm until I fell. I remember him on top of me. He took my head and banged once. I was laughing and laughing. He had me inches up by the hair and was ready to let me go again.

Tamara, my mother said. Your father is not going to work right now. He won't get out of bed. He's crying all the time.

That poet who whacked my head on cement was asking me if I wanted more. He seemed to be raving; he seemed really mad. Let's do the whole fucking thing again, he said. He really wanted to give me what I'd asked for. It was drama to him. I didn't have the stomach for drama.

We want to come visit you there, my mother said.

I imagined my father cocooned in a sheet. In Seoul I thought, I am a mean lone-wolf type like him.

Dion was African American, shaved bald, with hunted eyes. It looked like he used eyeliner. Kelly had picked him up at a party and bragged that he was a super-hot loner. I remember when Dion came with us one afternoon to some Latin barbecue on the base. I could tell that this person liked to set himself apart. He sat with his thighs wide, hands covering his knees.

At the army barbecue, I said yes to every soldier who asked me to dance. This was serious salsa. I had no idea how to do it. I just pumped my hips and let those guys spin me with a heart-racing laugh in my chest the whole time. Dion sat at a picnic bench, hulky and moping. I didn't think he was watching. I was busy flying. But later that night, Kelly tried not to be upset when she told me that Dion didn't want to sleep with her. She said, Dion thinks you're cool. He said to me, Tamara's cool.

Dion lived forty-five minutes out of Seoul. He had a full-time job at an elite middle school. He was one of the few English teachers I knew who actually had a contract. Once, I took a daylong substitute position at his school and he said I could stay over the night before. Dion put me in his spare room off the kitchen. There was nothing to eat. I couldn't even smoke. I lay on the bed reading with the door shut until Dion called my name.

I stood at the doorway of his bedroom, watching him at the computer. He didn't have a shirt on. His nipples were black.

Dion glanced at me in the doorway. Don't you feel like your life is over? he asked.

I laughed. Dion was twenty-six. It didn't occur to me that he was serious. My life was just fucking beginning. I was staring at the monstrous-looking scar on his arm.

What happened to you?

Not taking his eyes from the computer screen, Dion said it was like a tattoo.

This is branding, he said. It's my fraternity, man.

That thing was the size of my hand, bubbled black in the curvy parts with dull gray grooves that looked like worms.

Dion looked at my face. He said it was a good kind of pain.

Come here, he said. Why don't you come in?

Dion shifted over on his chair to make

room for me. I waited before I went to where he was, acting as if I wasn't sure. As soon as I sat down, I think he silently laughed. On the screen there were ads of oiled-up women in bright string bikinis.

Dion asked me where I grew up.

Toronto, I said. What about you?

Columbia, South Carolina, man. You know where that is?

I shook my head no. I liked just looking at him.

Have you ever seen someone get shot? Dion asked me.

We were sitting side by side on one chair. Our legs were almost touching.

I can't believe that you've never seen anyone die, Dion said. That kind of shit is just normal to me.

I giggled. I felt so inadequate.

Did you know that a woman can screw a dog? Dion said.

God. I kept laughing. I really didn't know that.

Dion had rabbit eyes that half-closed when he smiled.

So, you want to see? he asked.

The wallpaper in his room had colors like a nursery. The desk was formed of three planks. I took a quick breath. I said yes.

A long-nosed dog with a small black head bucked inside a living room. A woman was on her hands and knees. It was a tight-skinned Labrador. The woman's limp hair fell over her face. The dog held her back. It didn't have nails. She seemed slow, an old woman. The dog stood up and reared.

Fuck, it's disgusting, Dion said.

The video stopped. The screen filled with ads for telephone sex.

Sorry, shit. Dion stood up.

He was the electrical prince of all hate. I had no idea how to make something happen between us.

In Love Hotels men dealt with their mistresses by the hour. In Love Hotels students slept with each other because everyone lived at home until they were married. Travelers stayed in Love Hotels too. In Seoul I'd booked an upscale Love Hotel for my parents. The sheets were changed daily. Their room had a hairdryer, a minifridge, and a rotating TV.

Insook, one of my students at the travel school, took me and my parents for a weekend to the east coast. I didn't tell Insook that my parents weren't really talking to each other because if you didn't know, you couldn't tell. At the smelly beach my father would stare at my mother, sidle up to her on the boardwalk, and sometimes even take her hand. Once in the middle of dinner he broke into tears. My mother was embarrassed. Insook looked away. At Naksana temple, a fifty-foot-tall stone statue of the Buddhist Goddess of Mercy smiled down at all of us. My father's hoarse barks turned into guffaws.

After six days in the Love Hotel, my parents spent their last two nights at the Hilton. It turned out my mother was in love with someone else.

Dion quit his high-paying contract job in the suburbs and moved to Seoul. I started seeing him all over the place with a short Jewish girl who looked something like me. I tried not to care. I got laid by other freaks. But once, after Dion moved downtown, we found ourselves alone together, drunk and stoned at the end of the night. I thought it was auspicious. In the last hours of darkness we sat on the ground, cross-legged on the cement, our backs up against a shuttered storefront. Dion got hard under his sweatpants. I put my hand there, a confirmation. Then a woman walked by us. She was older and blonde, in some tight-fitting suit. In the growing pink light, the woman smiled down at us—me and him, the bottom-feeders.

Yeah, Dion hummed. This is so good.

My hand held on to his beating cock heart. I felt like a single-horned beast of benevolence.

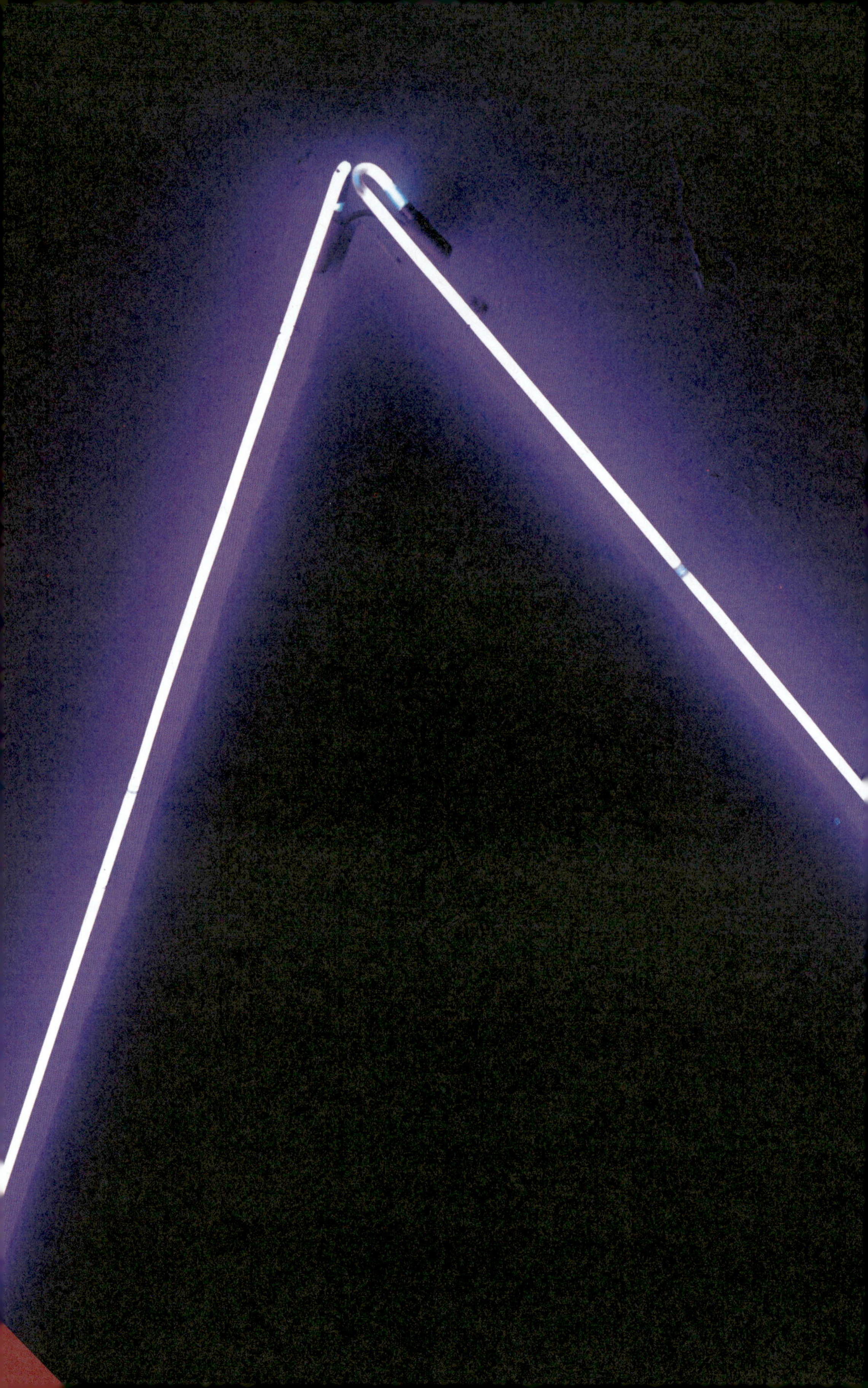

After Dion broke up with the first short Jewish girl, he actually began to live with another one, *another* short Jewish girl in Seoul like me.

It occurred to me that there were types of people in this world—there were people out there exactly like me, who did what I did and who even thought like I thought, who shadowed me and mimicked me and if I didn't step up, they would step up and in for me. ❧

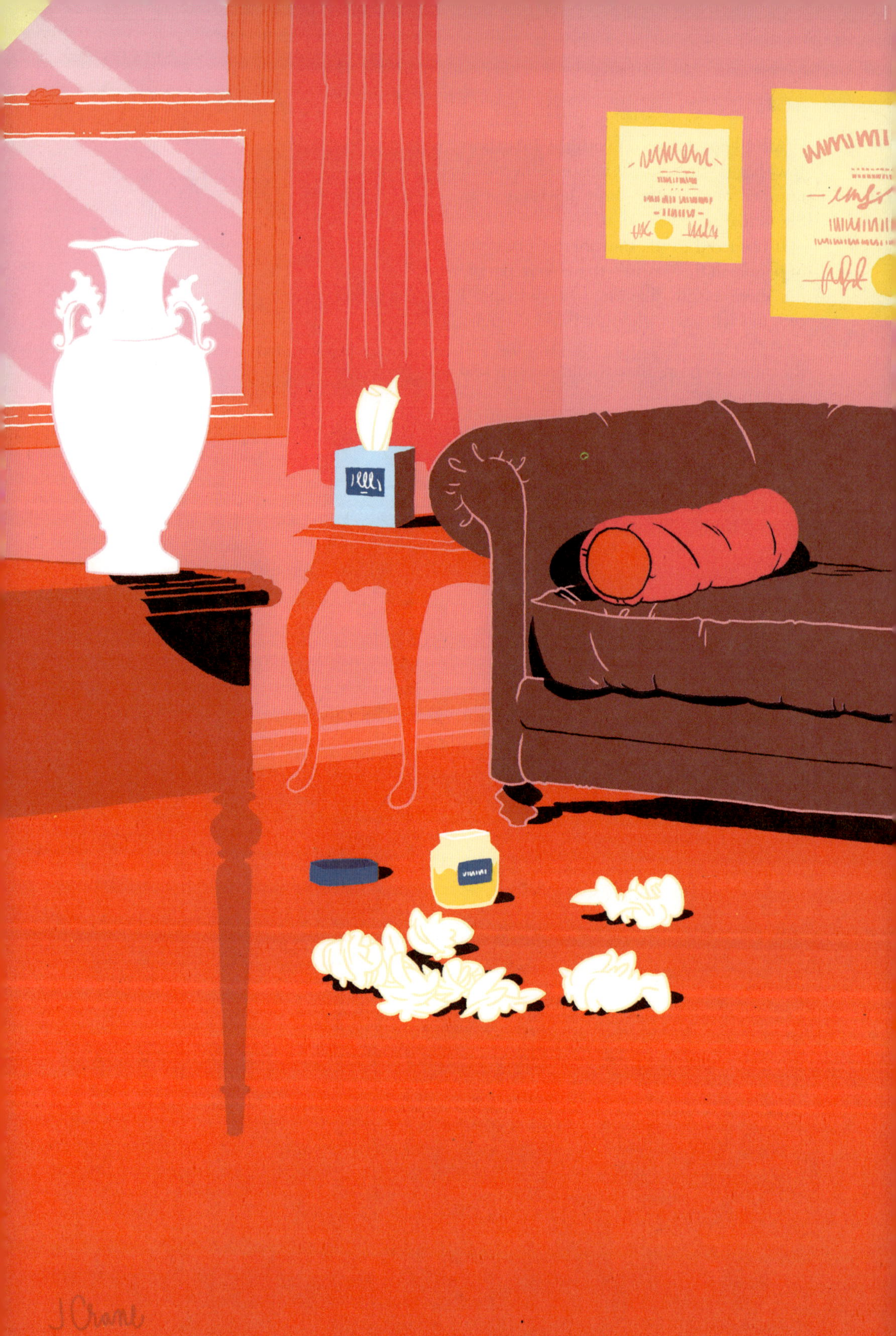

I NEED A DOCTOR

By Amie Barrodale
Drawings by Jordan Crane

A WOMAN WHO WAS lonely and depressed should begin by getting on some medication. She should then clean her house and throw out old knickknacks. After that, Dr. Sheppard told his patients to lose weight and wear dresses.

He was not taking new patients. This was in part because his schedule was full, in part because he was the newly appointed director of cognitive science and neuropsychiatry at Columbia, and in part because he and his wife, Isabel, were separated. More precisely, she had asked him to leave. She said that it was because he was arrogant. He suspected she was jealous of his professional success. She was respected in her field, but she had not won his accolades or his popular recognition. But what she said was true in its way: he did believe that what Isabel called compassion was vulnerability wearing a polite expression. What she called humility was just a wish to be liked. He didn't have those pretend qualities.

He and his wife had shared a practice and office for twenty years, and so they had—after some initial attempts to carry on as usual—made a short-term arrangement: he saw his patients in the mornings, and Isabel saw hers in the afternoons. She would not speak to him. Together they had agreed on a clean break.

His new academic appointment filled the downtime. Isabel wouldn't have believed it, but he was doing just fine. He was meditating in the mornings. He'd hired a nutritionist, and he was eating better than he had in years. His personal trainer had him down to 27 percent body fat.

Then Catherine Summer called. His secretary told him that Mrs. Summer had been referred by Columbia's dean and wanted to see him, or something. "She has anxiety." When Dr. Sheppard finally spoke with Mrs. Summer on the telephone, she explained that her daughter had suffered a panic attack at Morts Restaurant in St. Louis.

"Courtney's been in New York five years. She hasn't done anything. She interned at *Town & Country* and she volunteered at the Morgan, but from what I can gather all she does is eat and drink. We pay her expenses—we always have—but of course that is with the expectation that *eventually* she will find her way. Now it seems like she's developing these disorders."

"I'm sorry to say I've recently accepted a position at Columbia University, in addition to my private practice, so as you can imagine—"

"How nice. Courtney's almost twenty-eight years old, and she has no plans for a career, no boyfriend. Dr. Angel said you were the right one for us."

"Oh, you know Don? That's interesting, Mrs. Summer. You'll have to tell him I said hello."

"Call me Kitty."

"My wife, Isabel, is excellent with young women, Mrs. Summer."

"Call me Kitty," Mrs. Summer said. "Courtney didn't used to have a weight problem, or any problem, but her last boyfriend was overweight, and some of his eating habits rubbed off on her. Over Christmas she'd sit in front of the television with a sleeve of crackers and a block of cheese, and I'd say, 'Go out! Do something!' I know she could lose the weight easily, if she'd simply *do* something, but she won't listen to my suggestions, and I'm worried, with her father's metabolism, if she lets herself reach thirty without losing the weight it'll just stay on her. After a certain age, a woman's body just won't respond to diet or exercise—our estrogen levels change—and of course there are procedures, but *why* go down that road? She's just a girl! Of course I'm happy to pay for liposuction if she'll take it, but I tell her it's simple: don't eat. All the diet gurus in the world are peddling the same line of bullshit, excuse me, but if you want to lose weight, stop eating. You don't see any fat people at Auschwitz. Not to be insensitive, Dr. Sheppard, I understand you're Jewish—Don told me— but honestly."

Dr. Sheppard looked at the nineteenth-century Satsuma vase on the corner of his desk. It was one of two, about the size of a lamp, and had been commissioned for a Russian general, to resemble a lighthouse. It had been a gift from Isabel's mother to the couple when they married.

"Hello? Dr. Sheppard? The sooner the better, honestly. We need your help. I'm asking as a mother."

"Yes, sorry, I'm here." He asked if Courtney would be free to meet at lunchtime.

"Of course—she doesn't have a job. I believe I mentioned that."

He began to take notes.

C OURTNEY   THREW   HERSELF into the armchair opposite his desk. His first impression was that she was remarkably pretty. Her hair was almost blonde, and it was long and straight. She dressed mannishly—in jeans, a wool crewneck sweater, a worn-out blue oxford shirt, and high-quality, unpolished loafers—but she couldn't hide her looks. Each of her diamond earrings was big enough to make an engagement ring, and they caught his eye throughout the conversation.

Courtney *was* slightly overweight, and her posture was bad, but her manners were good. She looked Dr. Sheppard directly in the eye when she said, "Thank you for meeting me. My mother told me you made an exception for her. She's very happy that I'm here."

"How do you feel about it?"

"I'm doing my best to humor everybody."

"What do you mean?"

"I mean my mom wants me here, and so fuck it. No offense."

Dr. Sheppard nodded. He glanced over the intake questionnaire. No health problems, no smoking, no problems with alcohol. Asked to list her number of drinks, Courtney checked the box "four–five a night." So, a problem with alcohol. She didn't exercise. She slept between ten and twelve hours nightly. In answer to the question, "Why did you come in today?" she wrote, "I'd like to find a solution to life's mysteries."

"What about, do you have anxiety? Your mother mentioned something at Morts."

Courtney pressed her face into her hands and took a deep breath. "I had a panic attach, okay? I think they're pretty normal. My mom acts like I have a gnome or something."

"A what?"

"Ugh, a movie I saw. This schizo guy had a gnome that made him drink rye."

Dr. Sheppard didn't press her, but he made a note on what she had said. Of course she had intended to say "panic attack," but the word she spoke was "attach." He prescribed a low daily dose of Prozac, Ativan as needed for mild anxiety, and a monthly supply of ten four-milligram Xanax for severe panic. He asked Courtney to come back two days later, on Thursday, and to see him twice weekly until they were comfortable with each other. As she was leaving with the papers, he said, "Do you feel all right about that? How do you feel?"

"Compromised," Courtney said. "See you Thursday."

H E W A S I N H I S school office eating a Potbelly sandwich later that afternoon—he taught Tuesdays from 4:30 to 6:20—when Mrs. Summer called and asked if he had a moment to chat.

"Well, to be honest, Mrs. Summer, I teach in a few minutes."

"It's Kitty."

"I generally take this time to prepare."

"Well, this won't take any time at all. I'm calling to ask a favor. I understand things went well with Courtney, and I want to thank you, by the way. But the reason for my call is, my husband and I are in Stockholm just now and I wanted to have his secretary send you a check. So, just your best mailing address."

"Sure," he gave his address at the office. Then he couldn't help it. He said, "As it happens I'll be in Stockholm next month for an IHS meeting. I'll be speaking. How's the weather? Should I bring a coat?"

"Oh, hooray! We can meet. Courtney said you were wonderful, but I don't think you really know a person until you spend some time one-on-one."

"Well, that's nice to hear—about Courtney. You know, I shouldn't say this, but my impression was that Courtney was feeling ambivalent about her treatment."

He shouldn't have brought up Courtney's feelings with her mother, but he wanted to keep her on the phone. Apparently she was a stickler. Her tone got icy. She said, "I'm sorry to run on you, that's my other line."

T HE I H S M E E T I N G was held at a modern conference hotel outside of Stockholm. The lobby was full of young, excited doctors and pharmaceutical representatives, many of whom already wore their lanyard badges.

Dr. Sheppard made it through the lobby with a few handshakes. He had submitted a paper for presentation, but it had been accepted for the congress. What that meant was that he was not asked to speak before five hundred colleagues, but to compress his research to fit a poster, which he would hang among a thousand others and present to a panel of three evaluators. Ordinarily, researchers of his stature responded to congress selection by sending a nurse or a research assistant to the meeting. Some of his colleagues felt Dr. Sheppard was commercial, or a pop analyst, because he was a regular on Dr. West-Marchingham's program. They were jealous.

In his room, he sat on one of the twin beds, took out his phone, and looked at text messages from the dean, his secretary, a patient who was addicted to cough syrup, and his phone company (he was roaming). He contemplated taking a second Valium. He went into the bathroom and looked at the soaps, then splashed his face with water and scrubbed it.

He opened the split bottle of Chardonnay provided by the congress, poured it into a glass, and opened the window. A low, atonal song was being played downstairs. It comprised single notes. They were low notes, and so they were not disturbing, but Dr. Sheppard wondered why a hotel would play that kind of music. Who would make that decision at an executive level? He closed his window, finished the wine, and went downstairs with his poster.

The congress looked like a high school science fair. Cloth panels with pushpins in their upper left-hand corners snaked through the room, and youngsters ner-

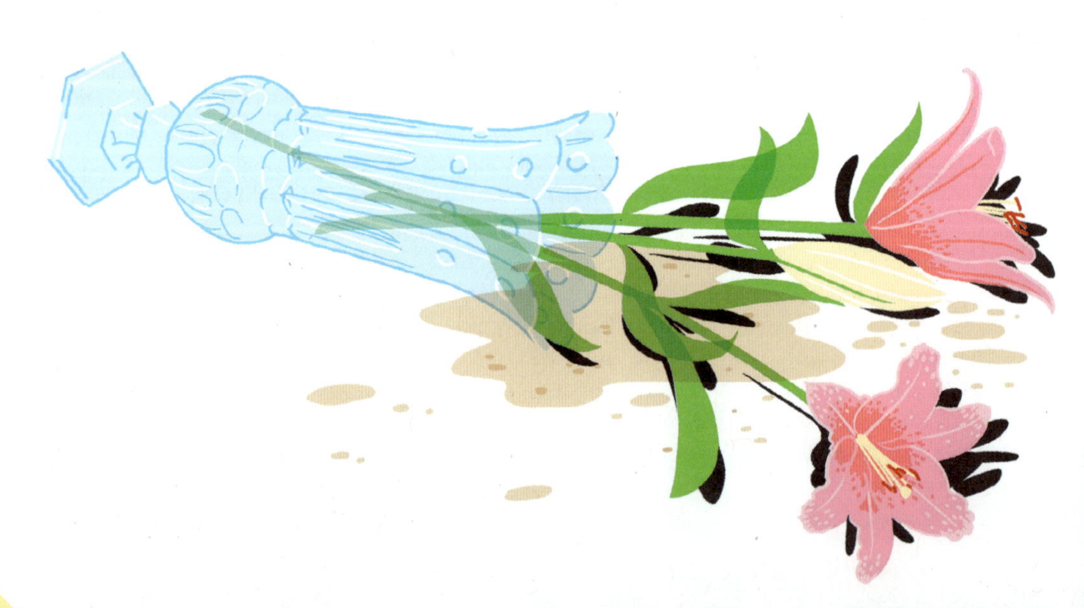

vously hung their work and pretended they weren't aware of him. He double-checked his packet and found his spot. He was beside a young, shaky Italian man who was so excited to be in the congress, he appeared to be having a seizure. Dr. Sheppard pinned one side of his poster, then slowly unrolled it. Before he could get to the other side, the pin came undone. He tried again. On his third try, a hand clapped the one side of his poster.

"Need some help?"

He looked up at the woman who had her hand on his poster.

"Kitty. Kitty Summer. In the flesh. I'm so pleased to meet you, Dr. Sheppard."

Mrs. Summer was more attractive than her daughter. She was greyhound thin, and she wore patent heels, a slim-waisted skirt suit, and a short string of extraordinarily large pearls. He pinned the corner of his poster and stepped back.

"Oscar Sheppard."

"This is my husband, Stephen," she gestured to a pudgy man in tweed. "We owe Dr. Sheppard money, Stephen. Dr. Sheppard, do you have a minute? Good. Let's feed you. You look hungry."

M RS. S UMMER GOT the waiter with a look. She said, "Stoli, one rock, and my husband will have the chicken sandwich."

"And a side of mayo?" Stephen said.

"And a side of mayo—please bring it in a ramekin."

Dr. Sheppard ordered a white-wine spritzer and the raw-vegetable appetizer. Over their drinks, the Summers asked Dr. Sheppard questions about his flight, his wife, his books, and his appointment at Columbia. He told them about Isabel and their shared practice. He explained that she didn't like the big meetings, or travel, and he praised Courtney's intelligence.

"I think our sessions are going very well."

"Oh, she says you're marvelous. Of course she doesn't show any improvement, as far as I can tell, but these things take time, one supposes."

"Yes, she's just barely started on the medication."

"Barely started," Kitty snorted.

"Generally speaking it takes a month for the brain to—"

"Ah."

The waiter put Stephen's sandwich and mayonnaise in front of him. Mrs. Summer took two Ziploc bags out of her purse. She put the bread in one and the lettuce and tomato in the other. She put both bags back into her purse, picked up a knife, dipped the tip of it into the mayonnaise, dotted the chicken, and put the knife back down precisely.

"How long are you in town?" she asked.

"'Til Sunday."

"Oh, that's too bad. We could have had you over for dinner, but at least you'll have time to go to the baths. Have you been yet? I don't really go in for museums. Do you? What do you go in for?"

Dr. Sheppard told Mrs. Summer about some of his hobbies. He worked out three times a week, he explained, and he was devoted to daily meditation. Kitty loved horses. While they talked about her long-time love of horses and her prize-winning dressage, her husband ate. When he choked on a bit of his chicken, Mrs. Summer gave him a glass of water, which made it worse. He was choking and snorting water out of his nose. "It's the mayonnaise," she explained to Dr. Sheppard. He pretended not to notice as Catherine Summer instructed her husband to raise both hands above his head, and made him stay that way while she talked about dressage.

"At home, I have my riding. But this year, during Stephen's appointment, I've decided I'm taking time off. So today, for example, I did a little shopping."

"Appointment?"

"Stephen is a diplomat," Mrs. Summer

said.

"Ambassador Summer?"

"Head ass-kisser Summer," Stephen said. "My wife fund-raised for the last campaign, and this is the reward."

"Well, it must be nice."

"Hmph. I spend half my day managing the Dunleavys."

"Stephen is talking about our caretakers. They're a charming couple, but they've never really been in service. I called last week asking them to take a bag of mine out of storage and mail it to Courtney, and they behaved as if it were a great inconvenience."

"They haven't met Kitty yet," Stephen said to Dr. Sheppard, and raised his eyebrows. It seemed like he was issuing a friendly warning.

Dr. Sheppard changed the flow of the conversation, "Does your daughter mind you being away for a year?"

"Are you putting us on the couch, Dr. Sheppard?" Mrs. Summer laughed. Stephen smiled politely. Mrs. Summer said, "I think she's glad. She has the opinion that I control her life."

"She never mentioned that."

"She wouldn't. She's too cunning." She stopped herself and then said, "When Courtney moved to New York I came up and helped her get settled. We looked at apartments together and when we found one she liked—emphasis on *she liked*, that girl, well, we're the ones who made her that way—we bought furniture. I didn't think about it when she didn't thank me because children tend to expect you to do that kind of thing, but three years later she called me blind drunk and told me that I was crazy and I'd ruined her life because I bought her three sets of kitchenware. Of course the parents are always to blame. I'm boring you?"

"No."

"You think it's odd that Stephen is eating boiled chicken. I'm sorry, it's his diet."

"No, I understand. But can I ask, why do you have the bags?"

"My baggies? You pay for the lettuce and tomato and bread whether you eat it or not, so I take it and put it in the fridge for Tove. Dr. Sheppard? While we're on the subject of diet and exercise: I think it's important that Courtney doesn't know we've met. Stephen, you agree. She would regard it as a betrayal. I bought her kitchen supplies and she still hasn't forgiven me."

"H OW   WAS   YOUR   weekend?" Courtney asked.

"It was all right."

"You look like shit, no offense. What did you do?"

Dr. Sheppard looked at his telephone. He righted his prescription pad so that it was in line with his blotter and said, "I went to New Haven."

"Oh, why?"

"I had my thirty-year reunion."

"Did you drink too much?"

"Very funny. How about you?"

"I'm just asking because I've never seen you look so tired. I mean, that's the polite word for it. You look like somebody beat you."

"I flew home on a red-eye."

"Red-eye from New Haven. Well. Did you have fun?"

"I saw old friends."

"See anyone I'd know? I know lots of people in New Haven. Not that I'm like a New Haven asshole. I went to Bowdoin. I got into Yale, but fuck them. I hate those people. I honestly do."

"Do you know the name David Kehn? He's an old roommate of mine."

"Senator David Kehn? That guy's so gay."

"We lived together freshman and sophomore years, until he joined the art frat."

"But you're like prehistorically aged, no offense. I mean, I didn't mean that as an insult. You're very attractive. I mean, not that I—I just didn't realize you two were the same age. Senator Kehn and Dr. Sheppard. He looks like twenty years younger than you. It's weird. Did you go to college late? Did you two get high?"

"Yes, occasionally we did. Why do you ask?"

"Ha! I have to tell my dad. He'll flip. Tell me everything."

"I'll tell you sometime, but I don't think we want to spend our whole hour gossiping about my friends. Why don't you tell me what you did over your weekend?"

"Oh, Christ."

Dr. Sheppard waited. Courtney said, "If you want to know, I hung out with friends."

"Tell me about your friends."

"Just friends. I hung out with Emily and Trip and Kris. Emily came over and—she does this thing, whenever she comes into my house, the first thing she does is she says, 'I have to go to the bathroom.' It's so weird. It's like, what the fuck? Once she went in there and a couple minutes later the fire alarm starts going off."

"I don't understand."

"She'd lit a match to cover up the smell of her shit, and she was so uptight about it she put the match in the bin full of Kleenex and started a fire. I mean, and I'm the one on medication."

Courtney laughed, and Dr. Sheppard watched her.

"I'm not avoiding the question, if that's what you're suggesting with that expression. Emily came over and we opened a bottle of wine. Trip called and invited us to the Wonkey Donkey so we went over there, and they had some red wine and vodka so we made Stalins. Have you been drinking Stalins, come to think of it? You look like it, no offense. That was a joke. You can laugh anytime. It's not a job interview. So anyway, Emily passed out up in Trip's loft, and Gandalf drank red wine out of my shoe, then I fooled around with Kris, and around sunrise Emily woke up and I got us a cab back home and she

stayed over in my bed. Kris's dad was a spy, or he says so. He's a pianist. Sunday afternoon me and Emily watched HBO, and around ten I figured she wasn't leaving so I ordered us Indian food and opened a bottle of wine, and then we went around the corner to Scratchers. My relationship to Kris is a secret, by the way. Not even Emily knows. So we went to Scratchers and I asked this guy if I could look in his wallet, and it was full of old ticket stubs so I told him he had a broken heart."

"What?"

"Seeing movies alone means you have a broken heart."

"How'd you know he saw them alone?"

"I asked him. Okay, your turn. Is Senator Kehn gay? I have a bet with my brother he's gay."

Dr. Sheppard looked at the ceiling and pressed his palms to his eyes. "Do you think maybe you could ask me something else?"

"Yeah. Why not." She thought for a moment. "Okay. Here's a good one. Do you look at pornography online?"

"Sure. I think we all do, these days."

"And…?"

"And what? I usually have trouble finding the kind of thing I like, because I don't want to sign up for any of the websites. It takes me a long time, looking at those tiny pictures."

"So it's something weird."

"What's weird?" Dr. Sheppard shrugged.

"I'm totally in shock here. I mean, I'm not shocked by your answer—of course it would take you a long time, you're like eighty-five—but just that you'd say it to me. It's kind of cool."

"What made you ask the question?"

"Oh, I don't know. It wouldn't be appropriate to talk about it with you."

Dr. Sheppard blinked.

"I can see that you can't tell when I'm joking. That's kinda funny, isn't it? Because you should be able to read me by now. That's like your job. Anyway, I just was thinking about porn because I used to never look at it, but since I broke up with Tom I'm not having sex with any-body, and then you started me on these medications, and my sex drive changed or something, and I started having less sex, like no sex drive at all, which weirded me out so I started off with online porn, basically nothing, but in about a day I fell down a rabbit hole, and now I look at the totally fucked-up stuff, and I feel weird about it. Sorry. But still I feel just kind of weird about it. I thought we're supposed to be honest. Did I gross you out?"

"It's normal."

"But I feel like a sex addict or some-thing."

Dr. Sheppard shrugged. He wanted to ask Courtney why she and Kris didn't sleep together, but he felt uncomfortable. That was unusual. He had many female clients, and most spent all their time in session discussing their sex lives and their romantic lives, and the ways those two things made them miserable. He had heard a lot of things. He did not usually shy from the subject of sex.

I T   W A S   U N S E A S O N A B L Y hot, nine-ty degrees in April. Dr. Sheppard was regretting a text he had sent Isabel the night before. He had been drinking at the bar below his apartment, and he'd had the opportunity to sleep with an attrac-tive young woman. She was twenty-three years old. He had texted Isabel to tell her. It was too embarrassing to look at the exact words. When his phone rang, he expected to be excoriated.

"Dr. Sheppard? Kitty here. Do you have a minute? Good. I'm calling because I'm concerned. I was in New York last weekend and I saw Courtney. We had given her a hammer—to be more precise, her younger brother had given it to her—and it was covered in rubber cement,

and paint, and I don't know what all else. Apparently she'd loaned it to one of her bohemian friends? And a chair from the set I bought her was missing. I asked her about it of course, and she told me she'd broken it apart for kindling. Now Dr. Sheppard, I don't want to get into a discussion about money, but what exactly is it we're paying for?"

"Well, Courtney doesn't seem to have a lot of friends."

"She's out with friends every night."

"Oh, I mean she has Trip and Emily and Kris—but to be honest, they aren't really friends. They aren't people she con-nects with, they are people she gets drunk with. I'm sorry if that sounds blunt, or difficult to hear. I mean, I think Emily is all right, if a little hysterical. And Trip seems like he basically shares some of her background. But I don't really care for this Kris. From what I can gather he's an editor or a pianist or something."

"Oh God. This is appalling."

"What? I've offended you. I'm sorry, it's wrong for me to reveal that kind of thing."

"The fucking pianist errant."

"The… I'm certain I misheard you. The penis what?"

"Oh God, I think it's the pianist errant. Listen, there's a kid—it's sad really—he was accepted to Rice in the architecture program, but he heard another student playing jazz music, and I think he must be manic, because he had the other stu-dent teach him a few riffs, and then he moved to Morocco to teach himself to play, and now he has a piano strapped to a pickup and the last time I heard it had rolled off and smashed up a Camaro."

"You mean the Wonkey Donkey." He laughed. "Well, that one's a bit compli-cated, actually."

"She's seeing him?"

"Well, not exactly seeing," Dr. Shep-pard said. "They 'hook up.' Let me rec-ommend an essay to you. It's by Tom

Wolfe, called 'Hooking Up.' It basically explains it to our generation. It's not nearly as bad as it sounds at first. I mean, it's not a morally blameworthy thing. That's how they see it."

It was with the intention of reassuring her that he began, but two hours later they were still talking, and he had told Kitty everything that he knew about Courtney.

OVER THE NEXT year, their shared secret evolved into a bond. They conspired. Kitty called to ask about Courtney, he waited for those calls. Sometimes he texted if there was a problem that was pressing, and within a few minutes his phone rang.

Courtney improved. She went from a size ten to a size four. She was still too big to borrow clothes from her mother, but she began to dress like a woman. She wore dresses, and when she did wear an oxford shirt, it was bright white and starched, and she wore it with tight jeans and riding boots.

But Courtney didn't seem to be aware that her shoes were unpolished. It was a pity because anyone could see at a glance that all of her boots were exceptionally fine—some designer and some handmade. He didn't know how to bring it up. During meditation one morning, he caught himself envisioning a trial. He was on the witness stand, defending himself. "And why," a female lawyer asked, "did you choose that expression?"

"WHAT ARE YOU over there thinking about?" Courtney asked.

"Oh, I was thinking about an apartment. I made an offer on an apartment. The seller accepted it. I'm supposed to hear later today if I can buy."

"A loan."

"No, it isn't a loan," he stopped himself. He hadn't told Courtney that he and his wife were separated, and he didn't know

how to now. It wasn't a secret he had meant to keep, but now he had known her for more than a year, and it seemed funny to say all at once that he was in the midst of a property settlement and divorce. He said, "What were you thinking about?"

"Oh, nothing."

He waited. She said, "When you make that face, I have to tell you what I'm thinking." And then she was quiet again. "Do you have bad credit or something?"

He let that go. He said, "What did you do over the weekend?"

"I reupholstered my couch."

"Oh? Did you take it somewhere?"

"No, I did it. It was this awful cream bouclé my mom picked. It's a good couch otherwise, so I just redid it."

"Did you do anything else?"

"You know you don't have to be a dick about everything. It's actually a lot of work. People go to school to learn how."

"Oh, I'm sure. I'm just wondering if you got out at all."

"Screw you."

"What?"

"You heard me: screw you."

Dr. Sheppard smiled with half his mouth. They both waited. Dr. Sheppard decided to go ahead and say it: "Have you ever heard of shoe polish?"

"I don't go in for patent leather."

Dr. Sheppard looked at his shoes. "It's a parade gloss. But you really can't treat your shoes like that. It's bad for the leather. Look," he got down to show her. He lifted her shoe and turned it. "See this cracking you're getting? You literally slap these shoes against the ground into water, salt, dirt, grease, and grime thousands of times a day. It's not like your skin—the leather of your shoes only receives the nourishment you give it."

She let him handle her legs and boots.

"Did you even condition these after you bought them? Surely your mother did."

He went around to his desk and opened

the top drawer. He dug around. "Shit," he said.

"Dr. Sheppard."

"Hold on—stay here, I'll be right back."

He went up front and came back a few minutes later with two rags and a jar of Vaseline. He closed the door.

"Don't start with me," he said, and he got down on his knees and worked Vaseline into her right and then her left boot. She was quiet while he worked.

When he was done she said, "Thank you."

"Oh," he waved a hand dismissively, but he couldn't think of anything else to say.

D R . S H E P P A R D W A S talking to Kitty while lying on the couch of his office. He said, "Kitty, I took them off of her feet before polishing them."

"Well, for chrissake, yes. I should hope so. I mean I presumed. But nevertheless. Wait, *you* took them off? You mean she took them off."

"Yes, naturally. She did. Anyway, I brought up marriage with her."

"Did she attack you?"

"No, actually. She cried. She asked me how she could meet men."

"Good. What'd you tell her?"

"I told her, you know," Dr. Sheppard didn't want to lie again, but the truth was he wasn't sure what Kitty wanted to hear. "I told her that she had to be open to it."

"Open… She needs to get out of her apartment. She needs to lose a few."

"She's a size four!"

"I know, I know, with Trish, the Paltrow nutritionist. Do you believe Gwyneth had a fat ass? That's the kind of thing a savvy woman can conceal. But I told her you can't be on 1,200 calories. It's just not effective. I want a daughter who can wear belts."

"I don't know, Kitty. There's a limit. Apparently Trish is over there, measuring out servings of butter. I don't eat butter, myself. My trainer doesn't encourage it,

but I mean, I think apart from the butter she's doing all she can."

"Don't knock butter. Butter isn't a problem food. The problem foods are fruits and veggies. If you start in on one of those party platters, there's no stopping. Watch next time you're at one of your little… functions. The fatties gather around the celery. I don't touch it."

"What, may I ask, do you eat?"

"Whataburgers. I have one a day."

"Kitty Summer eats Whataburgers?"

"It works. I order them dry. If I'm very hungry I'll get a packet of mayonnaise."

"Like with your husband in Stockholm."

"And then on my birthday I eat an entire white cake."

" D R . S H E P P A R D ? It's me. Can you talk? It's late here."

He looked at his watch. It was after nine, so it would be 1 AM in France. He was still at the office, but for all Courtney knew he was at home. For all she knew his wife could have been right beside him.

"Who is this?" Dr. Sheppard said.

"It's Courtney. Like you don't know," Courtney said. "You're the worst. But hold on. I've gotta keep my voice down. My mother's drunk. Hold on."

He heard Courtney shuffling around. She said, "I'm back."

"How is France?"

"France is cool. I mean, it's okay. You know how it is, you get to the hotel and after about an hour there's nothing to do but drink. It's hard to actually enjoy it. Listen, is it okay that I'm calling you? I miss you."

"Is there an emergency…"

"It's weird, I think I need a session. Can you do a telephone session? What time is it there? Are you in the office still? It's late here. Are you already at home? Are you in bed or something?"

"What was it you wanted to discuss?"

"I thought about you when I was taking my shoes off at security."

Dr. Sheppard settled down into his chair.

"Are you there?"

"I'm here."

"This security guard. Well, I mean I thought about you on the plane, too. Hold on."

Dr. Sheppard recognized the vacuum pull and clink of little bottles—she was in the minibar. He heard her unscrew and pour—was it three or four, surely three—bottles.

"I'm back. What were we saying? 'What wuz we sayin'?' Oh. Yeah, you're in trouble, man. I saw David Kehn and he doesn't even go to reunions, plus he said you already had your thirty-five."

"Courtney, are you mixing alcohol with your medication?"

"Hey, and speaking of which—no, Mom! I'm talking to Emily!" she yelled. Then she whispered into the phone: "She wants me to come back and watch *Steel Magnolias* with her. Hold on, I'll be right back—well, no, you can come with me."

Dr. Sheppard heard Courtney fumble with a door and curse. Then he heard a stream of water. It was interrupted by a toot. Courtney laughed, and finished peeing. She flushed the toilet.

"Courtney, are you all right?"

"Shh! I can talk in here in the bathroom. I locked the door and she can't hear."

"Why?"

"Don't worry, it's not weird. It's like the size of your whole office. It's got a swimming pool. It's got a Jacuzzi. The swimming pool here is carved out of the mountain. It's the best. You've got to come here sometime. We could come together if that wouldn't be weird."

Kitty was calling Dr. Sheppard on his other line. He said, "Courtney, could you hold on for a second?"

"Sure, I'll just sit here on the bathroom floor. Maybe I'll start a bath. For when we get off, I mean. Is that your wife?"

"Just a second."

"It's another patient?"

He switched over.

"Oscar? I'm sorry to call so late, but I'm worried about Courtney. She's very drunk. Is she calling you?"

"Hi."

"Courtney's not on the other line, is she?"

"No."

"Of course. It sounded like you were on the other line, and my daughter's drunk and hiding in the toilet. Listen. I've got a little questionarooni. I don't know how to put it delicately."

Courtney must have hung up and called him again: he had a call.

"Kitty, I have another call. Do you think maybe I could call you back?"

"I'll hold."

Dr. Sheppard switched over.

"Did you hang up on me? I'm just getting in the bath. I don't care. It's not weird. Who was that? You're always so weird. It's not very fair. Which is my point. I mean, that's why I'm calling, about this marriage thing, because I need to know. I don't want you to give me any of your professional act. What's up? Why do you see me?"

"It is my job."

"Cut the shit."

"Courtney."

"You're a liar."

Kitty had hung up and redialed. Dr. Sheppard said, "Can you hold on? I have this patient on the other line. It will just be a second."

"I called it!"

"Please hold."

He switched over and said, "I lied a moment ago. I'm going to level with you: I have Courtney on the other line."

"Still me," Courtney said. "What a total fucking giveaway. It is your wife! Listen, I'm running a bath, is that cool? If your wife's jealous I'm calling, just tell her I'm crazy. You should be home anyway.

It's late. Are you in the office? 'Tell me what you're wearing.' That's a joke! Do you do phone sex with your wife? Can you do a session with me if I'm naked?"

Kitty's call went to voice mail. She never left a message. He wondered if she would call again. A text message rolled in. It was from Kitty. It said, "I'm lying in bed right now and you're all I can think about."

She sent a second, "Tell me to take off my panties."

The other line beeped. It was Kitty. He said, "Can you hold on for one second?" and switched over.

"Dr. Sheppard, have you ever really been fucked?"

"Could you hold on a second?"

He switched back to Courtney and said, "Courtney, I think we should discuss this in my office. I appreciate that you've been honest, but I worry this isn't the time for us to have this sensitive of a, of a, of a… discussion."

"Look, Dr. Sheppard. Let's just tell the truth for once. I fucking love you, okay. I love you. I think about you all the time. I mean, tell me I'm wrong. I fucking talk about you. I fucking think about you. I jerk off to you. I'm sorry. Jesus, I'm sorry. I heard it's transference. It's transference, that's why I think about you—I'm messed up. I'm totally showing you my shit here. I'm fucked up. But the truth is you're in love with me too. I know it. And you're in love with my mother, which is fucking insane."

"It isn't transference," Dr. Sheppard said. "Our connection is real."

"Oh, good. Oh, that's really good. I know it is."

"But I think it would be wise of us to discuss this at a different time."

"I know, I know, I know," Courtney said. "I know. Don't start all that. What I want to know is, did you tell my mother you polished my shoes."

"No."

"Because that was this privately totally cool thing between us and you can't fucking share it with her. She's so fucked up. Now she's like jealous of me, because I'm not a size ten anymore and I can basically wear her fucking belts, and she's—old. Like I give a shit about her belts or the fucking maître d. You know? But it's like a contest who can nail the maître d. Fucking take the fucking—Jesus, is it my fault he comes on to me? I mean, who gives a fuck about the maître d, Dr. Sheppard?"

"Courtney. Can I have confidence you won't hurt yourself?"

"You think I'm suicidal?"

"I mean, could you stop drinking and taking pills for the night?"

Courtney hung up the phone. He switched over, and Kitty said, "Hello."

Courtney showed up on time Tuesday. She looked good. She was wearing jeans and a polo shirt, and she had gotten sun. She even had some freckles on her breastbone.

She took a seat on the couch—far away from him. He was going to ask her about her trip—something innocuous to diffuse the tension—but she cut in. She said, "I want to apologize for calling you, and for the things I said. I'd had a lot to drink, and I wasn't really myself."

"Oh, it wasn't anything serious." Dr. Sheppard waved a hand. "I mean, you don't need to apologize."

"I feel like I do. I mean I was serious. Everything that I said was true."

"I don't think I follow."

"I'm in love with you."

Dr. Sheppard didn't know what to say. He reminded himself that it was better, when he was uncertain, to say nothing. He said, "You don't have any real friends."

"I have a ton of friends."

"You have people you drink with, but no one you talk to. I'm your only real connection."

"That's not true."

"I'm the only person you interact with sober."

Courtney took a deep breath. She said, "That isn't true."

He raised his eyebrows. She said, "It may be true. Say that it is. What difference would it make?"

He argued that her love came out of loneliness, and she argued that all love came out of mutual loneliness. She said, "The deeper the loneliness, the deeper the love." He began to feel constricted and claustrophobic, and like all of this was not going to come out well. He thought he saw a way out.

He said, "I think if you're feeling this way, it might make sense to consider seeing a different therapist. I could refer you to my wife."

"Your wife," she said.

"We share a practice."

She stood up. She was getting angry, he could see. But there was no reason to be angry. This was a reasonable suggestion, under the circumstances.

"Sit down, Courtney, please."

"Your wife. You've got to tbe fucking kidding me."

What she did next surprised him. She picked up his Satsuma vase and threw it. Her aim was excellent and it soared across the room toward the large window. It hit the window, bounced off, and landed on the carpet. Dr. Sheppard had expected it to shatter, but he stood and went around the desk, and found it unharmed.

Courtney was looking for something else to throw. She picked up a glass vase of cut lilies—a gift from one of his divorced patients—and chucked it against the wall. It sprayed dirty, rotten flower-water across his desk, across the wall and the front of his shirt, but the vase did not break. It landed on the hardwood floor, the flowers still inside.

"Courtney," Dr. Sheppard said.

"Courtney, calm down. Sit down. Courtney, talk to me."

"Good fucking idea! I'll see your wife!"

She turned over an end table and lunged for his second vase. This one, she raised above her head with both arms and threw down onto the hardwood floor. One of the handles broke off.

Abruptly, unexpectedly, she got hold of herself. She looked around. She said, "I've got to go." Then her mouth turned down involuntarily twice. She opened the door to his office, and said, "Let's go."

"Is something the matter?" a woman's voice said.

"He said we can't see each other anymore."

"Whatever for? What on earth?"

Dr. Sheppard recognized Kitty's voice. She said, "Courtney, hon, wait. Courtney! Where are you going?"

Kitty was in the waiting room of his office. It was 11 AM and spring, but she wore stiletto-heeled boots, skin-tight leather pants, a cropped band jacket, and a matching polka-dot necktie and blouse. "Dr. Sheppard," she said. She walked to his office door and looked out into the hallway, turning her head both ways. "Courtney must have charged off," she said. Then she looked back at Dr. Sheppard, and smoothed her hair and smiled. "Dr. Sheppard, did you and Courtney have a disagreement? Why are you holding that vase?"

He realized he had the undamaged vase in his arms. He sat down with his arms wrapped around it. Kitty sat down next to him.

"Maybe I should try to call her?" she said. "I'm confused. Tell me. What just happened here?"

"So am I."

She smoothed her hair a second time. "Ever since we spoke in France, you haven't been answering my calls."

"I'm sorry, Kitty. It's been a very busy time. My school responsibilities have been onerous. I'm a bit overwhelmed."

"And do I understand correctly that you're saying you won't see my daughter? She must have been mistaken."

"No, I'm afraid I think that's for the best. I did give her an excellent referral."

"A referral? What on earth? Is this because of what happened between the two of us?"

Dr. Sheppard cringed. "I'm not sure what you're referring to," he said. "I'd like to discuss Courtney with you, Kitty. But I'm afraid I can't, as it would violate patient-doctor confidentiality. You understand that."

"Patient-doctor what?"

"Confidentiality. My professional ethics—I can't discuss Courtney's case with you."

Kitty nodded. "Confidentiality. I understand. Of course." She said, "There's something I've always meant to ask you, Dr. Sheppard. Since we're speaking… as professionals."

"Ask anything," he shrugged, and put the vase on the coffee table.

"Why did your wife leave you?"

He hadn't told Kitty that. But he didn't have to ask how she knew. Kitty knew things. So he started to explain to her about his professional success, and Isabel's suggestion that he was arrogant. Before he could fully express his thoughts, Kitty said, "Isabel is a very beautiful woman. I think it's much simpler than all that, Dr. Sheppard. Did you ever think it might have had something to do with your being fat?"

"I'm? I beg your pardon?"

Dr. Sheppard stood up and picked up the vase. Kitty caught him as he rounded the coffee table. He kept his arms around the vase. She pushed him down onto the couch.

He tried to get back up, and Kitty grabbed his shoulders. He shoved her, and the vase fell to the ground, but still it did not break. She punched him in the throat. She must have taken self-defense classes, because for a moment, he could not breathe. She gathered her handbag from his desk, brushed her hair with one hand, and walked out. Dr. Sheppard tried to catch his breath. "I need to go to the hospital," he said. "I need a doctor." 🐾

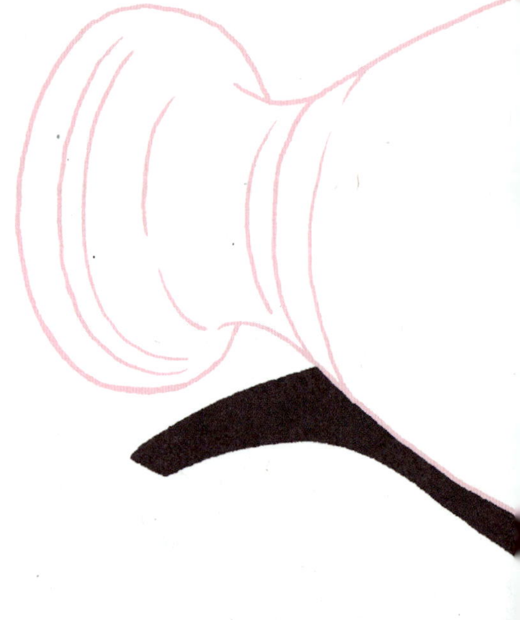

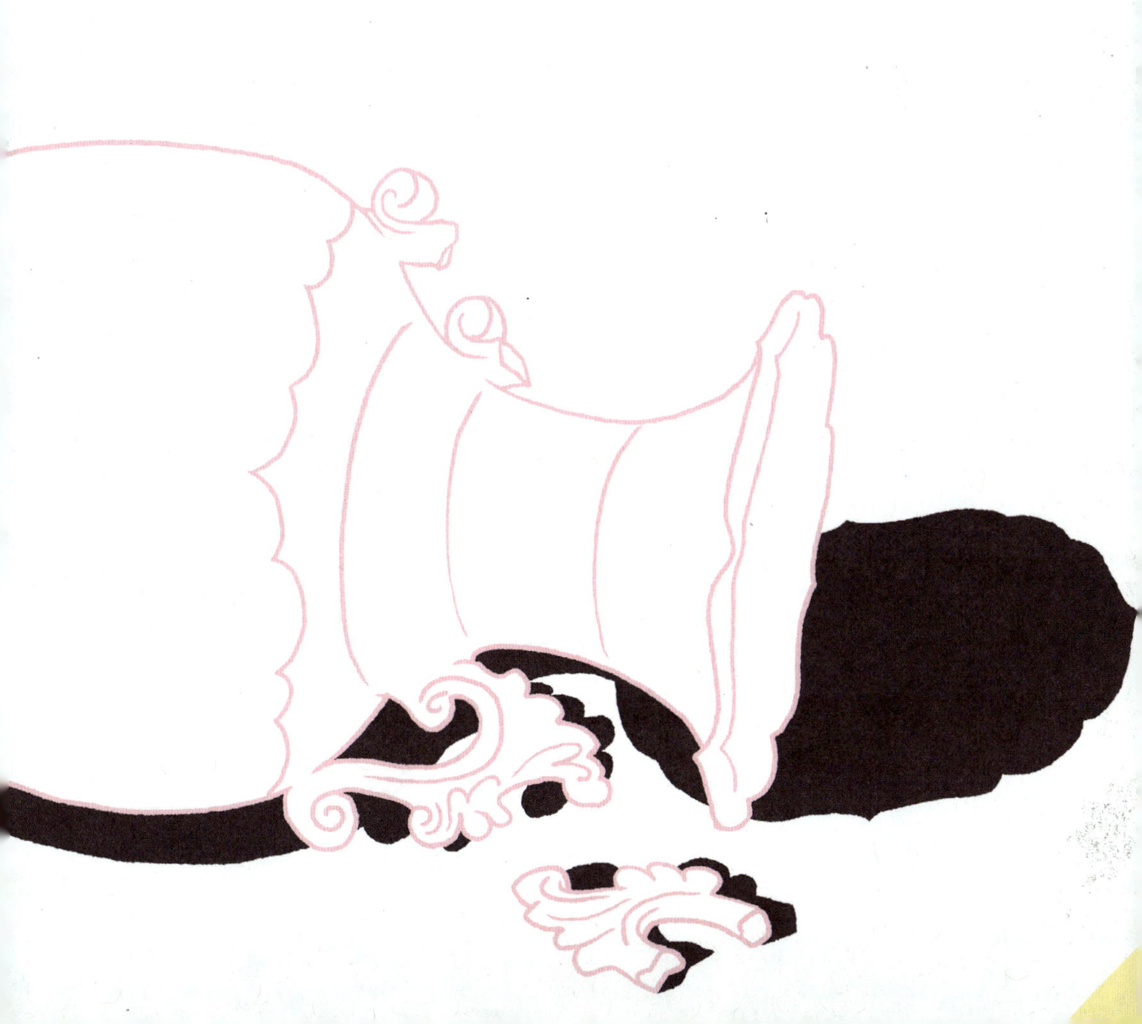

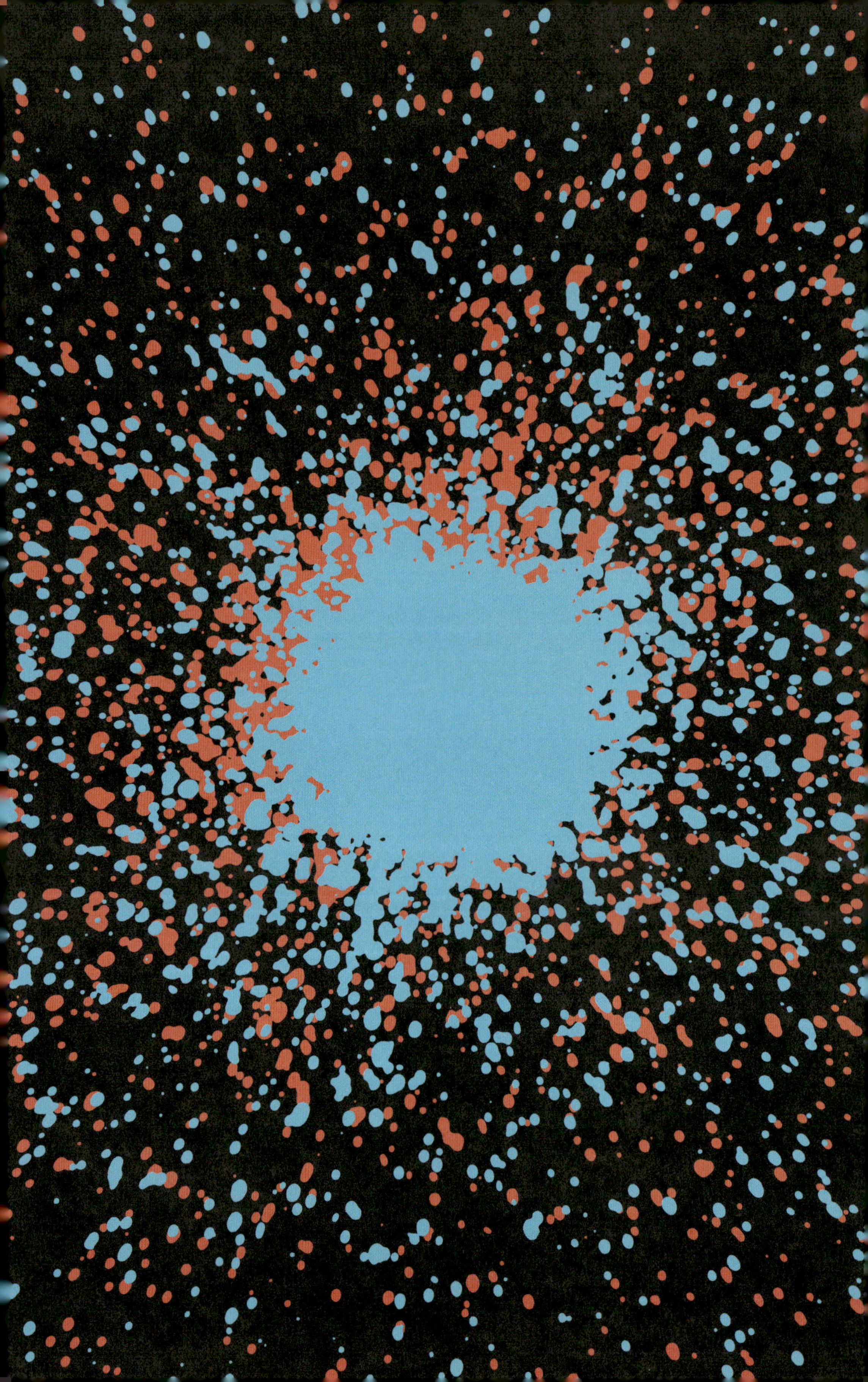

Baby's All Right

"… this sense that in spite of everything—
which of course is the ultimate, I suppose,
the ultimate mystical conviction—
in spite of pain, in spite of death,
in spite of horror, the universe is in some mysterious sense
all right,
capital A, capital R." —Aldous Huxley

146 Broadway, Brooklyn, New York
www.babysallright.com

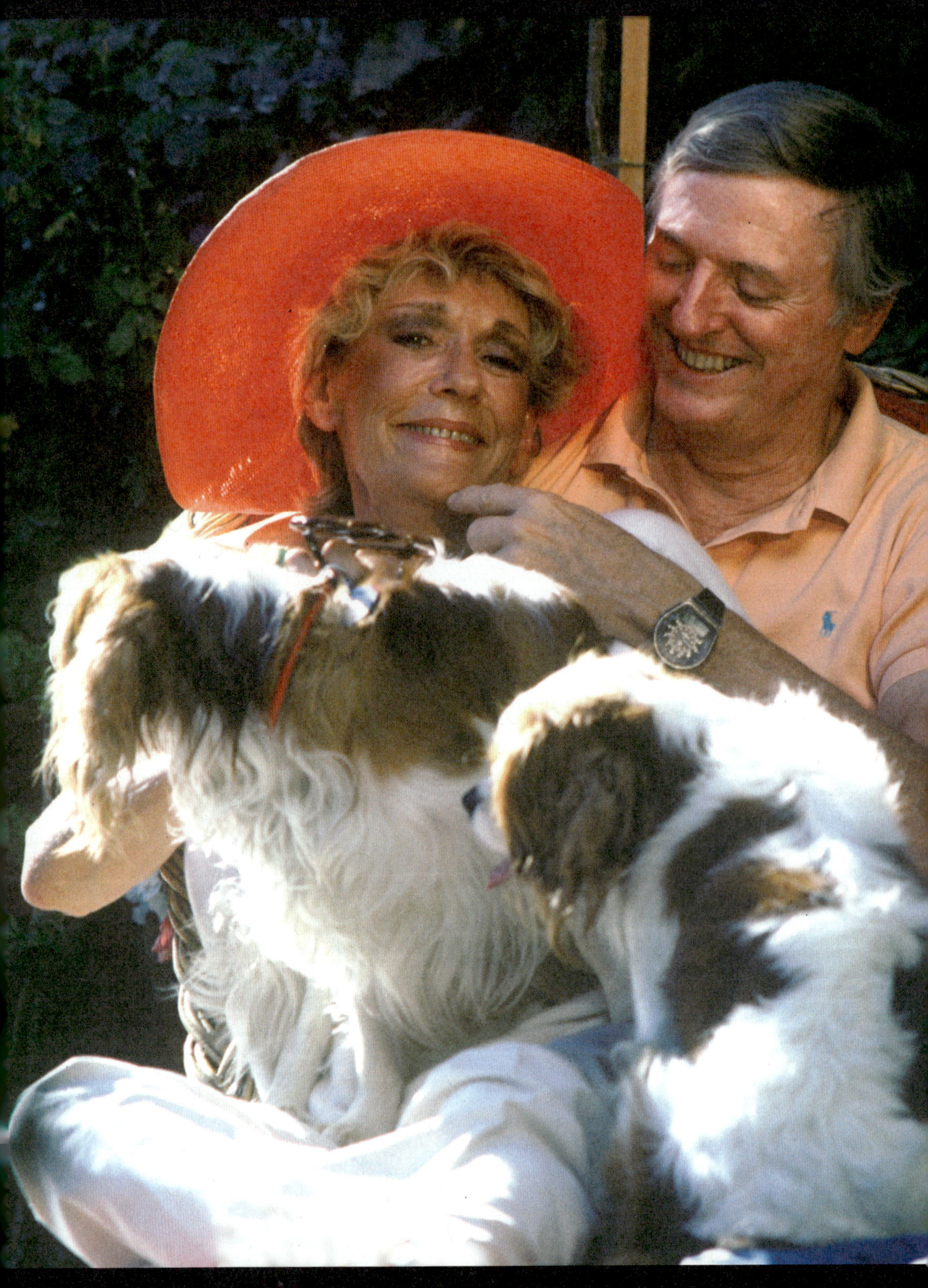

photographs by HARRY BENSON

MR. & MRS. B

BY ALEXANDER CHEE

HOW COULD YOU, my friends would ask, when I told them. How could you *work* for someone like him? Do you ever want to just pick up a knife and stab him in the neck? Poison his food?

You would be a hero, one friend said.

I did not want to stab him, and I did not want to poison him. From our first meeting, it was clear, he was in decline. And as for *how could I*, well, like many people, I needed the money.

And besides, *he* didn't really matter. I loved *her*. »

BEFORE I WORKED as a waiter for William F. and Pat Buckley, I knew them the way most people did—from Page 6 of the *New York Post* and its editorial page; from *Vogue*, the *New York Times*, and the back pages of *Interview*. When I first moved to New York, in 1991, Pat Buckley was the preeminent socialite if you were looking in from the outside—and I was.

Like many ambitious young New Yorkers, I had ridiculous fantasies that involved how one day I would run into her in the rooms I saw only in those pictures. Reading the *Times* on the train on my way to work, I imagined walking into the dimly lit salons where the rich and powerful met and determined the fate of the culture, if not the world.

When I say I really didn't think of him, I mean I didn't read what was referred to by her friends at their parties as "his magazine," the *National Review*, though I sometimes read part or all of his column in the *Post*. I tried to read him when I did because I thought of him as the opposition and I wanted to know what the opposition said and thought, or I thought I did, but too often it was too awful, too enraging, to finish. I knew civilized people were supposed to read the ideas of people who disagreed with them and at least think about them. In this way I was not so civilized.

When I met him finally, he was not as vigorous as she was, perhaps from drink or cigars or both, though she certainly drank and smoked as well. He was shorter and more rumpled, as if one day he had gotten tired and then never quite rested enough. She was tall, tan, and animated, with a wild shock of carefully highlighted hair. She wore a painterly face of makeup that at times resembled the portrait of her that hung in their home. She had the habit of filling the room, and then you might notice him somewhere in it, holding court in a quieter way. It was easy to imagine the woman she'd once been, handsome though not manly, a natural leader. And for those of us who worked there in their house, it was her we watched, always. For it would be her we answered to if anything went wrong.

IN 1997, I began working as a waiter for William F. and Pat Buckley. I was the picture of a New York cater-waiter: 5' 10", 165 pounds, twenty-nine years old, clean-cut. I took the job because I looked good in a tuxedo and couldn't stand the idea of office work unless it was writing a novel. It was the easiest solution to my money problems when I returned to New York after getting my MFA at the Iowa Writers' Workshop, and I'd already been doing it for two years when I was called to work for the Buckleys. Cater-waitering paid $25 an hour plus tips and involved working everything from the enormous galas in the Winter Garden to *People* magazine lunches to openings at the Guggenheim. The tuxedo and the starched white shirt—and the fact that each assignment was at a different, often exclusive, place—all made me feel a little like James Bond. Sometimes my fellow waiters and I called it the Gay Peace Corps for how we could come into places, clean them up, make them fabulous, throw a party, and leave. And I liked that when I went home, I didn't think about the work at all.

As a writer's education, also, being a cater-waiter allowed me access to the interiors of people's lives in a way that was different from every other relationship I might have had. When you're a waiter, clients usually treat you like human furniture. The result is that you see them in unguarded moments, and that, I liked. There was the Christmas buffet dinner where the host and hostess served their visiting family from a group of wines given to them by friends that they considered unworthy of being cellared. Or the Christmas party where the host took a friend into the coatroom to beat him in private (so badly he had to leave) to punish him for being a jerk to us, the waiters, and then handed out his friend's cigars to us afterward and said, "My friend said to say he was sorry." There was the party on the Upper East Side where we changed in a spare apartment we jokingly called "Daddy's Rumpus Room," as the walls were padded with gray flannel and the windows all frosted so that no one could take a photo from outside of whatever it was our host did in there.

And then there was the Upper East Side party for some wealthy closeted gays and lesbians who, to hide their sexuality and protect their fortunes,

*S*ometimes my fellow waiters and I called it the Gay Peace Corps for how we could come into places, clean them up, make them fabulous, throw a party, and leave.

had married off so they resembled straight couples. They looked on with a placid mix of despair and happiness at their sons and daughters, many of them openly gay and lesbian, who were there with their same-sex lovers.

The best thing I'd done for myself as a waiter was to have the cheap polyester tux we all had to wear tailored shortly after starting. I soon caught the eye of a private-client captain, who eventually brought me to the Buckleys. He was a funny, boyish older gay man whose expression could change from a warm smile to an icy stare in less than a heartbeat. He had an English face and complexion, with a last name that didn't match. I interviewed with him and left certain I'd failed. If he liked you, he never let on right away.

He worked for some of the wealthiest clients in New York City. I recall helping Martha Stewart pick out a favorite petit-four in the home of the Grubmans while Vera Wang and Tommy Hilfiger looked on. I learned, as I washed up afterward, that the plates had cost $3,000 a setting. I became used to climbing, at high speed, the back stairs at prominent homes all up and down Fifth and Park Avenues, and washing plates and glasses that cost more than my yearly rent.

The moment I describe next was not at the beginning any different from any of those other jobs, but I remember it because of a word: *maisonette*. It began with a phone message on my answering machine: "Come to _____ Park Avenue. It's a maisonette. Don't go to the front, but come around the side. But don't ring the bell. I'll be in front and take you in the service entrance. Tuxedo, plain shirt, bow tie. I want a fresh shirt—no stains on the cuffs or collars. And be sure to shine your shoes, as she'll know."

And then a pause. "When I say she'll know, I'm talking Pat Buckley. You're working at the Buckleys. Look your best."

I KNEW WILLIAM F. BUCKLEY in the same way that every gay man of my generation knew him: as an enemy. On March 18, 1986, the *New York Times* published an op-ed column by him that advocated for the tattooing of people with AIDS on their buttocks and wrists. He initially proposed something more visible, but then rejected it as an invasion of privacy.

There was a part of my history that made me an unusual figure in the Buckleys' home. I was a former member of the San Francisco chapter of ACT UP, the AIDS activist organization. I had driven to Maine to lie down in the street along with thousands of other protesters in front of President George H. W. Bush's house in Kennebunkport in 1991, for a die-in protesting his inaction on AIDS. I still had PTSD upon seeing policemen after being attacked by them in riots in San Francisco on International AIDS

I wondered briefly whether they ran background checks on the waiters, whether they knew of my past, whether someone like me could really work there.

Day in 1990. I had been a committed member of the group's media committee, appearing on television sometimes, determined to make a difference in the fight against a disease I was sure was going to devastate the world. This was an era when it was still shocking to hear that 10,000 Americans had contracted AIDS. But in just the six years between the die-in at Bush's house and the day when I walked up to the Buckleys' entrance, I'd watched the number of infected grow exponentially, each year, past all imagining.

So when I tell you that I thought of William F. Buckley as the opposition, I mean specifically, as regards to how he had given a powerful public voice to the belief that the illness revoked your basic humanity and placed you beyond help. The tattoo he suggested was to make sure you knew it. Whatever you might think of my friends who joked of my killing him, you may better understand the sentiment as a reaction to experiencing from him a denial that they were even *people.*

On the day I arrived at the service entrance to his Park Avenue maisonette with a waiter's tuxedo on my shoulder, I knew that we bitterly disagreed on the question of what it means to be human. I had never imagined meeting William F. Buckley at all, and so when my first day in the Buckley house began, the reality of what I was about to do to set in. I remember walking to Park Avenue from the subway and looking up at the enormous stone and brick tower in disbelief. I wondered briefly whether they ran background checks on the waiters, whether they knew of my past, whether someone like me could really work there. I drew a breath and put all of that out of my head.

And then the door opened and I was let in.

A MAISONETTE, if you didn't know, and I didn't, is a house hidden inside the walls of an apartment building. The owners share services with the rest of the building but have their own door. In the entrance to the Buckleys' maisonette, at that time, sat a small harpsichord of the most beautiful gold and brown wood. I was told that Christopher, their son, could play it very well. A portrait of him from when he was young hung on the wall on the right, near the entrance, and in it he looked supernaturally beautiful, like the child of elves. Next to the harpsichord was a tree made of metal and what looked to be cut glass or semiprecious stones for leaves, set in a bed of rougher stones in a low vase. There were trees like this all through the downstairs, chest-high, and the effect was like entering a forest grove under a spell, where the beautiful child from the painting might appear and play a song. The forest was also populated with expensive rugs, cigar ashtrays, lamps, and chairs covered in chintz. The house gave the appearance of having been decorated once in a particular style and then never updated again. Between the dark reds on the walls and the glittering stone trees, it felt warm and cold at the same time.

I was being auditioned, the captain told me. If I succeeded at this, one of his most difficult assignments, I would be a regular. "Mrs. B will watch you like a hawk," he said, "in general, but especially for this first one. So you have to be on your very best behavior if you want to be asked back." As the door closed behind us, he said, "That's what we call them: Mr. and Mrs. B."

I was introduced then to a kind older gentleman who, in my memory, ran their household. I don't recall his precise title or his name, but if it had been a palace, I think he would have been the chamberlain. He impressed me instantly as one of the sweetest and most elegant men I had ever met, with a full head of white hair and a wry look in his eyes that stayed whether he was regarding a martini or a waiter. He was busy with showing the cooks around the kitchen. The waiters were brought upstairs to change in a small room that sat at the end of a hallway near the entrance to the back stairs, which led from the second floor to the kitchen. It contained a single bed made up with a torn coverlet, and a treadmill covered in wire hangers and books. Dusty sports trophies lined dusty bookshelves.

"Whose room is this?" I asked the captain.

"Mr. B's," he said.

I stared, waiting for him to laugh.

He said, "Oh, honey. Sure. She's the one with all the money, after all. Canadian timber fortune, I think. Her friends call her Timberrr because of

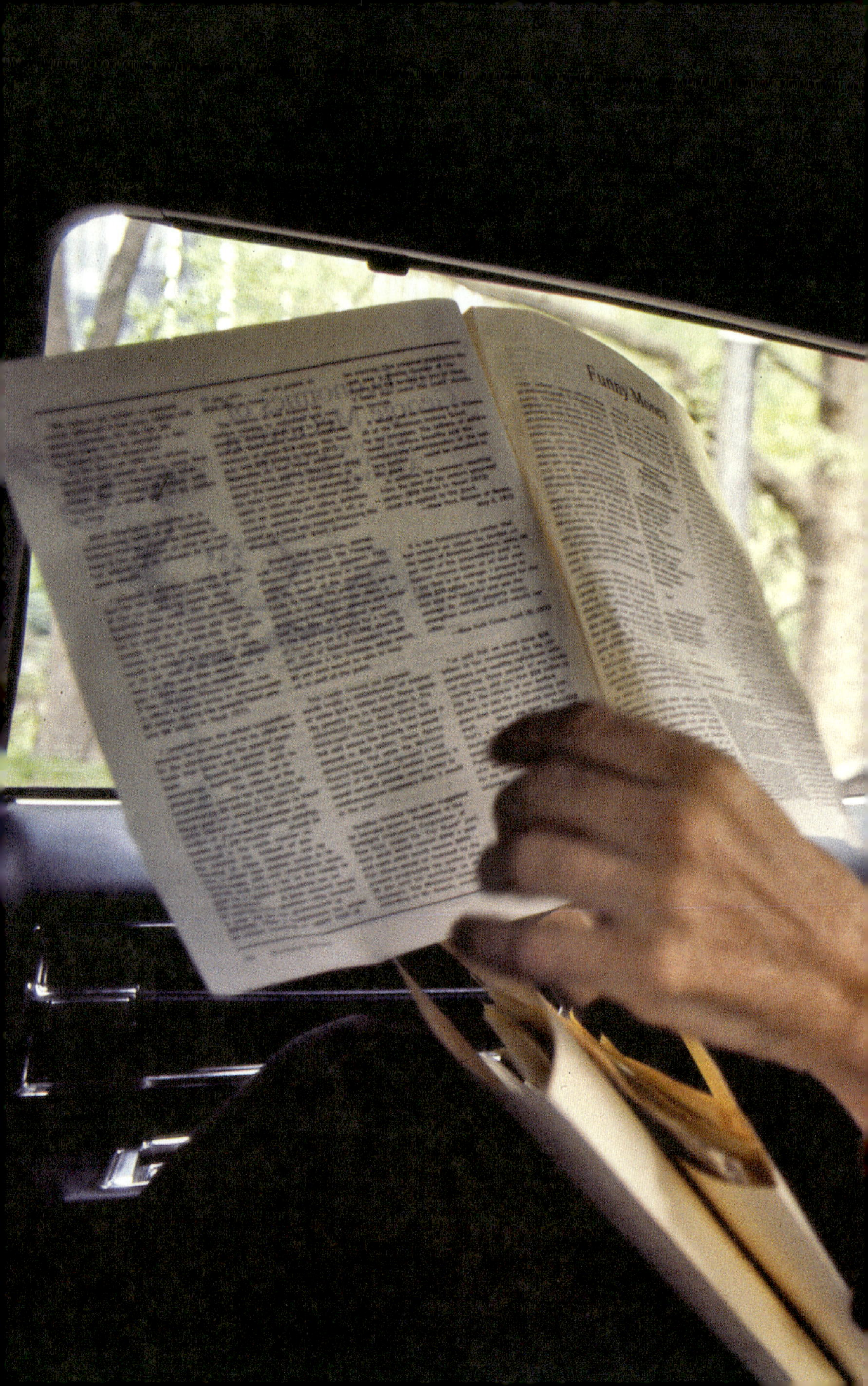
Funny Money

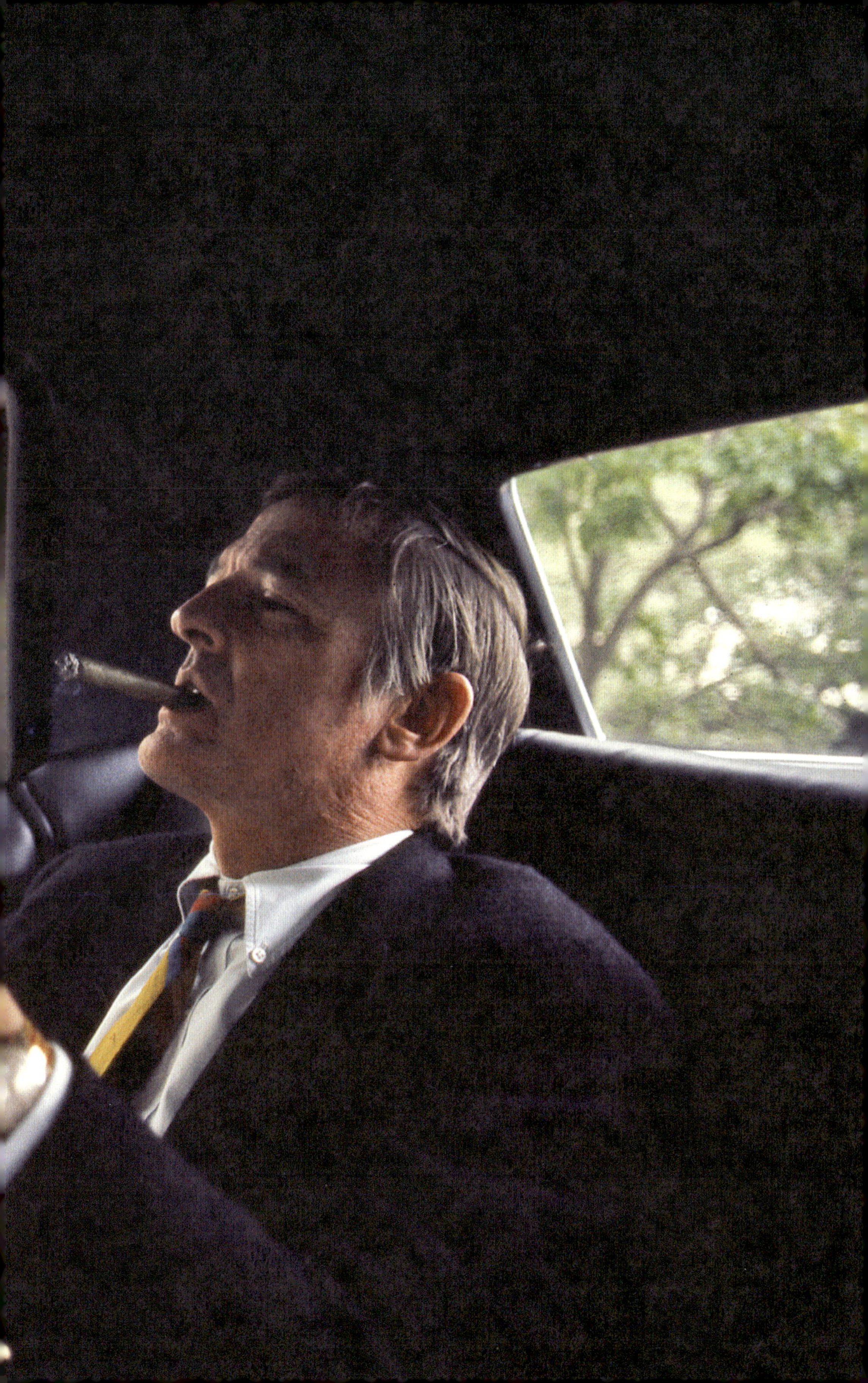

that and because she's tall and when she's drunk she falls over, because she won't wear her shoes." I thought of Madge Wildwood in *Breakfast at Tiffany's*. I laughed, he laughed, and then his face came over serious and flat and we both stopped laughing at the same time.

"Don't you dare write about any of this," he said. "Or I'll have to hunt you down and kill you. With my bare hands. Because I love them dearly."

THE PARTIES THE BUCKLEYS had in New York were typically attended by a strange mixture of her friends and his, which is to say, I remember holding out a tray of scallops wrapped in bacon toward the socialite Nan Kempner and the deeply conservative writer Taki Theodoracopulos, both of whom looked down at it as if it had insects on it, and then I moved on toward the magazine people, who swarmed the trays quickly, eating everything. It was her very rich society crowd mingling with the young writers Buckley was fostering, and they had very little to say to each other, typically drifting to different sides of the room, and yet never hostile.

Despite the way the writers condescended to me, I knew I made more money than they did. But it wouldn't matter. I was holding the tray they were eating from. The food was always from another era: the terrines, for example, which I never saw anywhere else I worked. The scallops wrapped in bacon. Gravlax salmon on Melba toasts. They did not go in for the new trends in cooking—there was never going to be a piece of charred tuna, pink on the inside, on those trays. The only pink was in the roast-beef appetizers. There would never be coconut-crusted shrimp. And dessert was often, perhaps even always, rum raisin ice cream, a favorite of theirs. I found that endearing.

On my first night there, when I was not supposed to make a mistake, I did. I remember very clearly being in the dining room and making my way through the thickets of chairs around the tables. Someone was speaking to the room for some reason as the courses were changing—we were doing a service where we came in with one plate and left with another, switching it out very quickly, in rows of waiters. I cleared from the wrong side and served from the wrong side, and while the guest didn't seem to notice, I was helpless except to look and see Mrs. B glaring at me as if I'd personally done it to hurt her feelings. Her dark, thickly lined eyes barely held in her fury.

I went to the captain immediately. He swore and glowered at me. "Chee…" he said, trailing off. And then he said, "It's okay. I mean, you're in for it now. But there's only one thing for you to do."

That one thing, it turned out, occurred at the very next party, and it was a part of my probation. Instead of passing food or drinks, I looked after her. Mrs. B typically sat talking to someone animatedly, her cigarettes, lighter, lipstick, glasses, and cocktail beside her on a small table. She drank Kir Royales, but with a light blush, not too dark. She would take off her shoes, setting them to the side. And when she leaped up to speak with someone she recognized on the other side of the room, she left everything behind.

Your job at that moment—should you have screwed up as I had screwed up—was to go immediately to the back and emerge with a fresh Kir Royale prepared exactly as she liked it. You never brought her the one she'd just abandoned. You then grabbed her lipstick, glasses, cigarettes, and lighter in your other hand, bent down to retrieve her shoes, and went over to where, by now, she was in conversation again. You did not interrupt, but waited until she looked at you, and then you said, "Mrs. B, you left these," and she would exclaim, take them from you, and sure enough, if the color of the Kir was right and you were appropriately chastised in your manner, and you did all of this exactly right each time she moved, you survived.

As I handed her shoes over that first time, I blushed a little, like someone in love.

For as much as William F. might have done to undermine the situation of people with AIDS, Pat seemed to do in their favor.

I'D NOT READ MR. B'S famous column on the AIDS tattoo before I worked for him. After I began working for him, I still did not read it. I felt it was somehow safer not to, because once that friend had asked me whether I'd ever imagined stabbing Buckley in the neck, it then flashed through my mind once I was inside the house. I remember serving him and watching his neck as I sat the plate down. The single thing I forbade myself to think of became, of course, impossible to ignore. I felt a little like the character in Chekhov's *Story of an Unknown Man*, who pretends to be a serf in order to work inside the home of the son of a politician he opposes. It's an act of political espionage that uncovers nothing, and soon the narrator despairs of what he's done. He eventually runs away with the neglected mistress of his employer.

This is not what I did.

For as much as William F. might have done to undermine the situation of people with AIDS, Pat seemed to do in their favor. In 1987 alone, for example, a year after the famous column, she was involved in raising $1.9 million for the AIDS-care program at St. Vincent's, a hospital at the epicenter of the AIDS epidemic in New York. Today, it might be easy to underestimate the value of that gesture. But at the time, no one wanted anything to do with people with AIDS. Pat was one of New York's greatest fund raisers for charity, and however many lives her husband may have put at risk, it seems to me she saved many more. If it was ever glamorous to raise money for people with AIDS, it was partly because she helped to make it so. And while the finances of their family are known only to them, it seems to me that Mr. Buckley would never condone the types of donations Mrs. Buckley likely gave. If there is a question as to whose money it was, perhaps the

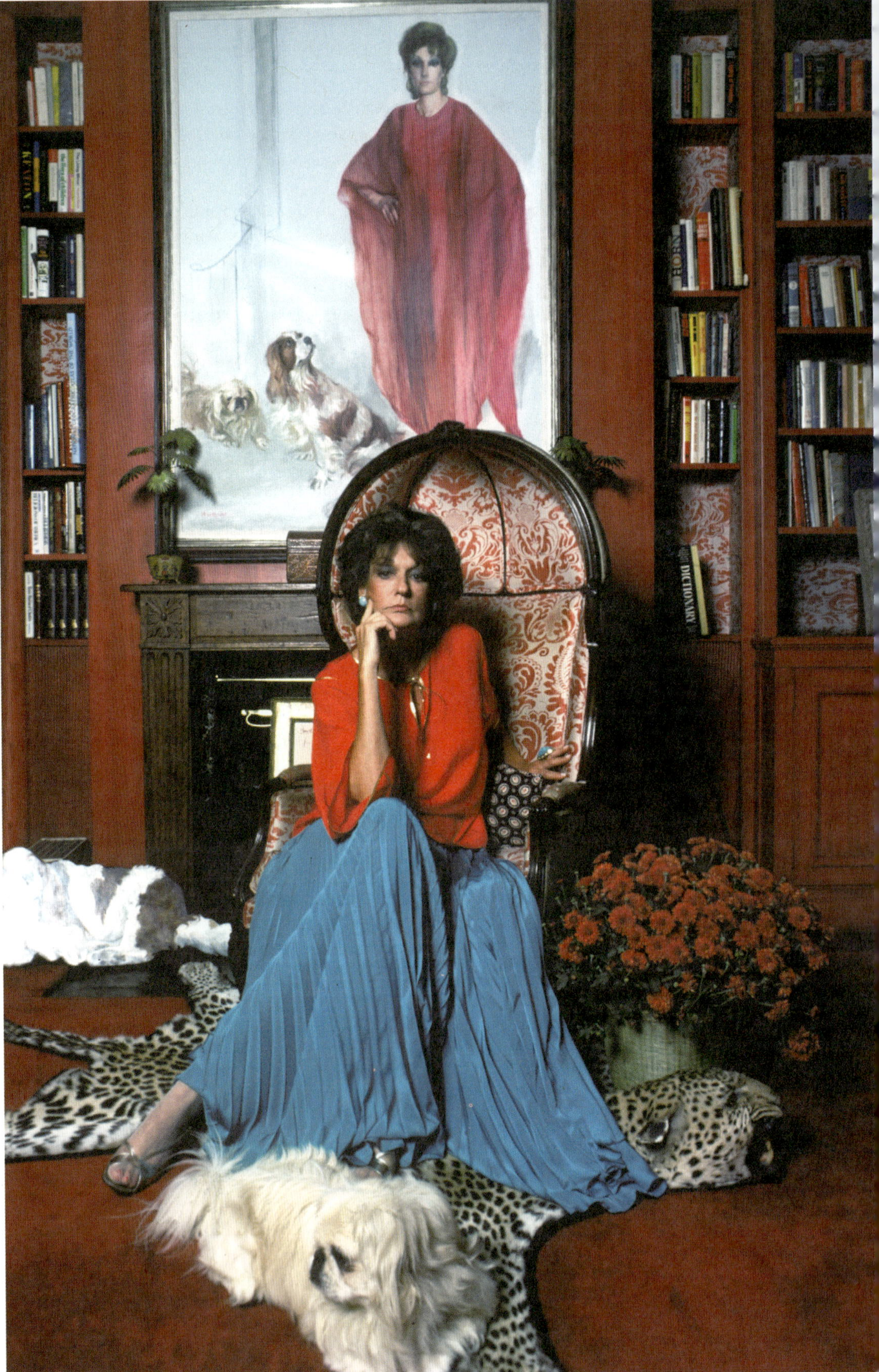

proof is there. She could, it seems to me, have afforded to go against him.

And so if it seems strange to you that one of America's most famous homophobes was married to a woman who was a hero to many gay men, if it seems strange to you that the household where she lived with him was sometimes full of gay men serving food and drink to her guests despite his published beliefs, well, it *was* strange. It was also complicated. And yet the times were such that we, her waiters, experienced the millions of dollars she raised for those who were abandoned to their fates as a kind of protection and affection both. It was not for us, per se, but it could easily have been us next. For gay men in the 90s, that thought was never far from mind. And so I think we could joke about killing him. But never, not even a little, about doing even the slightest thing to hurt her.

I REMEMBER BEING in the back of the Buckleys' limo, headed to their home in Connecticut for a party there. Their driver, our captain observed to me, kept a gun under the seat. A Cabriolet convertible pulled even with the limo and honked three times quickly to get our attention. It was Nan Kempner, waving wildly, girlish. She was still the beautiful icon, her hair held back in a scarf tied at her neck, the top of the Cabriolet down. This was just several years before her death.

"She thinks we're them," one of the waiters said.

I didn't think so. I was pretty sure she knew we were the waiters. Why wouldn't she know Mr. and Mrs. B were already there? She was a good sport, is the thing. It made no sense, of course, but it was easy to believe she was happy to see the men who carried around the food she so routinely ignored.

The Connecticut party invitation was a sign you'd arrived—both for the guests and for the waiters. To be asked to work there meant they trusted you the most. What I remember chiefly about the party is the roses, everywhere, carefully maintained. I first pictured Mrs. B tending them, before my imagination conceded to who she was and replaced the image with that of a gardener. I had a rose garden myself in Brooklyn, and well-tended roses have always impressed me. The country place was a large if somewhat unassuming house in Stamford, a city quickly becoming notorious for gang activity across the tracks from these seaside places. As Nan Kempner had sped away earlier, I wondered if she knew to worry about being carjacked in her convertible. Perhaps she had a gun under her seat too.

We changed clothes this time in an upstairs room with a view of the grounds and the pool before hustling down and attending to the needs of the hundred or so guests swarming the lawns. The party passed in its usual hustle, and was entirely unremarkable until the evening, as we went upstairs and changed to go. From the window, I saw Mr. Buckley head to the pool with a dark-haired young man we could see only from the back. I raised an eyebrow, and one of the waiters said to me, "It's a tradition. He always invites a male staffer to a skinny dip at the end of the night when there are parties up here."

"Really," I said.

We heard the splashes. My coworker smiled. "Really. That's how they used to swim at Yale, after all," he said. Before I could absorb this, Mrs. Buckley appeared in the doorway.

She was, as I've said, very tall, and she loomed there like a ghost. We all froze. We were in various stages of undress. I had my pants on, but my shirt and jacket were hung up, and I wore just a V-neck T-shirt. She had never once come to where we changed before. Her eyes were half-lidded as she looked down at me—I was very near the door. Nearest of all the waiters, who stared as she gave me a long, long look and walked slowly ahead until she was right in front of me. "Thank you," she said, very quietly, looking at me. "Thank you so, so much." And as she said this, she set her long fingers down into the hair on my chest.

"Thank you," I said. It was clear to me she couldn't see me very well. She didn't have her glasses on, and she was drunk.

I can only think I was very good with a Kir Royale. I wondered if perhaps Mrs. B had decided it was time for her to go make an invitation to a male staffer of her own. Why was she there that night, for what reason, when she had never come to us like that before? Was that night somehow unbearable, when all the others had been bearable? Whatever the reason was for her arrival in the room, all of us were shocked to see her.

*W*aiters and escorts both know that indiscretion is a career-ending move. You only reveal a secret if you are never going back again...

There was a terrible loneliness and sadness in her expression, and then it was gone, and she seemed to come back to herself. "Thank you, thank you all," she said, and turned and left the attic.

We finished dressing, and started back to New York in the car before the swimmers returned.

IN THE DAYS AFTER, when I thought of this evening, I could barely believe it. And then months went by, and years, and I could still barely believe it. I knew that, yes, if I ever wrote of it, my captain would throttle me—at the least. But more important, I'd lose my job. And for what? Waiters and escorts both know that indiscretion is a career-ending move. You only reveal a secret if you are never going back again, and at the time, I knew I had reached one of those accommodations one finds in New York—I had carved out a little place I could make a living, in a city where finding and keeping work has always been an extreme sport. I was also supporting my younger sister as she made her way through college with this money. I couldn't afford, in other words, to risk it—to become famous as a waiter who spoke of all this and then be blacklisted by New York publishing in the process. They were *monstres sacrés,* and I was not. Everything in my life would change, and nothing in theirs—I wouldn't be a hero, just an example, the briefest object lesson. And so it soon became a story that I told, instead, and to which people listened in disbelief, and at the end we laughed, as if it were only funny.

All these years later, the moment itself has come to represent some sort of peak, the climax of my life as a cater-waiter. It's as if I never did it again after that night, though of course I know I did. I'm sure I was back at the Buckleys' at least once more, for example, in New York. But in the way of these things, there was no good-bye—I didn't know in advance the moment I would leave, and there was no presumption of intimacy such that I would have written a note saying, "Thank you for the time in your service." I left the business, having finished and sold the novel I'd been working on. I transitioned to living off a mix of grants, advances, and teaching writing. I remember arriving at a party in Chelsea after the publication of that novel and finding my captain holding a tray. He smiled at me, we spoke, he congratulated me. Unspoken between us was that I still should never write of this.

And now Patricia Buckley is dead, William F. Buckley is dead, and the Buckley maisonette has been sold by the beautiful son. Even St. Vincent's Hospital is gone. The building is being slowly converted into a nest of luxury condos.

When I knew I would not return—could not return—I finally did read the famous column. And when just exactly what he'd written was there in front of me—the actual wish for tattoos for people with AIDS—I had numerous reactions. I was surprised to see there was not just one tattoo he wanted for them, but two, one on the forearm and one on the buttocks. I wondered if he knew, before he died, that this column would be mentioned in his obituary along with the names of his wife and son and his place of birth—that it would, in fact, tattoo *him.* And I couldn't help but imagine him in that pool in Connecticut with the young male staffer, swimming underwater, the walls glowing with light, their naked bodies incandescent, just like at Yale, and—maybe—wishing there was some mark on the boy he could easily see. ✿

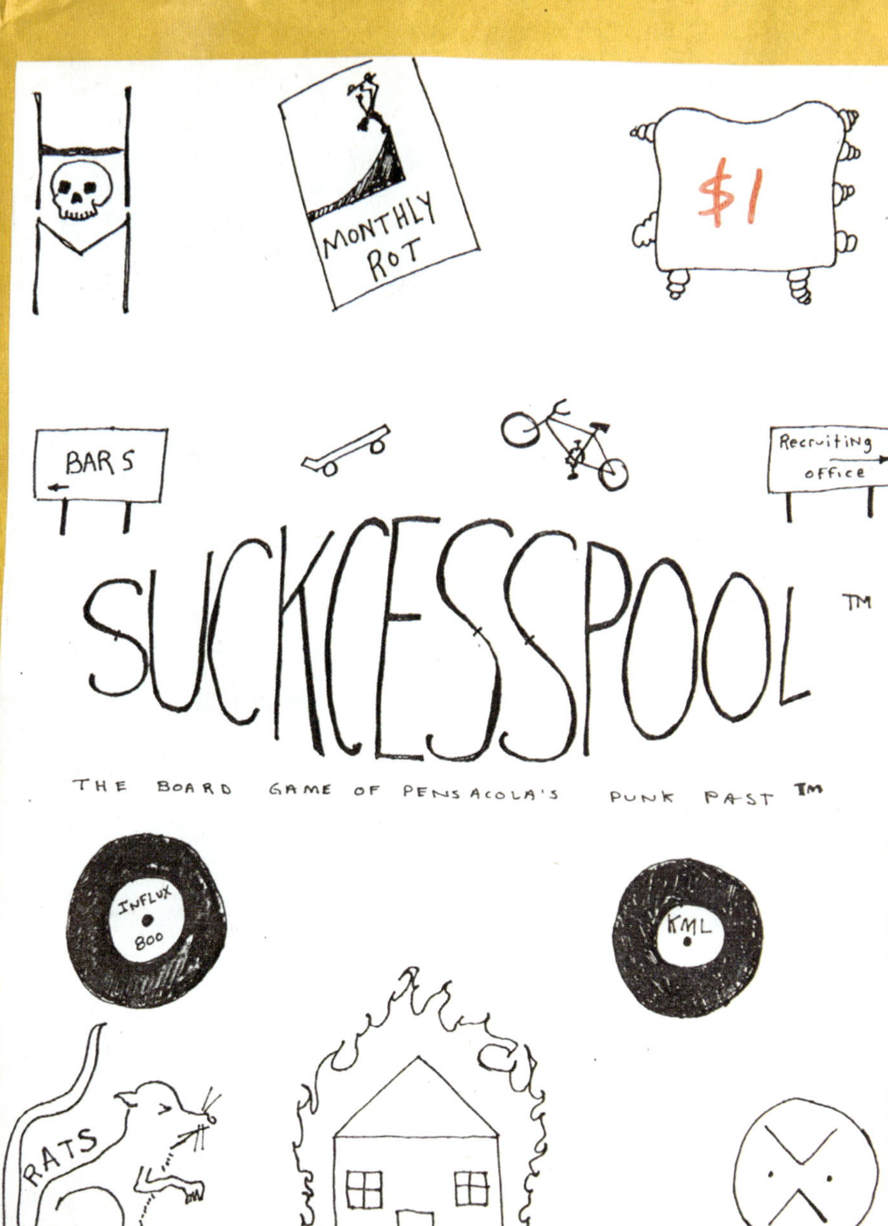

MONTHLY ROT
$1
BARS
Recruiting office
SUCKCESSPOOL ™
THE BOARD GAME OF PENSACOLA'S PUNK PAST ™
INFLUX 800
KML
RATS

SUCKCESSPOOL

By Aaron Cometbus

The writer, punk rock drummer, and Bay Area native Aaron Cometbus has been making the zine with which he shares his assumed last name since 1981. Since then, he's traveled and lived all over America and the world and has amassed thousands of pages of acutely observed, culture- and self-investigating, funny, and heartbreaking memoir, fiction, and commentary. His collected work is an essential piece of the contemporary American canon. (Sorry for the lofty praise, Aaron, but it's true.) Here we present *Suckcesspool*, a board game he invented while living in Pensacola, Florida, in the early 2000s. It tests the player's knowledge of local punk trivia, and therefore it is the most esoteric, quixotic, and functionally pointless game of all time. But there's something really beautiful about all that futility in this age of utility. And besides—as Aaron suggests in the essay that follows, and as we believe perhaps even more firmly than he does—*Suckcesspool* is more a piece of art or experimental fiction than a game.

—*Apology*

Suckcesspool in its original packaging. Photo by Aileen Son.

BECOMING A PUNK IS LIKE

marrying into a family or joining a law firm as a junior partner: its history and legacy become your own. You take on the debts and the responsibility for raising the kids.

That's why the deadbeat dads who've become punk's professional spokesmen—always *men*—bother me so much. They abandoned their child before it could walk, but they dismiss everyone who arrived after they fled. They miss the point, which is to include yourself, not to keep other people out.

I say this as someone who always felt like a latecomer to punk, and an outsider to many of the little scenes that make it up. I loved the history more than the natives did, precisely because I hadn't been there since day one. For the old-timers, it was personal and often painful. For me it was legendary—a mystery to uncover. Yet it was also a living, growing thing. Celebrating the past wasn't about freezing it in time, but showing it as one long, unbroken chain.

I moved to many different cities, looking for the spirit I'd lost in my hometown, or been too young to enjoy when it was around. There were places and people I liked, but rarely did the two coincide. More importantly, my attempts at transplanting didn't take. I formed friendships and bands, but my life and the lives around me didn't become deeply intertwined. Yet roots finally grew in a place I never intended to live, a city I'd never even heard of until I got dumped there on a corner downtown.

Ten days into a ten-week trip, the van pulled over on the side of the road and let me out. The best way to explain what I found is to quote Maggot Sandwich, Pensacola's classic and somewhat comical punk band:

200 city blocks of shotgun shacks along the street
The kids look hungry, the old they suffer from the heat
Old abandoned cars are the toys in which they play
The world that's made them mean just gets tougher every day
This aint no hot nightspot
This aint no fancy suit
This aint no heaven on earth
This is the Sunshine State
My Florida!

In short, Pensacola lacked the usual Florida archetypes. Rather than a tourist trap or a state college, its main draw was a Navy base. There was no Disney World or Everglades, few Cuban exiles or elderly Jews. Culturally, economically, and geographically it was closer to the Deep South. Alabama was a stone's throw away; Miami a twelve-hour drive.

Nothing important had ever happened here.* No one of note was born within Pensacola's borders—not even in the world of punk, where everyone is a star. Perhaps that's why I came to love the place so much. The stagnancy could be depressing, as could the feeling of living far from where the action was. But being off the map was refreshing, too. With no illusions of "making it"—even as far as Gainesville—everyone's expectations were more realistic, and the scene, by necessity, was completely self-sufficient (as well as self-referential, including a cover band that played only old Pensacola punk songs).

Coming from the Bay Area, I'd seen the other side of the coin: overexposure, an inflated sense of self-importance, and growth so rapid that it changed the character of the place, supplanting much of what made it—and its version of punk—unique.

Of course, getting my own house in Pensacola for two hundred dollars a month didn't hurt. But that wasn't the reason I stayed. In a time of crisis, I was taken in and welcomed by strangers. That's enough to make anywhere feel like home.

By 2001, when *Suckcesspool* was made, Pensacola really did feel like paradise. The underground culture was more vibrant than in cities ten times its size. The different sects cross-pollinated in ways I hadn't seen anywhere else: hippies, punks, poets, activists, artists, surfers, and veterans all hanging out together and finding common cause. Between us we had two dozen fanzines, a bookstore, a record store, a collective restaurant, two clothing shops, and three clubs where bands could play—and these were not just places we gathered, but places we *owned*.

We set up punk gigs but also weekly readings, protests, exhibits, and acoustic open-mic nights. When the local paper started printing my calendar of events—without bothering to ask—it was a confirmation that our small community was responsible for a large part of the city's civic life.

Making *Suckcesspool* (the name, like many other parts of the game, comes from a Maggot Sandwich song) was a way to include as many people as possible, especially the type usually overlooked by history, whose role is supportive but offstage. It was also a way to put several generations together on the same page, and show that our scene was just as sordid and disgusting as any other, even if for the rest of the world it didn't even merit a footnote, much less a coffee-table book.

Suckcesspool was a collective effort, with input and information from everyone who was hanging around. Rymodee was a particular help, a veritable storehouse of Pensacola punk folklore. He also drew the cover and gathered tracks for the accompanying compilation tape. Scotty Potty and Ichabod provided inspiration and assistance, without which the project couldn't have been done and wouldn't have been so much fun.

However, no project would be com-

---

* The worst moments in Pensacola's history are the only ones known nationally, which paints a skewed picture of the city. When friends from home said, "Isn't that where they murder abortion doctors?" I replied, "Isn't San Francisco where they murder mayors and gay supervisors?" When people came to visit, they were shocked to see the G&L (Gay and Lesbian) Bank on Pensacola's main street.

plete without the failure and despair that follows its release. On the maximum effort/minimum reward scale, *Suckcesspool* scored nearly 100 percent, an A+. Thirty copies were assembled in an elaborate package with wheat-pasted, hand-colored covers, game pieces, and a cassette. But the response was underwhelming, to say the least.

People complained that facts were left out or not quite right. They griped about the high cover price (a buck). Worst of all, they just read the quiz cards and chuckled. No one played the game—no one but Rymodee, Scotty, Ichabod, and me, crowded in my kitchen dressed in fake mustaches to resemble Captain Crap of Maggot Sandwich fame.

I should have known better, but who learns from their mistakes, except to raise the ante each time in order to achieve an even higher level of pain? I'd done a board game once before, an ill-fated collaboration with Sam McPheeters based on another depressing Southern town (albeit one that has since achieved some renown). It, too, featured elaborate packaging and a low cover price, and, like a fart, was either badly received or politely ignored.

Perhaps someday our Richmond board game will also see a proper rerelease. In the meantime, I urge and beg you to not just read the *Suckcesspool* game cards, but to cut them out and *play*. Don't feel left out if you don't know the names. You'll still recognize the likenesses, and the mixture of enthusiasm and impending doom. Just remember that all scenes and home-

towns are more or less the same. The only differences are the ways that everything goes wrong.

It has even been suggested that *Suckcesspool* is an experimental novel that you read by rolling the dice. You learn the landmarks as you go, and are introduced to the local legends, cartoonish villains, and lovable fools. The defining events of Pensacola punk—all disasters—unfold each time you make a move.

Though the people and events in *Suckcesspool* are real, I don't mind it being seen as fiction, because that's how it felt at the time. Me and Scotty would walk the tracks to Whataburger every week, reviewing the latest twists and turns in the plot as if they were chapters in a book. The narrator was the water tower in the center of town—immortalized in a song by This Bike is a Pipebomb—which looked down Sphinx-like on our lives. When me and Scotty got matching water tower tattoos, no fewer than thirty of our friends followed suit. It was too absurd— and too good—to be believed.

In hindsight, the era in which *Suckcesspool* was made was a golden age, right before the start of a war that decimated the local economy, followed by a hurricane that destroyed almost everything else—most notably, the sense of hope. The community didn't die, but it did change, and many of the major players moved away.

Suckcesspool stands as a document of that time and the scene some of us left behind, which continues on—unheralded and largely unknown—today.

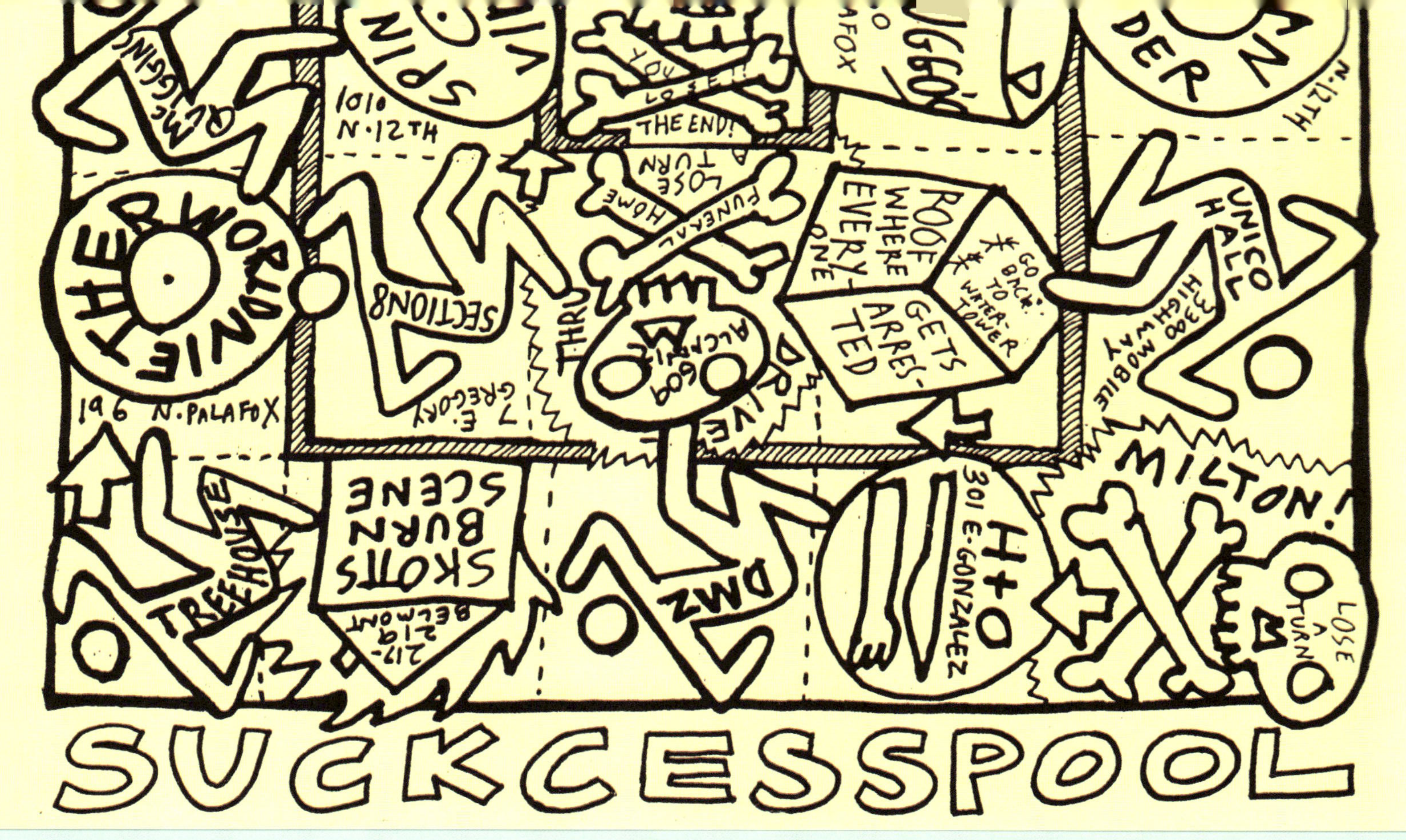

THERWORLDNIE
146 N. PALAFOX
1010 N. 12TH
SPIN C VI
DER
N. 12TH
SECTION 8
THRU
7 E. GREGORY
YOU LOSE!!
THE END!
FUNERAL HOME
LOSE A TURN
ALCUM609
DRIVE
GO BACK TO WATER TOWER
ROOF WHERE EVERY ONE GETS ARRESTED
UNICO HALL
3300 HIGHWAY MOBILE
JIGGO
AFOX
TREEHOUSE
SKOTTS BURN SCENE
217-219 BELMONT
DMZ
H+O
301 E. GONZALEZ
MILTON!
LOSE A TURN
SUCKCESSPOOL

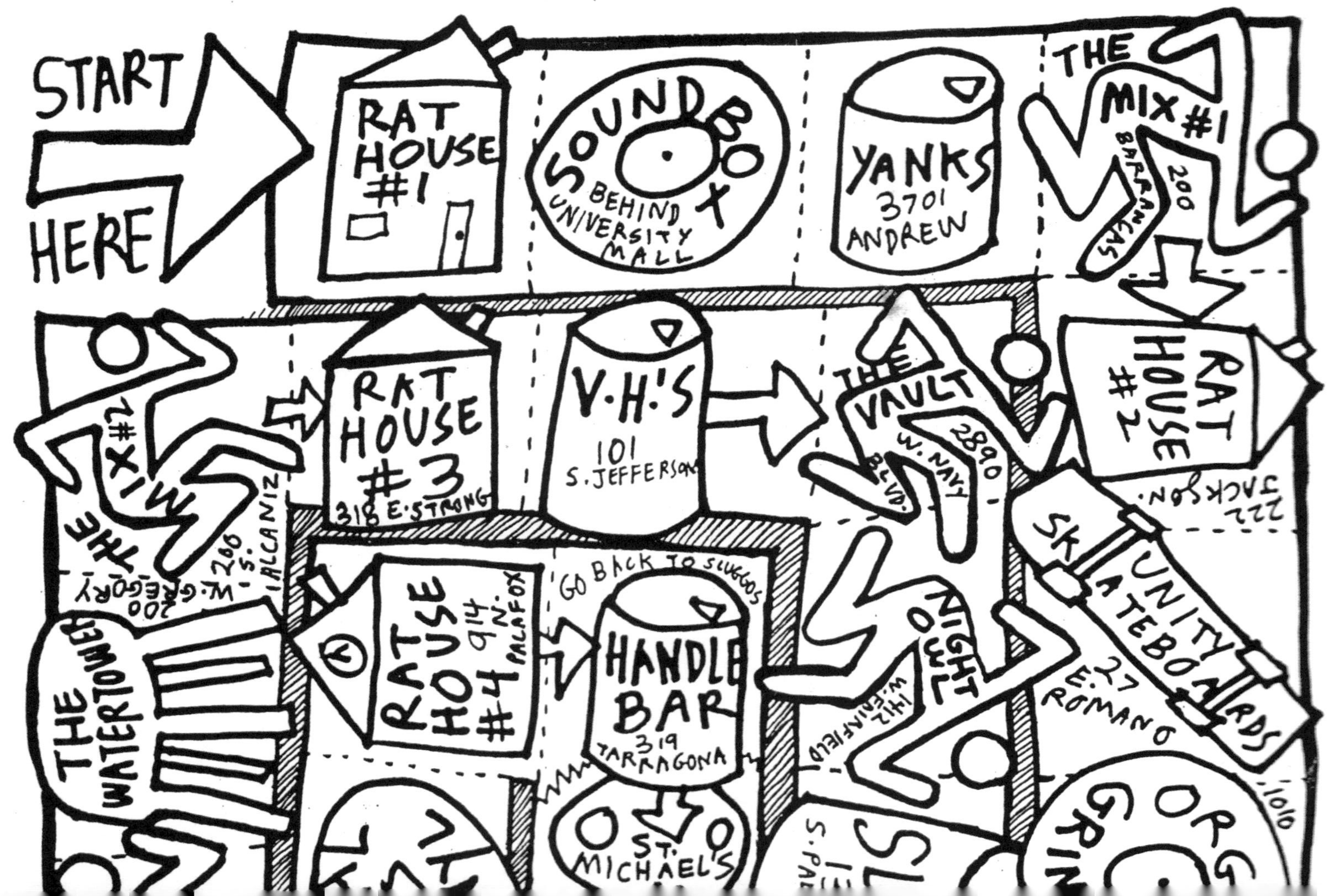

START HERE
RAT HOUSE #1
SOUNDBOX
BEHIND UNIVERSITY MALL
YANKS
3701 ANDREW
THE MIX #1
200 BARRANCAS
THE MIX #2
200 W. GREGORY
S. ALCANIZ
RAT HOUSE #3
316 E. STRONG
V.H.'S
101 S. JEFFERSON
THE VAULT
2890 W. NAVY BLVD.
RAT HOUSE #2
222 JACKSON
THE WATERTOWER
RAT HOUSE #4
914 N. PALAFOX
GO BACK TO SLUGGOS
HANDLE BAR
319 TARRAGONA
ST. MICHAEL'S
NIGHT OWL
1412 W. FAIRFIELD
SKATEBOARDS
UNITY
27 E. ROMANO
1010
ORG GRIN

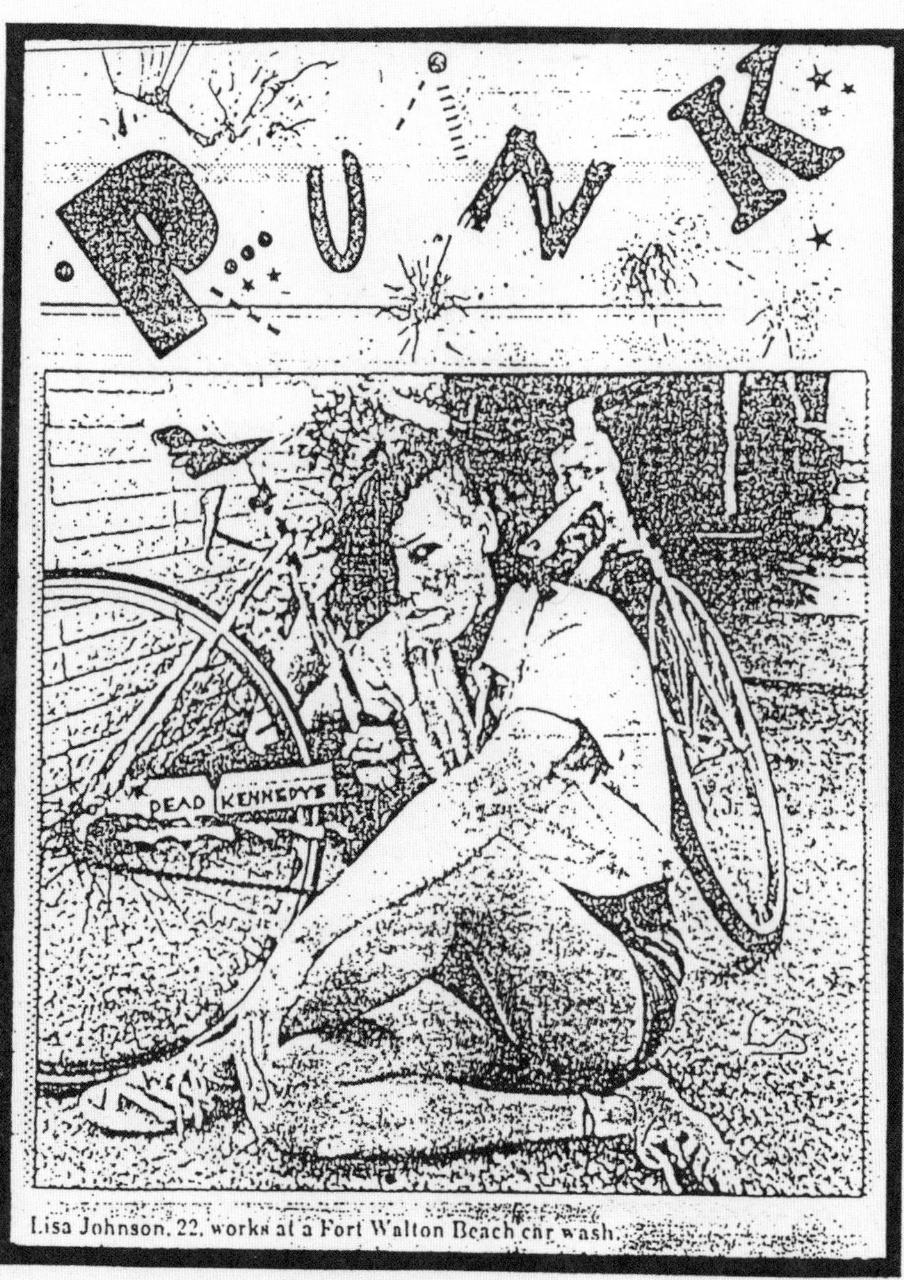

Lisa Johnson, 22, works at a Fort Walton Beach car wash.

WHAT THE REST OF THE COUNTRY THINKS WHEN THEY HEAR "PENSACOLA"

A) WHITEST SAND

B) SHARK ATTACKS

C) KILLING ABORTION DOCTORS

D) AWESOME PUNK SCENE

INVESTIGATING A LOCAL CAT-KILLING SPREE, THE POLICE MISTOOK SPRAYPAINT OF THIS BAND'S LOGO AS A CLUE

A) CRASS
B) BLACK FLAG
C) DEAD KENNEDYS
D) WOODENHORSE

If you answered C move ahead 5 spaces (the cops thought DK stood for Dead Kats)

'IN TRANSIT' GOT SHUT DOWN THE VERY FIRST WEEKEND IT OPENED BECAUSE OF THIS BAND'S NAME ON A FLIER

A) HEADLESS MARINES
B) THE FUCKING HORRIBLES
C) DUCT TAPE NECKTIE
D) WE HAVE PICTURES OF DEBRA DUNLOP HAVING SEX WITH A DONKEY
E) WE HAVE PICTURES OF BRAD VUCOVICH ON A WATERSLIDE WITH A UNICORN
F) WE HAVE PICTURES OF SPARKY TAYLOR RIDING A BROKEN BIKE WITH A SOCK MONKEY

If you answered B move ahead 1 space

MAGGOT SANDWICH'S KEYBOARD PLAYER WAS...

A) ANNA GRAM
B) MONA GRAM
C) HOLLIE GRAM
D) KANDY GRAM

If you answered D move ahead 4 spaces

MAGGOT SANDWICH GOT THEIR NAME BY POLLING...

A) READERS OF THE MONTHLY ROT
B) READERS OF MRR
C) CUSTOMERS AT DOGHOUSE DELI
D) HOBOS AT HOBO BEACH

If you answered B move ahead 2 spaces

WHO GOT BUSTED FOR LEWD AND LASCIVIOUS BEHAVIOR IN THE QUAYSIDE PARK BATHROOMS WITH A SUNDAY SCHOOL TEACHER FROM ATMORE?

A) MS. MULLET
B) COWBOY BOB
C) CAPTAIN CRAP
D) CHE-CHE LA FEMME

If you answered B move ahead 3 spaces

UNICO HALL WAS A BUILDING THAT HAD NOT ONLY PUNK SHOWS, BUT ALSO:

A) BOWLING
B) ANGRY VETS
C) BINGO
D) PIZZA

If you answered C move ahead 3 spaces

FLORIDA BLANCA + ROMANA BAR WHERE GAY PUNKS HUNG OUT CIRCA 1984?

A) THE FLAME
B) MR. B'S
C) PAPPY'S
D) VALHALLA

If you answered D move ahead 4 spaces

WHICH REDNECK GANG USED TO BEAT UP THE PUNKS?

A) HOT LEAD
B) COLD FEET
C) FOUL PLAY
D) LIGHTNING STRIKES

If you answered C move ahead 4 spaces

WHICH IS TRUE?

A) SLUGGO'S WAS OWNED BY SLUGGO
B) YANK'S WAS OWNED BY YANK
C) McQUIGGIN'S WAS OWNED BY THE BROTHERS McQUIGGIN
D) THE MIX WAS BOOKED BY SKOTT COWGILL'S GRANDMA

If you answered B,C, AND SORT OF D move ahead 4 spaces

NAME THE PENSACOLA PRO SKATER WITH HIS OWN ZORLAC BOARD (INCIDENTALLY, THE MODEL USED TO KILL THE BUM IN 1989)

If you answered SCOTT STANTON move ahead 4 spaces

WHO IS PENSACOLA'S BIGGEST STRAIGHT EDGE FAILURE?

A) SKOTT COWGILL
B) BRAD VUCOVICH
C) AARON COMETBUS
D) GABE SMITH

If you answered TRUE or ALL OF THE ABOVE move ahead 2 spaces

WHO BUSTED SLUGGO'S WINDOW WITH THEIR ASS?

A) PETE KELLY
B) IVAN FROM WAFFLE HOUSE
C) BOB NOXIOUS
D) JEN KNIGHT

If you answered A move ahead 4 spaces

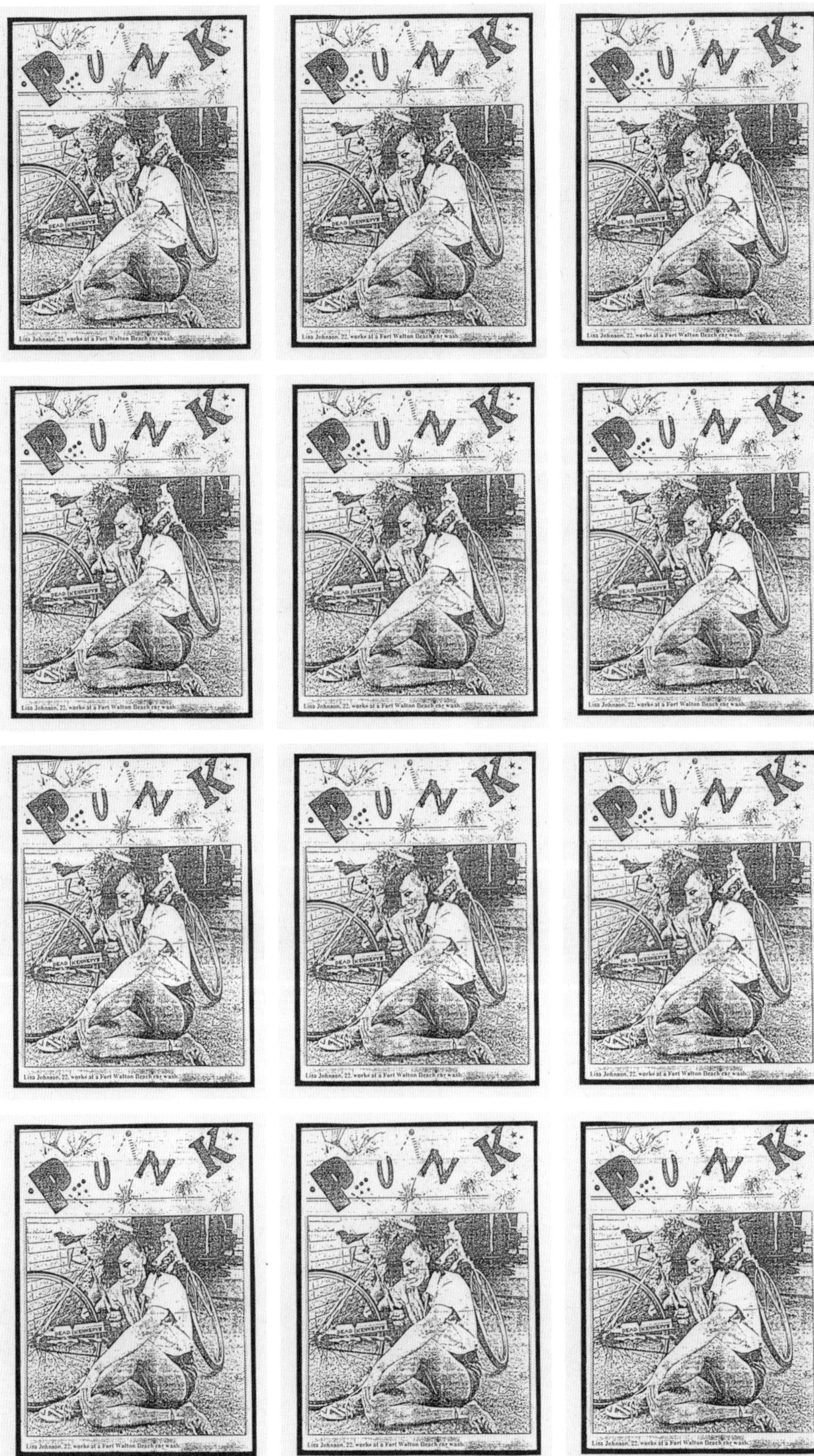
PUNK
DEAD KENNEDYS
Lisa Johnson, 22, works at a Fort Walton Beach car wash.

WHICH PENSACOLA ELDER STATESMAN GOT BEAT UP BY IGGY POP?

A) DAN PRETO
B) JAMEY JONES
C) ELVIS JONES
D) SANDY WHITEHEAD

WHAT DOES S.K.A.B. STAND FOR?

A) SKOTT KOWGILL AND THE BOYS
B) SKATING KURBS AND BANKS
C) SHOOT+KILL AMERICAN BOYS
D) STREET KONKRETE ASPHALT BASH

"THE HANDLEBAR" WAS NAMED FOR THE OWNERS LOVE OF...

A) MOUSTACHES
B) MOTORCYCLES
C) BICYCLES
D) THE AUSTRIAN COMPOSER OF "MESSIAH"

SKOTT COWGILL'S DAD WAS...

A) COP
B) FBI
C) IN MAGGOT SANDWICH
D) CRAZED BIKER

THE HANDLEBAR HAD A SHORT DOUBLE LIFE AS...

A) AN ART GALLERY
B) ARENA FOR JOURNEY COVER BANDS
C) WEEKEND HAIR SALON
D) FIERY INFERNO

AFTER A LONG ONSTAGE SPEECH ABOUT VEGETARIANISM, THE BAD BRAINS ORDERED THIS WHEN IN PENSACOLA:

A) RIB DOGS AND CORNBREAD FROM KING'S BBQ
B) CHICKEN AND BISCUITS FROM QUEEN BEE
C) CHITLINS AND COLLARD GREENS FROM H+O
D) LOBSTER AND BURGERS FROM RED LOBSTER

WHO HAD HER EMBARRASSING TATTOOS SURGICALLY REMOVED?

A) SHIELACORE
B) HOLLIE ROCKER
C) PAULA PAYPHONE
D) MAGGIE SANDWICH

NAME THE PEOPLE STUCK WITH THESE EMBARRASSING TATTOOS:

A) "WHITE TRASH"
B) "THE DOORS"
C) "STRAIGHT EDGE" WITH BEER GUT STRETCH MARKS
D) EXPLODING FIRECRACKER ON HIS PENIS

WHAT NAME IS WRITTEN ON EVERY SECONDHAND PUNK RECORD IN PENSACOLA?

A) LOBO
B) HOBO
C) PUTO
D) LOLA

"SMELL OF DEAD FISH" STARTED OUT AS...

A) A JOURNEY COVER BAND
B) AN ENVIRONMENTAL NEWSPAPER
C) A MISSPELLED TATTOO
D) A RESTAURANT

WHAT LOCAL CHARACTER IS A FAVORITE MASCOT OF THE PUNKS?

A) COWBOY
B) TURBO
C) SLIM
D) LARRY FROM WHATABURGER

MAGGOT SANDWICH'S DEBUT 7" WAS CALLED...

A) "TAKE A BITE"
B) "LIVE FOR TODAY"
C) "DEAD TO MY WORLD"
D) "THIS IS PENSACOLA, NOT TALLAHASSEE"

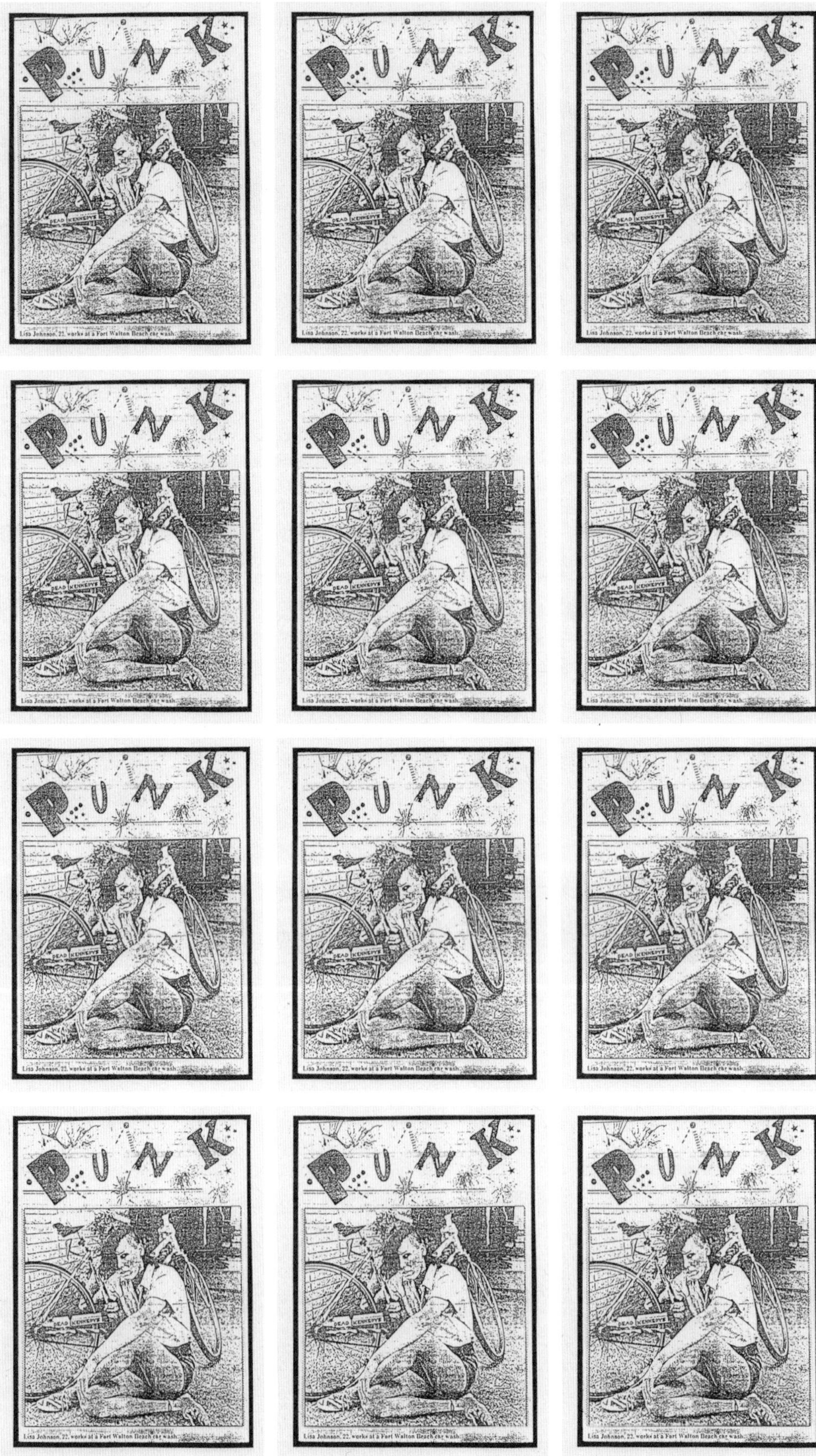
PUNK
DEAD KENNEDYS
Lisa Johnson, 22, works at a Fort Walton Beach car wash.

RYMODEE'S BIKE TATTOO WAS ORIGINALLY A...

A) BLACK FLAG SYMBOL
B) CIRCLE A
C) STRAIGHT EDGE X
D) DRI THRASHING GUY

BIG DAVE WAS ARRESTED AT SPRINGFEST FOR
A) OPEN CONTAINER
B) INCITING A RIOT
C) CONTRIBUTING TO THE DELINQUENCY OF A MINOR
D) SODOMY

WHAT "BEER CITY" BAND HAS THE DUBIOUS PRIVILEGE OF HAVING THEIR SONG SLAUGHTERED BY AN AGING FOLKER WITH AN ACOUSTIC GUITAR?

A) AMERICAN SUICIDE
B) RADIO 55
C) BULLETPROOF
D) GIMCRACK

WHAT DID THE INITIALS N.C.S. STAND FOR?

A) NUKE CHRIST SHIT
B) NO CLASS SURFERS
C) NAKED CAR SALESMEN
D) NOAM CHOMSKY SUCKS

SINCE TIME IMMEMORIAL, THE PENSACOLA PUNKS HAVE GATHERED AT...

A) THE FOUNTAIN AT PLAZA FERDINAND
B) THE CHIPLEY MONUMENT AT PLAZA FERDINAND
C) THE ANDREW JACKSON STATUE AT PLAZA FERDINAND
D) THE GIANT REINDEER AT PLAZA FERDINAND

NAME THE PENSACOLA 80'S PUNK ANTHEM.

A) I SCREAM
B) I WANNA SKATE THE RAMP
C) I WANNA FISH THE LAKE
D) I WANNA ROCK SO I CAN THROW IT AT YOU

NAME PLAID GIRL'S BIG HIT

A) "BITCH"
B) "LIES"
C) "DADDY"
D) "GET DOWN"

WHO STOLE LITTLE BILLIE BLASPHEMY'S METALLICA SHIRT AND DISAPPEARED TO LOUISIANA ON A CREDIT CARD SCAM?

A) PAT RYDER
B) PAT ROSS
C) PAT FROM THE RAGING DAISY
D) EDMUND G. "PAT" BROWN

ONLY BAND TO EVER MOVE TO PENSACOLA:

A) REDNECK MEATWAGON
B) THE BEACH MONKEYS
C) THE JAZZ ASSASSINS
D) GIMCRACK

MISGUIDED YOUTH, WHEN THEY PUT OUT THEIR FANZINE, "WHY I'M GLAD I'M NOT A GIRL"...

A) WERE HAILED AS LOCAL HEROES
B) HAD THEIR TIRES SLASHED, WINDOWS SMASHED, AND CAR TRASHED
C) WERE BANNED, SLANDERED, BRANDED, AND BANISHED
D) GOT SCATTERED, SMOTHERED, COVERED AND TOPPED

WHAT CLUB WAS A POTATO AND SALAD RESTAURANT DURING THE DAY?

A) THE MIX
B) SECTION 8
C) THE VAULT
D) McQUIGGIN'S

WHAT WAS MAGGOT SANDWICH'S ORIGINAL NAME?

A) SOAK
B) OAKS
C) A-OK'S
D) KAOS

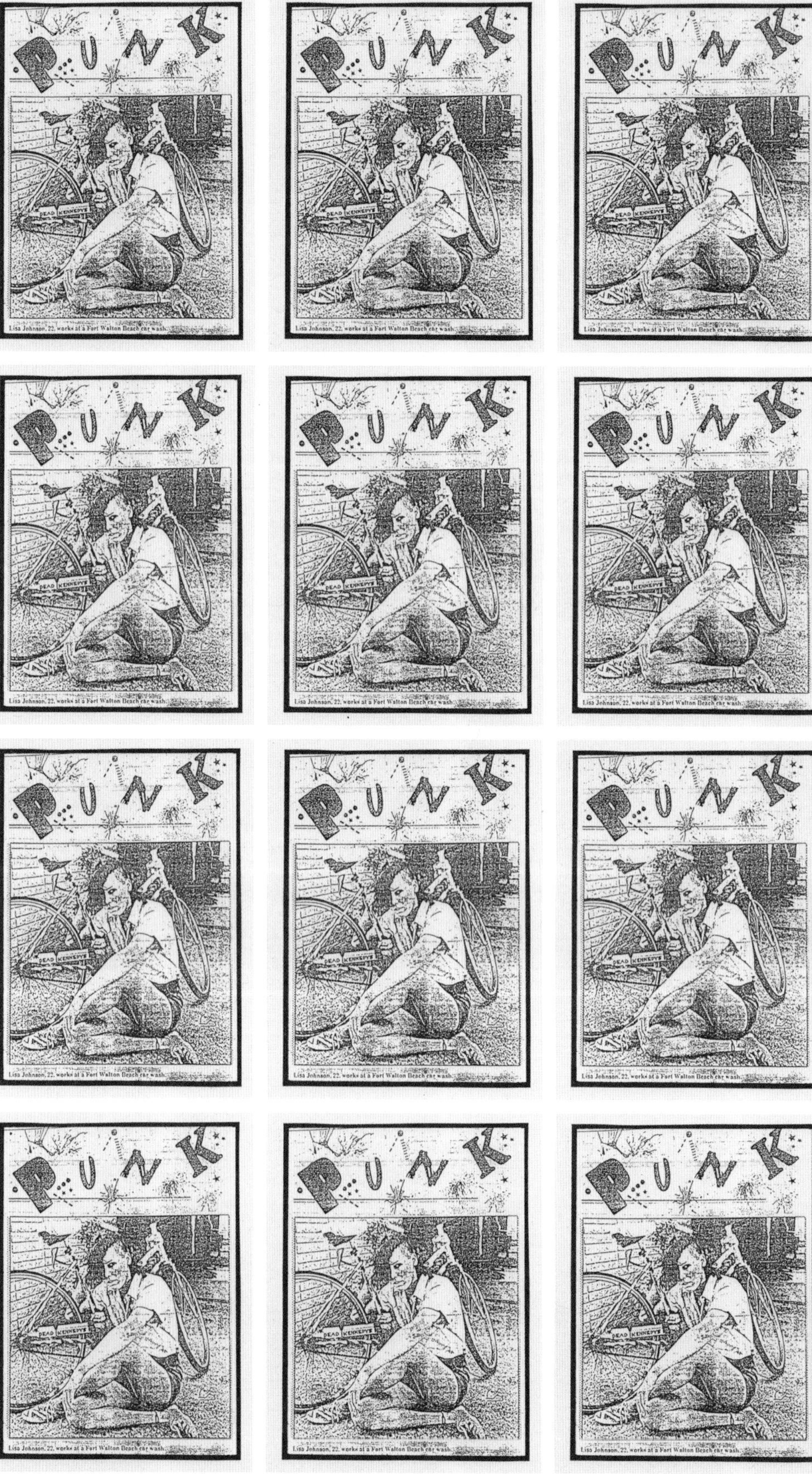
PUNK
DEAD KENNEDYS
Lisa Johnson, 22, works at a Fort Walton Beach car wash.

WHICH BAND'S VIDEO FEATURES BRAD VUCOVICH'S COUCH BEING STABBED?

A) VAN HALEN
B) GREEN DAY
C) N'SYNC
D) PAULA ABDUL

If you answered B move ahead 2 spaces

MAKE UP YOUR OWN QUESTION

STEVE WINFREY IS FAMOUS FOR WHICH LOCAL PUNK EVENT?

A) PUTTING ON THE GBH SHOW AT THE LION'S CLUB IN 1988
B) GETTING BURNED UP IN A HOUSE FIRE IN 1995
C) KILLING A BUM WITH A SKATEBOARD IN 1989
D) LIVING IN HIS CAR IN THE WALMART PARKING LOT IN 2000

If you answered A move ahead 2 spaces

WHICH OF THESE WAS P-COLA'S FIRST PUNK BAND:

A) THE GAMES
B) THE SHAMES
C) THE NAMES
D) THE DAMES

If you answered C move ahead 1 space

MAGGOT SANDWICH ARE NOW...

A) DOOR TO DOOR SALESMAN
B) MOWING THE PJC LAWN
C) IN THE PARK PLAYING WITH A BOOMERANG
D) STILL ACTIVE IN THE SCENE

If you answered ALL BUT D move ahead 2 spaces

SLUGGO'S WAS ORIGINALLY CALLED:

A) VICTOR HUGO'S
B) EMILE ZOLA'S
C) ANDRE MALRAUX'S
D) JEAN-PAUL SARTRE'S

If your answer was A move ahead 1 space

HEADLESS MARINES WERE ORIGINALLY A COVER BAND OF...

A) THE CLASH
B) THE EAT
C) THE SEX PISTOLS
D) THE THOMPSON TWINS

If you answered C move ahead 4 spaces

WHO IS CAPTAIN CRAP'S BROTHER?

A) THE INCREDIBLE BUZZ SAW
B) THE NOTORIOUS BUZZ ERD
C) THE INFAMOUS BUZZ ZERK
D) THE NEFARIOUS BUZZ COX

If you answered C move ahead 4 spaces

WHICH PCOLA PUNK NOW WORKS AT THE "RIOT HYATT" IN L.A.?

A) "PSYCHO" CINDY
B) LENA "SWAYBACK"
C) "PLANET" JANET
D) ANNA "HANDJOB"

If you answered D move ahead 4 spaces

BLOUNT, APATHETIC BAND, THE UNEMPLOYED, DISTANT SILENCE. MATCH THE BANDS WITH THESE FACTS:

A) HENRY ROLLINS PROMISED TO SIGN THEM
B) ALL THEIR STICKERS WERE PRINTED ON THE WRONG SIDE
C) ONLY PCOLA BAND TO RELOCATE
D) INVOLVED IN BLOODIEST BAR BRAWL IN GULF COAST PUNK HISTORY AFTER THEIR SOUNDMAN GOT BITTEN ON THE NOSE.

If you answered A) DISTANT SILENCE B) APATHETIC BAND C) BLOUNT D) THE UNEMPLOYED move ahead 6 spaces

---

WHEN FANG CAME TO P-COLA THEY...

A) BROKE EVERY RULE AT 6-4
B) HAD TO INSTITUTE A "NO MORE SEX IN THE VAN" RULE
C) PLAYED "PUFF THE MAGIC DRAGON"
D) RECEIVED BLURRY TATTOOS FROM CRIMPSHRINE, WHO'S MEMBERS ARE ONLY ALIVE TODAY BY LUCK OF HAVING USED THE SAME NEEDLE BEFORE, NOT AFTER, FANG

If you answered ALL OF THE ABOVE move ahead 3 spaces

"CRUD" WAS PART OF

A) THE "SLOB SQUAD"
B) "ESPRESSO YOURSELF"
C) "THE CLAY CAFE"
D) SLUGGO'S 86 LIST

If you answered ALL OF THE ABOVE move ahead 2 spaces

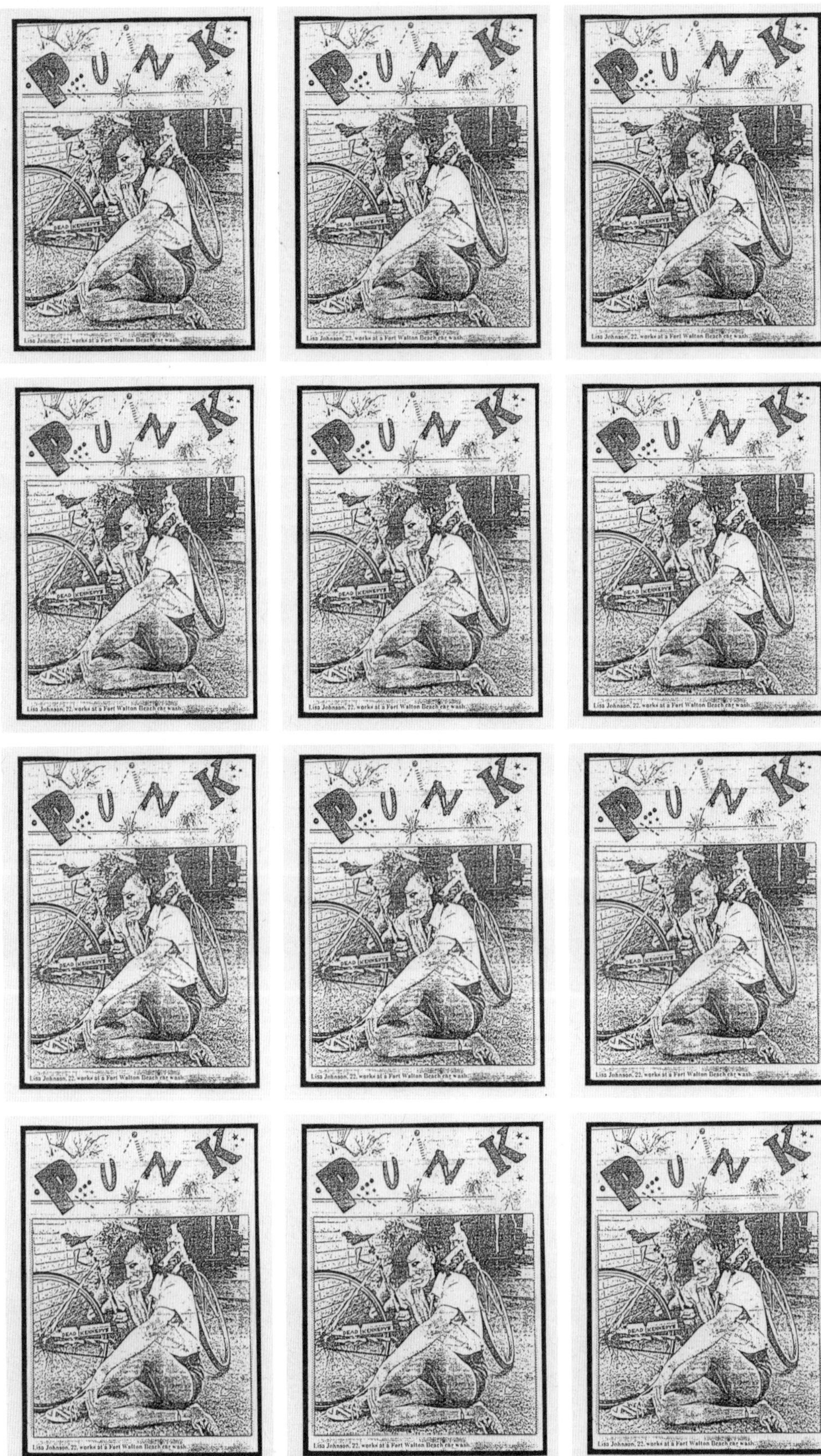

PUNK
DEAD KENNEDYS
Lisa Johnson, 22, works at a Fort Walton Beach car wash.

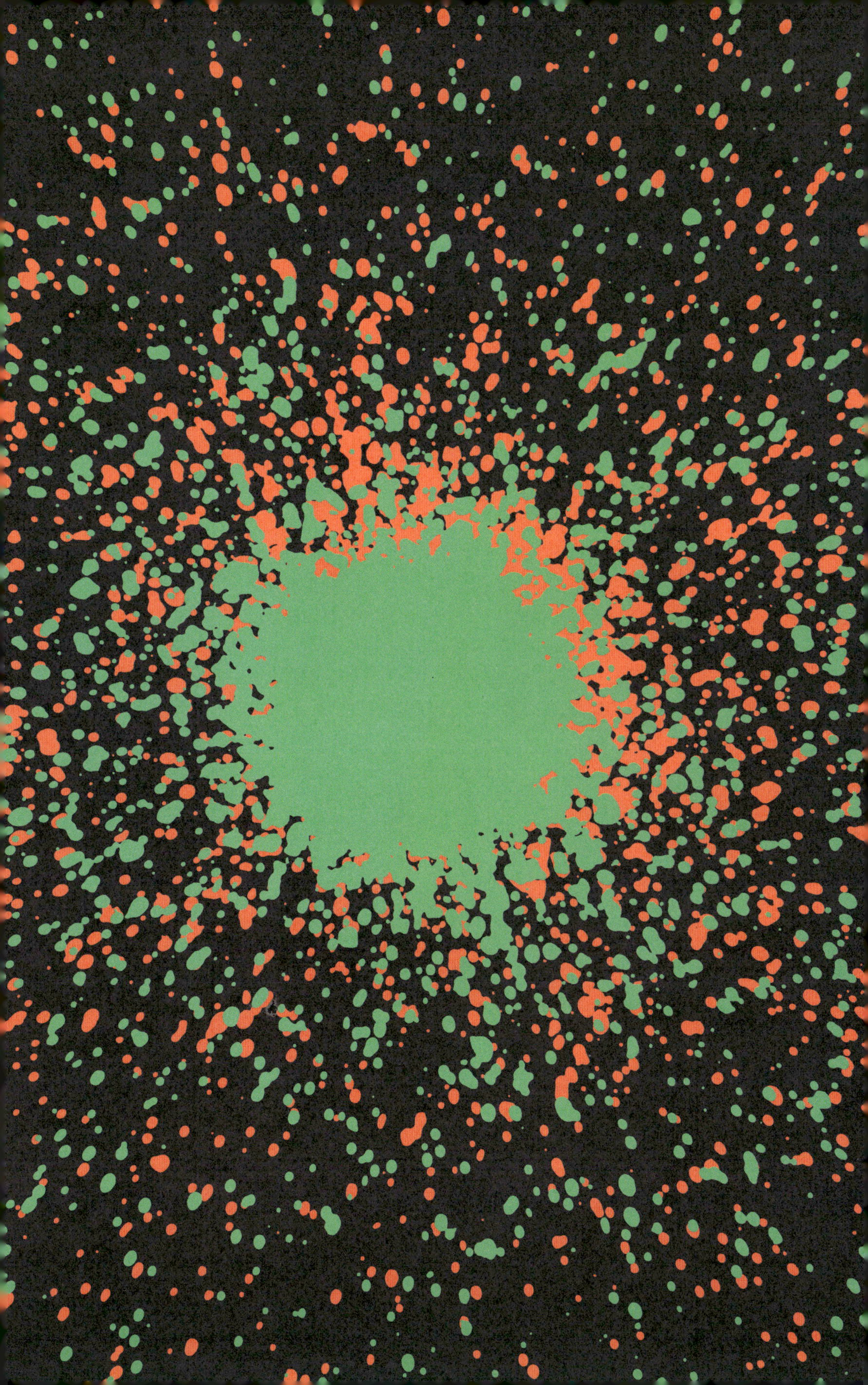

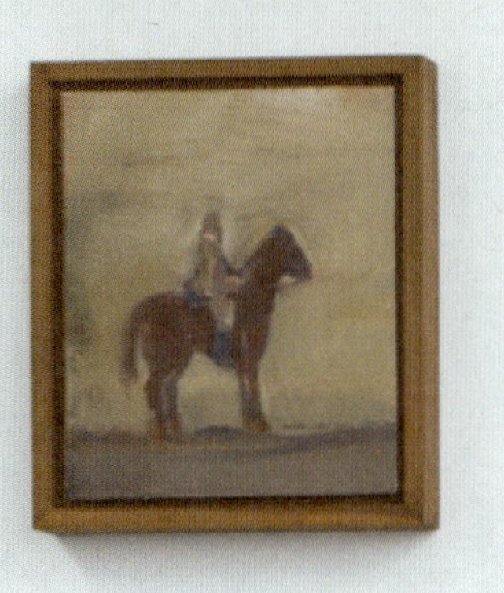
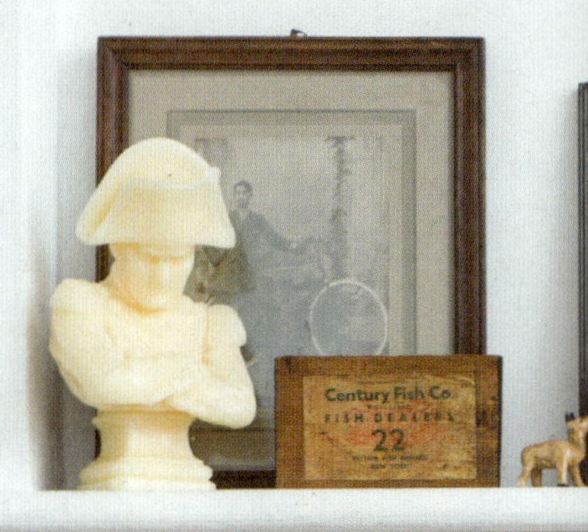
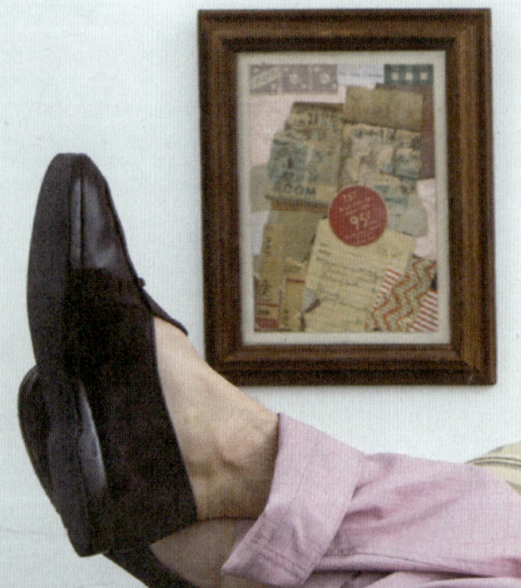

SLEEPY JONES

pajamas, underwear and t-shirts designed for pondering, plotting and procrastinating
available at Colette, sleepyjones.com,
and Sleepy Jones at

the

312 Bowery, NYC

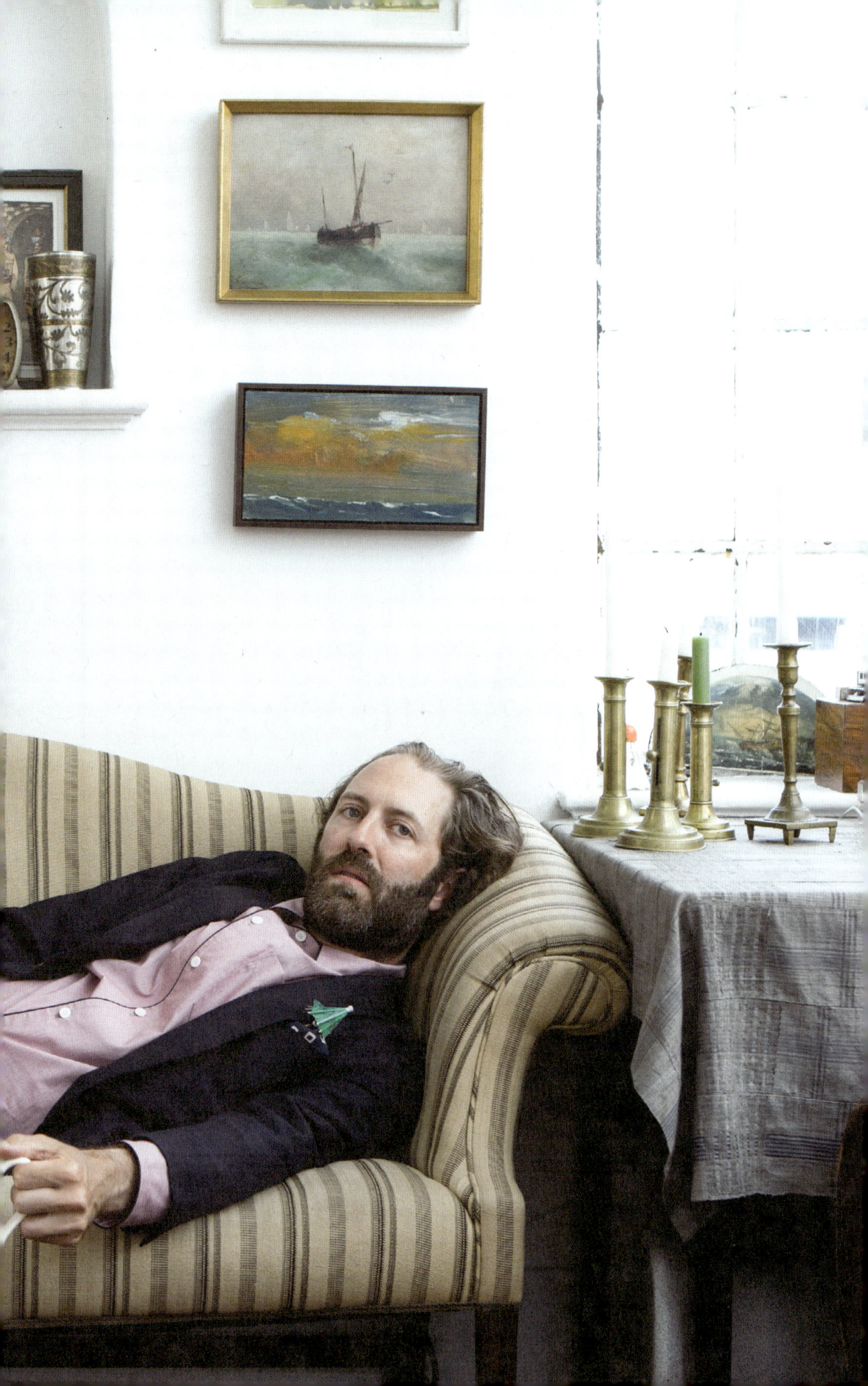

Crypts

by

Paul Maliszewski

with illustrations by

Jim Krewson

Lately I've been thinking about dying. An art-history professor I had in college died last March, and I hadn't thought of him for a while, years maybe. His class was called Art and the Mind, and we met one evening a week for three hours, us sitting in this dark hall, looking at his slides, and listening to him speak. "It's the history of everything," he said, and the class did seem that way, the slides encompassing everything from early human artifacts to contemporary art. A lot of the material was beyond me, like much of college. I wish I could travel back through time and retake his class. I'd want to arrive as I am now, with what I know, or just be someone other than the guy who was painfully self-conscious even about his socks and who spent hours alone, listening to R.E.M. on cassette, hitting rewind and then playing back certain bits, trying to decipher the lyrics. "It's the End of the World as We Know It (and I Feel Fine)" was challenging, but parts of *Murmur* proved impossible. Much of what I wrote down was sheer guesswork, stabs in the phonetic dark. I kept at it, though, kept rewinding and playing. I scratched out words and wrote in others. When I finished, I monkishly recopied the lines onto clean pages. I took considerable pride in this work. Pretty much the only reason I think about time travel is this desire to return to college, smarter. I found videos online of lectures the professor gave and bookmarked them to watch later. But now that I could perhaps better understand them, I have less time. I did watch one video of him in his apartment, talking about his art collection. He looked older, which shouldn't have surprised me, though that was the first thing that came to mind, that and how the skin on his neck was loose, his cheeks sunken. It'd been more than twenty years since I took his class. (I had to think, just then, what year I graduated, and do the math. I'm often doing this age math now, counting off the years, performing the addition and subtraction of time, trying to figure how old I was when and how long ago whatever was.) The professor's apartment was thick with books. Shelves rose to the ceiling, each packed to bursting, with books stuffed sideways between the shelves as if they were a form of insulation, keeping out the cold air. Art was everywhere the books weren't, lining a hall, hanging above doorways.

I recently emailed an old friend, saying how sorry I was to have been a crummy correspondent. I hadn't written her in it seemed like forever. I'd kept a bunch of her letters, though, hers as well as other people's, preserving them in boxes. I used to think I'd read them one day and remember what I'd forgotten, be like Krapp in the Beckett play, listening to recordings of his younger self. But lately, I don't know. I tried to go through my papers, tried to be honest about what I really needed, and I did get rid of some stuff, a little, but after a few evenings of sifting through the old mail, all that accumulated past, I gave up and closed the boxes. I tell myself I'll get back to it still, at some point, that I really need to, that it would be good for me.

When we were in school, my friend and I stayed up nights at this diner, keeping each other company while we wrote our papers. There was a guy, another regular, who sat at the counter with a stack of newspapers, going through them with his pen, circling words and phrases. We were curious about him, about what he was doing and why, and I think at some level we suspected that one or both of us were going to become like him, that he was us further along, in the future. One night, my friend asked if I'd put a hibachi grill into the story I was writing. I turned back a few pages and showed her that I already had one.

Another night, we decided to drive out to see the USS *Texas* battleship. It made sense at the time; the country was ramping up for the first Gulf War. In the middle of the night, though, even a battleship can be hard to locate. We drove around, looking for any sign, but all we found were refineries, lit up and loud. The *Texas*, it turned out, was not far, at the end of a road, docked by the edge of this state park. We decided to board the ship. We had to. It was an obligation. It had something to do with the war. Something about how if the country were going to war, if they were going to be killing people—if we were going to do that—then we needed to understand the military. And here was this ship. I was convinced the war would drag on, that there would have to be a draft instituted, and that I would be drafted. It didn't matter what any reasonable person told me.

We scaled a chain-link fence and just walked up the gangplank. It was too easy. Then we tried to go belowdecks. There was a doorway and steps leading down. No lock or barrier, maybe a dinky rope stretching across the opening—I can't remember—nothing in any case that would keep us out. The lights were even on. My friend was ahead of me, almost to the bottom of the stairs, when an alarm sounded, a piercing, shrieking thing. We turned and ran, hands covering our ears, yelling at each other just to be heard. We climbed back over the fence and headed for the car. Another car was coming, though, and we thought cops for sure, so we dropped to the ground and lay there, quiet. A minute passed, and my friend whispered to me did I think it was okay to get up. It seemed like no one else was around.

We were, I think, best friends. She deserved better than my occasional emails. I asked if she'd heard the news about our professor. I wanted to know what she recalled. He'd seemed exotic to us, living this life we envied. He got to talk about art all the time. He flew in from New York to lecture about the Venus of Willendorf.

I think about how I might die, too. How old I'll be, how my wife, younger, will be with our sons then, or alone, our sons moved out, living somewhere else, and what will they be doing, where will they be, if they'll be okay. I think sometimes they'll be happier without me around, better off. And if that's true, don't I owe it to them to remove myself, to exit? Wouldn't that be the right and kind and decent thing to do? I've imagined this time, years from now, when our older son is a teenager, maybe in college, and he's talking to a friend, who's visiting, maybe a girlfriend, and I hear her say, "You never told me your dad was a writer," and then I hear our son laugh, and he says, "Well, I mean, he is, I guess, sort of, but nobody's heard of him, you know?" I've thought of killing myself. Not because of that, but maybe because of what underlies it? This sense of myself as an embarrassment or a disappointment, a failure, really.

It doesn't help that there's so much money being made around us, so many lawyers here. We live in D.C., on the Hill. The other day, I overheard these two women talking, one a lawyer, the other I don't know. We were at the park. I was there with our younger son, helping him into this plastic car he'd had his eye on, which happened to be right in front of these women. They were watching their kids play or whatever, when the lawyer started in about how she was up for some job, and I guess they asked her what she wanted in the way of a salary, what she needed, and she told them whatever the figure was, and then she said to her friend, "At first I didn't know what I'd say, but then I told them, and I don't know where that number came from, or how I arrived at it, you know, it just came out of my mouth and there it was." She wouldn't say the number, of course, she was all cagey, coy, the way people get about money, saying her number without having to say it, saying in effect, It's a really large number, as we all know. Her friend said, "How did they react to your number?" The lawyer said, "They were fine with it, they know that's what it will take to hire the best." She actually said "the best." She paused then and said, "But there are four people up for this, and what if one of the others says a number and it's $80,000 less?" My son wanted to open the door of his car, and then he wanted to get back in, and he did that for a while, opening and closing the door. Her idea of an incidental amount—a mere $80,000 separating her from the less pricey attorney—is more than I've ever made by a factor of I don't want to even think about it. Later, I told my wife all this. She knows it upsets me, but she just thinks there are values that go along with that much money, and it's the values that are important to her, and I understand that, but money's such the dominant culture. It just gets to the point where if you're not making it, what are you doing? My wife asked me if I want our sons to make $400,000 or whatever a year when they grow up, and I said, "Not really. It's not the most important thing." And my wife said, "You want them to do something they love, right? Find their own way. Figure things out for themselves." And I said, "Sure, of course, but I also want them to have shoes, you know? Whatever they do. And yet I don't get them shoes." My wife said she gets them the shoes, and I give them everything else. Which is flattering, though not true. I don't know. Sometimes I want to be the person who takes care of the shoes.

I don't think about killing myself all the time, but the thought does occur, and I'll follow it for a while, considering hypothetical particulars, places and means, but then the thought's gone. I feel bad—depressed or whatever—but not that bad. It's like how I imagine anything, really, how I let stuff play out in my head, these concocted scenes or long what-if's, where I'm thinking about what I would say if she says whatever I think she's going to say. It's an extension of dreaming. It's just that some dreams are not good dreams.

I ask my wife if she ever thought of hurting herself when she was depressed. She felt pretty bad last year. It's been a hard couple of years. I leave it

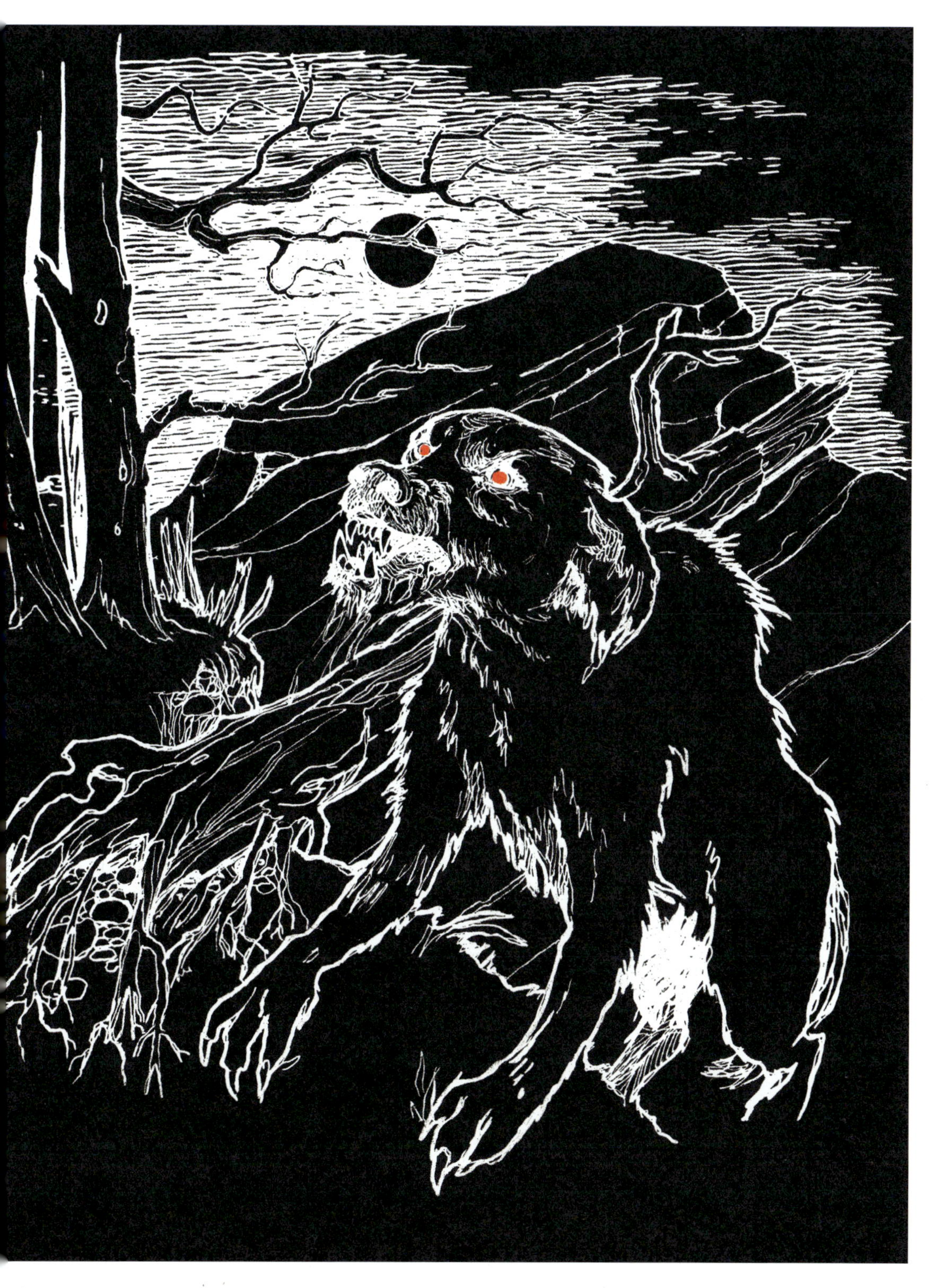

The black dog, also known as the hound of hell, patrols forests and execution sites. To see him portends a dark end, and soon.

like that, at hurting herself. I think we both know what I mean. She says, "No, never." I ask again, later, and she tells me the same thing. Part of me doesn't believe her. I tell her that, too. Because doesn't everyone think about it?

Other times, I think this is a pretty good life, decent, you know, and I don't want it to end. Nothing all that particularly great has to even be going on. Like this one morning recently, I drove our older son to school. He's in kindergarten, and it had finally started to get cold here. Like we'd busted the coats out already, but that day was the first day I thought I should have brought gloves, why didn't I bring gloves? As I drove, my son was asking how many days it was until Christmas, and I said it was a lot of days still to Christmas, that we had Halloween coming up pretty soon and then Thanksgiving and then most of the month of December and that's when it would be Christmas. He started talking then about the calendar, how he wants to make his own calendar. He's been talking about this now for a few days. It's his next big project, and I told him I'd look on the computer and see if I could find him some monthly calendars. At first I was like, "Why don't we just buy a calendar? If you want animals, we can get you a calendar with pictures of animals. They have all different types at the store. We can look at them." But the boy knows what he wants: He wants the whole month on a page, and he wants to make his own pictures.

Later, after walking him to his classroom, I had to get gas for the car, so I stopped at the station near the school, and it was as I coming around the side of the car, and I was looking down at the flap thing you have to open on the car, and I opened it, and as I twisted the gas cap, the thought came to me just then: "It's not a bad life, you know." Like just those words went rushing into my head. I was staring at the gas cap, or that nozzle part, the opening to the gas tank, whatever it's called, and I remember all this, because I actually thought at the time that I should remember it, that I needed to, because I thought it was funny, to be thinking this while getting gas, like why then, after all? It's so monumentally incidental, and maybe that was the appeal of the moment, I don't know. I told myself I should tell my wife this, tell her what I'd thought. I think she worries sometimes that I'm never happy, or not often happy. Later still, when I was home, I thought how nice it was that our son was looking forward to the future, whenever it might be, whether it's Christmas or his grandmother—Bah, he calls her—coming to visit. He wants to count the days and keep track of them. That forward march through time, which I occasionally dread and worry over, he looks to it with real expectation. I asked him how many months he wanted me to print out, and he said, "I want the whole year."

My grandfather was going to die. I'd figured that out somehow, through whispers, or maybe I was told he was sick and realized what that meant. I don't know. My mom was in the kitchen, though, on the phone with one of her brothers, and then she was off the phone and talking to my dad, and he was saying maybe they should wait to fly up. To see what happens, or what the doctor says, and then maybe go tomorrow or the next day, depending. It had to do with the price of plane tickets. I could tell that somehow. He was hoping my grandfather would get well, just like that, and then they wouldn't need to go. I was in the seventh grade. Sixth or seventh, I think. I would have been twelve at the time. Maybe my dad just came out and said something about the expense, or maybe we all just knew. My dad can be cheap at the exact wrong times, and then turn around and be lavish to the point of embarrassment. What I remember is my mom was crying, and she said to my dad, "What are you going to do, wait until the hearse drives by?" I can still hear how she put that, how angry she was and how quickly she spoke. So much else I've forgotten and now don't know for sure, but I can hear her saying that, and I think it has stuck with me because it's how I talk, and how I am, when pushed to that point and feeling powerless. We always come back, she and I, with claws.

My grandfather died not long after the phone call, and my parents flew to New York, to Fredonia. My brother and I were to stay at home. This was in Houston, in a subdivision where all the streets had long, florid names describing natural features that did not exist there and never had. We lived on Rolling Timbers Drive. Nearby was Whispering Falls, Echo Canyon, Rippling Water, on and on. My parents had decided the funeral was no place for kids, that we were too young. Maybe my cousins weren't going either. I don't know how I feel about that. I guess I don't agree, but it doesn't matter now. My dad arranged for a man he worked with, a man also called Paul, to stay with us while they were out of town. Before they left, my dad sat down with me and my brother and gave us our instructions, telling us that Paul was coming and that, as a condition of his staying with us, he was going to be bringing a gun. He'd told my dad that he didn't feel he could properly do his job—taking care of us, watching the house—without having his gun with him: As if it wouldn't be wise to come to Rolling Timbers Drive unarmed. "Nothing bad is going to happen," my dad said, "but the gun is in case something does."

We had no guns in our house, and never had. Once, I shot a rifle at a paper target hung from a clothesline as part of this father-son camping-type thing known as Indian Guides. We wore vests my mom sewed for us and knew each other by Indian names. I was Thunder Bird, of the Kiowa tribe, and my dad Thunder Hawk or Eagle, I can't remember. I'd also shot friends' BB guns and maybe one pellet gun, pumping them full of air, as much as I could, and then pinging mailboxes, sides of cars, trash cans, whatever. That was the extent of my experience with guns.

The first thing my brother and I wanted to know was where the gun would be kept. We couldn't contain our excitement. Our babysitter was bringing a gun! This would be cool. My dad frowned and said he didn't know where the gun would be, that would be up to Paul, but wherever he kept the gun, and he would probably keep it in my parents' bedroom, my dad said, where he'd be sleeping, we were not to handle the gun. "Just leave it alone," he said.

The next day, when my brother and I came home from school, Paul was there to meet us. We had chips and French-onion dip, our usual, and I'm guessing we watched *The Brady Bunch* in reruns or *Scooby-Doo*, but who's to say? As soon as I politely could, I scooted out of the room and went looking for the gun. I found it, a shotgun, under my parents' bed, a box of shells beside it. The gun was pushed way under the bed, to the middle, but if I lay on the carpet and squeezed partway under the box spring, if I reached as far as I could reach, I was able to touch the gun. I slipped a couple of fingers under it, under the trigger guard and just lifted it, holding it there. I didn't want to move it, let alone get it out, because I thought it would be obvious somehow, that Paul had put it just so. I only wanted to know how heavy it was, what it felt like. I thought it was pretty heavy, that's about it. I think I must have shown it to my brother, and I'm sure I went back to look at it myself, when I knew Paul was occupied, making

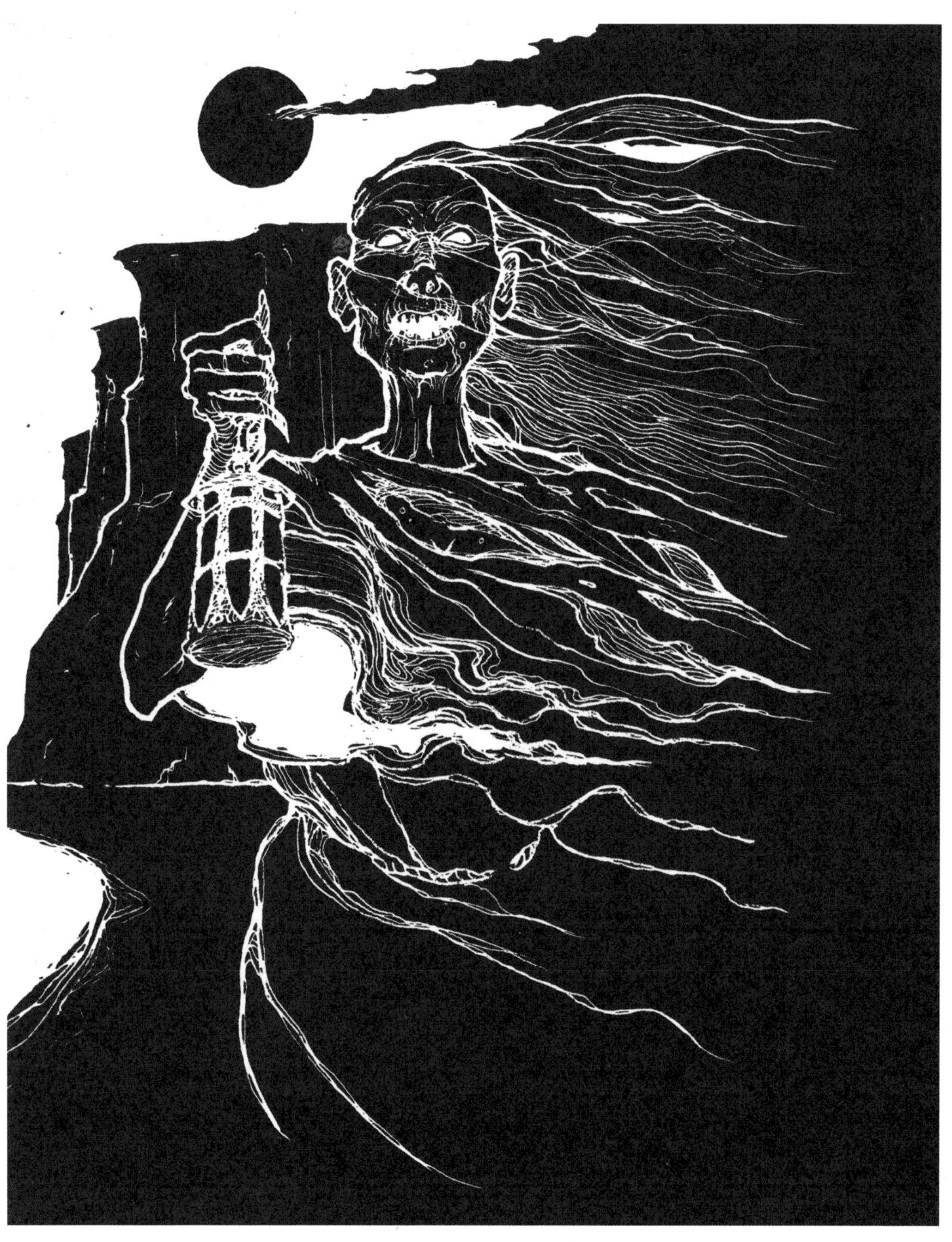

The banshee haunts the Irish coast.
Her wail heralds death for those who hear it.

dinner, say, but all I remember is lifting it that one time, weighing it in my hand, too terrified to do anything else, but too curious to leave it be.

I have this memory of a guy in junior high school dying. I didn't know him. People said it was a car accident, that he was with older kids, and they were all drinking. A car accident is what I recall. When he was buried, what everyone said about his funeral is that his mother placed inside his casket two items: a bottle of Jack Daniels and his Mötley Crüe ticket. He loved Mötley Crüe, and they were coming to play, and now he'd never be able to see them. This is what was said. Crüe was big at our school. This would have been 1983 or so, *Shout at the Devil*–era Crüe. I remember this one kid at lunch, relating the detail of the buried Crüe ticket, or maybe he was hearing it from someone else. In any case, this kid said he wanted to find where the guy was buried and dig up his casket, so he could get that ticket. It seemed wrong to him. To have this unused ticket, just sitting in the ground.

When our yearbook came out that year, we got a slip of paper with it that said something like "In Memoriam" and then the guy's name, which I'm sorry I can't remember, followed by his dates, and I think the idea was you were supposed to tape or glue the slip of paper into your book on some blank page, and we could all remember him by that. The yearbook editors or whoever said that, unfortunately, the yearbook was already done, sent off to the printers, when the guy died. It was too late to make a correction.

I asked my one friend from these years, the one person from back then I'm still in touch with, and he remembered almost none of this. What he recalled was a guy in high school getting in a car accident, probably our freshman or sophomore year, he said. "He was," my friend told me, "a troubled, troublesome kid, who eventually took to wearing a short Mohawk like Travis Bickle in *Taxi Driver*." I wrote back to say that I thought I remembered the guy he was talking about. No name, just a vague recollection, and no Mohawk, but that's my memory for you. The thing is, I think this is a different guy. "For some reason," I said, "I'm picturing him in an Army coat, a green canvas thing." But he was a bigger guy, this guy my friend was talking about, and the guy I was thinking of, who I'm pretty sure died in junior high, was thinner. It's like I have these gray faceless forms in my mind, and they have different sizes to them, as if all that's left in my memory now are the relative shapes that people once occupied.

My friend said he also has a weird memory of a rumor that someone we knew "got in a car wreck after high school that mangled his face badly." He mentioned the other guy's name and then said, "I have every confidence this absolutely did not happen." Together, with both our memories, we could almost be dangerous. The name seemed familiar to me, maddeningly so, but his face in my memory had been obliterated by time. I kept thinking of that name, though, hearing it in my head, hoping some image or salient detail would emerge and then join with the name, that a person would begin to take shape. But there was nothing, just the name alone.

My dad's brother was dying of a brain tumor. It had gone undiagnosed for too long. Years probably, the doctors thought, and now nobody would operate, or could. My dad was with him, my dad and his other brother, and they were visiting regularly, staying for as long as they could. Everyone knew it wouldn't be long. They were trying just to keep his spirits up, but they were also saying good-bye. This was in 2006. My dad called me one of those times. He sounded beyond excited, just like hyperventilatingly happy. I wondered what was wrong with him. He asked me about "that character you have who writes all those letters to the president." Since April 2001, I'd been writing and mailing letters to President George W. Bush, signing them all "Harvey Strub." The letters were fiction, just stories from Harvey's life. I tried to send a new letter out every week, on Mondays. I wrote about the food he ate, his warehouse job, his separation from his wife. I didn't know where exactly Harvey was going, but I liked making his life up. "They're stories," I told my dad. "The character writes letters, but they're just stories." I wasn't exactly sure what this distinction was that I wanted observed, but the truth is, it's never long before I get testy with my dad. "Right," he said, still wildly upbeat. He asked was I still writing the letters, and I allowed that I was, not sure where this was going, since we never talk about my writing, which is fine, believe me. My dad said, "Your uncle really doesn't like President Bush." And that's when he asked if I would read to him. "I'll put your uncle on," he said, "and you can read the letters to him." I said no. There are like eighty of these letters. I'm not sure how I put it exactly, or even if I came up with some meager excuse, such as that I wasn't done with them—I'm still not—or that the letters weren't about liking or not liking Bush, that couldn't be more beside the point. I'm sure whatever I said, I didn't put it well. My dad was trying to stay chipper, though, acting like even my refusing his request was a source of further excitement. Then he said okay and we hung up. I don't know why I didn't just do as he asked. It would have made my dad happy. Maybe it would have made my uncle happy too, I don't know. And I liked my uncle; that was the thing. I hadn't seen or talked to him in years, but I really liked him. He took my brother and me to see *Star Wars* and *Raiders of the Lost Ark*. He worked at this scrap-metal business. My brother and I loved going to his work. Just row upon row of stacked-up metal junk. Burned-out cars, some smashed into cubes or flattened into sheets. My uncle gave us these power-ful magnets. They had the name of the business on them—I can't remember it now—and I carried mine around, testing stuff, seeing was this or that magnetic. That's sort of what my uncle did, just test metals in different ways, try to deter-mine the value of whatever metal there was in, say, a wrecked Buick LeSabre. It would have been nothing for me to read one of my letters, to pick a short one and just read it, and then my uncle might have said that was nice, it's good to hear from you, and I might have said thanks and ask how he was doing, though I knew he was doing awful, and then he might have told me he was okay, in that way people do when they're not, and I might have said something else in return, but instead there was nothing and he died not long after.

My grandmother was in the hospital, in a coma. My wife and I drove up to see her. We had our son with us. This was in 2009, so our son would have been a year old? A year and change, I guess. My grandmother was living then with my uncle and my uncle's wife—I should call her my aunt, I know, except that it's his second marriage and I persist in thinking of his first wife as my aunt and am still in touch with her. They have a lot of land, my uncle and his wife. It's kind of like a farm without the farming part. My uncle had given it a name—it's that kind of place, and he's that kind of person. He named it after the village in Poland where my grandmother was

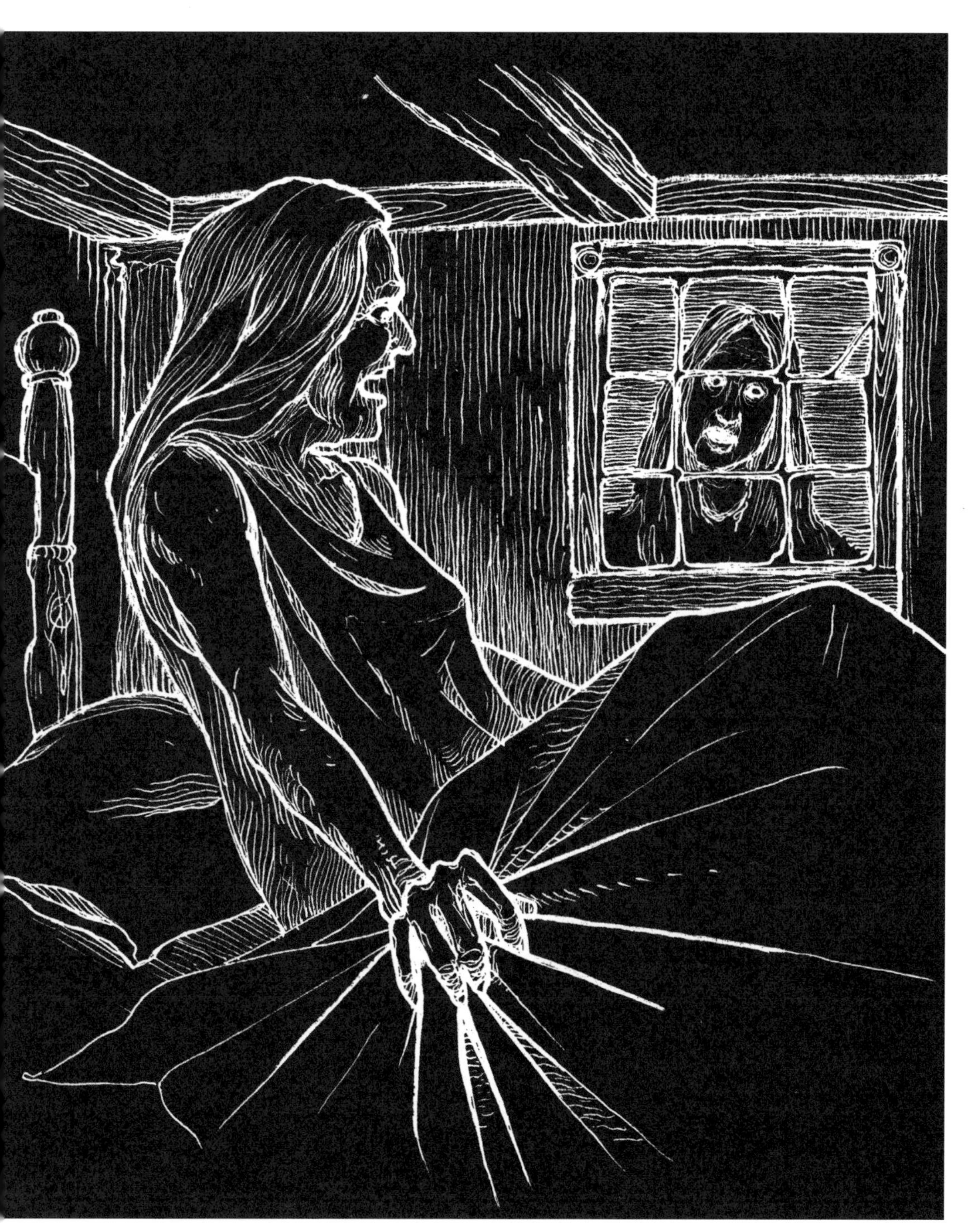

Beware the doppelgänger, the ghostly double image of one's own self. If you see it, your time is close at hand.

born. They had a logo designed for themselves, and they put the logo on their towels and napkins. It's all a bit much, to be honest.

I had visited my grandmother once since she moved in with my uncle. It wasn't far away, but it was far enough—sixty or seventy miles or something. My wife and I had our son and he was young yet and hard to travel with. Or maybe we were bad at traveling with him, I don't know. It just wasn't easy to deal with him in places that weren't baby-proofed to the nth degree. The breakables put up high, the electrical outlets fitted with those little caps. But we made the trip, and it was nice. My wife had never met her. My grandmother hadn't been able to travel to our wedding, or didn't feel up to it, whichever. And my grandmother met our son, and after all that, after lunch—I think we ate lunch—and then we walked around their property, and then we said we had to go, we were sorry, but we really had to be going, because we had a drive still, an hour and a half, and we'd be getting home late, and our son would probably lose it at some point, because that was how it went when we got home late. We were heading out to our car, and my uncle's wife was walking with me, and I was carrying our son up against my shoulder, and she was saying how much it meant to my grandmother to see us, for us to visit, and how I should come back with my family. "It's going to be what keeps her alive," she told me. "You know that," she said, and I started crying. And later, she wrote a note, thanking me for visiting and telling me again how much it meant to my grandmother. But it was in that moment of walking to the car, when she said that seeing family was going to keep my grandmother alive, that I knew I wasn't going to be back.

The doctor at the hospital had this way of saying strange things that could almost sound encouraging. My grandmother had had a severe stroke. But the doctor said, "She has all her faculties still, and her mind is in perfect shape; it's just that her conscious mind doesn't know it should wake up." I had never seen anyone in a coma. I held her hand between my hands, and her hand was not cold. I had thought it would be cold. I told her that my wife and I were there. I just talked. I said obvious things, facts. We had come to see her. Our son was outside. He was with the woman who had been caring for her, I said.

After we left, I called my dad and said we'd been to the hospital. I told him what the doctor had said, about her faculties and her conscious mind, and

I think it confused him, like it confused me, and he asked me to repeat it, and I tried to use the same words the doctor used, so there would be no confusion, so I would create no error. My dad said, "Has the doctor tried to give her some water?" I said, "I'm sure they're keeping her hydrated." I told him I thought she was on one of those drip things, an IV. I was pretty sure I had seen a drip. My dad said, "It's just that the last time she went to the hospital, she was really out of it when she got there, but all she needed was a glass of water, and she was ready to go home, and I just wonder if the doctor knows about that, if it's in her records, if he knows to try that." I said I didn't think it was a glass of water she needed. "It's serious," I told him. "Okay? The doctor said what he said, and I know how it sounds, but I don't know, you know? She's in a coma."

Later, after my dad and uncle talked to the doctor, they decided it was time to take my grandmother off life support. My cousin was there, and she said when they took all the tubes out and turned the machines off, my grandmother moved. I guess it looked kind of like she was struggling even. And my dad said, "She's trying to breathe. We made a mistake. She's trying to breathe." But I guess that's just what happens. The body struggles and then it doesn't. The other thing my cousin told me is that while they were all there in the room with my grandmother's body, my dad and uncle were talking about Mama, as they called her, and Tata, their father, who died years before, and my dad said to my uncle, "Remember how Tata used to force himself on Mama, and how we'd be in our bedroom, listening to her screaming?"

I pictured the layout of my grandparents' house. I hadn't been in years, but I remembered the stairs taking a turn near the top, and then the bedrooms all there, on the second floor. The bathroom at the end of the hall. The bedroom my uncles shared was just across the way from where my grandmother and grandfather slept. My brother and I always slept in my uncle's old room when we visited. College pennants were tacked to the wall, and there was this string—I remember this string—that went from one of the bedposts, across the wall, up to the ceiling and then over to the light, just so a person could give the string a little tug and switch the light off without getting out of bed. I always liked that string. My grandfather had rigged it up. He was smart like that. In Poland, during the Second World War, he supposedly took a regular rifle and turned it into a semiautomatic and then used it to fool some soldiers into thinking a bunch of men were hiding in the woods, firing at them, not just one lone man with his gun. I have a padlock he made that was on the trunk they brought with them from Poland. He made a padlock with a working key. I wouldn't know where to begin. He had old home movies, and we'd watch those. In a lot of the movies, the three brothers would be wrestling. My grandfather liked the wrestling movies, and there was always needling when, in the movie, one of the brothers ran away, like he wouldn't fight. I remember sitting on my grandfather's lap, and he showed me his bicep—his arm muscle, as I thought of it then—and it looked like a tennis ball popping out of his arm. He'd flex his arm for me, and it'd look like the ball was bouncing, moving up and down, and he said to me, "Your grampa is strong."

One night, my brother and I were asleep in that bedroom. My parents had gone out with my uncle. My brother and I played with their old Lincoln Logs and maybe watched a little television, I don't know. I guess my parents came home late, or late according to my grandmother, and so they all got into an argument downstairs, and my brother and I woke up to their yelling. I remember my grandmother saying that my parents had been drinking. "I can smell it on your breath," she said. "Big deal," my mom said, "we were drinking." And maybe she said something about all we had was some wine, but I'm not sure. My mom came upstairs, and she said we were leaving. We were going to my uncle's to sleep. Downstairs, the fight was still going on. I was carrying one of our suitcases. We had packed everything up. Maybe it was the day before we were to leave anyway, I can't remember now. I was pretty young. My grandmother tried to take the suitcase away from me then. She grabbed at the handle, and I pulled it back. "I paid for that suitcase," she said. Maybe she did. It was news to me. I said, "You gave it to us."

The next morning, I woke up at my uncle's place, and I remember the room was bright, and my grandmother was there, trying to give me money. I tried to give it back to her, tried not to take it, said that she didn't need to give me any money, that it was okay, but she insisted. She pushed it into my hands. "Take the money," she said. "Save it."

That was the last time I saw my grandmother until, I think, I was in

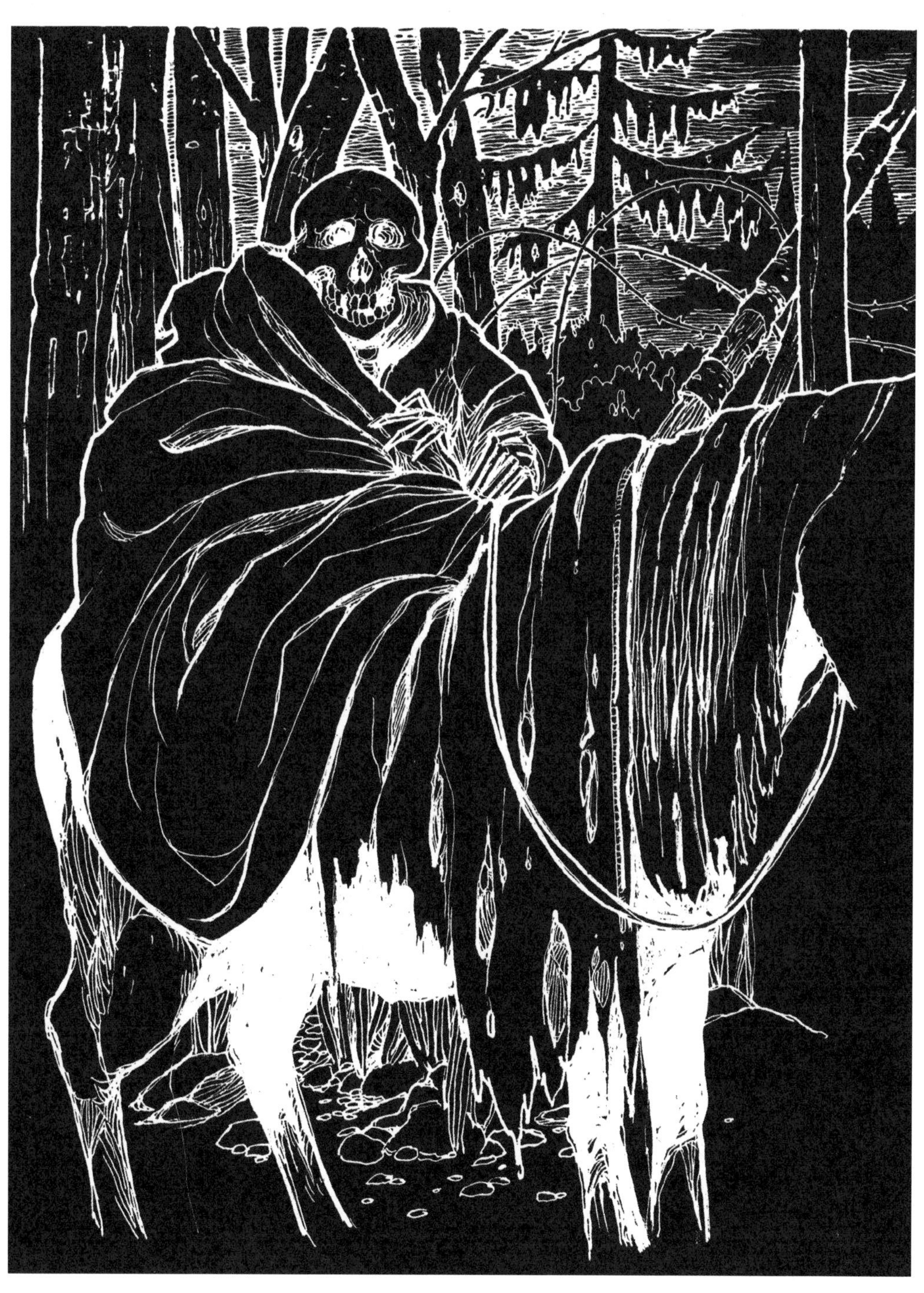

The final of the Four Horsemen of the Apocalypse is named Death.
With him comes plague, strife, and tribulation.

college, when we had a big anniversary party for her and my grandfather. We did write to them in the intervening years, short notes mostly, bits of personal news stuck to the end of a thank-you. And we always called on Christmas morning. We just didn't visit them, for a long time. We got birthday cards, Easter cards, and Christmas cards from my grandmother, all with money stuck inside. That money mattered, but we weren't ever to mention it. The first word of Polish I picked up from listening to my grandparents and my dad talk was *pieniądze*. I asked him—I was a kid, however old—Daddy, what is pee-en-zee? You and Grandma and Grampa keep saying pee-en-zee. My mom laughed. She knew what pee-en-zee was. "*Pieniądze*," my dad said, "is money." We were never supposed to thank her for the money. That was the deal. We sent thank-you notes, but we just had to say thanks for the great birthday card or whatever. My grandfather didn't want her sending anyone any money. Never mind that it was her money. She'd made it cleaning houses, and she kept some for herself, separate. I can remember my mom instructing me on the finer points of this subterfuge. "Your grandmother will know you got the money," she told me. I asked my mom if I also couldn't mention money when writing to her parents, and she said, "No, that's fine, you can thank them."

Do dogs or cats think about dying? Do other animals? They must know or have some deep instinct. You hear stories about an old animal going off by itself, crawling into the woods when it knows it's about to die. But maybe those are just stories. If an animal's sick, though, or hurt, they must know something's wrong. The dog with the hurt paw realizes it's painful to walk. But does that dog grasp the consequences? Or fear them? Or worry about what's next, about what worse ailment may follow the hurt paw? Do animals understand where all this sickness is leading? Are they aware that life is limited, that all the time they're here, they're getting closer to death? Is the rattlesnake concerned about how much life remains? Does the sockeye salmon think about how he's squandered what life he's lived so far? Does the black bear or the red-tailed hawk? Do gorillas contemplate suicide? Do orangutans, animals I've always thought seem inclined to introspection—maybe it's the look on their faces, those sad eyes, or the way they sit at the National Zoo, leaning against the cement wall of their enclosure, longish red hair hanging down—do they wonder how long they have and what will come after them and how their sons and daughters will fare, if they have sons and daughters, and if they don't, should they and how soon, or is it just too late? As the day ends, after they've eaten their fill, do they ask themselves what has this life been worth, finally? Anything? Or are humans alone so lucky, to face more or less every day, some thought, some nagging reminder, of our mortality?

When I was a kid I was obsessed with extinction. Not just dinosaurs, though that was part of it, and not just the theory that the earth would one day become uninhabitable and that people, some people, would leave and travel into space and live in torus-shaped colonies. For several years, I wrote research papers in science classes about the feasibility of space colonies. How could we sustain plant life in space? What would the most efficient method be for simulating gravity? How many people will live in each colony? In one report, I described how people would need to adapt to the radically new conditions. Space, physical space, would be limited on the colony. People would, I said, have to work and sleep at different times and take their breaks at different times, eat lunch at different times, all according to a strict schedule, which I laid out. Living in space would be a bit like attending school, with the sixth-grade lunch period and then the seventh-grade lunch period. Maybe several families would share an apartment, using it at different times. I drew up floor plans, squeezing as many units as I could into the torus shape, which for some reason I now can't recall was considered by several experts to be the optimal shape for a space colony.

Around this time, my grandmother, my mom's mom, came to visit. I'd brought home a copy of the school's literary magazine, for which I'd written a short mystery story about a guy who got his bike stolen in the first paragraph and who then, in the second and final paragraph, found the guy who stole the bike, case closed. My grandmother, I remember, took the magazine to bed with her and read it that night, and the next morning I overheard her saying to my mom how surprised she was. "So many of the kids are writing about nuclear war," she said. And I remember thinking how that had never occurred to me as the least bit odd. Not that it wasn't true, what she said. Once she'd pointed it out, I paid particular attention to the poems about nuclear winters and fallout, about mushrooms clouds blossoming on the horizon. I just wasn't surprised by them. This was 1982. My friends and I talked matter-of-factly about nuclear arsenals, the Soviet Union's and ours. We said ours, as if we owned some piece of it, and I suppose we did. We spoke of mutual assured destruction, warheads, ICBMs, the threat of MIRVs. In the fifth grade my dad taught me how to recognize Russian names by their several common endings. "Names ending with -sky," he said, "are Russian names." My math teacher that year had a -sky at the end of her name. "Names ending in -ski, like our name," my dad said, "are Polish." I needed to watch out for the Russian names.

The sort of extinction that interested me was personal: the disappearance of my family from the earth. The way I looked at it, if I chose not to have children, and my brother also chose not to have children, there would, at some point, be no more of us. I believed that extinguishing the Maliszewski line, or at least our little branch of it, was for the best. I didn't like our family. I didn't want us to continue, and I didn't think we should survive. I didn't like how my dad treated us, how he punished my brother and me, hitting us, giving us the belt, or else making us kneel on the floor as if praying until he said we could get up, and then it was hard to stand and my knees hurt and I felt wobbly as I went to my room. My brother and I threatened to call the police on him quite a few times, but my dad just laughed at us and said, "What would you do about money? Did you ever think of that?" Mom stayed at home and took care of us. We told him we'd do something, we didn't know what, and then just let the matter drop. Extinction was my fail-safe plan, though. I had to get my brother to agree with the idea, but that wouldn't be hard. He was younger, I could convince him. Then a couple of cousins came along, my uncle's kids, and that complicated the situation. A larger pact was required, but how? We hardly ever saw our cousins. I couldn't put my idea in a letter. I decided to keep it to myself, make it like a secret wish. If I told nobody, maybe it would come true. That's how it was supposed to work. Anyway, now my wife and I have two kids, lovely boys.

I N the year 8113, humans, if there still are any humans, may gather in Atlanta, Georgia—if such a place even exists in the eighty-second century—to open the Crypt of Civilization, a time capsule—a chamber, really, measuring twenty feet long by ten feet high and ten feet wide—containing, among other things, a plastic savings bank; miniature male and female mannequins enclosed in glass vitrines; a package of six miniature panties, five miniature shirts, and three drawers; samples of aluminum foil, artificial rubber, gold mesh, and upholstery textiles; two albums of bird songs; six recordings by Artie Shaw; the same number by someone named Richard Himber, with whom I am unfamiliar, though his obituary in the *New York Times* describes him as a bandleader, composer, magician, and "formidable practical joker," and that does, I admit, intrigue; one quart of Budweiser beer preserved in a special ampule; six packages of wooden forks and spoons; a set of Lincoln Logs; a cigarette lighter; and much more. The Crypt, with all this stuff inside it, was sealed in 1940, its mammoth stainless-steel door welded shut. A plaque explains:

> This Crypt contains memorials of the civilization which existed in the United States and in the world at large during the first half of the twentieth century. In receptacles of stainless steel, in which the air has been replaced by inert gases are encyclopedias, histories, scientific works, special editions of newspapers, travelogues, travel talks, cinema reels, models, phonograph records, and similar materials from which an adequate idea of the state and nature of the civilization of 1900 to 1950 can be ascertained. No jewels or precious metals are included.

The Crypt was the idea of Dr. Thornwell Jacobs, then president of Oglethorpe University, a small liberal-arts college originally founded in 1835,

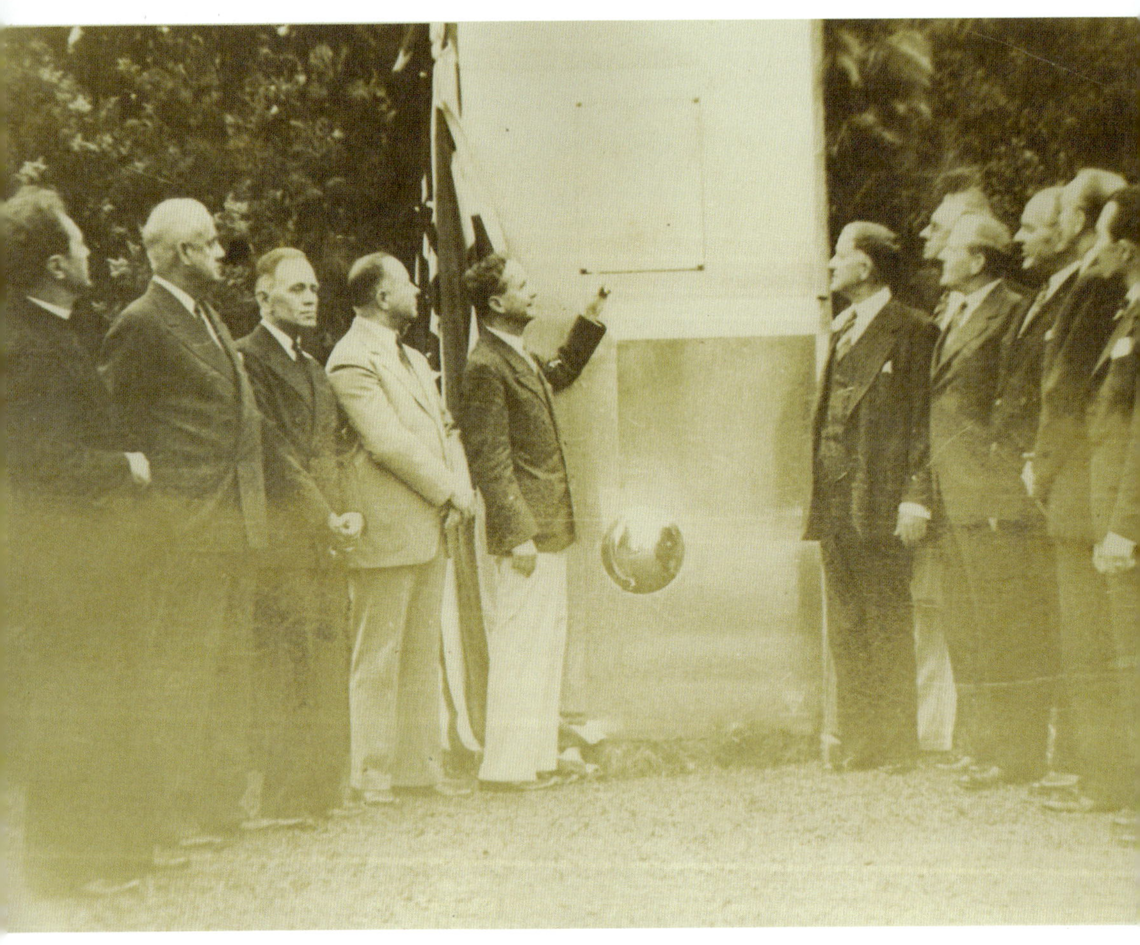

The dedication ceremony for the Crypt of Civilization's door in 1938.
Dr. Thornwell Jacobs points to the plaque above the Crypt door. T. K. Peters stands third from the left.

outside Milledgeville, Georgia, best known as that place where Flannery O'Connor lived. After the Civil War, the school had to close on account of investing heavily in Confederate war bonds. Then, in 1915, Jacobs refounded Oglethorpe in Atlanta. His grandfather had taught mathematics and astronomy at the first school and so, growing up, Jacobs heard stories about it and wanted to attend. As a professor, Jacobs taught a class called Cosmic History, a three-term course that was required in order to graduate from Oglethorpe with a bachelor's degree. Historian Paul Stephen Hudson said Jacobs's class dealt with "the overpowering magnificence of the universe in which human beings are only small parts." In lectures Jacobs discussed everything from anthropology and archaeology to biology, chemistry, geology, and physics as well as, for good measure, mythology and prehistory. The final exam took two days and covered everything "from before the beginning of time to views of the end of the world and after." Sample questions:

- What is matter?
- Do you see any conflict between Science and Religion? If so, state and explain.
- Do you believe in immortality? If so, why? If not, why not?
- How long do you expect the world to last and by what causes do you expect its life to come to an end?

Jacobs could find no book suitable for his Cosmic History class, so he wrote one, called *The New Science and the Old Religion*. Note the conjunction. For Jacobs, science and religion went together like bread and butter. He believed they didn't have to be opposed to each other or viewed as competing alternatives, an idea which could not have been popular in the South at that time, and which seems all the more progressive in light of the fact that Jacobs was also an ordained Presbyterian minister. He had little patience for those who would pit science against religion. "It is preposterous," he writes, "to suppose that the teachings of the Son of God could contradict the teachings of the suns of God." Scientists and believers, he felt, should "warn themselves against overconfidence."

While working on this book, Jacobs was bothered by how little was really known about past civilizations, particularly the lives of people who didn't happen to be pharaohs. As he says in *The Stream of Knowledge*, a 1938 movie that he wrote and appeared in and later stored in the Crypt, he was "impressed with the extreme difficulty of reconstructing the history of man's laborious and fascinating ascent to the ordered complexity of modern civilization." But, he continues, "one civilization after another had risen, flourished, perished, and been forgotten." It was the forgetting that worried him, what he called "recordless oblivion." Jacobs hired T. K. Peters, a photographer and audiovisual consultant, to work as an archivist on the Crypt project. Peters, who came with quite a varied résumé, was the inventor of a microfilm camera that used 35-mm motion-picture film and had served as a technical adviser on D. W. Griffith's *The Birth of a Nation*. He also worked on archaeological digs at Karnak and Luxor and was the only newsreel photographer to capture the 1906 San Francisco earthquake. Explaining Jacobs's rationale for the Crypt, Peters writes,

> Practically our entire knowledge of ancient life rests upon two very incomplete sources, the first being deposits obtained from the tombs of the long forgotten Pharaohs of Egypt and the kings of ancient Sumeria and Babylonia, and the second from rock inscriptions, and clay tablets excavated in ancient Assyria.

The discoveries were great, but the gaps, Peters argues, were as many and as significant as the finds themselves. Jacobs, with Peters's help, intended to redress this problem, by "preserv[ing] a complete cross sectional picture of the entire life of our world today for the people of the future." He decided the Crypt should be opened in the year 8113, because at that time most scholars put the earliest fixed date in history at 4241 B.C., when the Egyptian calendar was created. Since 6,177 years had passed between that moment and 1936, when Jacobs formally announced his project in the pages of *Scientific American*, then the Crypt should, he felt, remain sealed for just as long, 6,177 years. From readers of the magazine and from industrialists and philanthropists as well, Jacobs sought suggestions and assistance, but he also addressed them as, one imagines, he did his students in Cosmic History class, saying:

> It may be difficult for most of us to realize that our present civilization and all of its technical advances occupy only a few seconds, as it were, in the vast spread of geological time. We are living in a geological epoch just as truly as did the brontosaurus and the pterodactyl. Time will last just as long in the future as it has lasted in the past; our present-day civilization will eventually fall; our tall buildings and huge dams of which we are so proud will be reduced to ruins. This may not be a pretty picture to contemplate but it is one that will be just as true as the story of the downfall of the mighty empire of ancient Nineveh.

The Crypt's contents, what Jacobs in that first announcement calls "a complete record of how we live," would be as old in 8113 as the relics of the ancient Egyptians were to him and his contemporaries. As for what the future held or would look like, Jacobs knew only that it would appear, in Hudson's words, "unrecognizable to its present inhabitants." In *The New Science and the Old Religion*, Jacobs concludes, "What living conditions will then be we can no more picture than could the Cro Magnon man draw upon the wall of his cave his vision of the sky-line of New York."

In Atlanta, the project got under way. Jacobs chose a location for the future Crypt, a room in the basement of Phoebe Hearst Memorial Hall, on the Oglethorpe campus. The room had formerly been a swimming pool, so the floor was already impervious to water. Jacobs had additional concrete poured and a layer of damp proofing installed. The walls, made of granite, were covered, Hudson says, "with vitreous porcelain enamel embedded in pitch." The floor (two feet thick and made of stone) was complemented by a stone ceiling that was seven feet thick. What's more, Hearst Hall lay on a foundation of bedrock Appalachian granite. It was solid. Jacobs felt it would stand for "two to five thousand years." Which is longer than he gave the

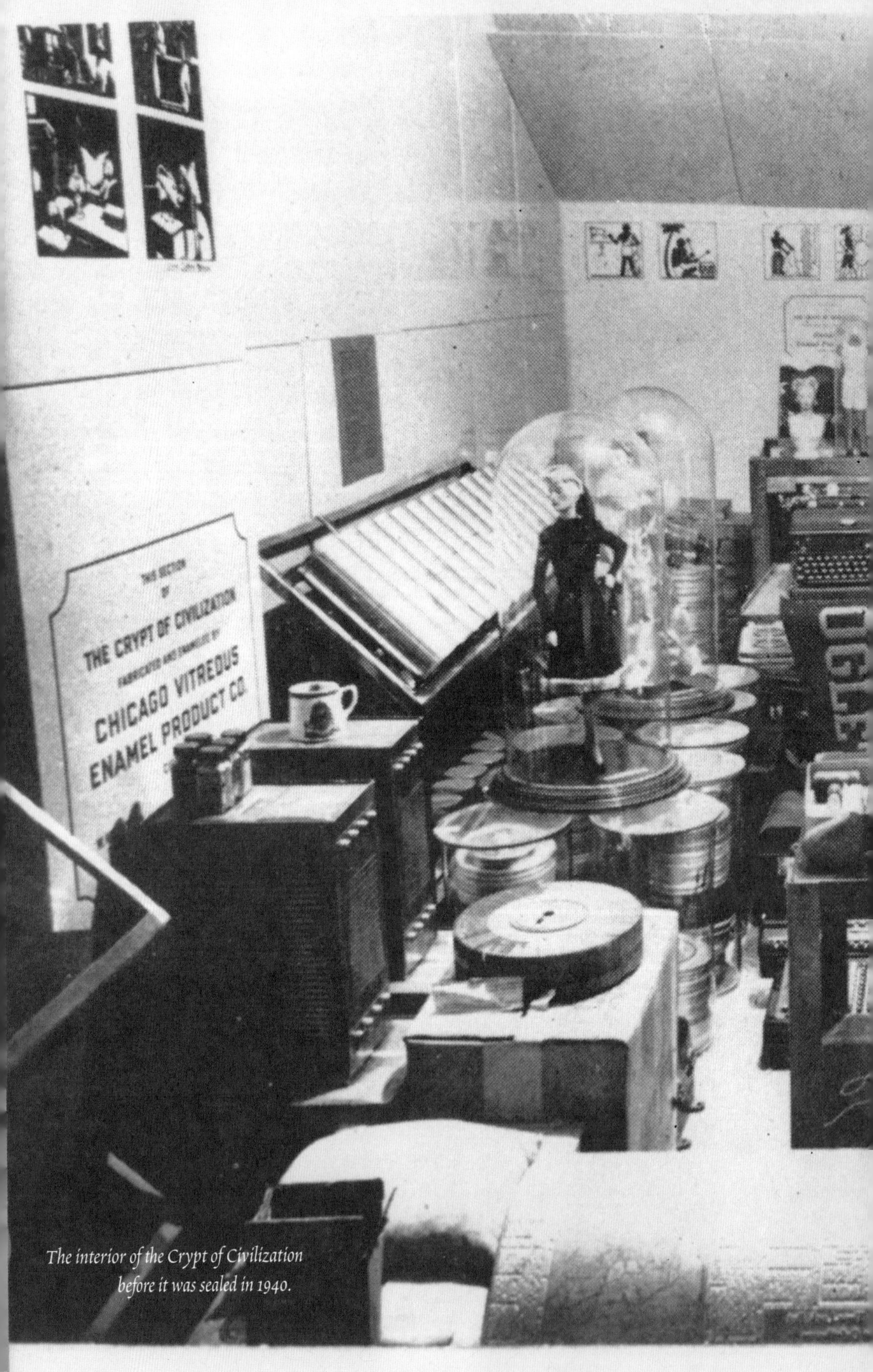

The interior of the Crypt of Civilization
before it was sealed in 1940.

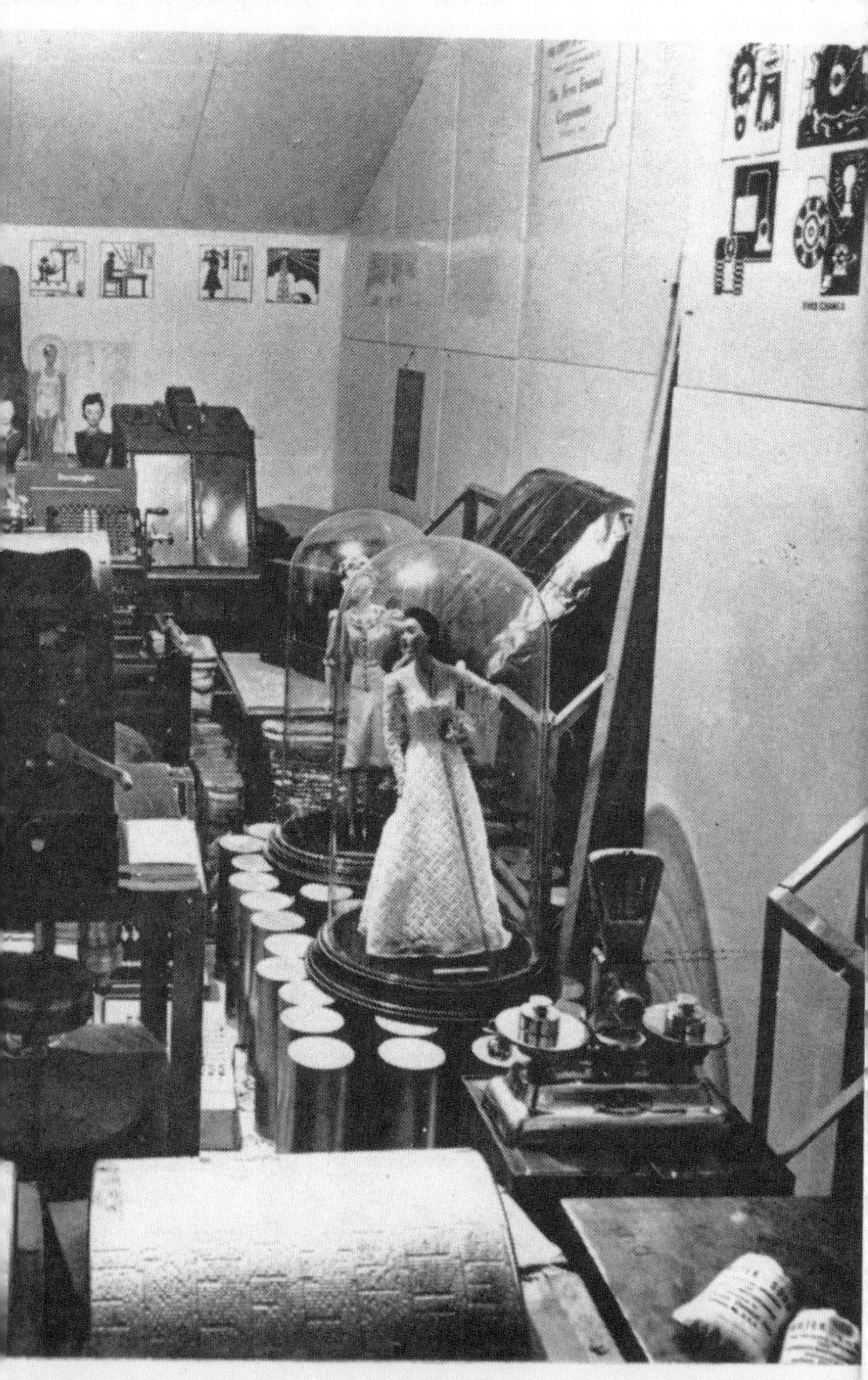

U.S. Capitol, speculating that it "will probably have disappeared completely" within six hundred years.

Peters meanwhile began microfilming the world's great books and documents. Students worked around the clock, in three shifts, putting in eight hours at a time, photographing all the pages that needed to be stored. Peters claimed they could photograph a page every second, sixty pages a minute, in other words, 360 pages an hour, which sounds more than a little optimistic, the sort of thing you say when your boss asks how quickly you can get the job done. In all, Peters and the students worked from 1937 to 1940, and the Crypt now includes the result of all that labor: over 640,000 pages stored on microfilm, taken from more than eight hundred books, including encyclopedias, dictionaries of modern languages, dictionaries of some ancient languages, the Bible, the Koran, the *Iliad*, and *Inferno*. Hollywood producer David O. Selznick donated a script—an original copy, it's said—of *Gone with the Wind*.

That script could be the one great work that survives the six-thousand-year wait. Provided, that is, Peters stored it as it was donated, on paper. Peters was well aware of the limitations of microfilm. As a precaution, he had a duplicate made, a copy of all the film, etched onto pieces of metal, which, Hudson says, were as "thin as paper." Peters also took extraordinary measures to extend the life span of the microfilm. In an address he gave to the Society of Motion Picture Engineers in 1939, he described how, once the film was printed and processed, they put it onto hundred-foot rolls, with eight rolls placed into a glass cylinder and glass spacers separating each roll. After the cylinder was packed full and closed, a vacuum pump removed the air and replaced it with helium, containing, Peters said, "sufficient moisture to keep it in a flexible condition during the time it is sealed up." The glass cylinder was then fitted into an asbestos cylinder, which was itself sealed inside a stainless-steel cylinder. I have no idea if any of this will work. Nobody does. There is, however, good reason to be doubtful. Peters hoped that the film—cellulose acetate, the state of the art at that time—would last as long as rag paper. Because four-thousand-year-old scraps of Egyptian papyrus had been discovered intact, Peters concluded that his film would therefore last just as long. And so his preservation methods protect the film from environmental threats, from fire, moisture, cold, and insects, all worries, to be sure. But what about the film itself?

Since the Crypt was sealed, industry standards for microfilm have changed, several times, most notably in the 1960s and the 1980s; cellulose acetate is no longer considered the best material to use. Microfilm itself, of course, has largely been replaced by digital scanning and images, with all the usual pros and cons there. Meanwhile, old rolls of cellulose acetate film, many in libraries, are not aging well. Nicholson Baker, in *Double Fold: Libraries and the Assault on Paper*, points out that the acetate in the film releases acetic acid. "As the decades pass," he writes, "afflicted microfilms can begin to shrink, buckle, bubble, or stick together in a solid illegible lump." And, Baker adds, "Microfilm's emulsion—the soft layer of gelatin and silver that holds the image—has vulnerabilities as well." The National Archives has reported finding strange spots on its master negatives, some red or yellow, some with concentric rings around them. Citizens of the future could well throw open the door of the Crypt and find there hundreds of steel cylinders, gleaming, each one containing a perfectly preserved plastic blob.

I wish I could be optimistic, at least for a moment. I would like to assume that the microfilm, that spooled record of its day and all the time that came before, survives. How will it be read, though, or viewed? Peters considered that problem as well and so, stored inside the vault are "electric machines, microreaders, and projectors." In case electricity is no longer used in the eighty-second century, Peters also included "a generator operated by a windmill to drive the apparatus." But what if these machines break down? Or what if the bulbs, after sitting unused for six thousand years, fail? Will some Etsy of the future sell antique lightbulbs for a microfilm reader manufactured in the 1930s? Will anyone in the eighty-second century know how to repair a twentieth-century anything? Consider the plight of video art. In 1986, the Los Angeles County Museum of Art acquired *Video Flag Z*, a piece by Nam June Paik, consisting of a six-foot-high stack of eighty-four white Quasar monitors, together creating, according to a *Los Angeles Times* article, "an American flag in pulsating red, white and blue." The piece was operated almost continuously until the late 1980s, but then many of the monitors began to fail, and spare parts could not be found. As

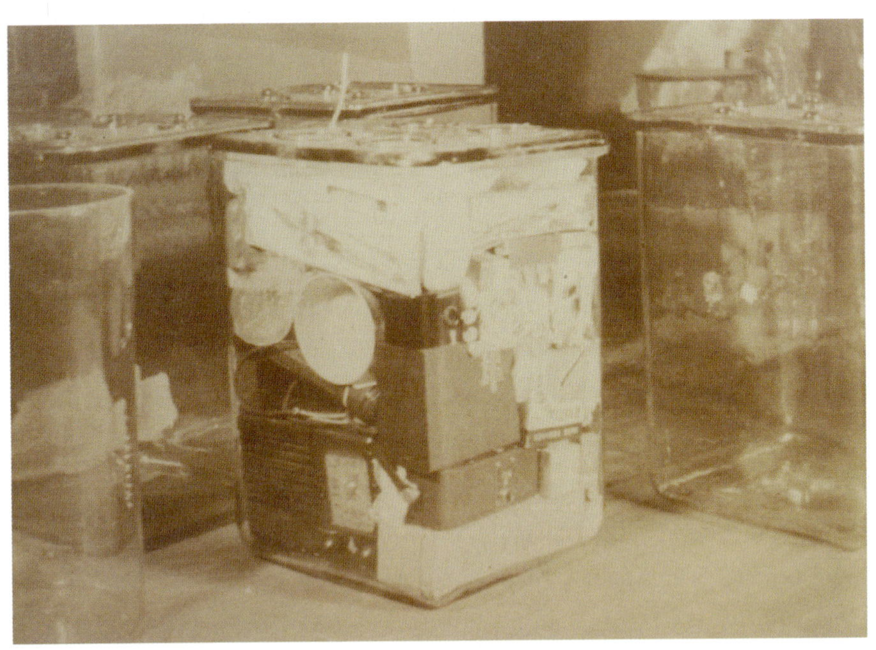

One of twelve large glass vitrines in which sundry items were hermetically packed for storage in the Crypt. A clock radio and a plastic bowl are visible in this one.

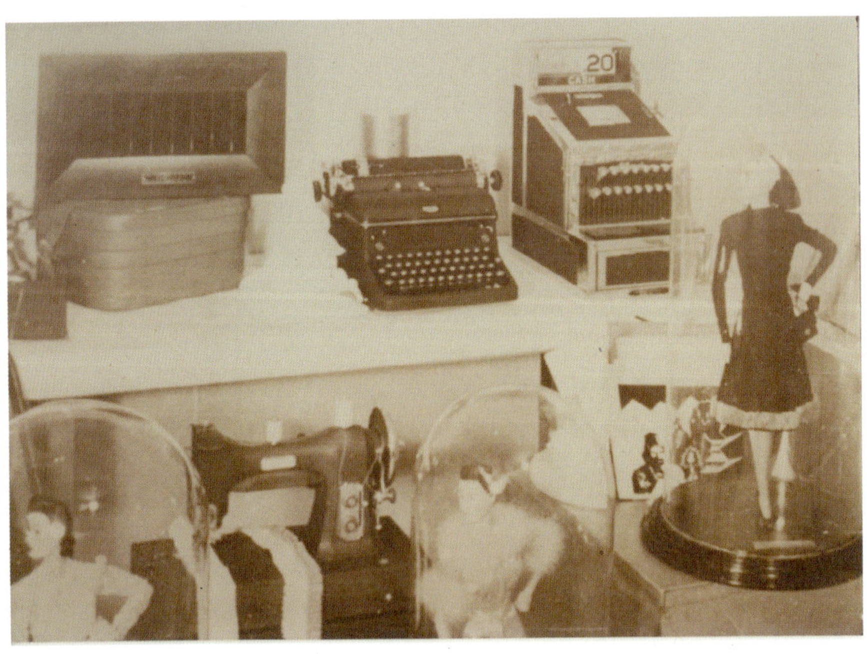

Various twentieth-century artifacts that are stored in the Crypt. On the right are figurines dressed in late-1930s fashions. Nearby are 1940 models of a Royal typewriter, a National cash register, and a sewing machine.

museum conservator John Hirx said, "We're a museum. We're not a TV-man-ufacturing plant." In 2000, Paik's piece was removed from display and placed in the museum's warehouse. And this was the fate, remember, of technology that wasn't even twenty years old. It's not easy to be optimistic. If the machines inside the Crypt similarly fail, Peters stored a magnifying glass with which to try to read the microfilm. And if the film's ruined, there's the metal backup copy. Also, at the front of the Crypt, one of the first objects future visitors may notice is the "language integrator," a machine that Peters made to teach the rudiments of English. It consists of a mutoscope attached to a phonograph and operates at the turn of a crank. A person looking into it can view film of, say, a man holding an apple and then see and hear the word *apple*. The machine is able to depict and pronounce fifteen hundred words in all.

On May 25, 1940, the day the Crypt was sealed, Jacobs and Peters found it difficult to sound upbeat. War was roiling Europe. Earlier that spring, Germany had invaded Denmark, which surrendered on the day of the attack, as well as Norway, where fighting was ongoing and would continue until June 10. In May, Germany had attacked France and occupied Luxembourg and the Netherlands. Belgium, too, was invaded and would surrender in three days, on May 28. Among the final objects placed inside the Crypt was a steel press plate from that day's *Atlanta Journal*, on which, as Hudson notes, stories of war domi-nated. Jacobs, meanwhile, addressed his remarks to an audience in the distant future, saying in part, "The world is engaged in burying our civilization forever, and here in this crypt we leave it to you." His speech was recorded, with the tape placed inside the Crypt. A reporter at the *Journal* overheard Atlanta mayor Wil-liam Hartsfield ask Peters, "Suppose if there's an air raid?" Peters noted that the Crypt already lay under seven feet of stone. "It would just be deeper buried," he said, "and better preserved." The quote ran in the next day's newspaper.

It would take the invention of the atomic bomb to shake Peters's confi-dence. Hudson says that by 1950, just a decade after the Crypt was closed, doubts about its ability to survive a nuclear blast were becoming widespread. Jacobs by then was retired and offered no comment to reporters, except to refer them to Peters. Peters gave the Crypt only a fifty-fifty chance of surviving a nuclear attack. In 1948, he'd already decided a second Crypt of Civilization should be built, this

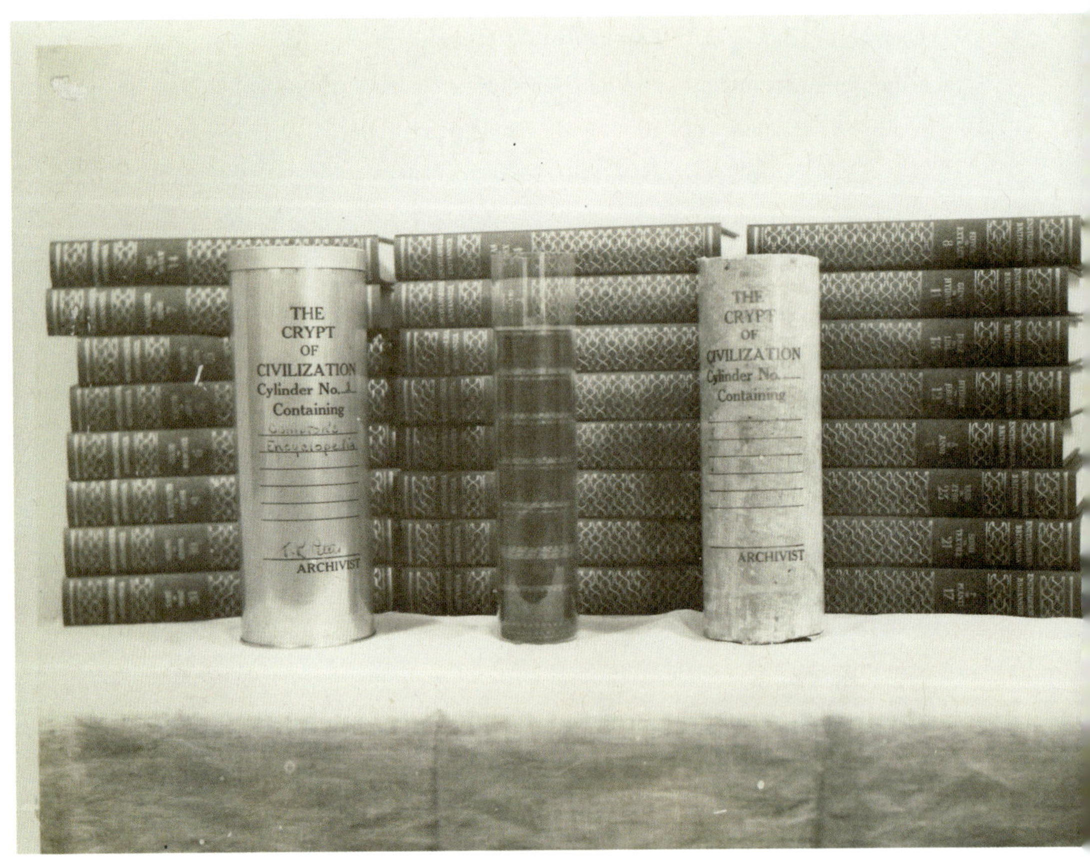

Books, microfilm reels, and canisters. On microfilm in the Crypt are classics in the arts and sciences totaling over 640,000 pages.

one designed to withstand the destructive power of an atomic bomb. This new and improved Crypt would need to be constructed from reinforced concrete and buried deep underground, in Stone Mountain, Georgia. It was just an idea, however; Peters could not find a sponsor or generate much enthusiasm.

In the end, the Crypt may be done in not by fiery apocalypse, but by something as ordinary as the passage of time, which, in its own steady and implacable way, can be plenty brutal. In 1971, just a little over thirty years after the Crypt was sealed, it was already forgotten. Hudson was an undergraduate then at Oglethorpe, and said there was no mention of the Crypt among students. It had no place in the lore of the campus. It might as well have vanished. In the 1960s and early 1970s, the school faced difficult times, financially. "It was always beautiful, with the granite," Hudson recalled when we spoke in 2006, "but the buildings were almost shells." Hearst Hall, where the Crypt is located, sat in disrepair. The first floor was used for classrooms, but the other floors were sealed off. The basement lay deserted and unlit. Hudson, though, was curious about what lay beyond the barriers and locked doors. And somehow, he got downstairs. "I was alone, with a flashlight," he told me. "I was in a place where I shouldn't have been." Hudson stumbled along and then he saw the stainless-steel door. "There were cobwebs on it," he said. He shone his flashlight at the door and saw a plaque there and then he read the text. "I didn't quite know what it was," he said. Hudson left and, though he was fascinated by what he'd seen, he too forgot about the Crypt. "The Vietnam War was going on," he told me. "It was the Age of Aquarius, the season of the witch, there was too much really to think about."

In 1984, Hudson returned to Oglethorpe, working as the school's registrar and also teaching history. A few years later, in 1989, he paid another visit to the Crypt. Hearst Hall in those days was in better shape. "The lower level," Hudson said, "was operational again." When I asked if that meant the Crypt was enjoying renewed interest, he told me, "It wasn't forgotten then, it was ignored." Hudson decided he would write about the Crypt. It wasn't, as he thought of it, a life-altering decision. "I was a writer," he said, "and I was looking for something to write about." That article, "The 'Archaeological Duty' of Thornwell Jacobs: The Oglethorpe Atlanta Crypt of Civilization Time

Capsule," appeared in *The Georgia Historical Quarterly*, in 1991. It's still the definitive treatment of the project.

In the years since, Hudson has continued to write about the originator of the Crypt, including an article about Jacobs's Cosmic History class. He's also helped get republished *The Law of the White Circle*, a novella, long out of print, that Jacobs wrote about the 1906 Atlanta race riots. In addition, Hudson and three fellow enthusiasts founded the International Time Capsule Society, which today maintains a registry of time capsules—if you make one, you can fill out their form online—as well as a list of the nine most wanted time capsules, "most wanted" because they've been "lost due to thievery, secrecy or poor planning." Two have since been found, including the one buried by the cast of the television show *M*A*S*H* somewhere on a Hollywood lot. In his memoir *Never Have Your Dog Stuffed*, Alan Alda revealed all:

> Late one night, we had sneaked over to a patch of dirt next to the commissary and buried a medical chest with a red cross painted on it. The chest contained a memento from each of the actors, something connected to his or her character: dog tags, a rosary, a surgical clamp. It was a kind of time capsule, and we left a note in the box explaining to whoever found it years in the future who we were and how much meaning these souvenirs had for us. The sentimentality of this gesture was undercut somewhat by the financial activities of Twentieth Century Fox. A couple of months later, they decided to saw the commissary in half and sell the land under one of the halves to a company that wanted to erect a high-rise office building. A construction worker dug up the box and called us, asking what he should do with it. We had thought the box wouldn't be found for a hundred years or so, and we thought when it *was* found, it would be regarded as some kind of treasure. "I found your box," he said. "You want it?"
>
> "No," I said. "It's yours."
>
> "Well, I mean, don't you want it? What should I do with it?"

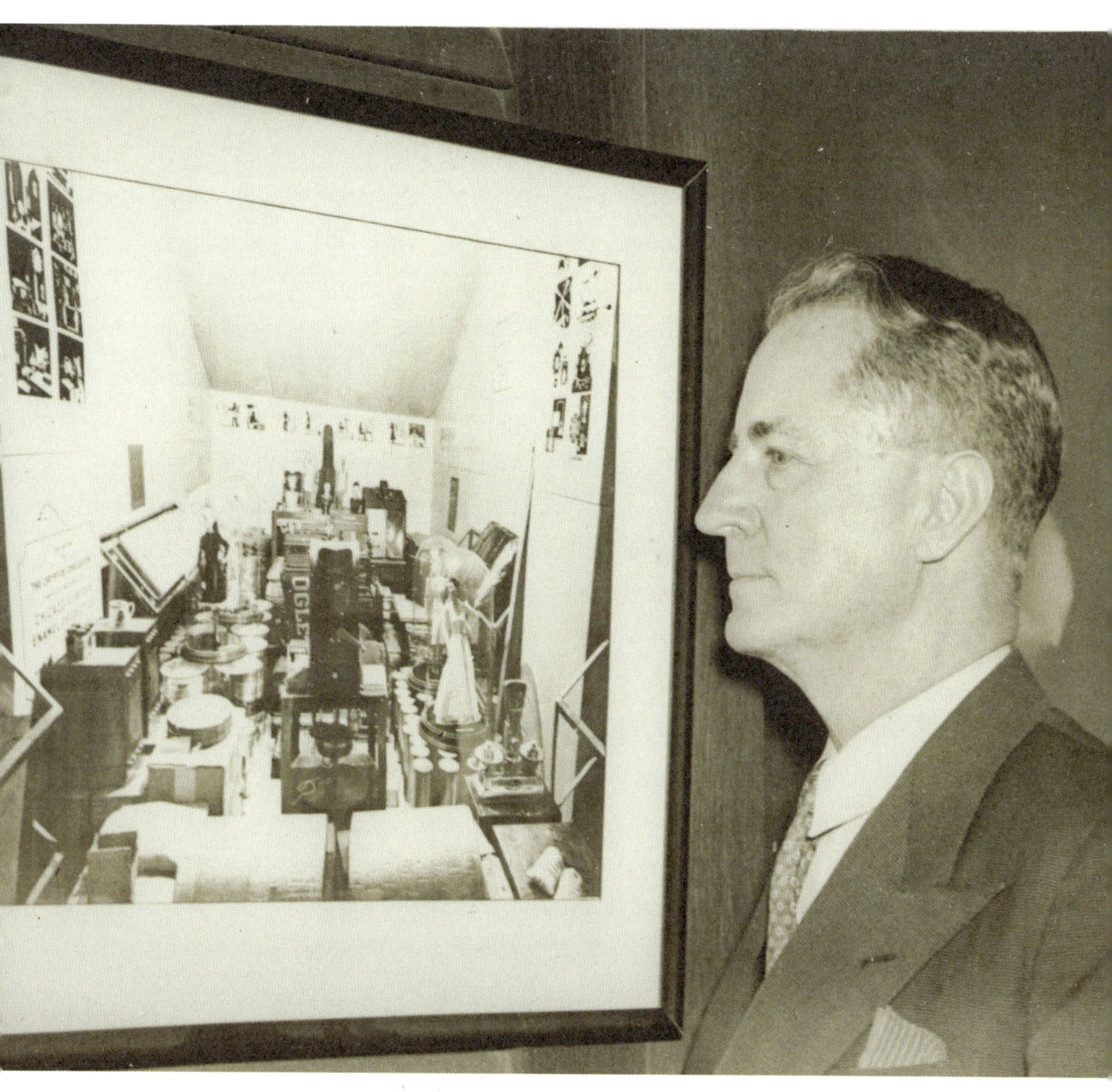

Dr. Thornwell Jacobs looking not at, but sort of beyond, a photo of the Crypt's interior.

"Keep it." *Keep the damn thing,* I thought but didn't say. Having your time capsule opened while you're still alive is not a good idea.

Though Hudson has written about non-Crypt-related subjects, he's become something like the unofficial spokesperson for the Crypt. Inquiries to Oglethorpe about its time capsule get referred to Hudson, who is a professor of history at Georgia Perimeter College. While at Oglethorpe, Hudson worked hard to keep alive some memory of what he has called "the granddaddy of all time capsules." "When I was there," he told me, "it was more part of the culture, because I just wouldn't let it die." The students, he said, called him the Crypt Keeper.

I asked Hudson what interested him about the Crypt. "I thought it was living," he told me, "pulsating with life." When we spoke, he pointed out that the Crypt was sixty-six years old, and said he'd always been taught to respect his elders. "It's just starting on its mission," Hudson said. As he talked about the Crypt, it was possible to forget that, to visit it, to look upon Jacobs's project, is to see, basically, just a fancy stainless-steel door with a plaque. Everything else lies hidden, left to the imagination. I wanted to see more. I wanted a window set in the door, so that I could peer inside. What does it look like in there? A photograph was taken just before the door was sealed, but how does the Crypt appear today? Have the contents been as well preserved as Peters promised? Or were the precautions he took not sufficient? The great door could guard a room full of dust and mold, slow-motion deterioration. Perhaps even now thick blankets of moss cling to the walls, while silverfish and termites have their way with the wood and the paper. We will never know.

A remodel job on the basement, completed, I'm guessing, sometime in the 1980s, installed fluorescent lighting and a drop ceiling that now obscure the top quarter of the door. Somehow it doesn't look as if the building is encroaching on the door, though. It just looks like the door has grown, become larger than its opening. It could be an epigram about history, written not in words but architecture, something about how a thing occurs the first time, but then along comes the drop ceiling, until eventually some knowing wag arrives to bemoan

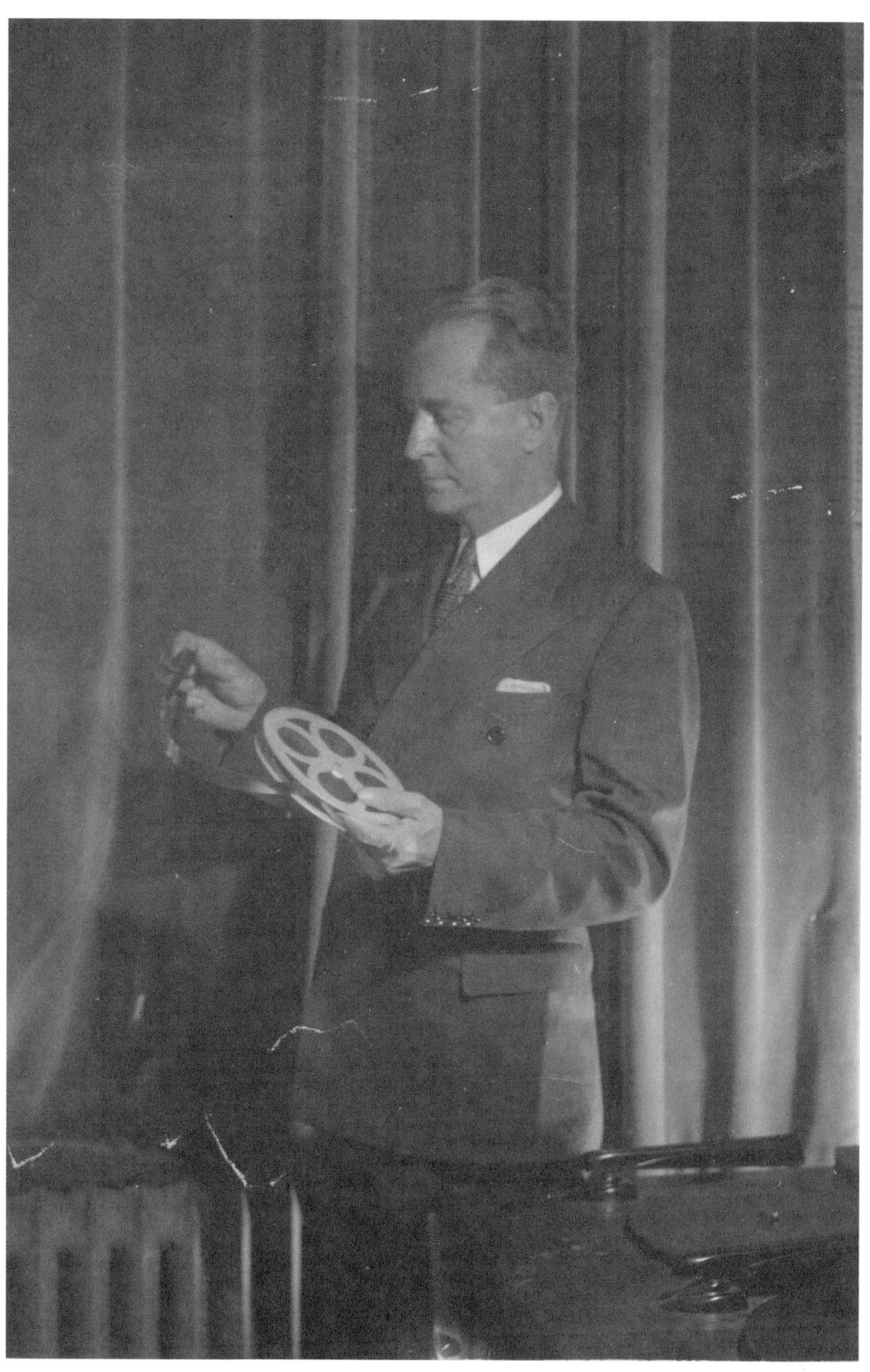

Dr. Thornwell Jacobs with a reel of film that was placed in the Crypt of Civilization.

This and all preceding Crypt of Civilization photographs courtesy of the archives, Philip Weltner Library, Oglethorpe University.

the aesthetic tragedy of the drop ceiling. Beside the door, to one side, I saw two chairs with wicker seats, as if someone might want to sit and wait for the year 8113. To the other side, Career Services maintained a bulletin board with a scalloped edge in bright rainbow stripes. Postings at the time I visited were limited: one job opportunity and a single internship. A piece of paper with an arrow drawn on it was taped to a nearby wall. "THIS WAY TO THE PSYCH LAB," it read. Outside the building, a sign for Phoebe Hearst Hall listed what was inside:

> Bookstore
>
> Classrooms
>
> Faculty Offices
>
> Crypt of Civilization
>
> University College

In such company, Jacobs's dream could seem downright average, the Crypt rendered normal, just something you'd expect to find on a campus, like another coffee shop with a kooky name. But Hudson sees the Crypt differently:

> I see it as something with a personality and quirks and ups and downs…. It's on a journey, and it's a journey that's going to take eighty-two generations. And it's stationary, yet it's moving through time. There's really nothing you can do but wait.

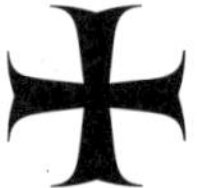

I've been thinking, though, that it might not be necessary to wait, that the Crypt, in fact, is already working. Imagine that the Crypt is a kind of a machine. It's spring-loaded and ready to run, ready to reveal its secrets, except, by design, at least as Jacobs intended it, this machine won't actually operate for a long time. But still, there's the fact of the Crypt itself, its physical appearance, its luminous presence, this giant, polished door, closed, welded shut, and then there are the stories about it, the partial inventory of its contents, and the photograph of its interior, taken before the door was sealed, which makes it look like the well-preserved tomb of an Egyptian pharaoh with eclectic taste. All these facts, I think, create something other than Jacobs intended, a machine that is already working, even while sealed.

For me, the Crypt generates thoughts, questions, feelings. In one respect, the Crypt is a machine that invites easy retrospective judgments, the sort that give hindsight its dismal reputation. When I read over the inventory, for instance, I found it hard not to question the need for storing those samples of textile upholstery or, for that matter, any of the other industrial samples—the plated plastics, the aluminum foil, the gold mesh. But then, maybe it will be an important revelation to some eighty-second-century researcher to establish that in the mid-twentieth century, people could in fact fabricate aluminum into very thin sheets and then wind those sheets around a cardboard spool. But those easy judgments are a bit of a trick, because the Crypt also encourages me to look anxiously toward the future. Whatever fun there is to be had questioning the wisdom of our ancestors, circa 1940, stops when I ask myself what I would save or preserve for the future. What would you put into your swimming-pool-size time capsule? I've thought about it, but have no good answers. I'm still thinking. Even if I were to set aside any grand ambition of including in a time capsule as much of civilization up to this moment as can fit, even if I just challenged myself to represent me or my family, what would I store? I'm surrounded by stuff, my desk a mess, but I'm not sure any of it is worth saving.

The Crypt is also a worry machine, sparking doubts and fears about the future and the very survival of the planet and us on it. I can't contemplate the eighty-second century without immediately wondering if there will even be an eighty-second century. Will the planet exist? Will it support and sustain life? For humans? Or will people—what people remain and those who can afford it—be floating around in space, colonizing some new, as yet undiscovered planet, or living high in space stations? Wherever people are then living, by the year 8113, I'll be gone—long gone—and forgotten. We all will. And all of our children, if we have children, will be dead as well. All of our nieces and nephews, and all of their children, and all of their children's children, will also be dead. Everyone now here, everyone we know—look around, everyone—will be gone. And probably everything we know, too, will be gone. Every building, every bridge, every road. Maybe they will be replaced, superseded by something greater and shinier, or maybe not. Maybe there will just be piles of rubble and wide fields of ash, or water, lots of water, or maybe all that will exist is a narrow band of nature, scrappy plants and scrappy animals, the sort of species that creep back in and flourish once everything else has died or left: crabgrass and bindweed, roaches, rats. My family lives in a brick town house a little over a hundred years old. All the houses on our block were built around 1910 or so. Will our house last another hundred years, even? I'm doubtful. And so, what will be here in 8113, a time so far in the future, so distant from us, that writing the numbers looks wrong, less like a year than a typo?

The Crypt is a humbling machine, too. To read a plaque that says this chamber shall remain locked until the eighty-second century is to be invited in frank terms to consider the length of one's life. You have to do that math, and the math is not pretty. How long will each of us live? Maybe a hundred years if you're genetically lucky. So to be realistic—to err on the side of rough averages—I'll figure on seventy-five years, more if you're a woman. For me, born in 1969, that means thirty-some years, come January. I don't even want to compute the precise number.* And then I think of our older son, because I've talked with him about time capsules, telling him what I've been working on, and now he wants to make one himself. I asked him what he'd put inside it, and he wasn't sure. He said he needed to think about what he'd want to see in the future. He was trying to figure out what he'll be into then, like right now he's into mummies and giant squid and building forts out of blankets and pillows, but what will he be into when he goes off to college, which is his handy marker for something a long while off yet, but also something he senses is a big step? Later, he told me maybe he wanted to stuff his time capsule full of pinecones. But on another occasion when I asked, he said he'd write a letter and put it in the time capsule, which I thought was nice. He's only just learning to read, trying to sound out the words and write down how he thinks they're spelled. Mostly, it seems to him

---

* I just did. It's thirty, exactly. How depressing.

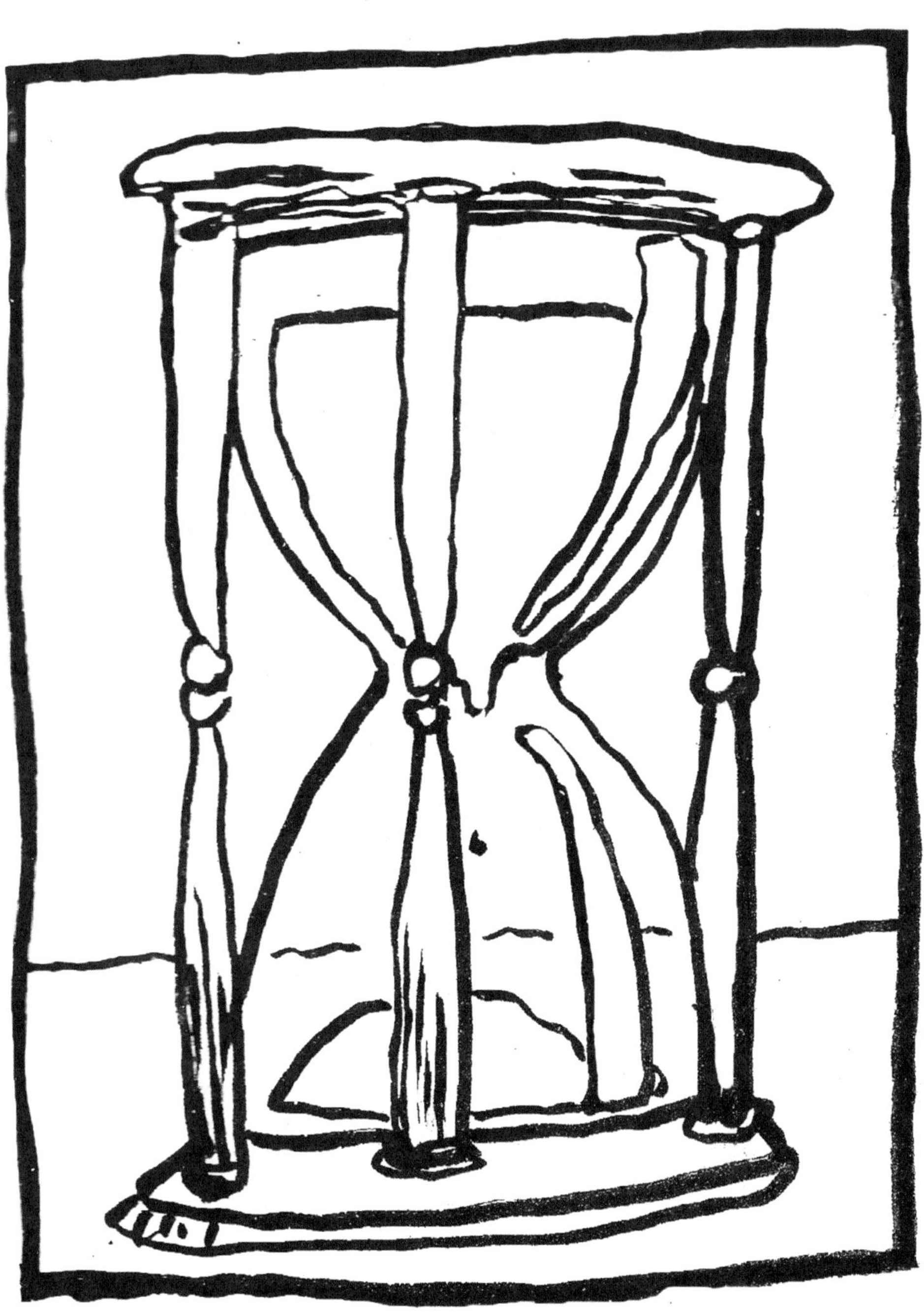

that words don't need so many vowels cluttering them up. "Answer," which he wrote the other day, could get along perfectly well as "ansr." I get teary-eyed when he tells me in school he wrote one complete sentence, and I ask him what the sentence was, if he remembers it, and he says the sentence was "I like dogs." I say how great that is. He wrote it all himself, he says, and then he tells me how he found the word *like* on a poster hanging in his classroom, and how he saw the word *dog* in a book, but he wanted to make it plural, so he added the *s*.

I have to follow through on the grim math. Let's say I live my allotted thirty more years, and then, after I'm dead, my older son has maybe forty-four more years to live. I'm just guessing, and figuring his generation will live slightly longer and that he will exercise and eat well and take better care of himself than I have myself. I'm trying again to be optimistic. But in years, in terms of time, this is nothing. We are just a burp in the great expanse of time during which the Crypt of Civilization has to remain shut. We won't even make it out of the twenty-first century.

And so the Crypt is also a powerful sadness machine. I get down just thinking about how nobody I know, not my family, my friends, not their children, not even the newest of newborns, will be around when that door of the Crypt swings open. We will all be gone. It's the sort of total sadness that understandably prompts some people to reach for consolation. Peters, the Crypt archivist, for instance, was a believer in reincarnation. He told one Atlanta reporter, "I will be back. I do not doubt it. I will be there in some form in the year 8113 A.D." He imagined he would be needed then, continuing, "I hope to have a part in explaining to the visitors of that remote time what we put into the crypt and what our purpose was."

I think, too, of the consolation Cormac McCarthy offers in *The Road*, his postapocalyptic novel. In it, a young boy and his father are trying to survive in a hellish, ash-covered world. Winter is approaching, and they hope to reach the sea, where it may be warmer. Food is scarce, however, and thieves prey on travelers. Others are turning to cannibalism. *The Road* is a novel written by someone who knows he probably doesn't have long to live. The book—particularly in the character of the father—seems determined to face the looming certainty of death with honesty. McCarthy was seventy-three when it was pub-

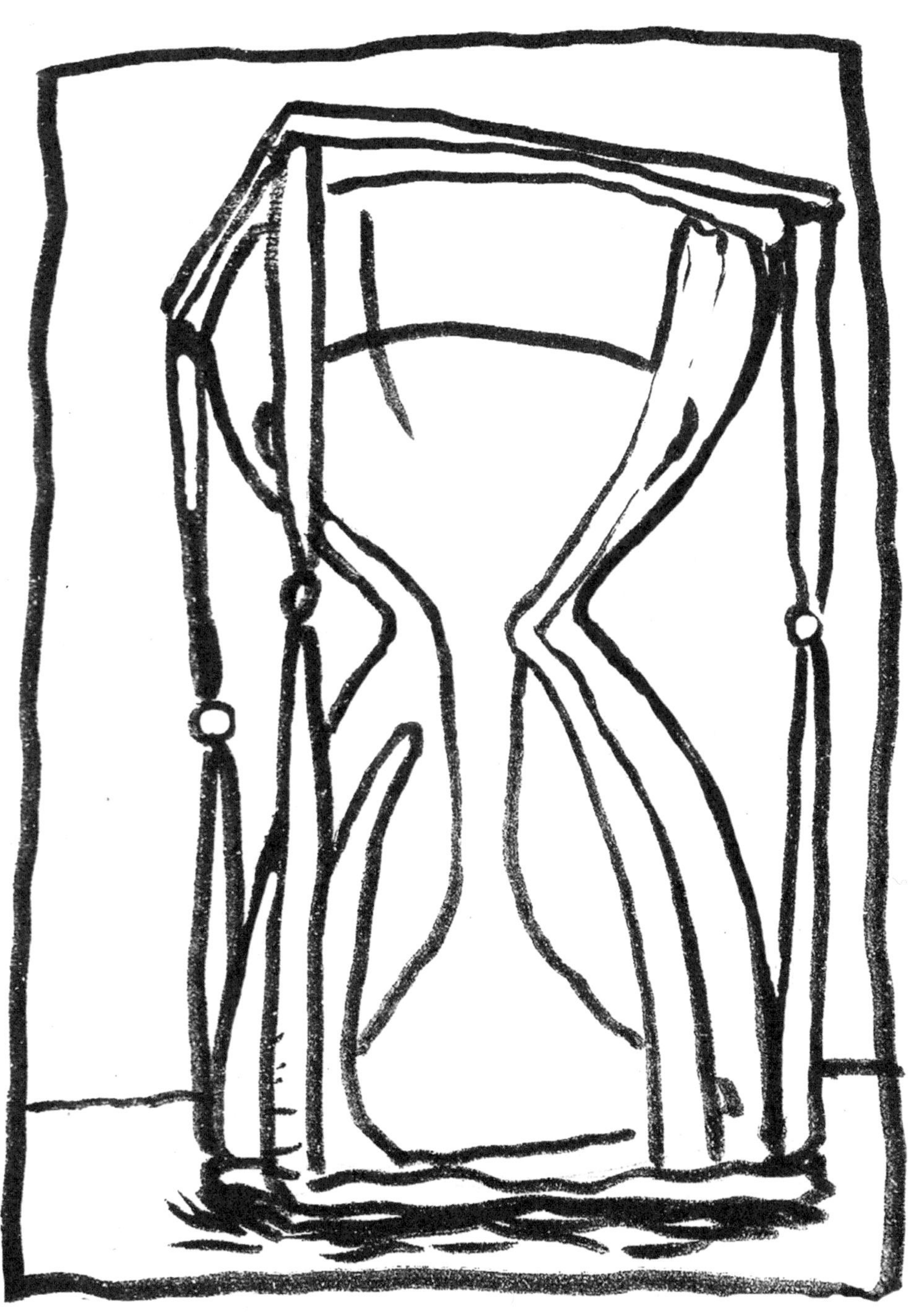

lished. McCarthy is the father of a young boy, too, John, born in 1998, and *The Road*, which he dedicated to John, does seem like a book written by someone who had a little kid running around the house. McCarthy said in an interview with Oprah Winfrey that the idea for *The Road* came to him when he and his son were traveling:

> My son John, about four years ago, he and I went to El Paso, and we checked into the old hotel there. And one night, John was asleep. It's—it wasn't night, it was probably about two, three o'clock in the morning, and I went over and I just stood and looked out the window at this town. There was nothing moving, but I could hear the trains going through, and that very, very lonesome sound. I just had this image of what this town might look like in fifty or a hundred years. I just had this image of these fires up on the hill and everything being laid waste, and I thought a lot about my little boy.

The book also pays loving attention to the boy, with his curiosity and his unending questions, which sometimes seem merely inquisitive and at other times go questing hard after some disturbing truth that he can sense but not name. One night, the boy is talking to his father:

> We're going to be okay, arent we Papa?
> Yes. We are.
> And nothing bad is going to happen to us.
> That's right.
> Because we're carrying the fire.
> Yes. Because we're carrying the fire.

This fire, the idea of it, is something the boy holds on to, a seeming bit of certainty in an otherwise bleak world. They are believers, the father and his son, and the fire is a symbol for their religion, whatever it may be. McCarthy doesn't elaborate. At times, the boy struggles to understand the fire. His father

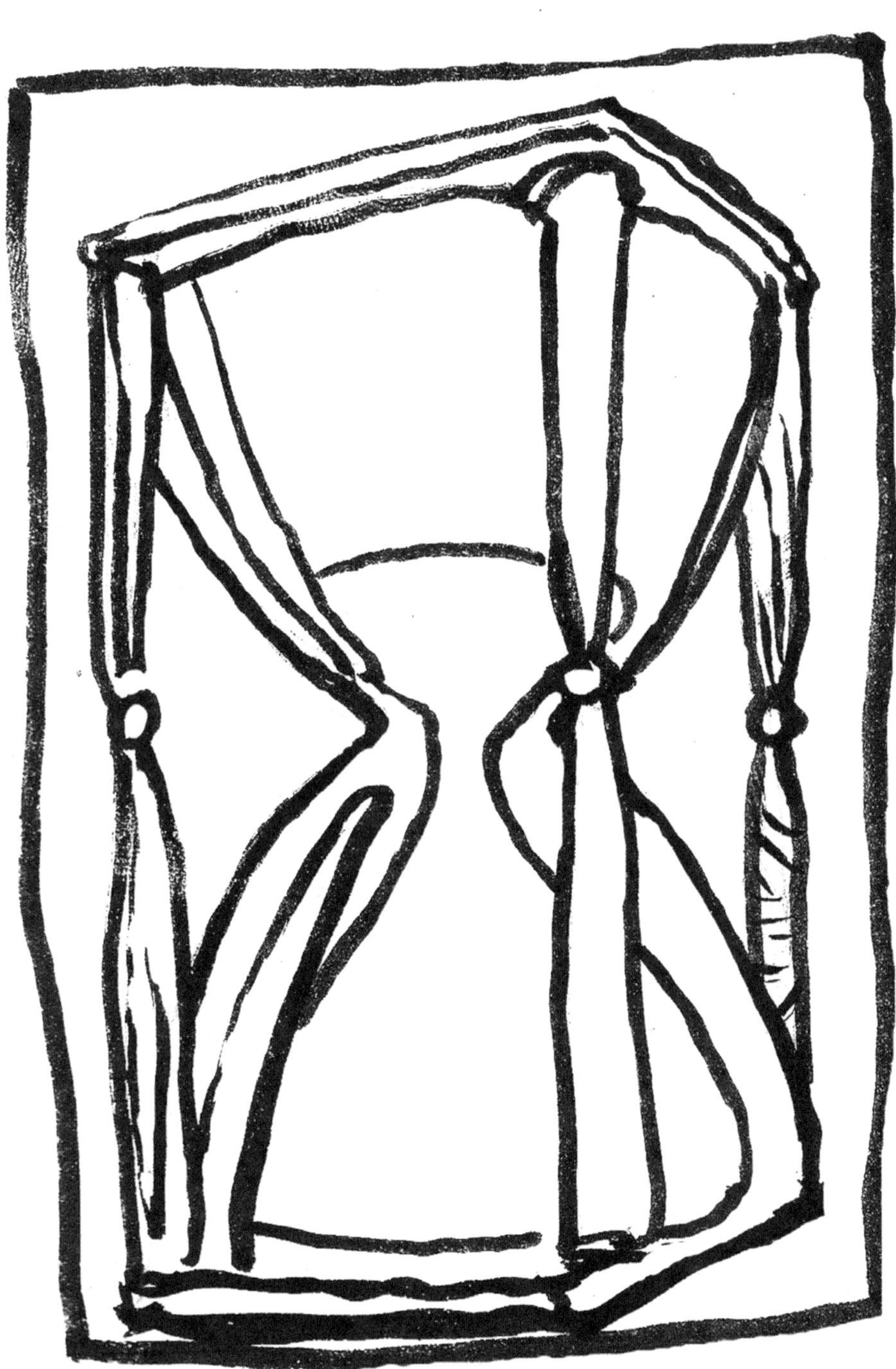

tries to shore up his faith:

>You have to carry the fire.
>
>I dont know how to.
>
>Yes you do.
>
>Is it real? The fire?
>
>Yes it is.
>
>Where is it? I dont know where it is.
>
>Yes you do. It's inside you. It was always there. I can see it.

I finished *The Road* shortly after my grandmother died. I think I'd been reading it already, before, but perhaps I picked it up when I was going to her funeral, because I wanted a book for the plane and because it seemed somehow apt. I can't remember anymore. I liked the novel, and I ended up talking about it with friends, more than I usually do with books. Almost always though, I got around to saying that I did have one reservation about it: I felt that the consolation, this fire they're carrying, was a cop-out, like a packet of artificial sweetener dropped in to cut what's bitter. I understand others might disagree. I know there are people who believe they too have the fire, in a manner of speaking, and I don't begrudge them that. I just think I'd rather suffer through the sadness, personally.

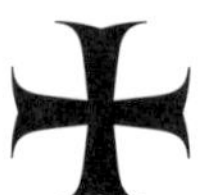

Last summer, while we were at the beach, my wife was saying how some of the beaches she went to as a kid are no longer there, or if they are still there, you wouldn't want to go to them, because there's so little beach left, and our older son heard this—we were in the car, driving around, looking for something to do other than go to the beach—and he wanted to know why all the beaches were disappearing. He has especially sensitive ears, I've always thought, for calamity. Any sort of disaster piques his interest, the more current the better, and so he started asking more questions, probing, taking the measure of the awfulness, but also looking for a handy culprit. "What's erosion,

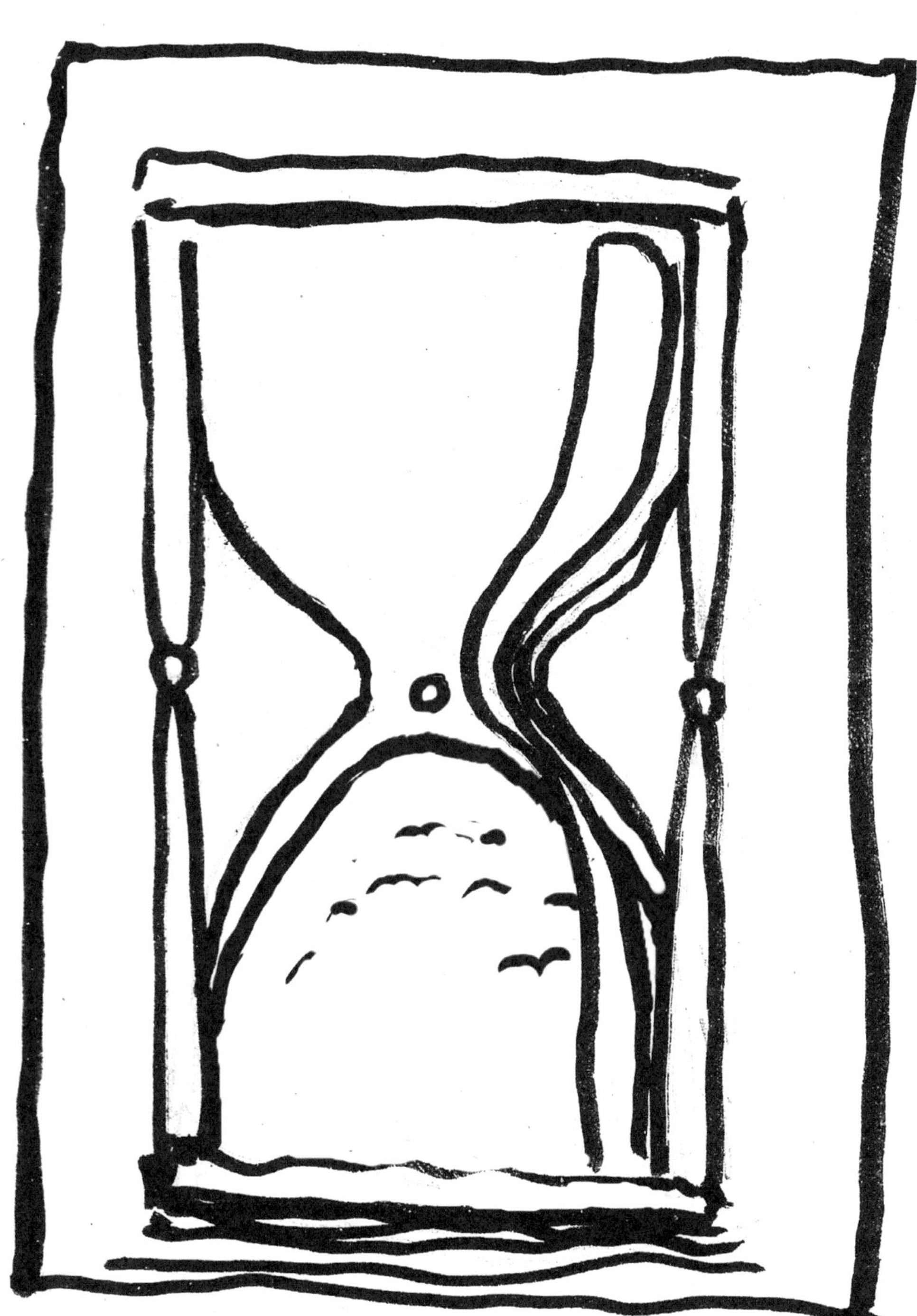

Mommy?" led pretty quickly to "What's causing it?" and "How can I stop it from happening?" And so talk of beach erosion spread into a broader discussion about environmental destruction and from there, I think, we were on to global warming. Once our son felt he had all the information he needed about the latest disaster, he was ready to fix the problem. He'll take it on by himself if he has to. "Here's what I'll do," he said. Which, pretty much, sums up how all our disaster discussions proceed. It's at once heartening and exciting, because he understands that these are problems and he wants to do something, and as I always tell my wife, he does unerringly come down on the right side of issues; at the same time it's also more than a little depressing, because as jaded adults, we've seen often enough how politics works, and how policy gets made, how bold proclamations to change this or end that are succeeded, sometimes years later, by minute gains or, all too frequently, meaningless symbolic victories, and no, we jaded adults are not so jaded that we want to tell our son all this, we don't want to say that these problems are never going to be solved, that things are only going to get worse, that the beaches will continue to erode and the world is going to get warmer and the oceans will rise, but still, it's hard for jaded adults to be terribly optimistic.

With regard to beach erosion and global warming, our son's first idea was that we needed to kill all the people. Which is not unlike how, last fall, he proposed solving the government shutdown, saying, "President Obama should call up the Army and all the police and kill all the Republicans." We do try as parents to temper his enthusiasm for mass murder with something more reasonable, like a letter to our member of Congress. And once we remind him that it's illegal to kill a bunch of people—and not nice besides—he's onto his backup ideas: such as that he, personally, will disable all the cars so that they can no longer run, and then he, personally, will make, as he put it, "a new car that is not a car, and that car will be better."

We talked it all out, until something else came up, like stopping for ice cream or wanting to listen to "Yellow Submarine" again, but it was his first idea I kept thinking about over the next few days. Because, leaving aside what's alarming about it, which as a parent, I've concluded, you just have to get used to doing, he's not incorrect to think that people—a lot of people, all of us, let's say, to spread the blame around evenly—are causing these problems, some more than others, sure, but we're all responsible to a degree. And so if you took the people—us—out of the equation, the problems would, you might conclude, stop. I do see the logic.

In college there was this guy who lived on the same floor as I did, real crunchy type, into Greenpeace and whatnot. He had all these bumper stickers stuck to the door of his room, slogans for his various causes. He also had a dry-erase board and a magic marker hanging there. A lot of people did then. The idea was—this was during the dark period, before the age of the cell phone—a person would leave messages on the board: So-and-so stopped by; your mom called; I'll be at the library; etc. I never had a message board, which, looking back, seems not at all surprising. I also didn't post things on my door. Anyway, one night I was walking by this guy's room, and I stopped and actually read all the slogans, and while I can't recall them now, I do remember that one sticker, posted front and center, directly above the message board, said simply, "Save the earth." It was late, the floor quiet, and I was tired, having just come back from hours spent writing in the computer center (very few of us owned computers then). I don't know why, but I picked up his pen and, under the sticker, I wrote, "Kill all the people."

I told my wife about the crunchy guy and his message board, and she shook her head in that now-I-see-where-he-gets-it way. I'd never told her the story before. It hadn't come up, or just never seemed relevant. I thought about telling our son, but then decided maybe I better wait a while on that yet.

My message stayed up on the board for several days. Some thought it was funny, and others found it disturbing. I told friends that, of course, I'd intended the message as some blunt provocation, a joke, albeit a sick one, but that I also believed it was kind of true, in a way, if you thought about it. Not long after, parents' weekend rolled around, and this other guy who lived on our floor had his mother and father visiting. They were coming back from dinner, when his mother stopped to look at the message board and then she read aloud in this quavering voice what it was I'd written. "Honey," she said to her husband, "come here. This says, 'Save the earth, kill all the people.'" My roommate and I were in our room. Our parents weren't visiting, which also doesn't seem that surprising, and so we were just hanging out. We overheard all this, and while it was easy to detect the concern in her voice, we just about died laughing. ❧

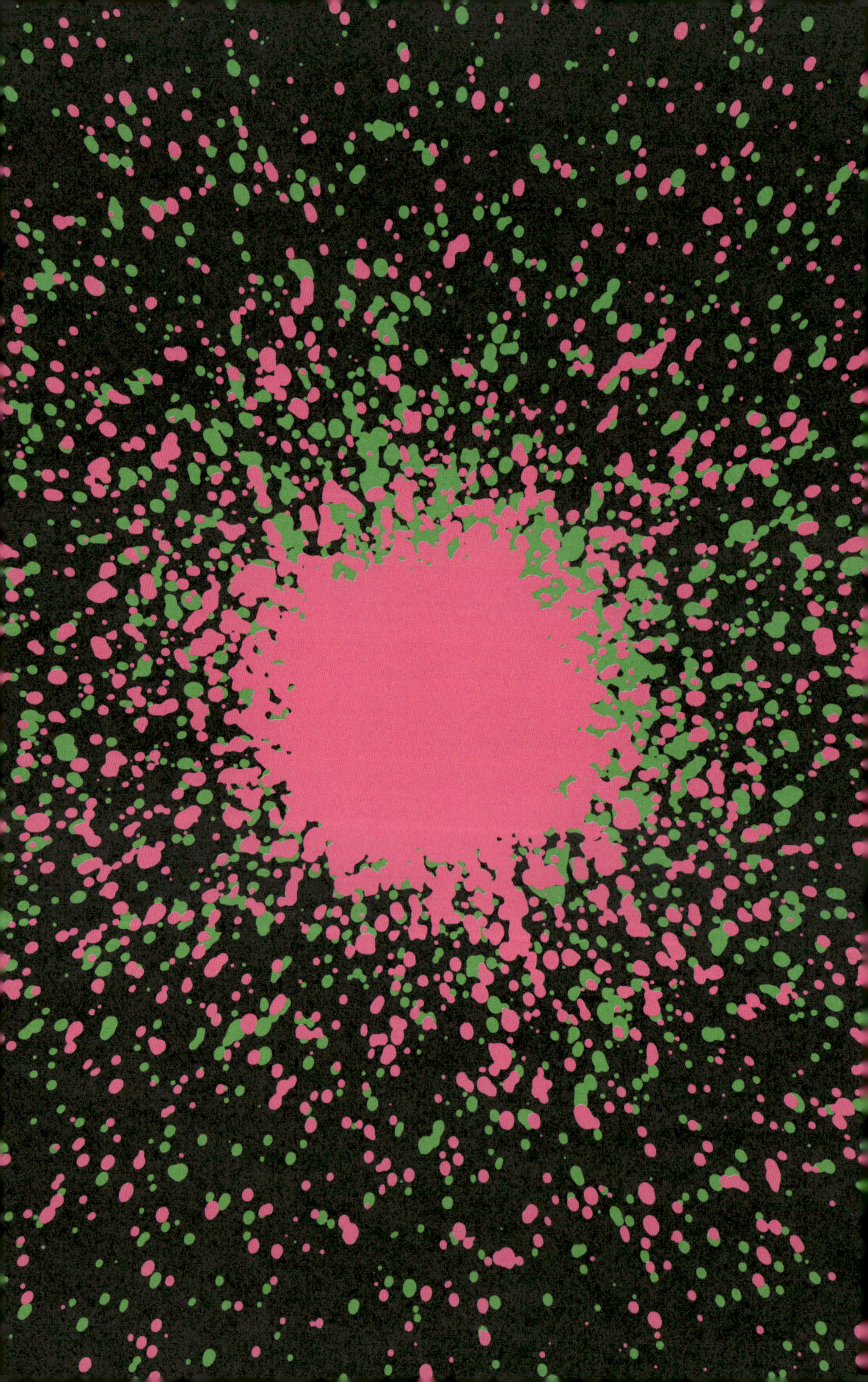

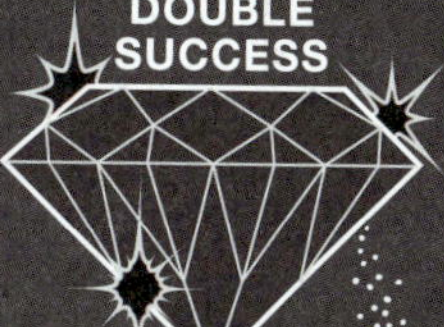

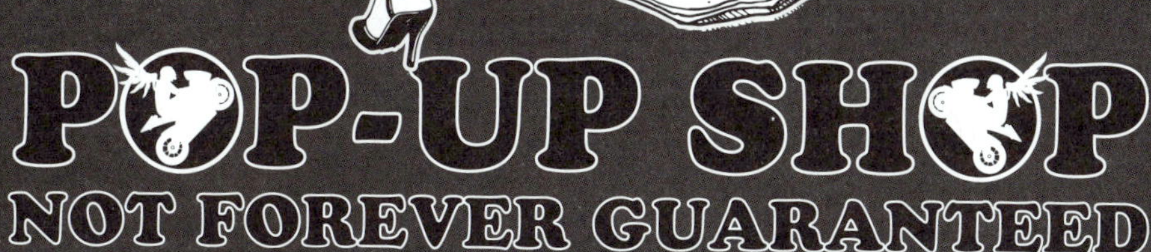

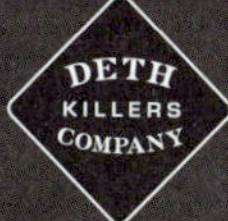

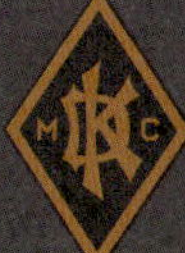

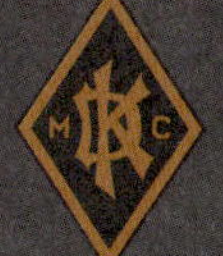

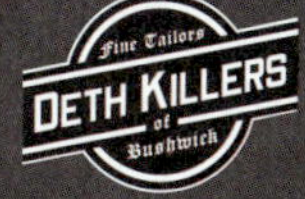

DETH KILLERS

ASPHALT "Resistant" JEANS

PRACTICALLY GUARANTEED

"IT'S ALWAYS A PUSSY AVALANCHE IN DETH KILLERS ROBOT SKIN PANTS"
-MICHIO KAKU

COME HARD

348 BOWERY, NEW YORK, NY
FEBRUARY 2014

BUSHWICK SINCE 2002
DETHKILLERS.COM

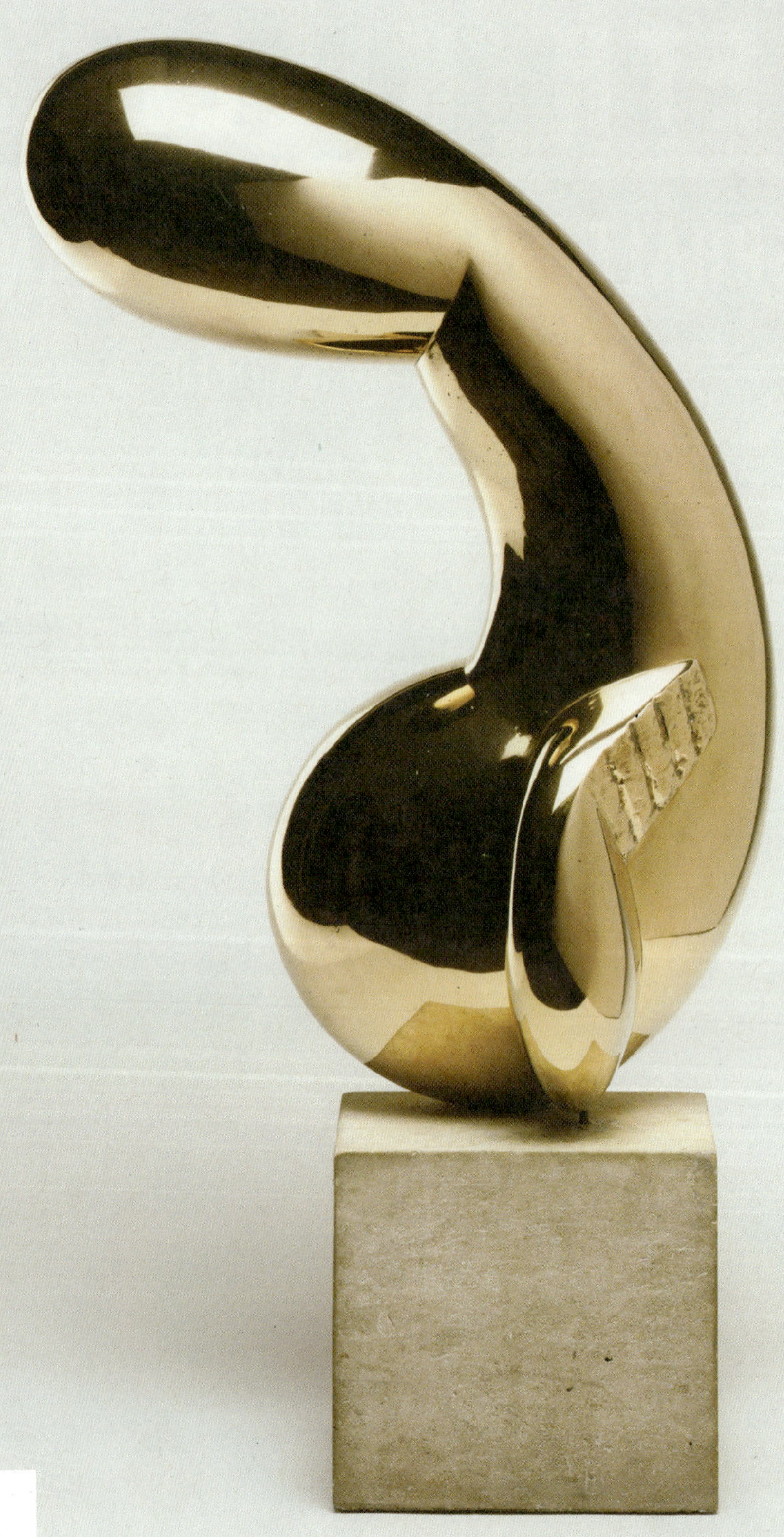

PRINCESSE X,
1915–16 BY
CONSTANTIN
BRÂNCUSI.

The Princess Diaries

THE GREAT QUESTION THAT HAS
NEVER BEEN ANSWERED,
AND WHICH I HAVE NOT YET
BEEN ABLE TO ANSWER,
DESPITE MY THIRTY YEARS
OF RESEARCH INTO
THE FEMININE SOUL, IS,
WHAT DOES A WOMAN WANT?

—SIGMUND FREUD

I'LL TELL YOU WHAT I WANT,
WHAT I REALLY REALLY WANT,
SO TELL ME WHAT YOU WANT,
WHAT YOU REALLY REALLY WANT
I WANNA, I WANNA, I WANNA,
I WANNA, I WANNA REALLY
REALLY REALLY WANNA
ZIGAZIGAH.

—SPICE GIRLS

Jamieson Webster & Ben Kafka

What does a woman want? What does she really, really want? It was a question Freud had been asking from the start of his career. Describing his early influences in an essay on the history of the psychoanalytic movement, Freud told an anecdote about his medical-school days, when one of his professors, a gynecologist named Chobrak, sent him a female patient suffering from hysteria. It turned out that, in her eighteen years of marriage, the patient had never had "successful" intercourse with her husband, who was impotent. "The sole prescription for such a malady," Chobrak told Freud, "is familiar enough to us, but we cannot order it." The prescription?

$$R_X \text{ Penis normalis}$$
$$\text{dosim} \quad \cdot$$
$$\text{repetatur!}$$

The brilliance of psychoanalysis was to take this idea seriously without taking it literally. Had Freud taken literally the role of sexual frustration in the origin of the neuroses, he would have ended up a massage therapist or some other kind of professional masturbator. His insight was that the physical stimulation of the genitals was only one component of a much larger field of sexuality ruled by unconscious wishes, fantasies, conflicts, and defenses. Even the most repetitive dose of "penis normalis" would not cure neurotic symptoms.

We still ask what women want all the time, and even though there's nothing especially sexual about the question, it always seems to be a question of sex—perhaps because that's what men most want women to want.

Freud apparently posed this question in its most famous form to his patient and patroness Marie Bonaparte, one of the odder characters in a profession full of them. Born in 1882, she was related to Napoleon Bonaparte on her father's side and the Monte Carlo casino fortune on her mother's. When she's remembered today, it's usually for a handful of notable events: marrying Prince George of Greece in 1907, cofounding the Paris Psychoanalytic Society in 1925, publishing a psychobiography of Edgar Allan Poe in 1933, rescuing the Freud-Fliess correspondence in 1936, negotiating Freud's move to London in 1938, and pushing for Jacques Lacan's exclusion from the International Psychoanalytic Association in 1953. She is also known for her distinguished list of lovers, including the sociologist Gustave Le Bon, the politician Aristide Briand, the psychoanalyst Rudolf Loewenstein (who was also Lacan's analyst and, briefly, Princess Marie's as well, also her son's), and quite possibly the artist Constantin Brâncuşi, whose sensational sculpture *Princesse X* supposedly depicts the princess studying herself in a mirror. Catherine Deneuve played her in the made-for-TV movie.

PRINCESS MARIE BONAPARTE IN HER GARDEN IN 1905.

The princess's archives, most of which are contained at the Library of Congress, are under seal until 2020. Until then, we must make do with her long list of publications: books, essays, translations, none of which are in print any longer. These range from the trivial (a children's book about her chow Topsy) to the intriguing (her collection of wartime myths with names like

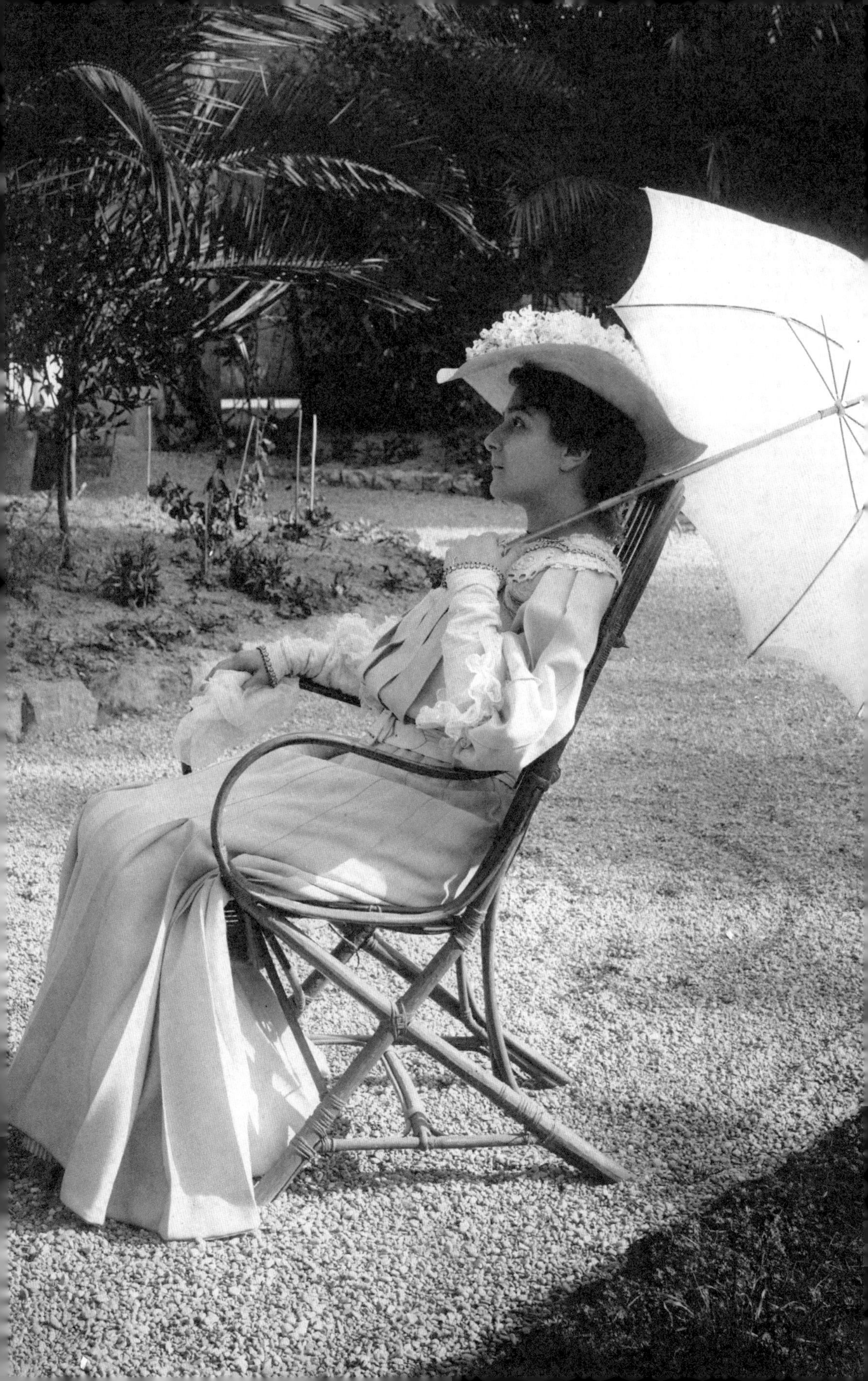

vichar.
KK mach.
linette
Mimi
mi mo too dans une
il chartier.

"The Myth of the Corpse in the Car" and "The Myth of the Doctored Wine") to the very significant: her childhood diaries, which, counterintuitively, are the most important work in her oeuvre. A lonely, morose child, she began keeping the copybooks at the age of seven and a half and kept up with them until she was ten or so. She brought these diaries with her to her analysis with Freud, which began in 1925 and continued intermittently thereafter. In 1939, she published a limited-edition set of exact replicas of the copybooks, along with five volumes of transcriptions and commentary based on her conversations about them with Freud.

These diaries provide a fascinating record of the life of a fabulously wealthy, precociously sexual French girl at the fin-de-siècle. The commentaries offer insight into the sexual frustrations of a mature woman. In fact, her lack of physical pleasure during intercourse had been one of her principal motivations for seeking the analysis in the first place. Sex had been a huge disappointment for her. At first she thought it was her husband's fault. "I hate this as much as you do, but we must do it if we want children," he told her on their wedding night. She soon discovered that his most meaningful relationship—which was almost certainly sexual—was with his Uncle Waldemar, who had a castle outside Copenhagen. But her liaisons were no more satisfying.

𝕭𝖔𝖓𝖆𝖕𝖆𝖗𝖙𝖊'𝖘 𝖒𝖔𝖙𝖍𝖊𝖗 had died shortly after giving birth to her; her father, an amateur geologist, preferred the company of rocks. She was thus raised by a series of nannies and tutors, variously well meaning and wicked. The copybooks include vocabulary lists in French, English, and German, but above all they contain stories—mostly written in English, which Bonaparte thought of as her "secret" language, that is to say, a language not understood by the servants who raised her. One of the most striking of these stories was at the center of Bonaparte's analysis with Freud.

The story is dated fall-winter 1889, when Bonaparte was not quite eight years old. It's called "The Mouth Pencil."

> Far far away lived a woman who name was Gretchen Holinneck. She was a servent and her brother "John Holinneck" also, they had a mistress who was very sever for them the mistress had a farm named "for all the bulls" or "the three stars." Once the mistress said "you must go out in the garden of the "ring bell" and now if you see the "sarquintué" you will not forget to the him good morning from me." "Yes" replied Gretchen and she went away and she met a good fairy who told her in giving her a Mouth Pencil "this will protect you from my enemie the fairy that you will meet" and she vanished.

To make a short story even shorter, Gretchen encounters the bad fairy, who tries to drill a hole in her neck. Using the mouth pencil, however, Gretchen is able to conjure up a necktie, which protects her, though only briefly. The bad fairy summons up some sort of monster, who digs a hole in the ground, through which the heroine and her brother fall until they get to hell. They manage to escape only to find themselves in the clutches of another monster, the Sarquintué. We are

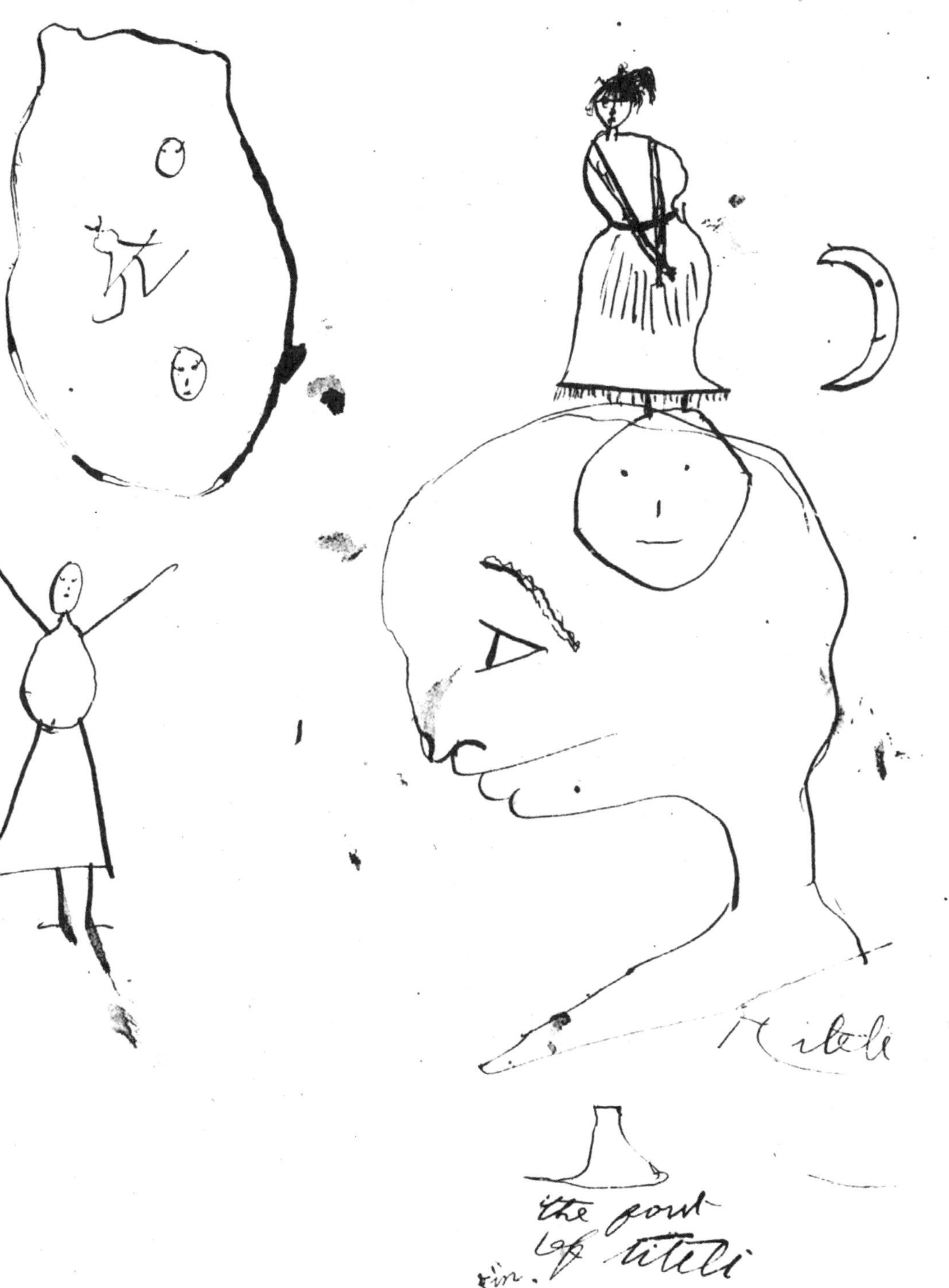

Ritchie
the part
in. of titeli

THE GHOST
AND THE QUEEN OF FAIRIES

The queen of fairies once went out
of her Kindom to go to a ball of
the ghosthess she had a black dress
in muslenn and silvers stars were
on it   she had a silver star in
her hairs and was beautifully dressed
the ghosthess had white dresses
with silver all was beautiful then
in the ball the queen of fairies
met a man and she dans with this
man and this man was the ESCAMOTEUR
then mimi the queen of fairies loved
him wery much and   maried
him

END

A CHILDHOOD STORY BY
THE PRINCESS (L) AND HER
OWN ADULT ANALYSIS OF IT
FROM DECADES LATER (R).

THE GHOST AND THE QUEEN OF FAIRIES
(I. 89)

The process of reconciliation continues. Mimi, queen of the fairies, goes to a ball of the ghosts, at which everything is beautiful, from her own black muslin dress, adorned with silvery stars, which make her a true queen of the night, identifying herself with her mother, to the beautiful dresses worn by the ghosts. I am thus reconciled with the dead—that is, the dead women. When Nounou departed (never to return again) she must have become assimilated in my mind to my mother, who had made the greatest of all departures—to the next world. Then, with the implicit acquiescence of the ghosts, I meet the Escamoteur, love him 'wery much' and, in final Oedipal triumph, am married to him.

not sure exactly what happens next, but whatever it was made them "very miserable," the narrator tells us, until yet another creature arrived to deliver them to a golden star. There is a nightmare involving bulls and frogs, a rescue by two more characters, a marriage between Gretchen and one of those characters, and then a transformation back into what the narrator tells us is "human form."

"When I showed Freud this page," Bonaparte writes in the volumes of commentaries on the diaries, "he said 'this mouth pencil seems suspect. You must have seen fellatio as a child.'" She protested, accused him of lazy interpretations, and so on, but gradually "yielded"—her word—"to the evidence." He used it to reconstruct a primal scene, that is to say, her first encounter with adult sexuality, in this case a dalliance between her nanny and her father's Corsican head groom. Bonaparte later confirmed this memory by seeking out the groom. It turned out that the scenes had actually repeated themselves not once or twice but regularly from the age of three or four months until the age of four years. To keep the child quiet, the nanny would administer her doses of sirop de flon, which a pharmaceutical guide from 1901 describes as a cough medicine made up of a "very weak syrup of morphine, colored with cochineal and flavored with cherry laurel." Yum.

Her encounters with the mysteries of adult sexuality make many other appearances in these diaries. It appears that what menaced—and excited—the princess most was the possibility of what she called "bursting." In her commentaries, she linked this fear back to hearing that her deceased mother was terrified of thunder. One suspects that there was more to it. Consider, for example, this story, "The Bursting Woman," about a little girl named Mimi:

> I know a woman that wanted to burst and she made this regime to burst: every morning she heard the noise that made the bursted ink by the left ear, and put a little on her tongue, then something went of her nose it was some ink that was going to burst and in bursting a juggler came and shutted in her ear a littler water of horse (in the right one) then she sweld a little melt a little and to burst goes what she made? She… she…... it is so terrible I can not say it. She swallod up a …. No, it would make you cry. I will not say it she swallod up…. No, I muss not say it she swallow up a…. … a knife, and she.. … made…… she made burst the…. Oh! How it is terrible I muss not say it you have anof of the emotins I occasioned you…. She made burst the house where fairies… fai…. Fairies…. And it is like that we have no more fairies…. Fai…. Fai…. ries…. Fairies!…..

The story is structured around a conflicted relationship to desire. It opens by acknowledging that the woman "wants" to burst. Whatever guilt, horror, and shame Mimi might experience, this doesn't stop the quasi-orgasmic appearance of the rhythmic ellipses, along with the swelling, melting, swallowing, and bursting, all of which finally ends with the fai, fai, fairies! Far from the frigid woman in analysis with Freud, little Princess Bonaparte is coming apart at the seams with excitement; much as, we would say, most children are. In this vein, the stories are less of an encounter with sexuality on the outside—the suspected, dreaded primal scene—but on the inside.

Marie's diaries are often stunning in their naive sensuality, the moments of

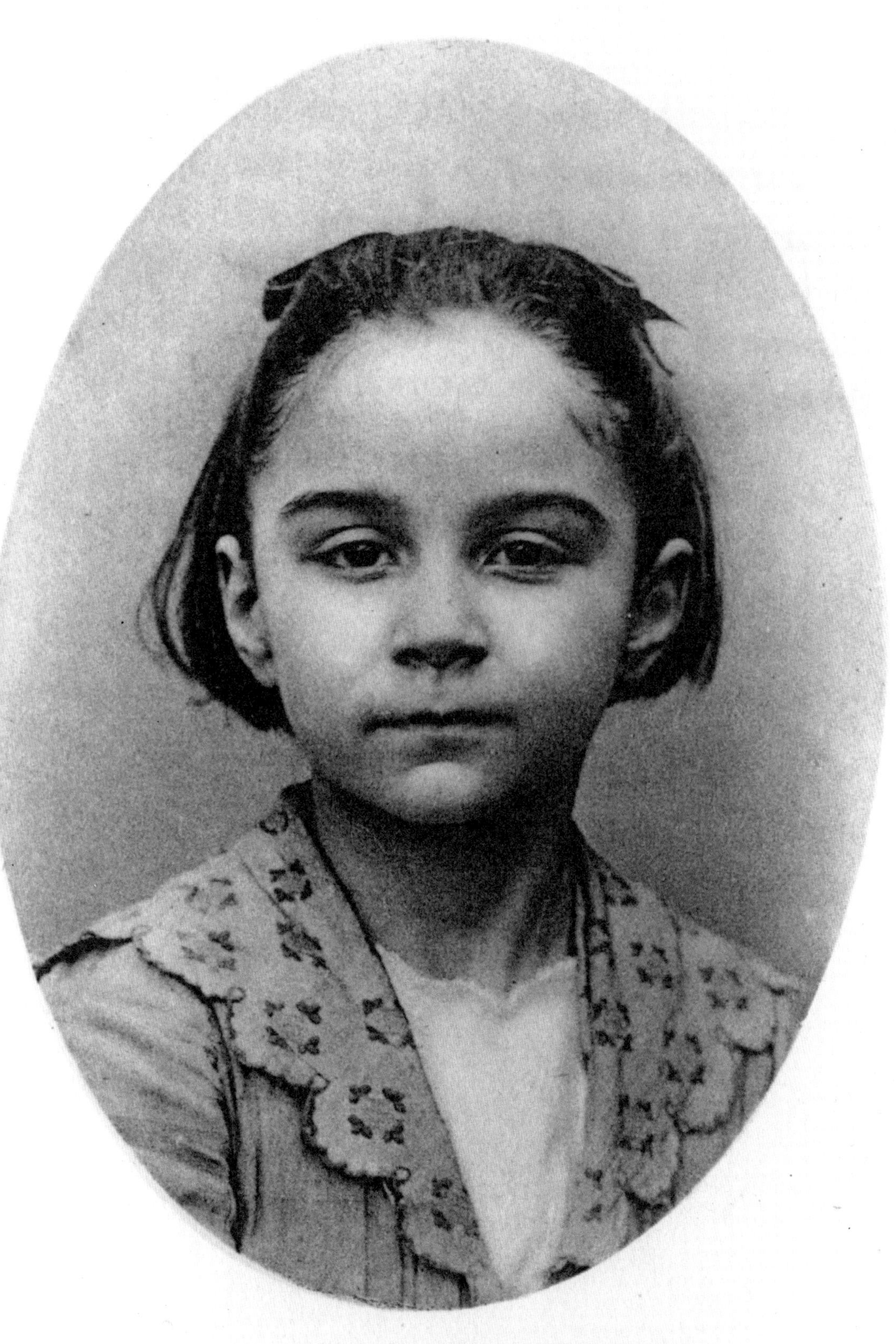

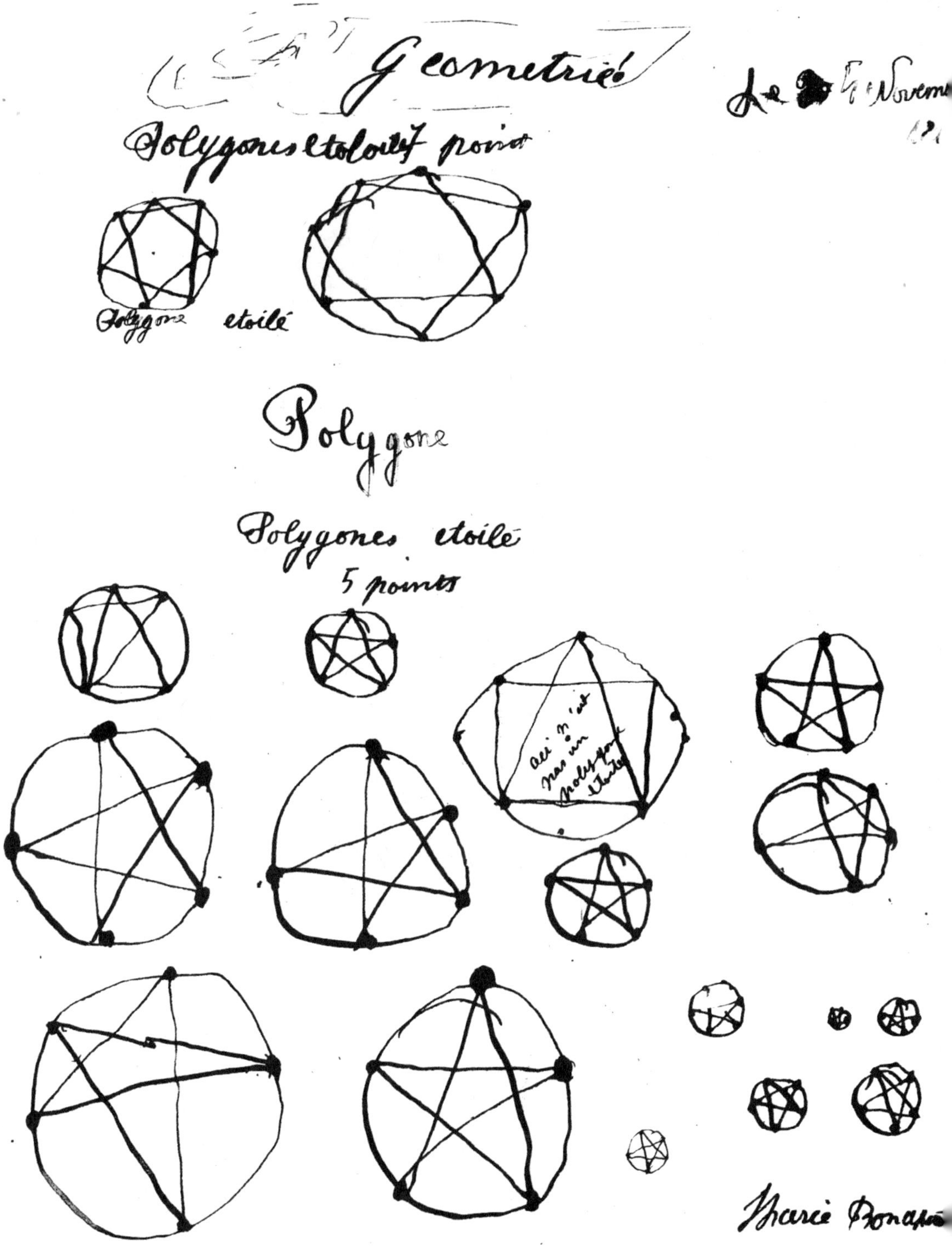

Geometrie!

Polygones etoiles poins

Polygone etoilé

Polygone

Polygones etoilé
5 points

ceci n'est
pas un
polygone
etoilé

Marie Bonaparte

bursting that break through. She writes, "My hand is all wet. What good spitting!" with an explanation that, as a child, "if I had no handkerchief and felt I was being watched, which meant that spitting on the carpet was impossible, what was I to do if I suddenly felt a compulsion to expel something from my mouth? What I sometimes did was to pretend to wipe my lips with the palm of my little hand and then surreptitiously to spit in it. The problem was then to wipe it, but how? On my dress? The curtains? The tablecloth? Meanwhile my hand would be wet, at first with a warm wetness which, however, gradually grew tepid and then cool. The warm sensation at first was quite agreeable."

In young Marie's drawings, bursting is given beautiful figure and form in the unfurling women who finally take their wide stances with raised, open arms, substances emanating from their bodies and, most often, the top of their heads. And scattered throughout her copybooks, a black mark with outward-bursting rays is a constant feature, a kind of compulsive doodle. Brâncuşi couldn't have been more right to give the contradictory interpretations of his *Princesse X*—both a woman gazing down at herself in a closed loop and the erect penis, her preoccupation with the object of desire.

There is another, more worrisome motif in these diaries. Alongside the wild stories and illustrations are a series of quasi-obsessive maps of French towns. The bursting pattern is still there in the crossroads and roundabouts, but it seems altogether more constricted. Similar things happen in the text. The young girl's joyful sensuality must contend with these staid attempts at mapping, diagramming, and charting.

Indeed, these maps seem to anticipate Princess Marie's later fascination with mapping women's desire. Bonaparte's book *Female Sexuality*, which appeared in French in 1949 and English in 1953, collected her essays on the subject. It was published by the psychoanalytic publishing house International Universities Press in 1953, wrapped in a band that proclaimed, "The Kinsey Report gives the facts—this book explains the why and wherefore." But it's less about wherefore, really, than where. In fact, the where for Bonaparte was always the clitoris. She undertook extensive research measuring the distances between women's clitorises and their vaginas, eventually categorizing them as para-, meso-, and tele- clitoridienne. Female libido, she believed, was inevitably lost as it navigated the canyons and crevices of the female genitalia: "Power is generally lost when rivers change course," she wrote. The further the clitoris from the vagina, Princess Marie believed, the more likely the orgasm will fall into the gap.

In Bonaparte's work, we see the contradiction between fantasy and anatomical reality that has always hampered investigations of sexuality—particularly female sexuality. Among the many things that Freud did right was to enlarge the sphere of sexuality while trying to remain closely tied to the body. Perversions weren't simply sexuality outside the norms, nor excesses or deficiencies, but the fixated arousal of particular vicissitudes of normal sexuality: mouth, anus, phallus, eye; and the sensations of the skin that always border on pleasure and pain. The routes traveled by sexuality had many more dimensions for Freud than the single one described by Marie Bonaparte, with her fixation on the clitoris. As Freud wrote in his third preface to the *Three Essays on the Theory of Sexuality* in 1920, "as for the 'stretching'

	Stages of Libidinal Organization	Stages of Object-Love	Attitudes Towards the Subject	
			Boy	Girl
PRE-AMBIVALENT — 1. Early Oral Stage (Sucking)		Auto-Eroticism (Without Object)	Pre-Oedipal Position. Primary oral passvity and activity towards mother.	
2. Late Oral Stage (Cannibalistic)		Narcissism (Total Incorporation of Object)		
AMBIVALENT — 3. Early Sadistic-Anal Stage (Or Sadistic-Cloacal)		Partial Love (With Incorporation)	Primary cloacal and phallic passivity towards the mother. Diffuse muscular activity.	
4. Late Sadistic-Anal Stage (Or Sadistic-Cloacal)		Partial Love (With Possession)		
5. Early Phallic Stage		Object Love (With Affirmation of Phallus and Partial Exclusion of Cloaca) — Castration Complex	Primary phallic activity towards the mother. **Active Oedipus Complex.** Positive Oedipus Complex of Boy	Negative Oedipus Complex of Girl
6. Late Phallic Stage		Object Love (With Exclusion of Phallus and Reopening of Cloaca) — Latency Period	Secondary cloacal passivity towards the father. **Passive Oedipus Complex.** Negative Oedipus Complex of Boy	Positive Oedipus Complex of Girl
POST-AMBIVALENT — 7. Final Genital Stage		Object Love (Puberty)	Ultimate genital activity towards the female (Penoid)	Ultimate genital passivity towards the male (Vaginal)

of the concept of sexuality which has been necessitated by the analysis of children and what are called perverts, anyone who looks down with contempt upon psychoanalysis from a superior vantage point should remember how closely the enlarged sexuality of psychoanalysis coincides with the Eros of the divine Plato." What this means is that from the sexuality of children and perverts, we stretch and enlarge our concept of sexuality. Indeed, sexuality should look and sound and feel more like the diaries the princess wrote as a girl, not the essays she wrote as a woman.

But between her and Freud's many hasty and generic interpretations of her childhood journals, there is little wonder that Bonaparte's analysis was a failure. Not only were the duo's readings of the material overly casual, so was the handling of the inevitable transference. A year into the analysis there was an extraordinary *passage à l'acte*: In an effort to experience sexual pleasure, she underwent an operation to have her clitoris relocated closer to the urethral passage. The surgery was performed by a certain Dr. Halban of Vienna, whose work she also promoted in various medical journals under a pseudonym. Freud was furious, refusing to visit her during her recuperation, accusing her of having a "wild imagination," of "stupidity." Eventually he relented and came to see her at the clinic, which, in retrospect, could only have compounded the disturbances in the transference. The operation had been unsuccessful; she was filled with remorse. But this did not prevent her from repeating the procedure while still in analysis.

We see in Bonaparte's dilemma the contradictory ideas about the nature of

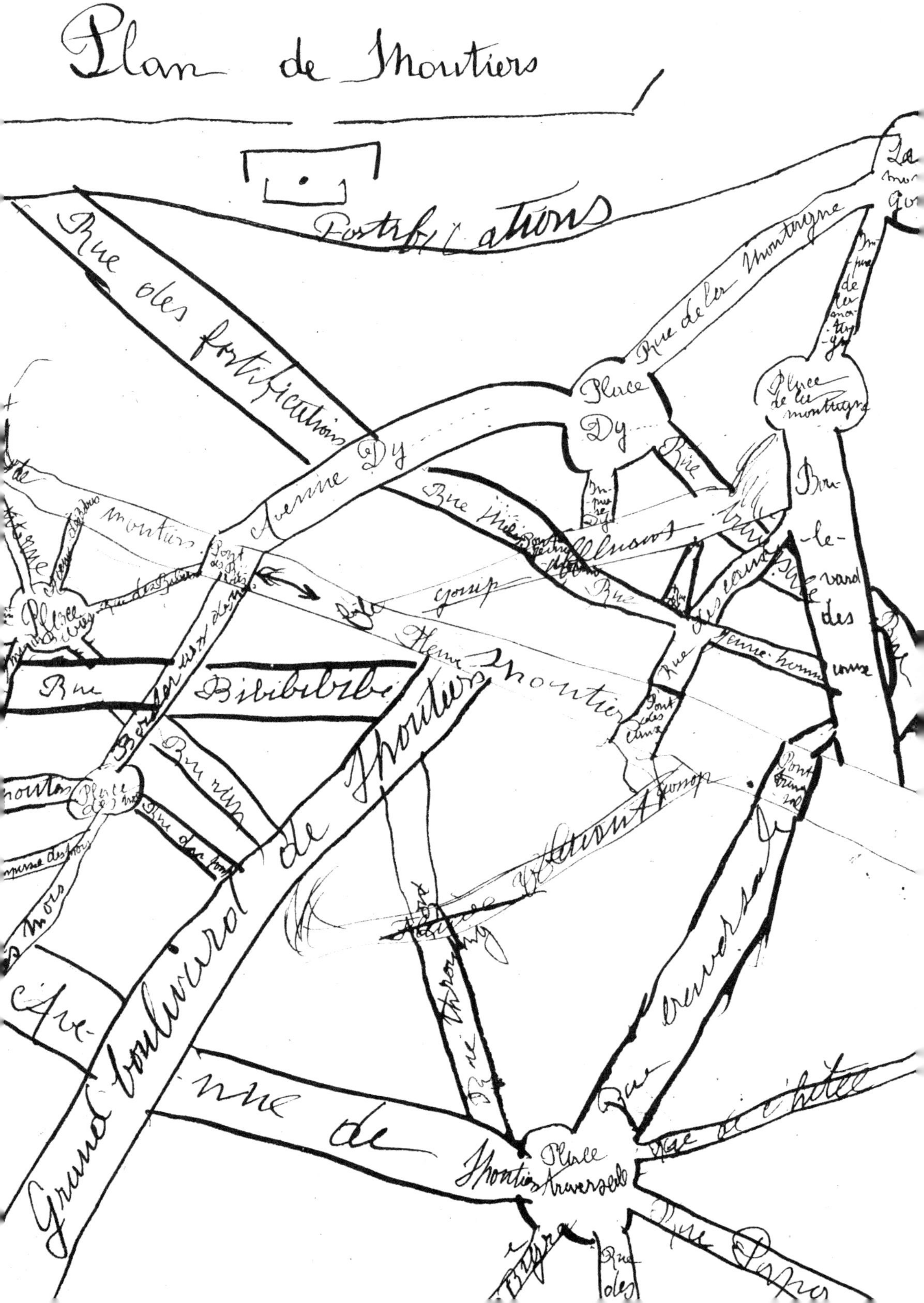

Plan de Moutiers
Fortifications
Rue des fortifications
Rue de la Montagne
Place Dy
Place de la montagne
Avenue Dy
Rue thé
Moutiers
gossip
Rue des
Boulevard des
Rue
Bibibibibi
Henri Moutiers
Rue
Grand boulevard de Moutiers
Ave-
rue de
Place Moutiers traversée
Rue de l'hôtel

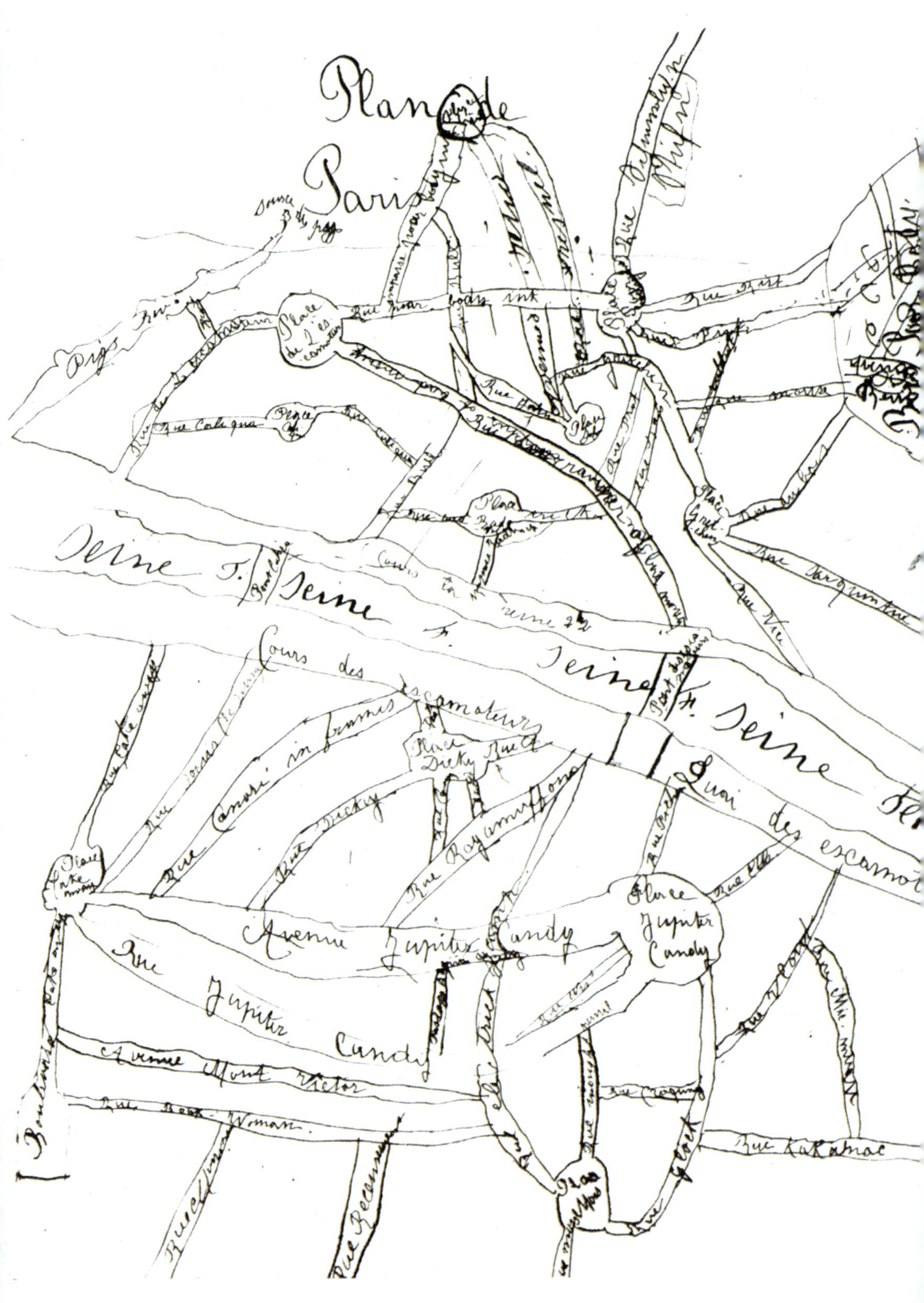
Plan de
Paris
Place de l'es...
Seine
F. Seine
Seine
F. Seine
Cours des
Rue des escamoteurs
Place Dicky
Rue Dicky
Rue Royaumittora
Avenue Jupiter Candy
Place Jupiter Candy
Rue Jupiter Candy
Avenue Mont Victor
Rue Katahac

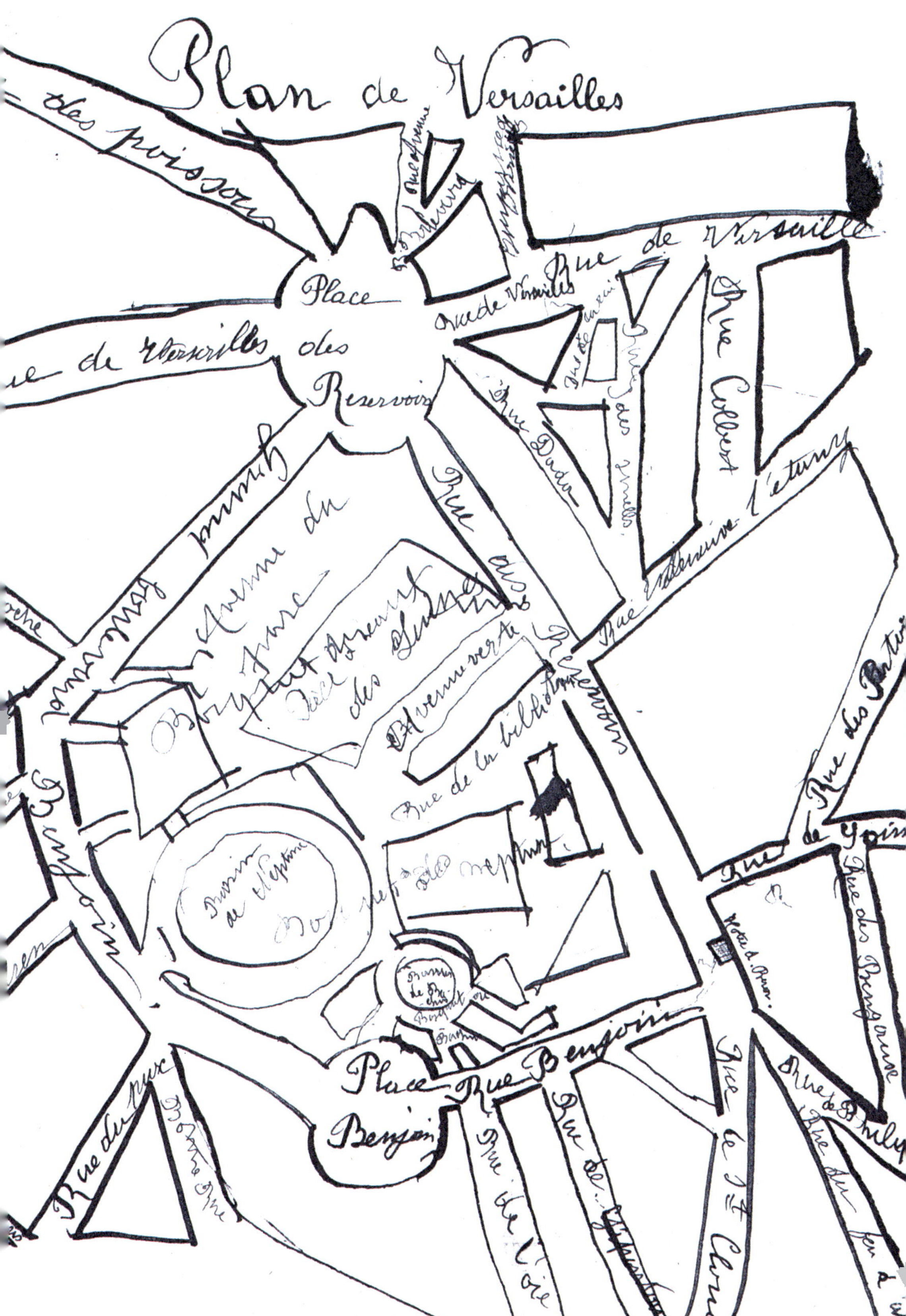
Plan de Versailles
Place des Reservoirs
Rue de Versailles
Rue Colbert
Rue des Poissons
Place Benjoin
Rue Benjoin
Place Benjoin
Rue des Portes

GOOD AND NONSY
SPITTING

My hand is all wet

What good spitting!

A SHORT POEM
ABOUT SPITTING BY
THE CHILD PRINCESS.

interpretation that are at work in psychoanalytic thought. One style of interpretation moves between particulars, from the detail of a dream to its latent meaning through a series of associations specific to the analysand, while another moves between genera, from a mouth pencil to fellatio. The truth is that both of these possibilities belong to psychoanalysis, but in the story of Princess Marie and Freud we see only a victory for generic interpretation.

"The real fact of my mother's death and my father's survival made a strange impression on me, which still survives in my unconscious," Bonaparte reflected in the copybooks. This unconscious fantasy consisted of the idea that "all women are more or less dead, or at least candidates for death, while men, the bearers of the phallus, are immortal. Sometimes, in certain semi-conscious, hypnagogic states, I still find myself astonished that there are innumerable women on the face of the earth, and not men only." This is an important insight, albeit melancholic and misogynistic. The problem is, if all women were more or less dead inside, how to revivify them? Bonaparte's thought is that this is possible only through the clitoris. Ours would be that they need to go back to bursting and spit.

That said, Freud never quite rid himself of the idea that "anatomy is destiny." It's one of those phrases that we wish Freud hadn't said, or at least hadn't said quite so memorably. For feminist scholars in particular, the phrase represents that aspect of Freud's theory that we find most troublesome, namely, the anatomical conception of sexual difference—a man is the one with a penis, a woman the one without one—that persists throughout his work. Such essentialism is not merely politically incorrect but psychically incorrect—incompatible with everything Freud discovered, and everything we have rediscovered, about the way sex and gender are lived, perceived, performed; fluid, mutating, and always contradictory.

The phrase made its first appearance in Freud's 1912 essay "On the Universal Tendency to Debasement in the Sphere of Love," where he set out to explain why some men have such a difficult time sustaining sexual interest in their wives. "Has one ever heard of the drinker being obliged constantly to change his drink because he soon grows tired of keeping to the same one?" he asks. "Why is the relation of the lover to his sexual object so very different?" As the essay proceeds, Freud offers a series of explanations for why men move from one object to the next: the incestuous wishes of childhood, the sexual frustrations of adolescence, the ethical strictures of civilization.

Finally, near the end of the essay, still not entirely satisfied by any of these explanations, Freud has another thought. Perhaps the problem isn't with the object of desire, but with desire itself, that is to say, with the sexual instinct, including the sexual organs, which are kind of... gross. "One might say here, varying a well-known saying of the great Napoleon: 'Anatomy is destiny'," Freud writes. "The genitals themselves have not taken part in the development of the human body in the direction of beauty: they have remained animal, and thus love, too, has remained in essence just as animal as it ever was." Objects of desire, the genitals nevertheless leave much to be desired.

Why did the question of female sexuality inspire such concreteness in early psychoanalysis? Why was their instinct to construct a veritable mapping of the body?

Marie Bonaparte's work reveals the impasse reached by so many theorists of female sexuality. By the 1970s, it had become common for feminists to critique the myth of the vaginal or "correct" orgasm, advocating instead for a broader understanding of sexuality. But they, too, often remained captivated by *la chose génitale*. Are we any closer to thinking in a more interesting way about orgasm or sexuality? Especially feminine sexuality? A colleague once said that the most subversive paper she could think to write today would be entitled "Bring Back the Vaginal Orgasm!" Naomi Woolf's monograph *Vagina* perhaps tried to fit that bill. And while it is subversive, it misses the point. There is always something impenetrably obscure about sexuality, as Freud wrote in the *Three Essays on the Theory of Sexuality* in 1905, and the fluidity and mobility of female sexuality—vaginal or otherwise—are exemplary of this.

Emerging from the failures

of all these experiments, where are we now? We would argue that once you remove the question of orgasm—in particular the female orgasm—from the dimension of anatomy, you are left with the essence of the sexual. And that, frankly, is terrifying, especially for men. Essence is by nature amorphous and impossible to contain, and if you can't map sexuality, does that mean that you are simply lost inside it? As Jacques Lacan said, the mistake is to believe that sexuality is "ready at hand," which is a problem that's particular (but hardly exclusive) to men.

We wish that psychoanalysts, after 100 years of listening to patients, would as a community have something more interesting to say about this. But while we've just suggested that we all stop trying to map the terrain of orgasm, we know that you (and we) will only with great difficulty not be able to search Princess Marie's drawings and diagrams—much less our own young imaginings of these things—for an answer. Perhaps the best guideline we can provide is the idea that the devil is always in the details and that if we are to recover a sexuality or a sensuality that we have lost, it is there that we should look, reading ourselves like a childish diary. 🐾

SIGMUND FREUD IN HIS OFFICE IN VIENNA CIRCA 1937. PHOTOGRAPH BY PRINCESS EUGENIE OF GREECE, DAUGHTER OF MARIE BONAPARTE.

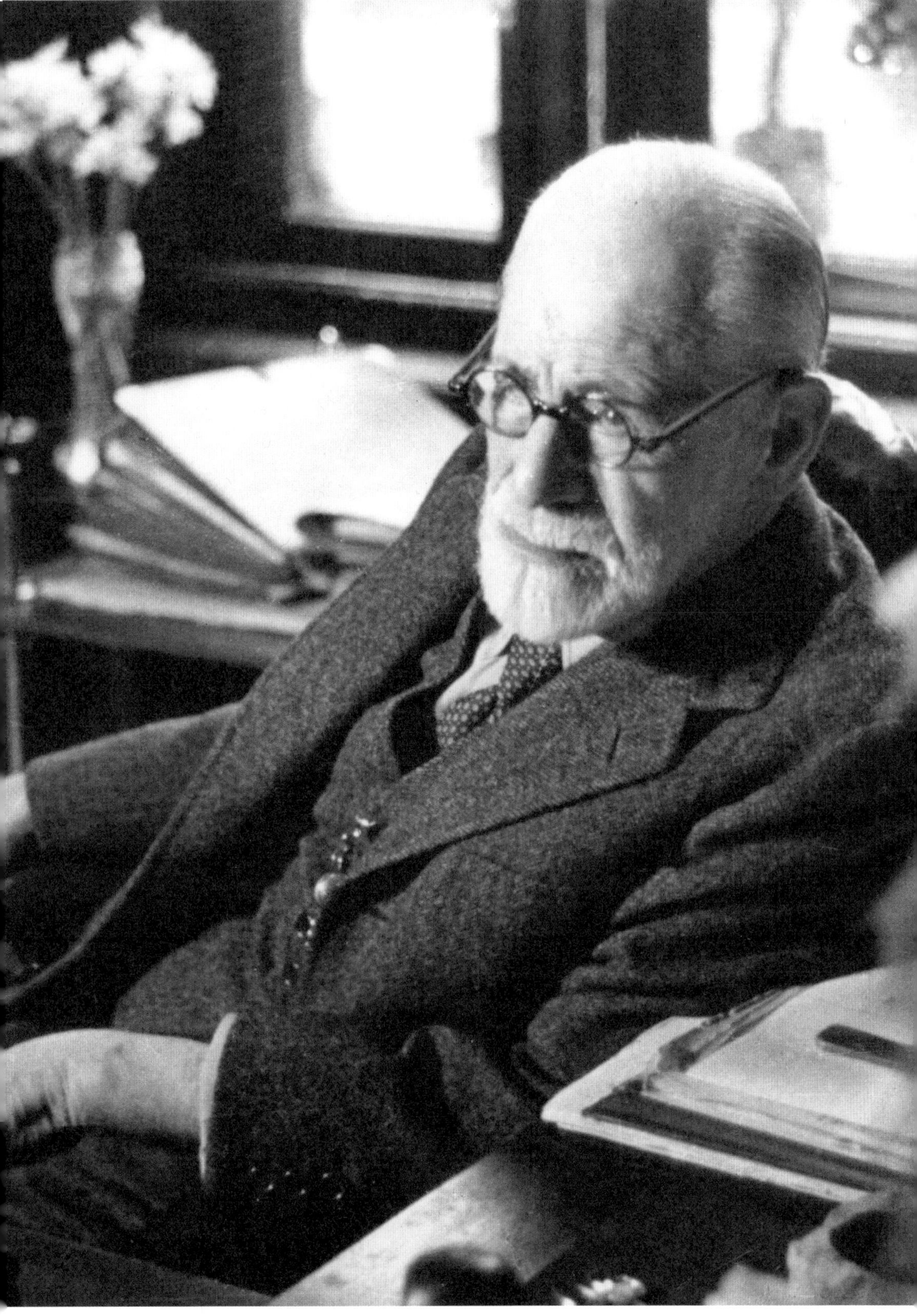

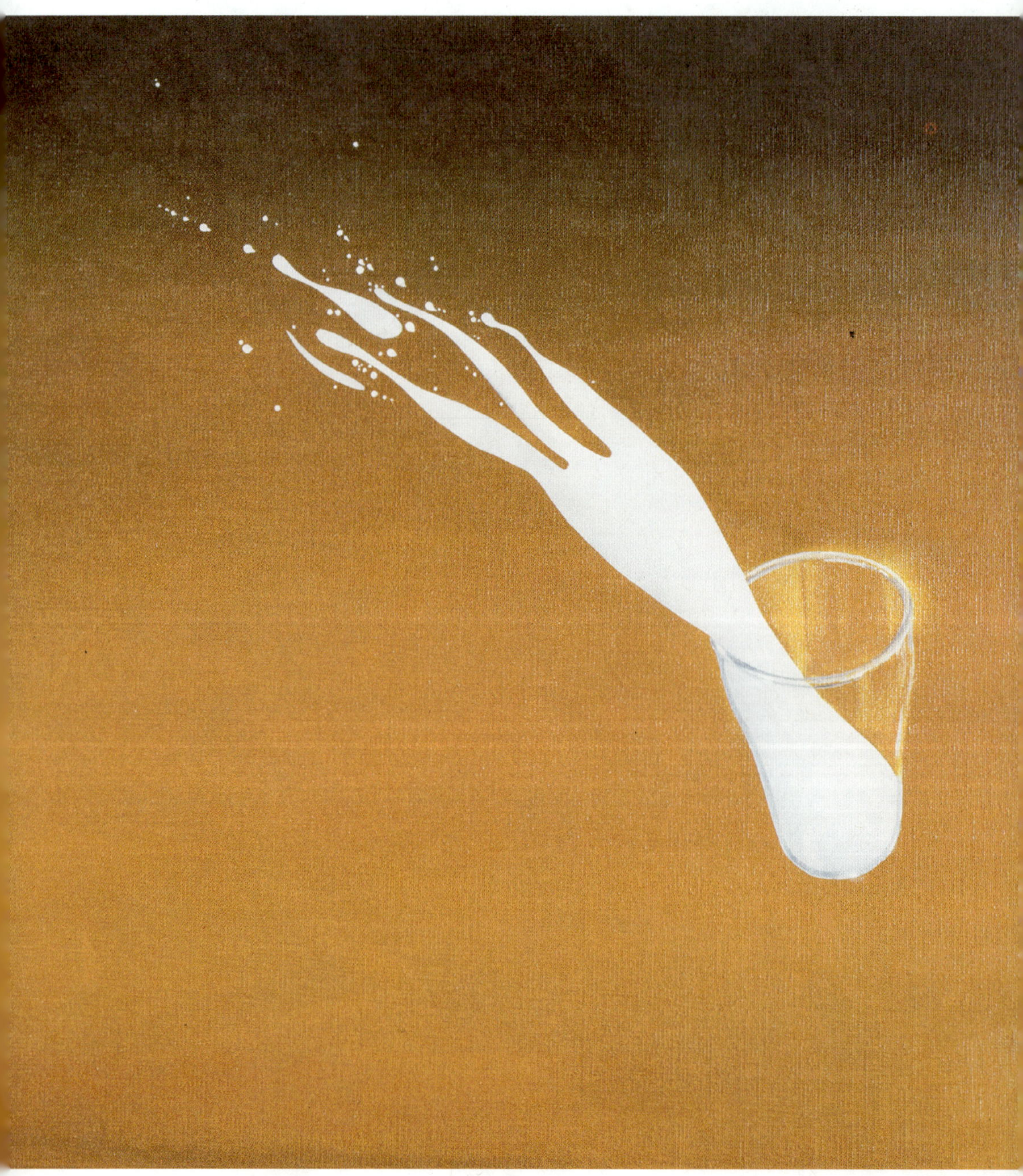

ED RUSCHA: *Glass of Milk, Falling*, 1967

Apologetic Climaxes

over the orgasm in all its various facets. This is a selection of art that's at least partially about anatomy, apocalypse, anxiety, bonding, climaxes, explosions, expulsions, eruptions, face-sitting, fecundity, fucking, gaps, goo, heat, love, martyrs, oil, penetration, phalli, pistils, pollination, protrusions, raptures, ruptures, scent, seduction, snakebites, spillage, stamens, sublimity, vulgarity, wilting, workouts, and wounds.

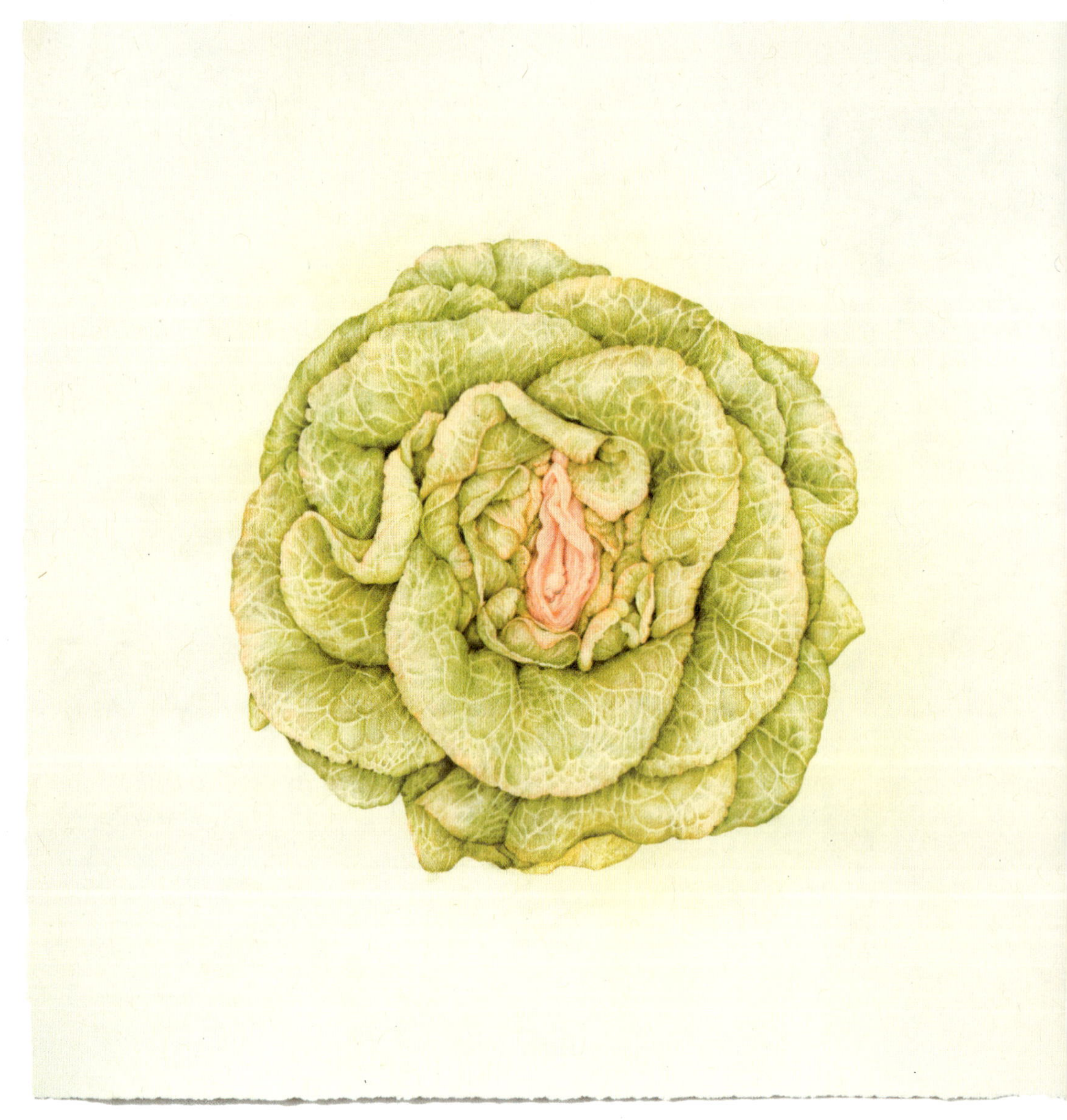

AUREL SCHMIDT: *Lettuce Vag*, 2013

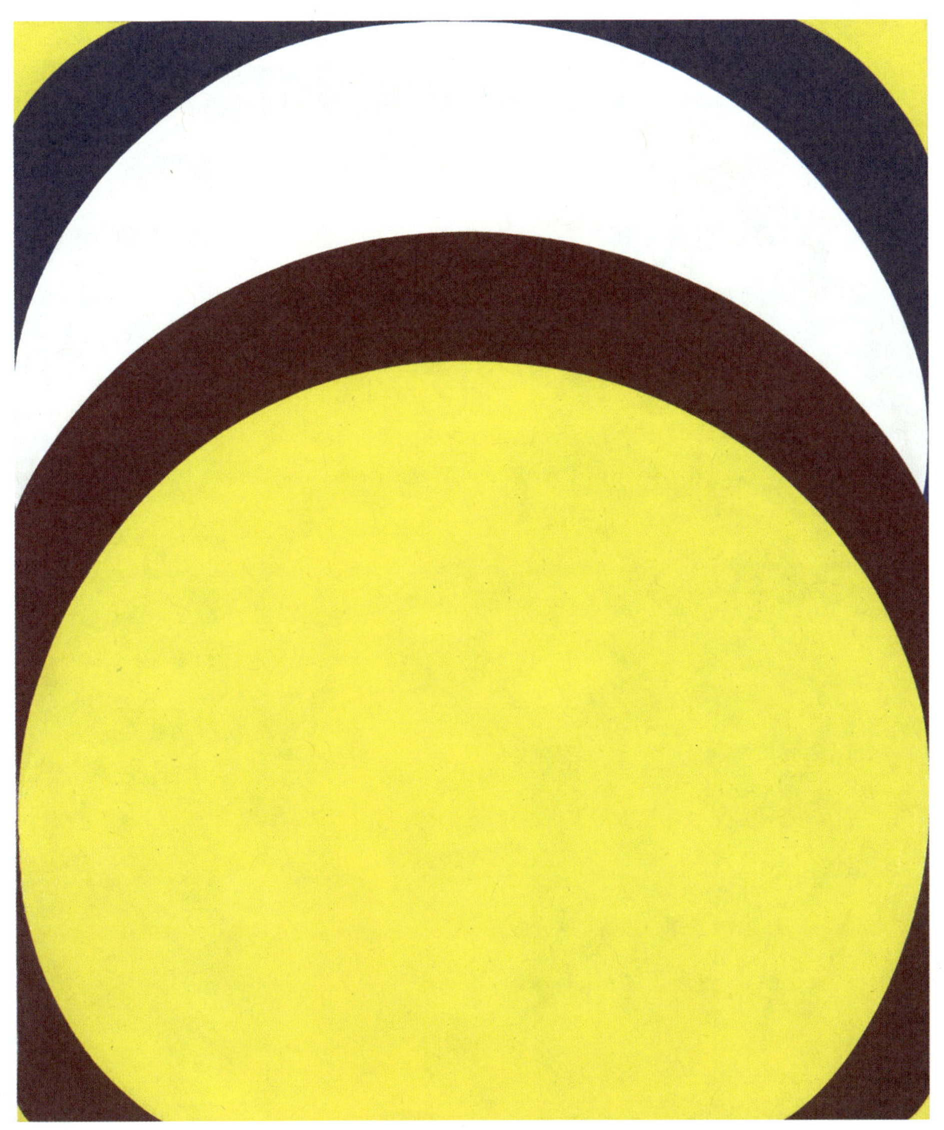

AL HELD: *Echo*, 1966

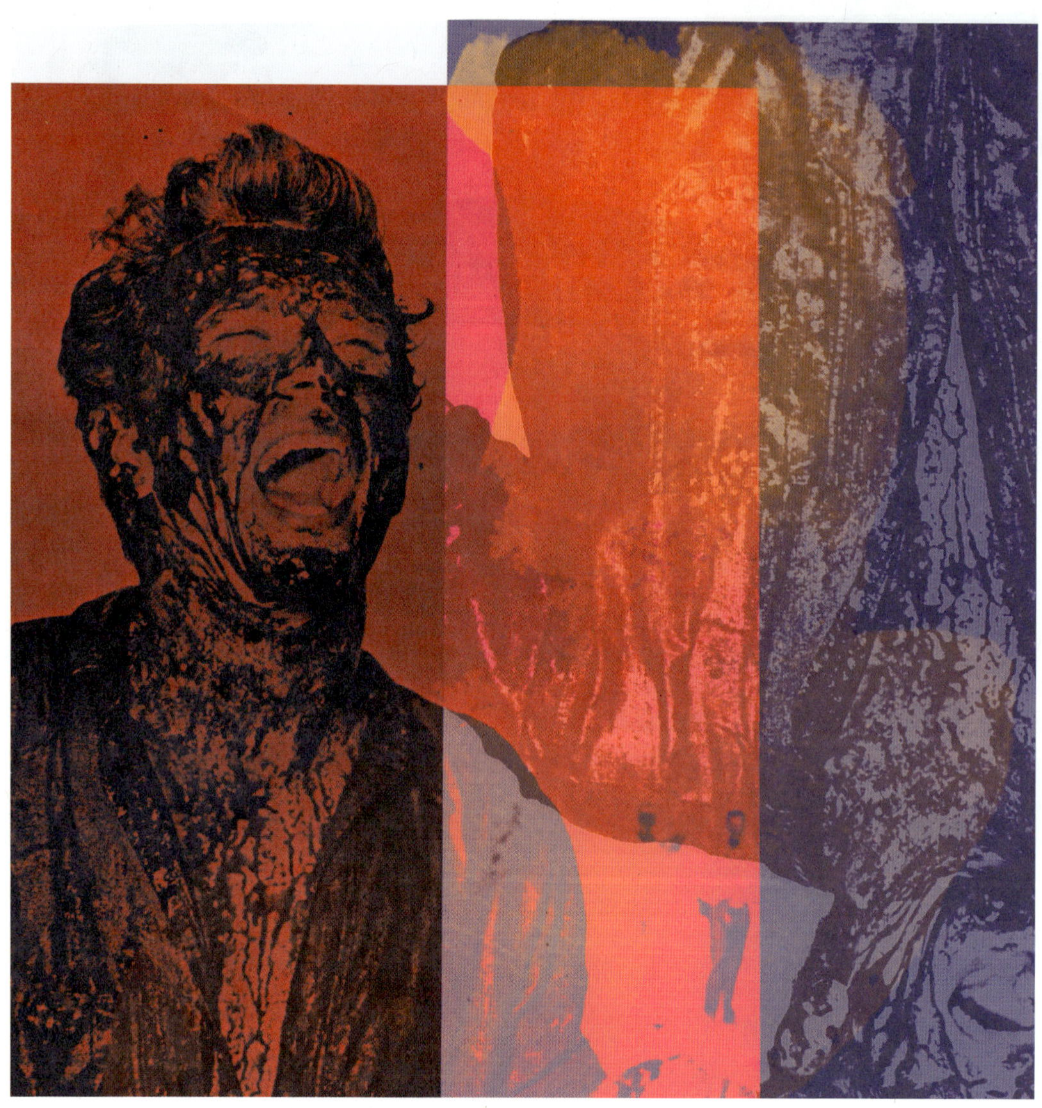

TARA SINN: *Untitled*, 2013

JOE DeNARDO: *Untitled*, 2013

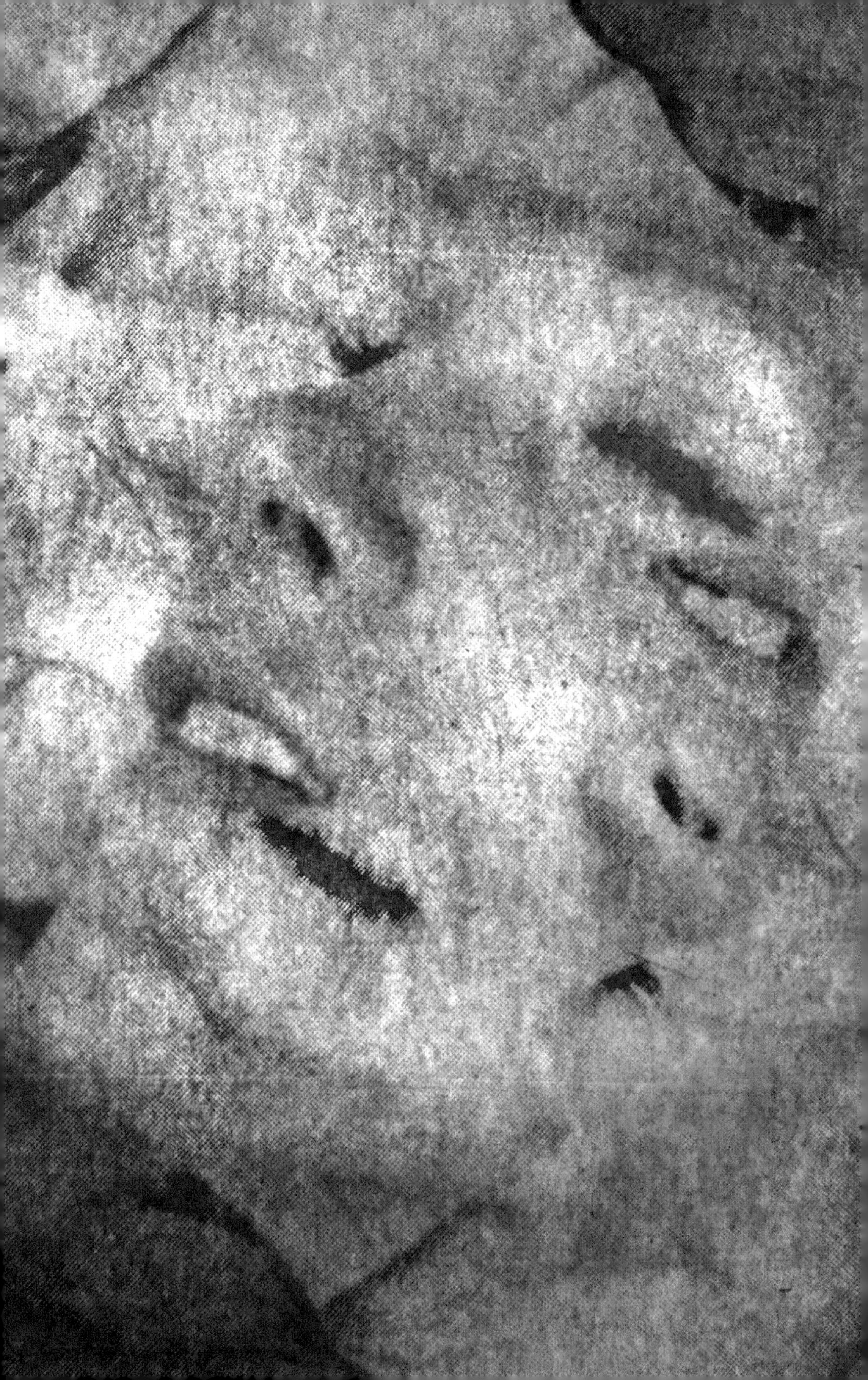

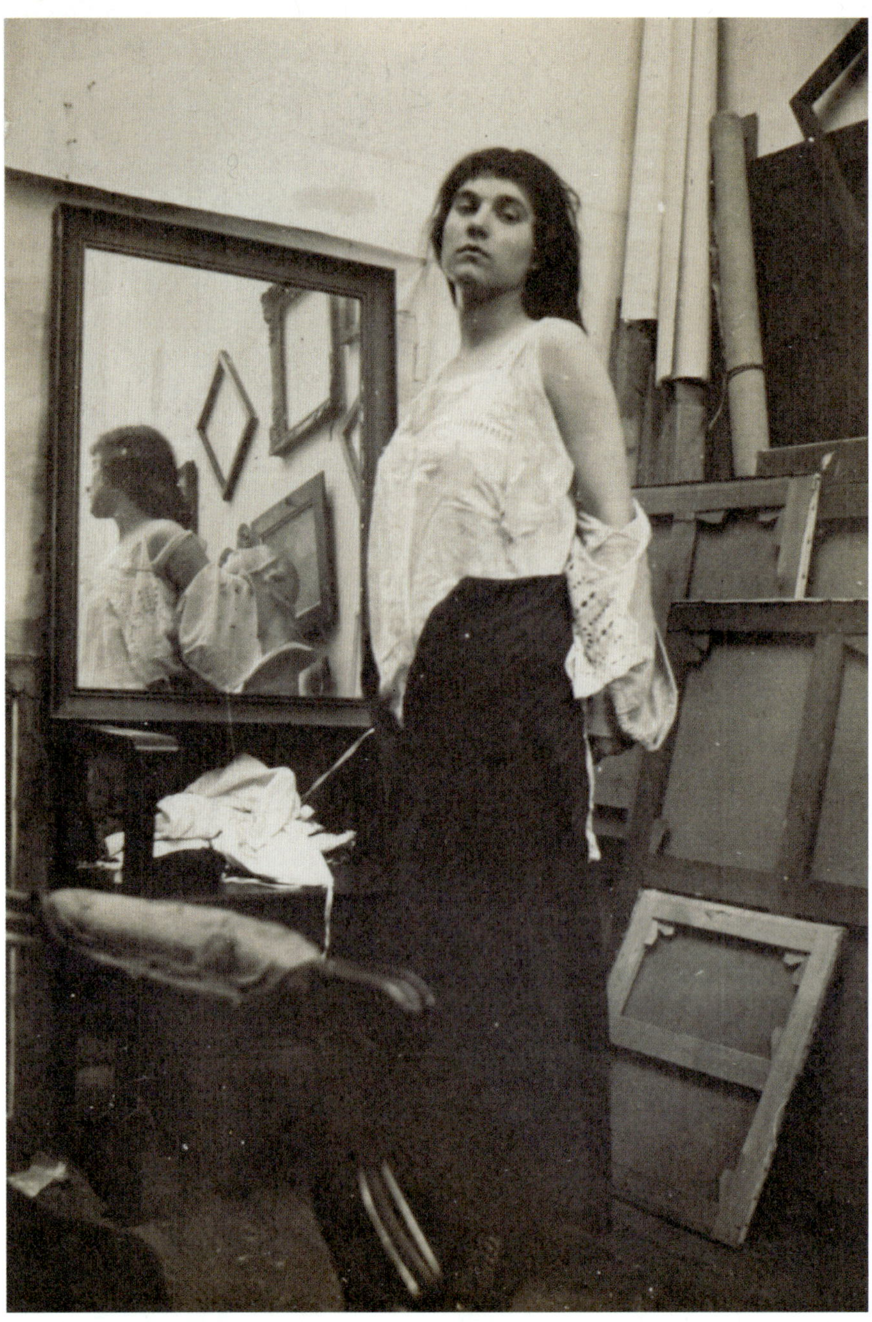

PIERRE BONNARD: *Model in the artist's studio*, ca. 1916

ROE ETHRIDGE: *Chanel No. 5 with Yellow Jacket*, 2009

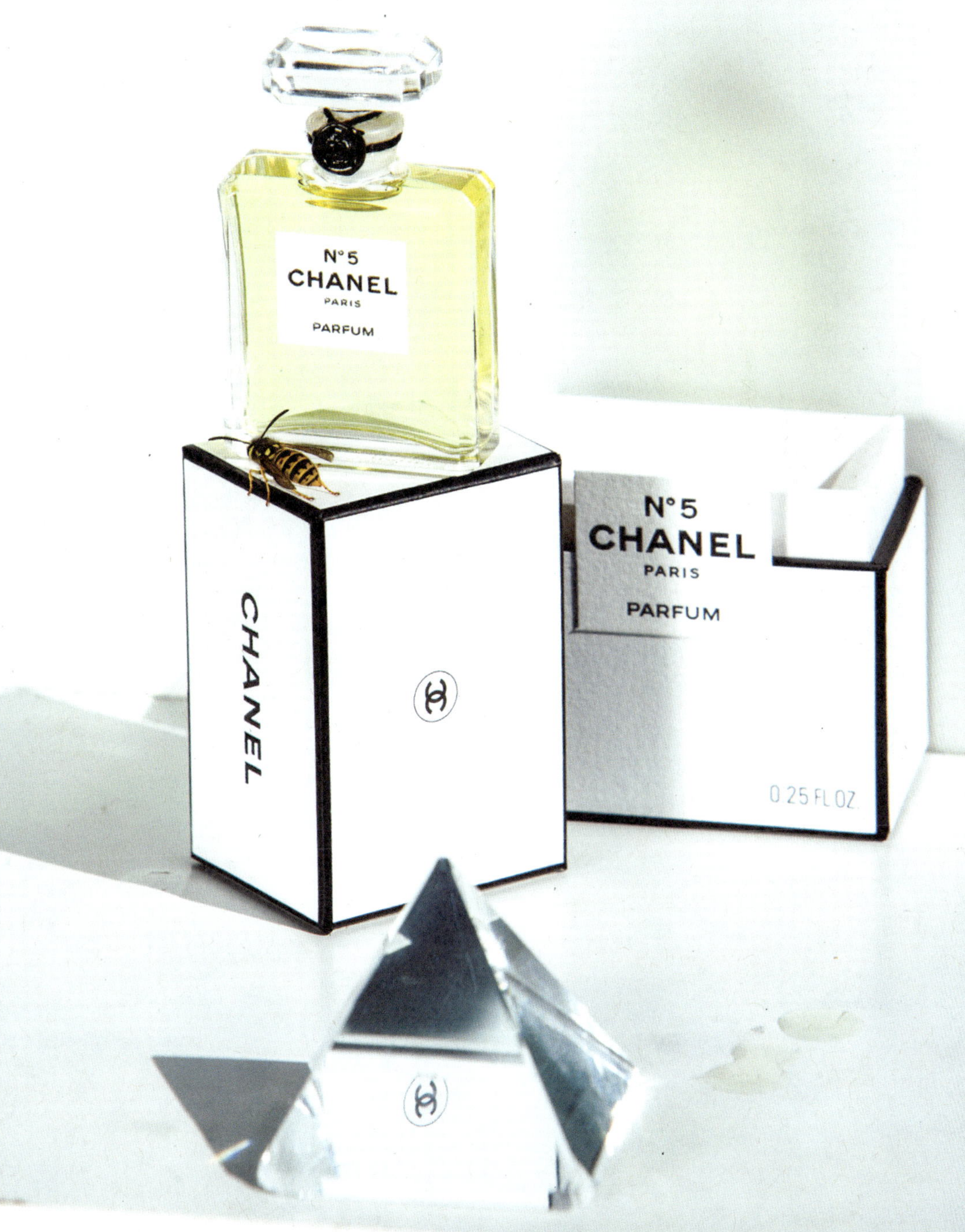

N°5
CHANEL
PARIS
PARFUM
CHANEL
N°5
CHANEL
PARIS
PARFUM
0.25 FL OZ.

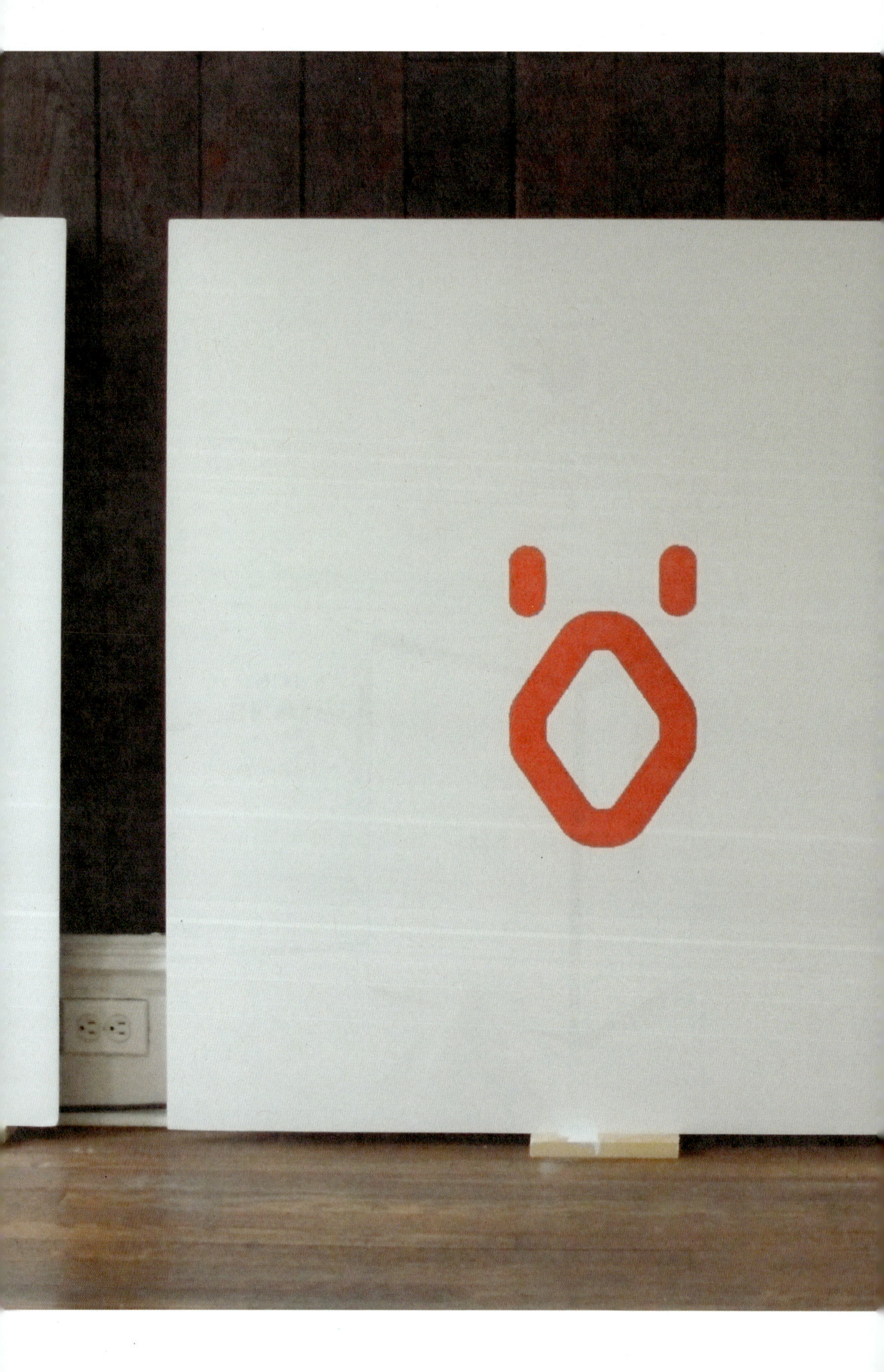

MICHAEL ZAHN: *MZ_651.12 (Version)*, 2012

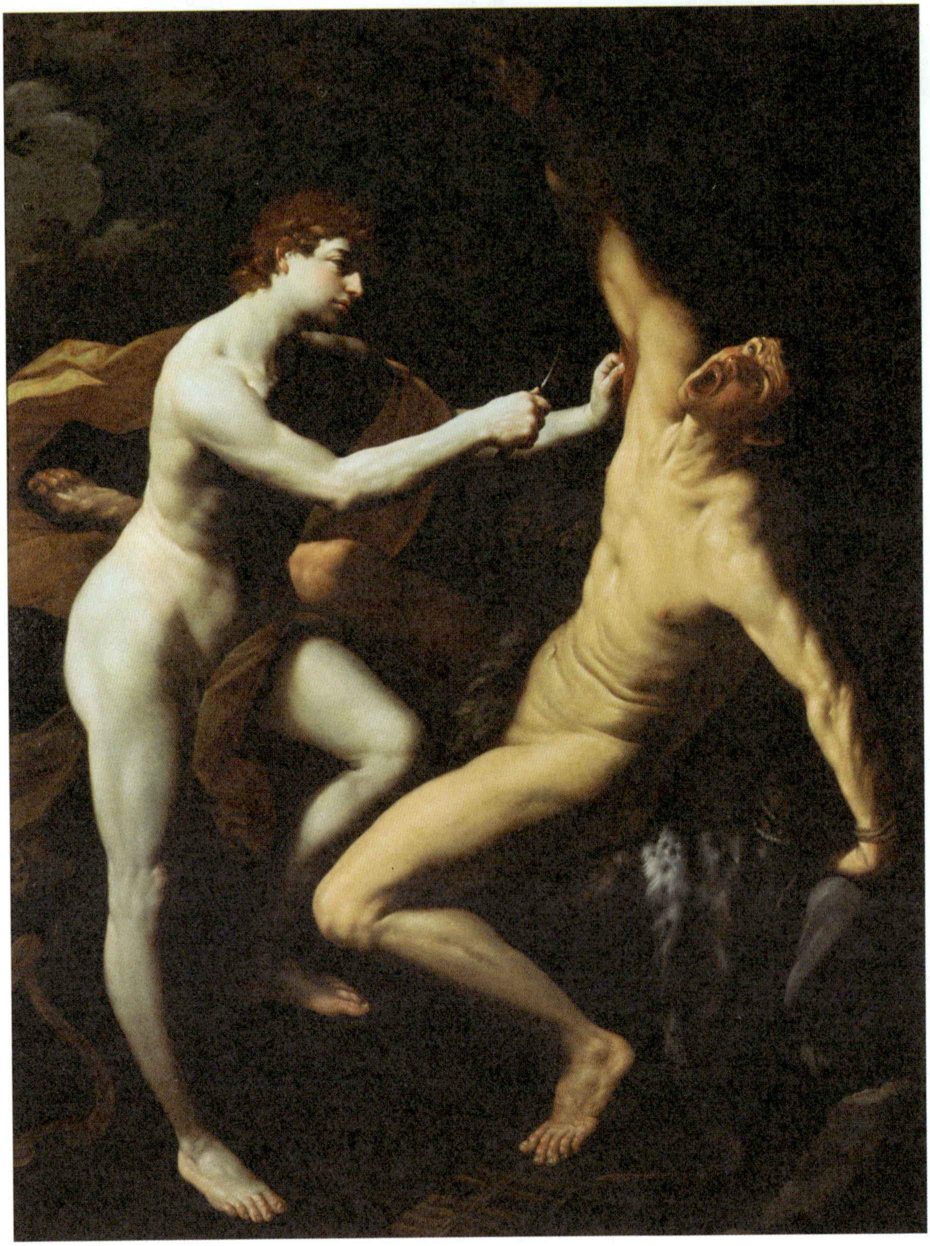

GUIDO RENI: *Apollo flaying Marsyas*, 1620-25

SANDY KIM: *Titty World*, 2013

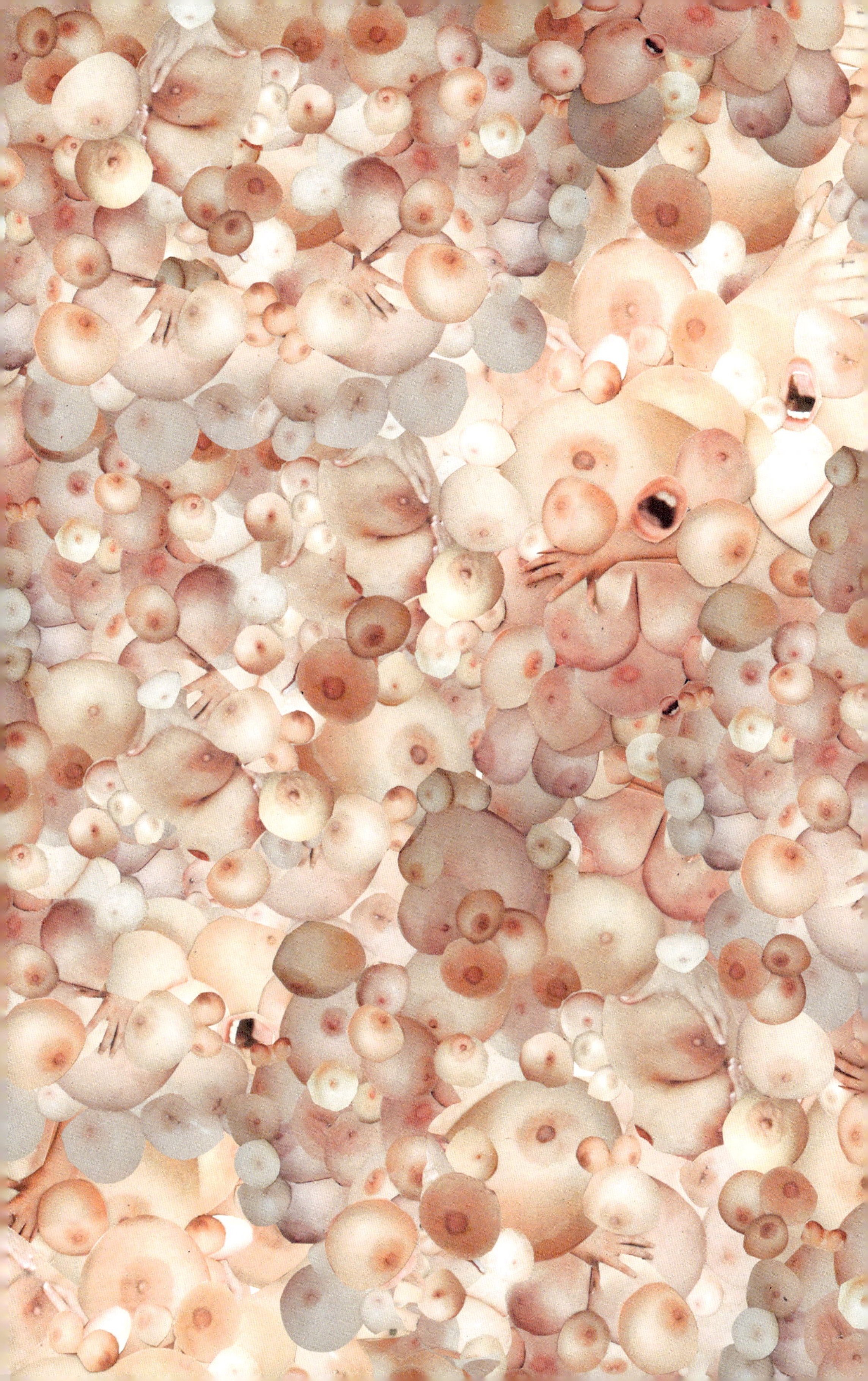

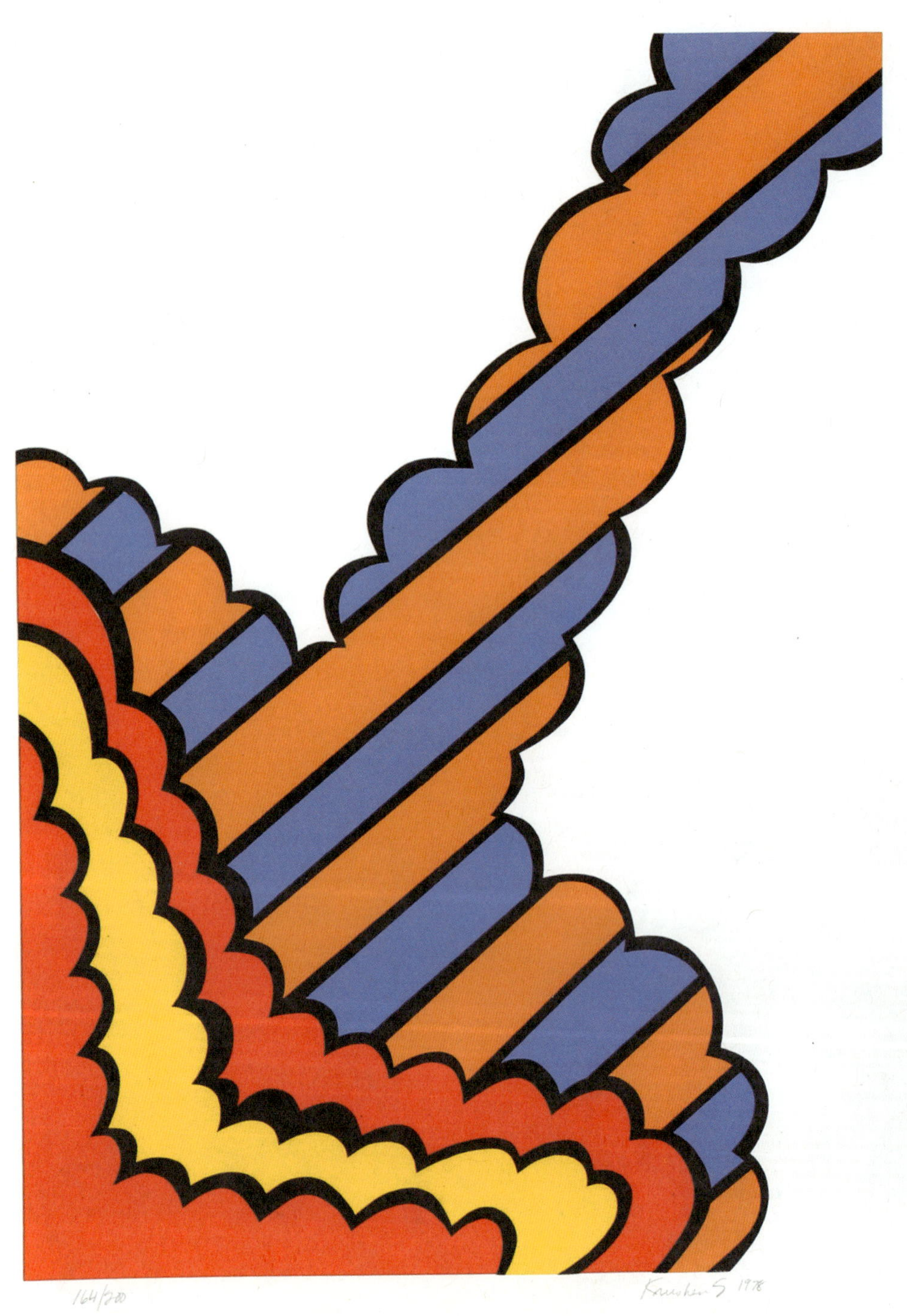

NICHOLAS KRUSHENICK: (left) *North End*, 1978; (right) *Big Sky*, 1980

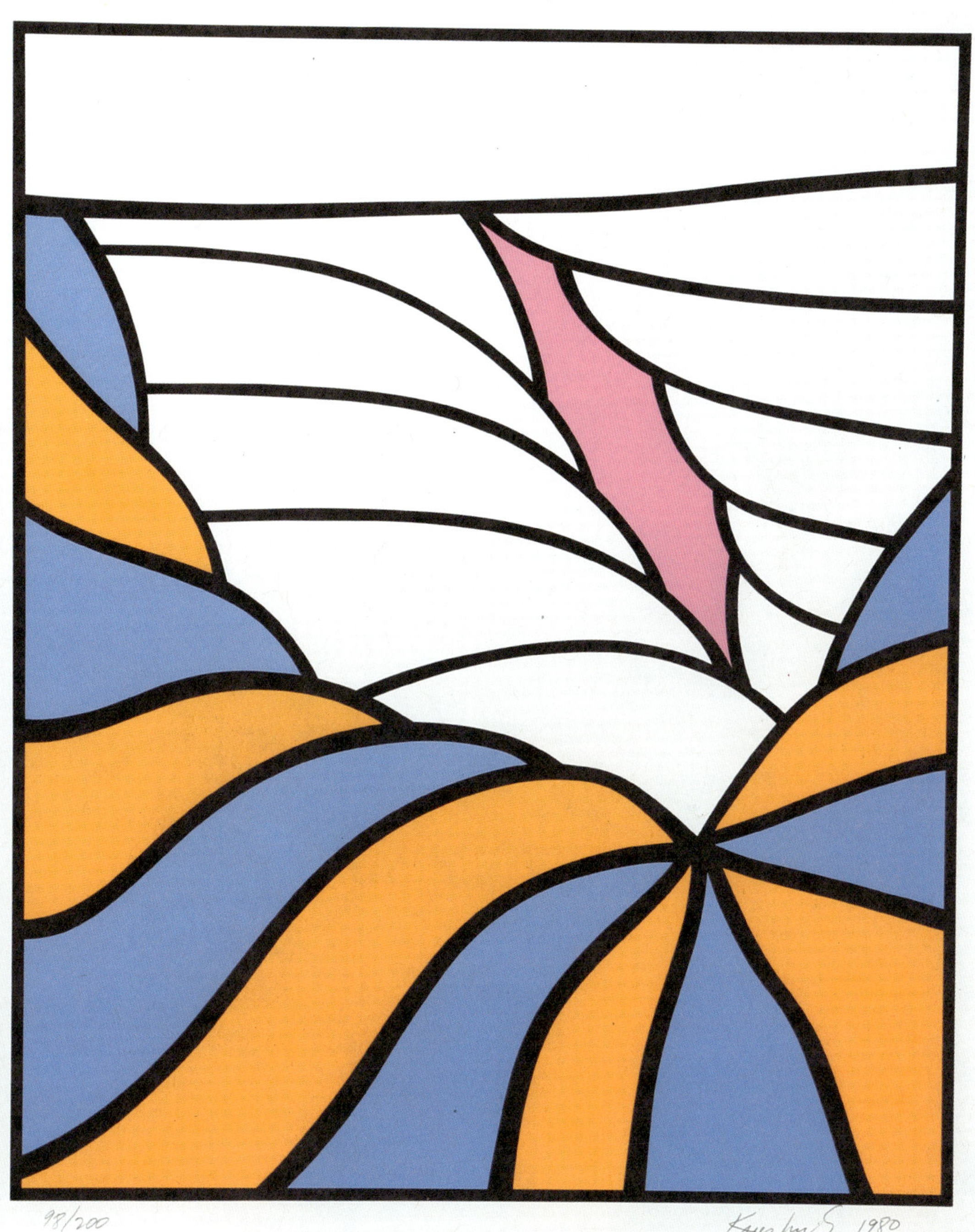

98/200
Kushner 1980

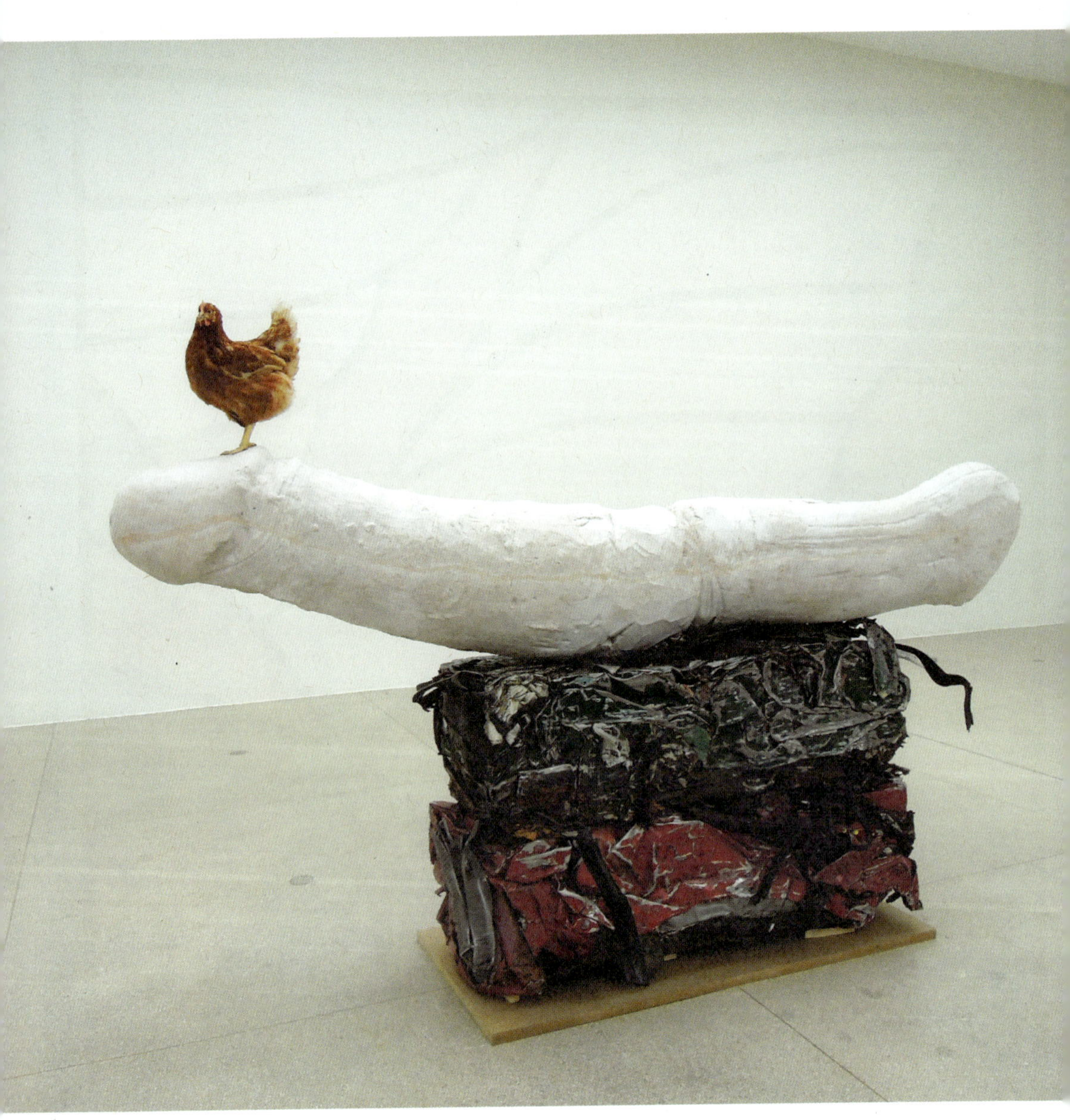

GELATIN AND SARAH LUCAS: *Eros*, 2013

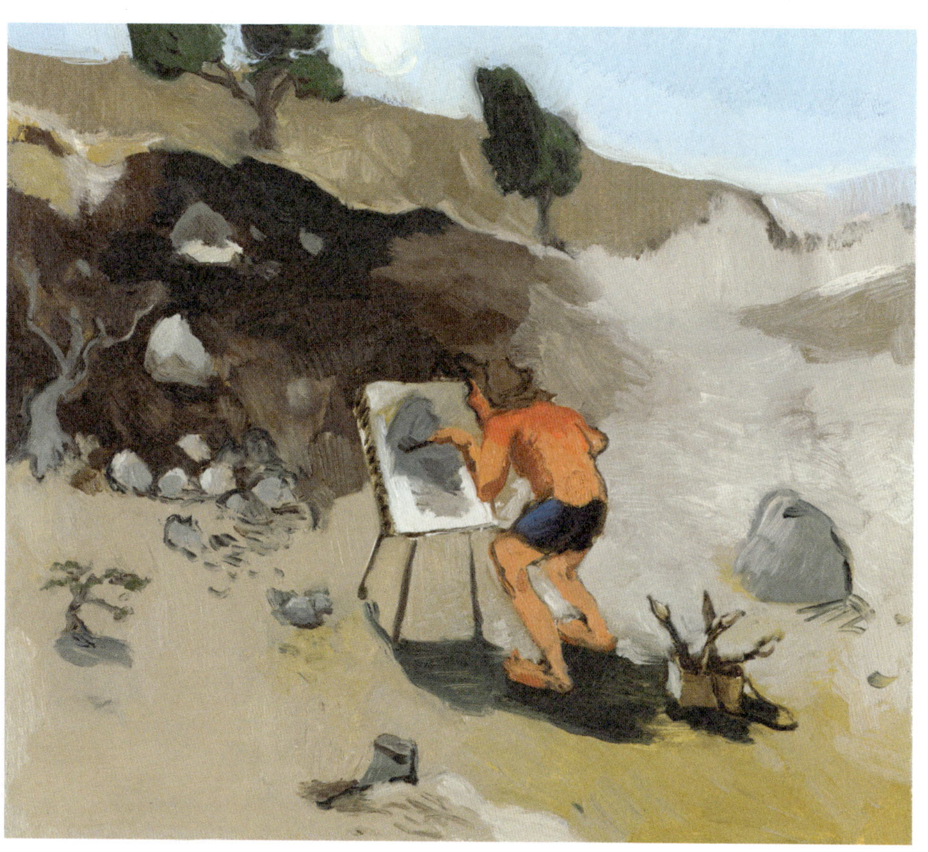

JANE CORRIGAN: *Painting in the Heat*, 2012

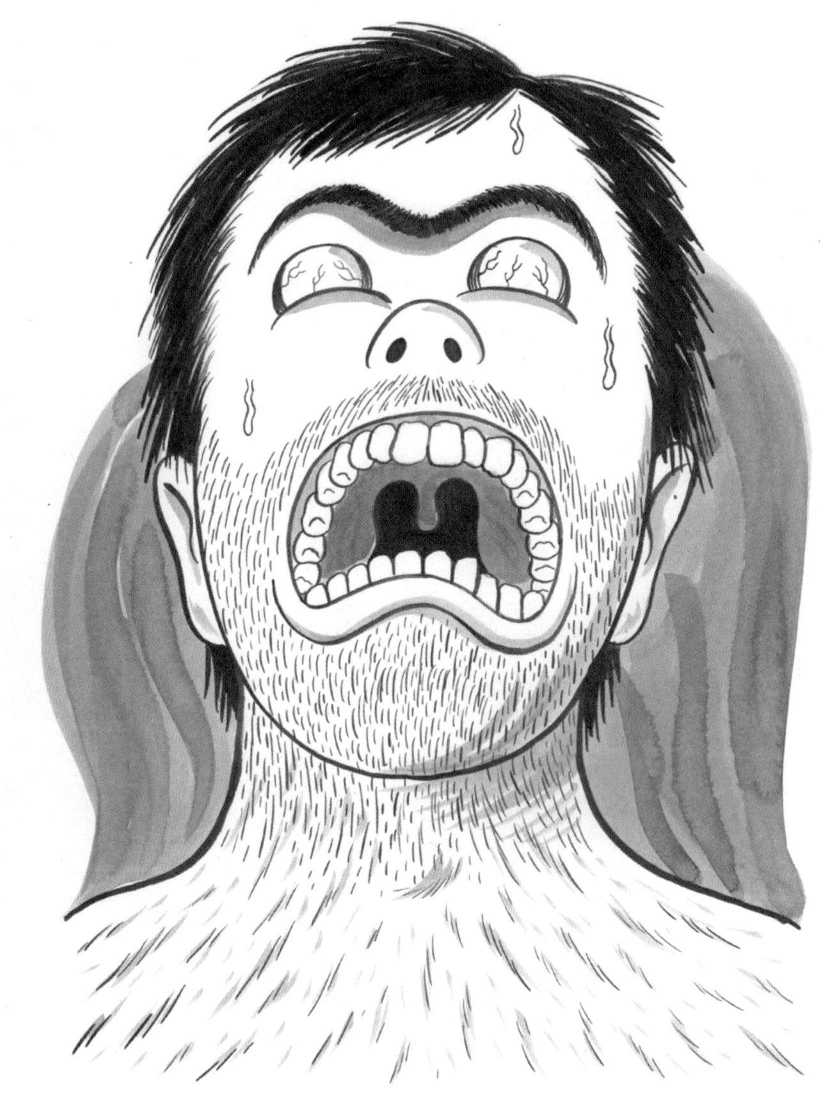

JOHNNY RYAN: *Untitled*, 2013

LEON FRANCOIS BENOUVILLE (1821-1859): *A Nun in Ecstasy*

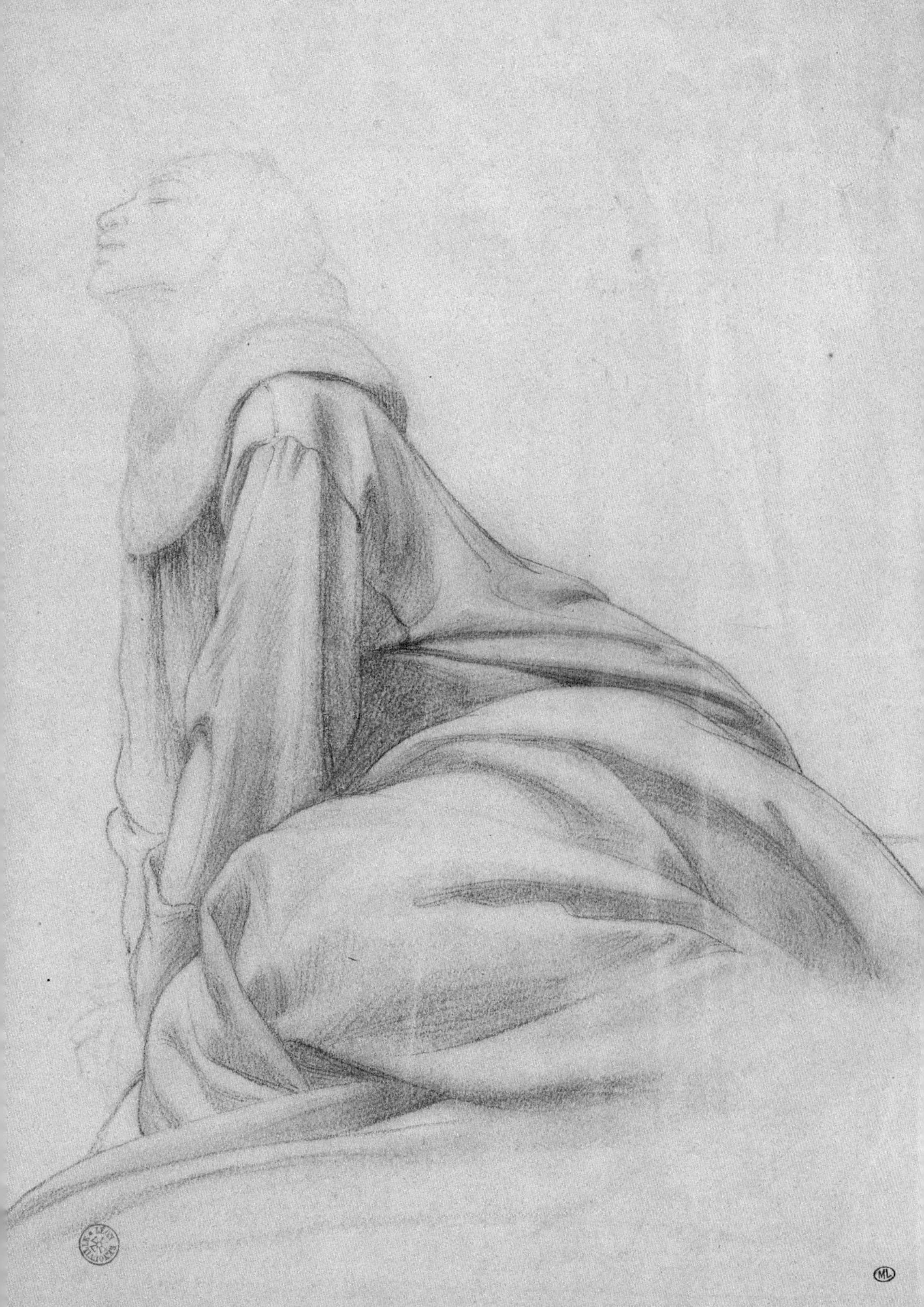

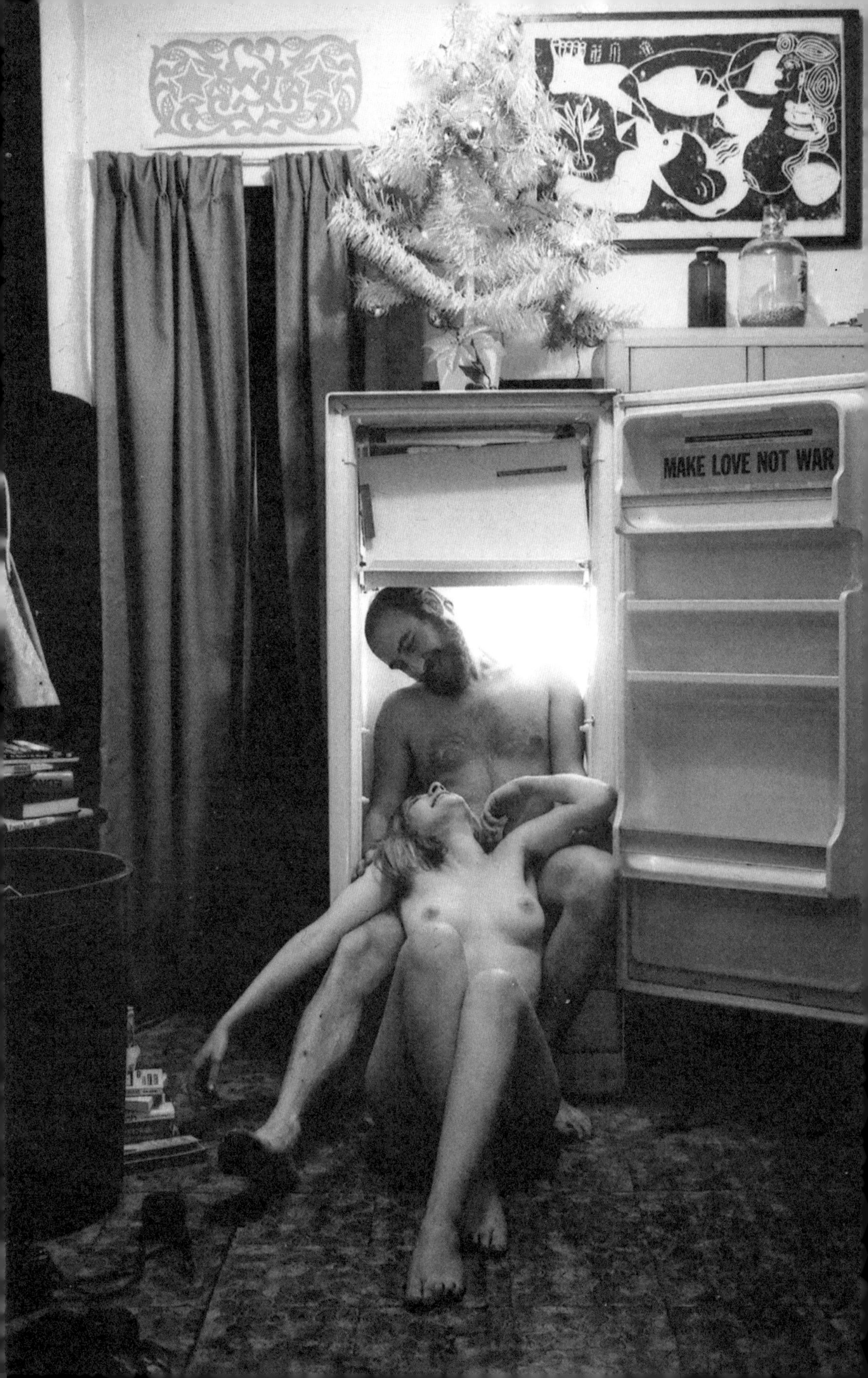

MAKE LOVE NOT WAR

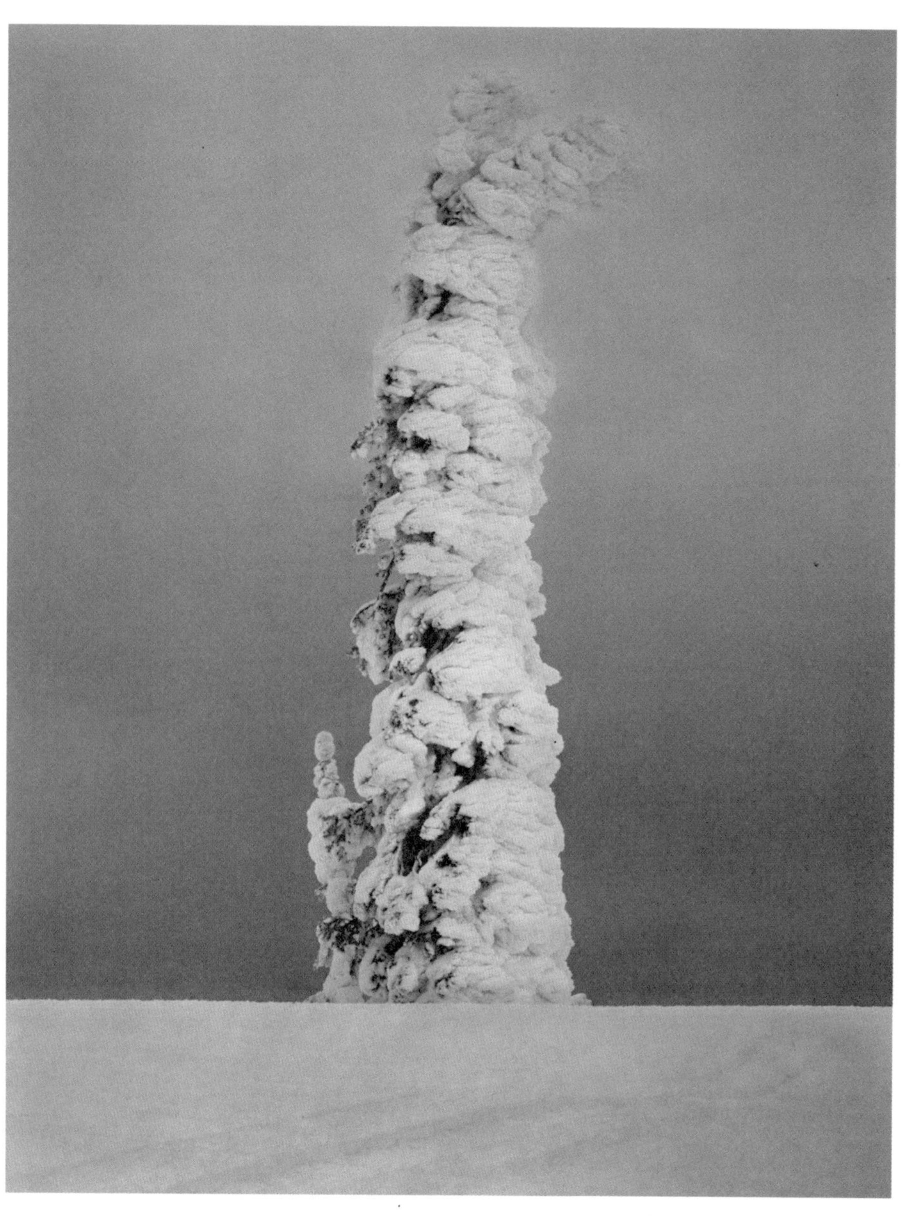

JASON NOCITO: *Ghost Hole*, 2013

CHARLES GATEWOOD: *East Village*, 1966

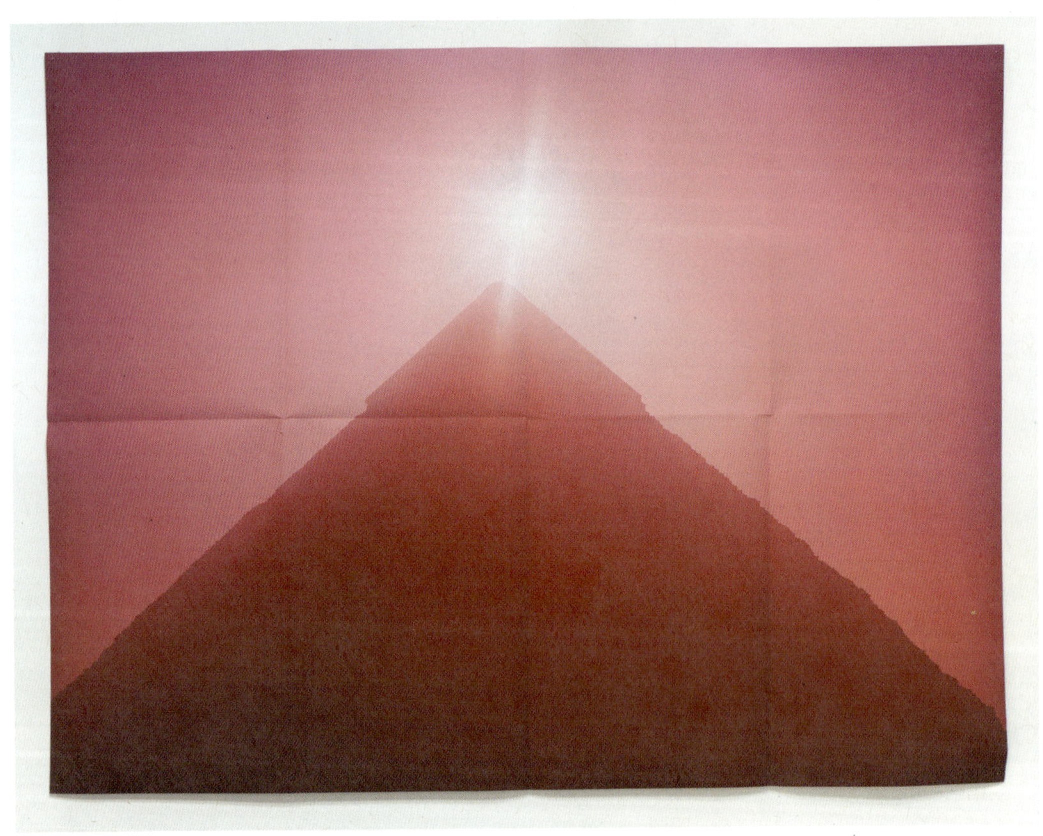

JACK PIERSON: *(PYRAMID, PINK)*, 2010; *(TORSE D'ATHLETE EN MARBLE)*, 2010

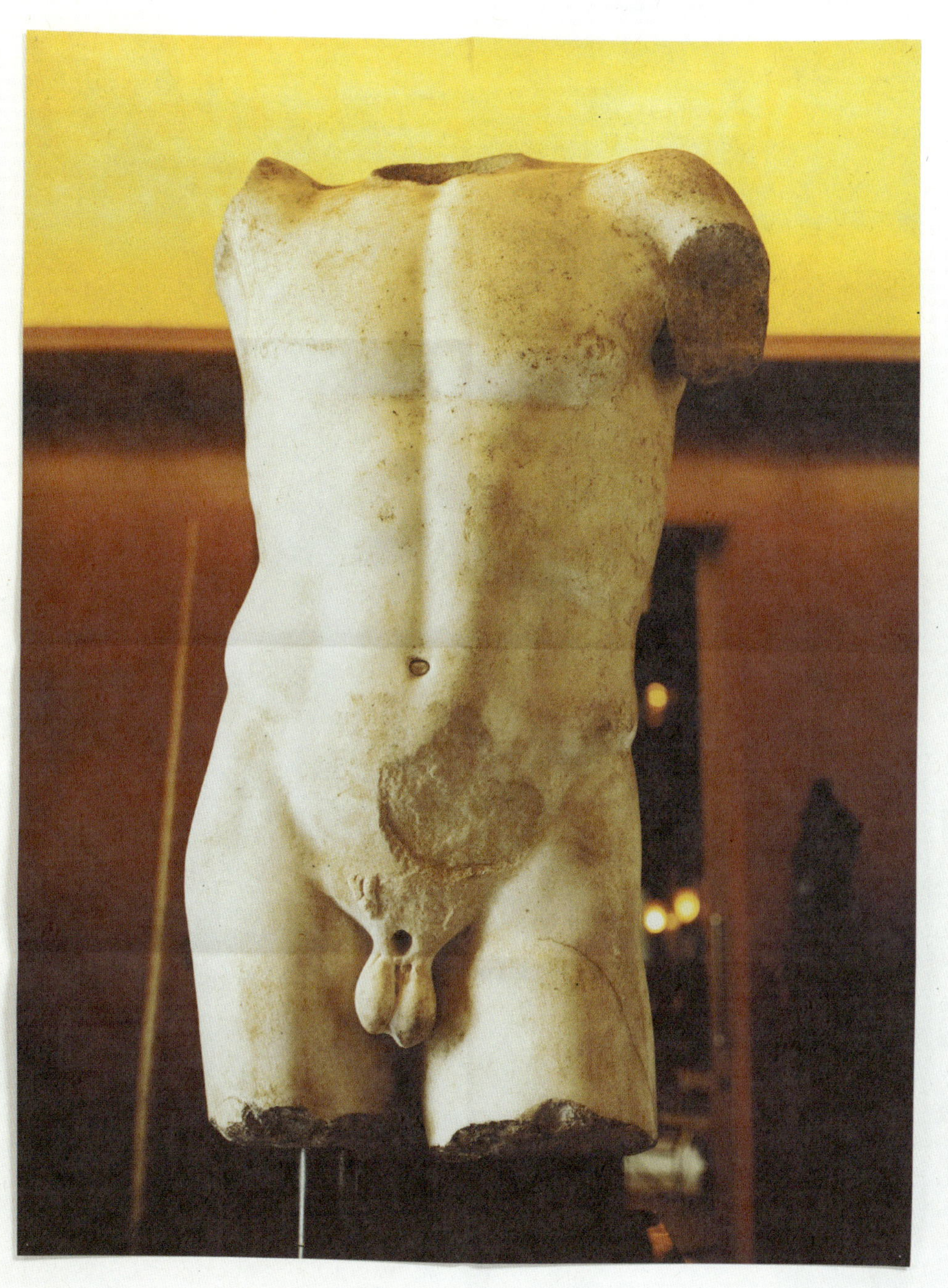

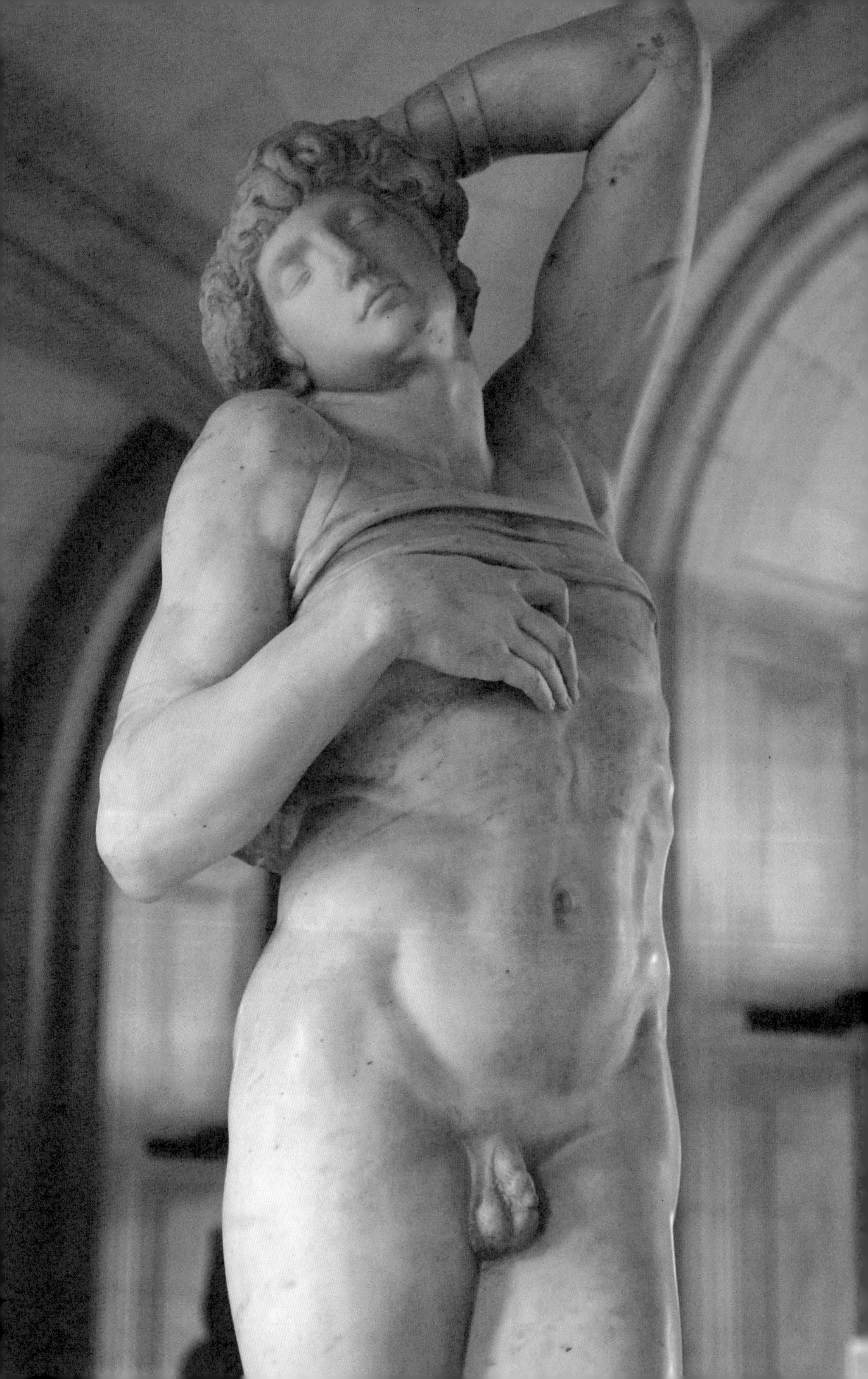

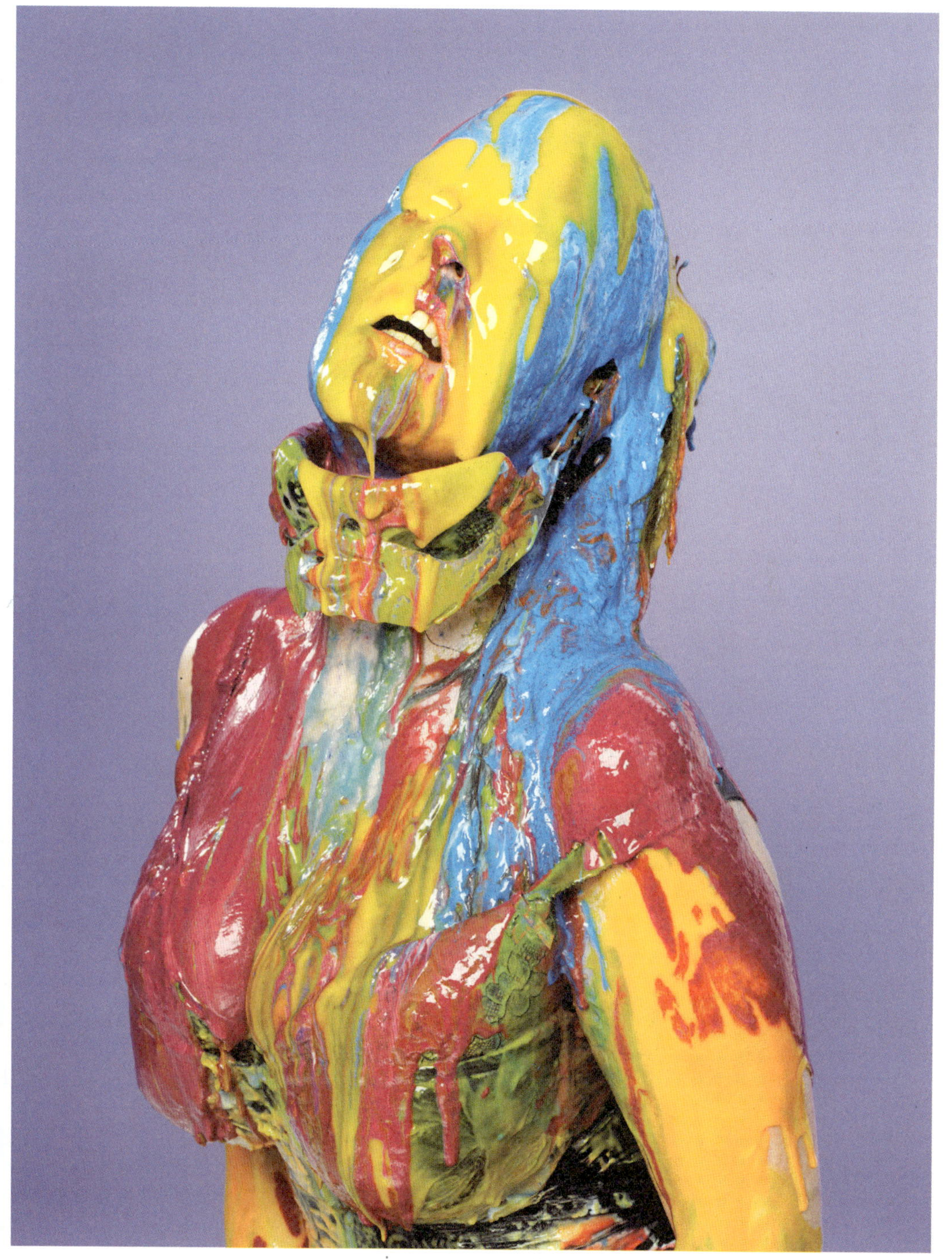

LINDER STERLING: *Glorification de l'Élue*, 2011

MICHELANGELO: *Dying Slave, for the tomb of Pope Julius II*, 1513-1516

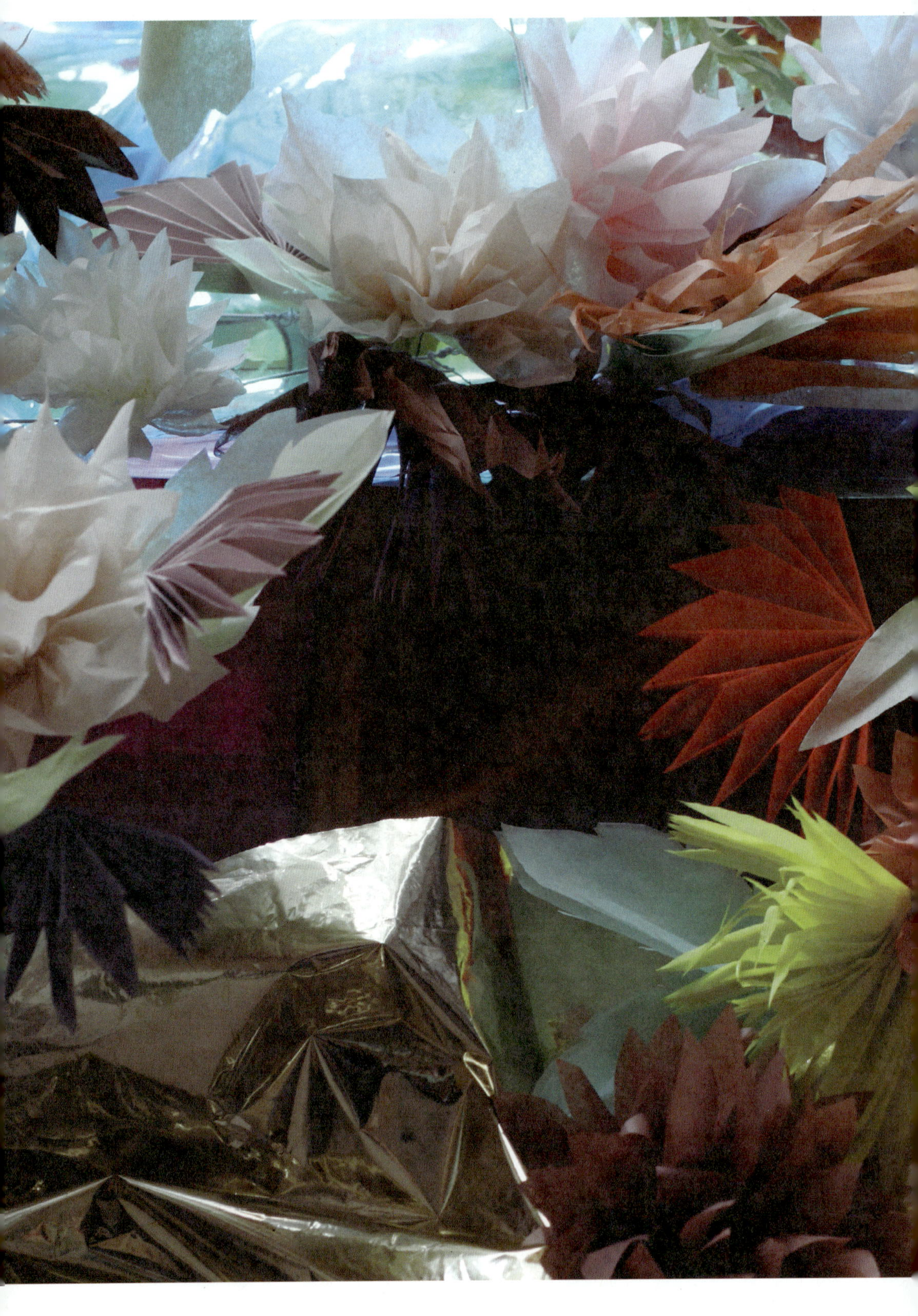

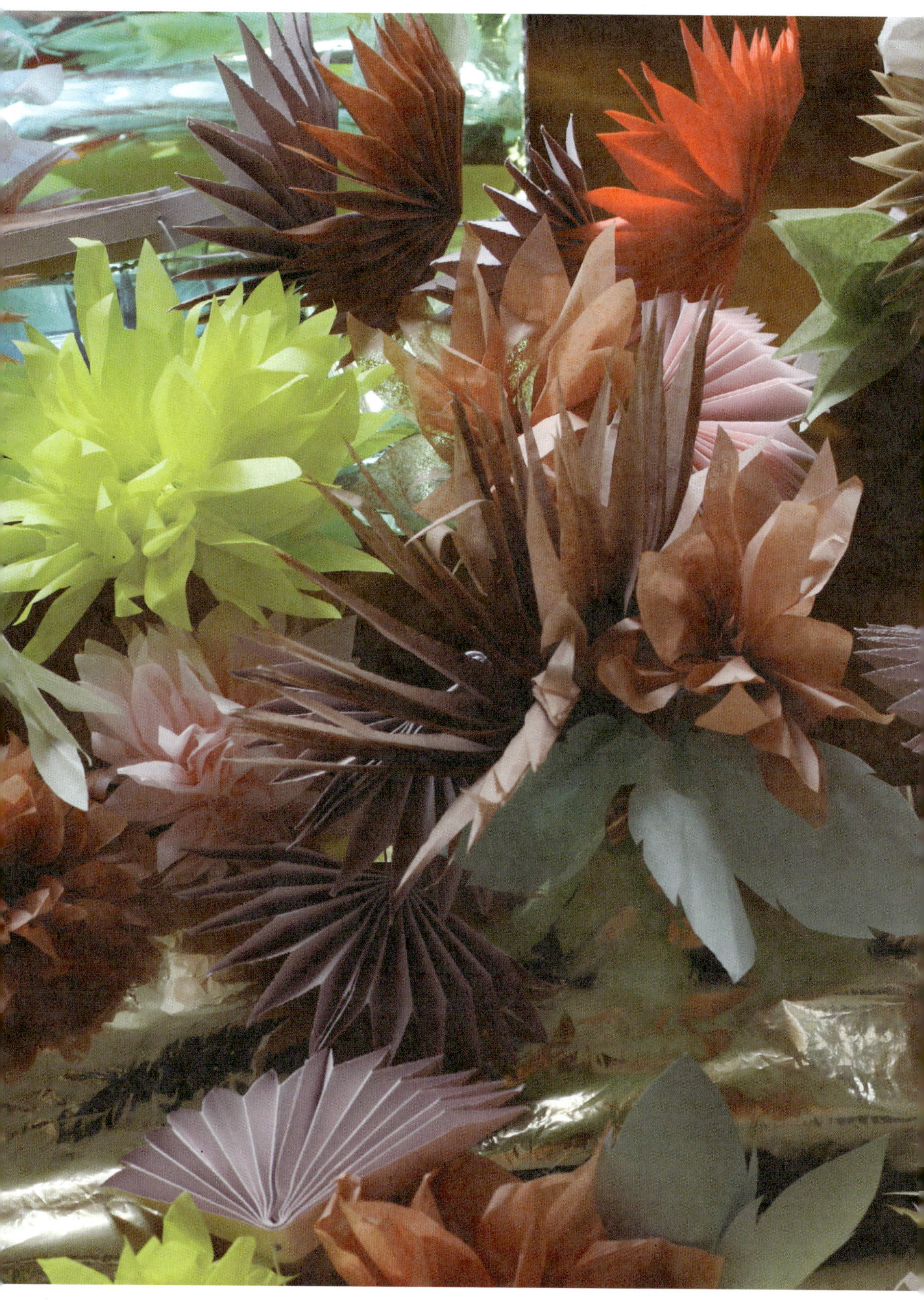

CONFETTI SYSTEM: *Arrangement 02, 2013*

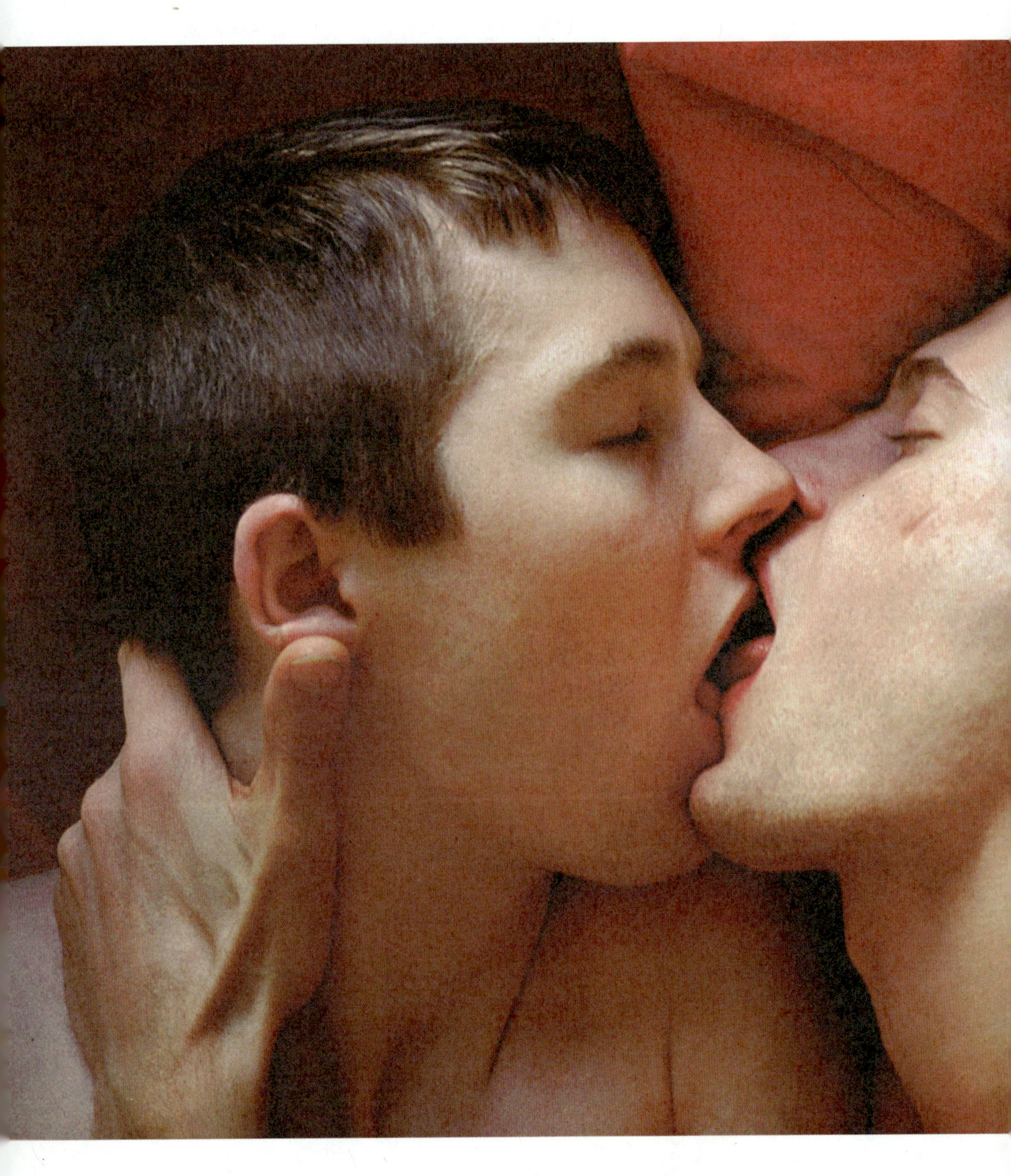

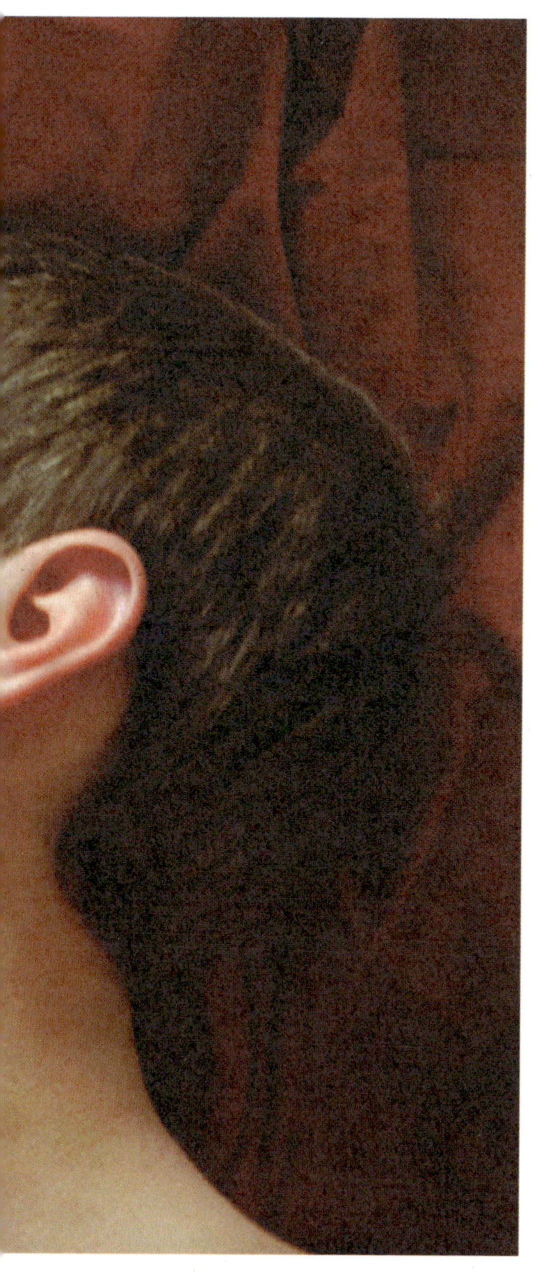

RYAN McGINLEY: *Ryan & Marc (Red Kiss)*, 1999

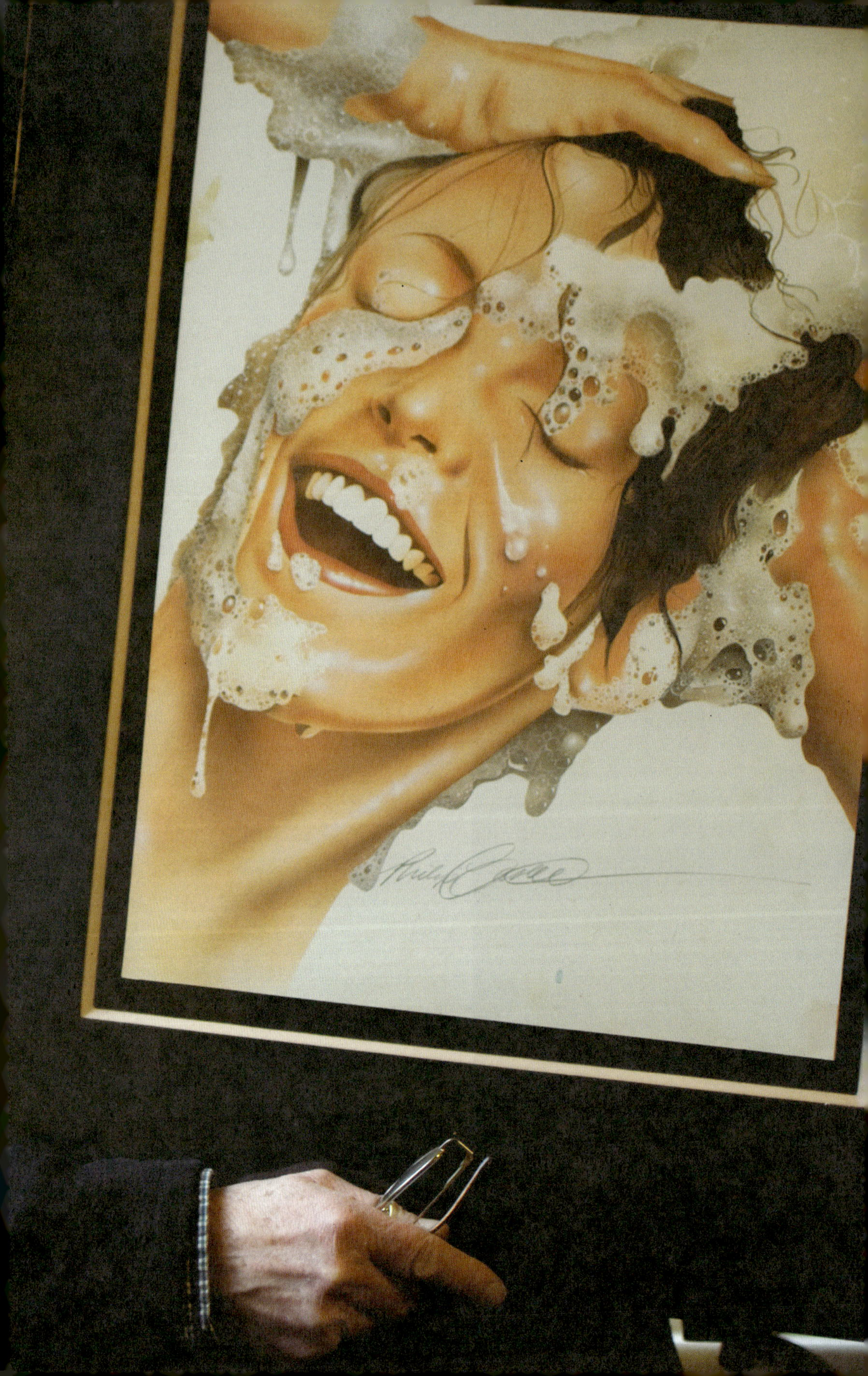

Projet d'un livre sur la sexualité
~ A projected book on sexuality

A young couple comes into my compartment and sits down; the woman is blond, made up; she is wearing big dark glasses, reads *Paris-Match;* she has a ring on each finger, and each nail on both hands is painted a different color from its two neighbors; the nail of the middle finger, a shorter nail painted a deep carmine, broadly designates the finger of masturbation. From this—from the *enchantment* this couple casts upon me, so that I cannot take my eyes off them—comes the idea of a book (or of a film) in which there would be, in this way, nothing but secondary sex character-istics (nothing pornographic); in it one would grasp (would try to grasp) the sexual "personality" of each body, which is neither its beauty nor even its "sexiness" but the way in which each sexuality immediately lets itself be read; for the young blonde with the har-lequin nails and her young husband with his tight pants and warm eyes were wearing their couple-sexuality like the legion-of-honor ribbon in a buttonhole (*sexuality* and *respectability* relating to the same kind of display), and this *legible* sexuality (as Michelet would certainly have read it) filled the compartment, by an irresistible me-tonymy, much more certainly than any series of coquetries.

ROLAND BARTHES: from *Roland Barthes par Roland Barthes*, 1975

The artist PHILIP CASTLE holding his 1976 painting *Shampoo* at home in South London in 2014.

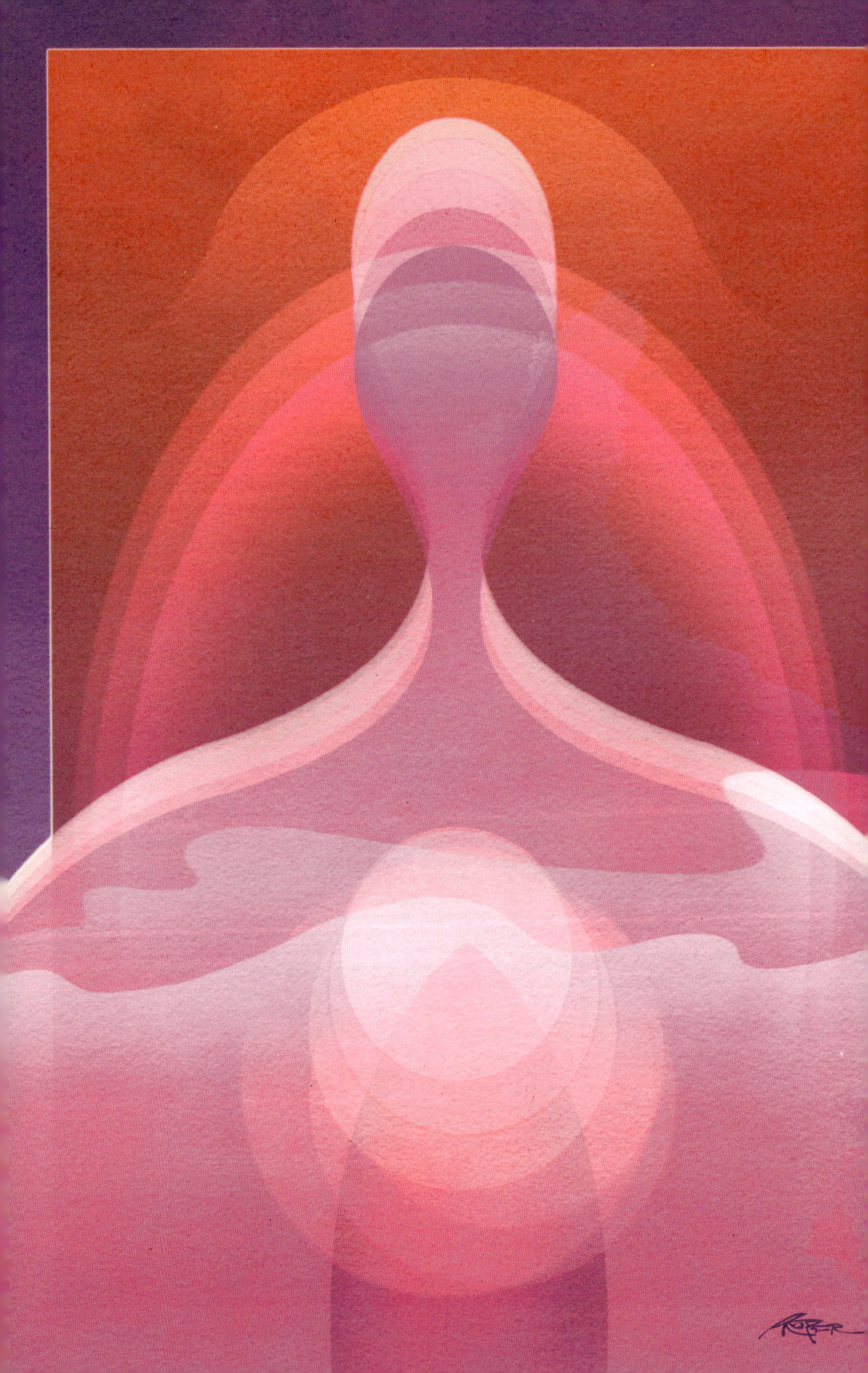

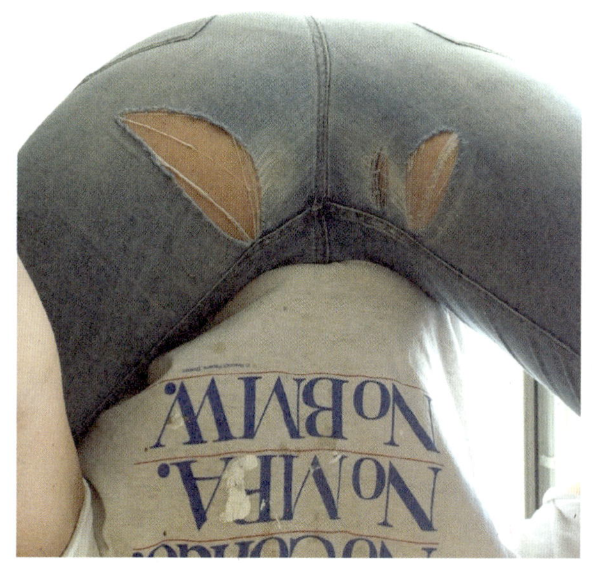

K8 HARDY: *Chub Rub*, 2013

ARIK ROPER: *Untitled*, 2013

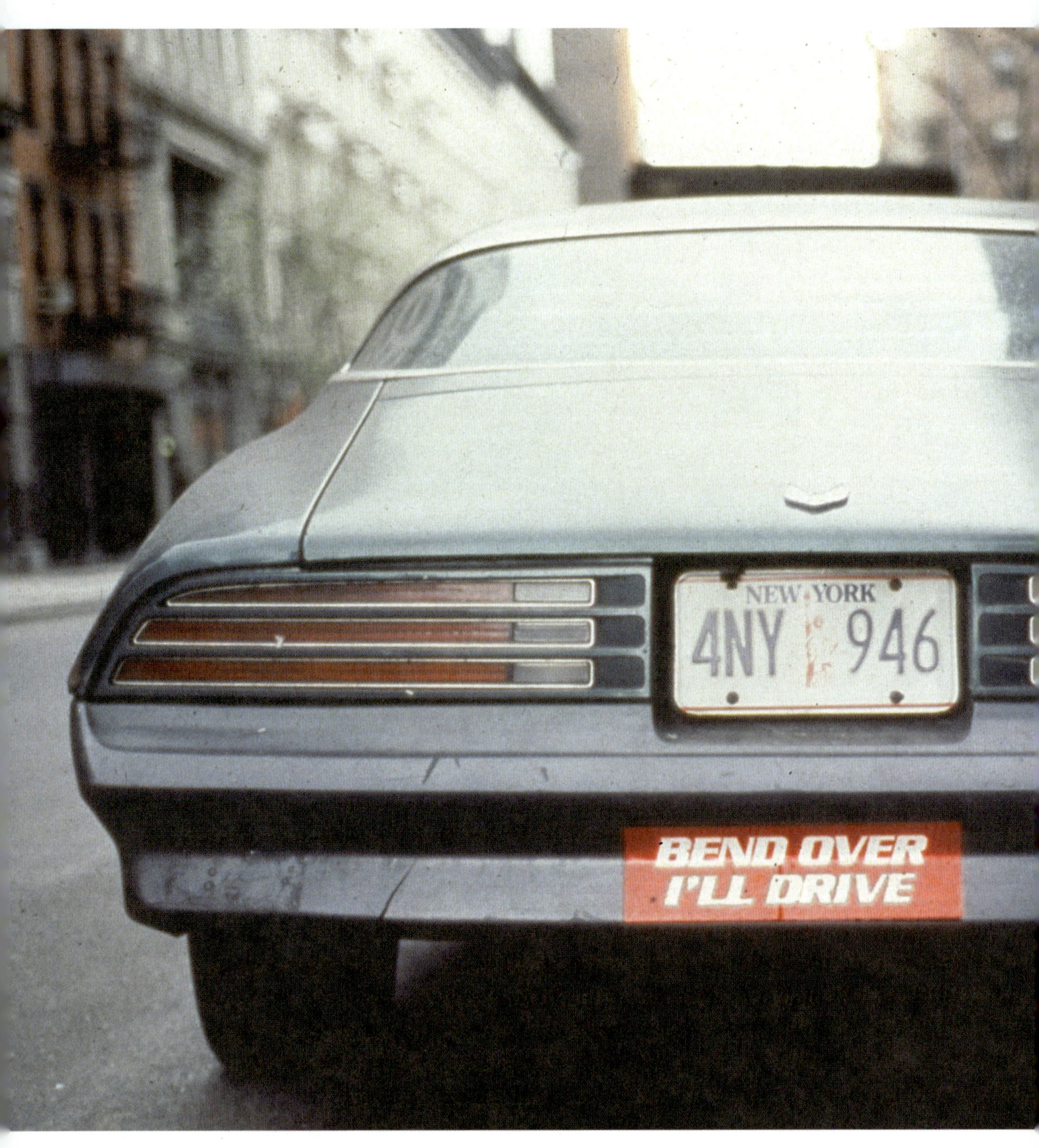

NEW·YORK
4NY 946
BEND OVER I'LL DRIVE

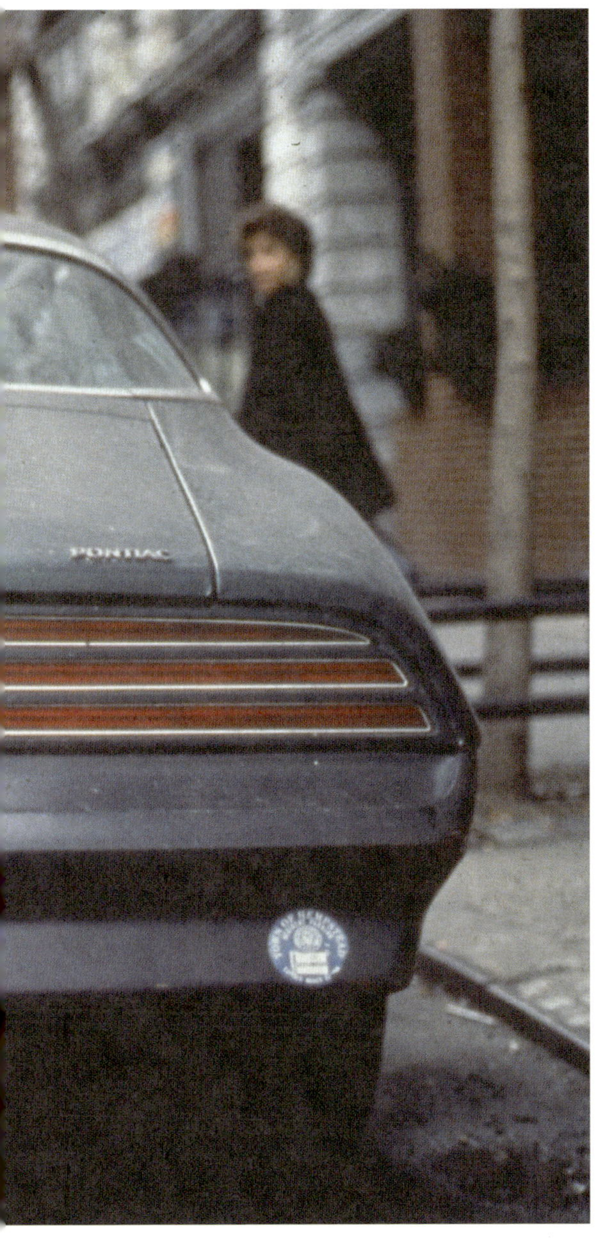

MARLENE McCARTY: *Bend Over I'll Drive*, 1990

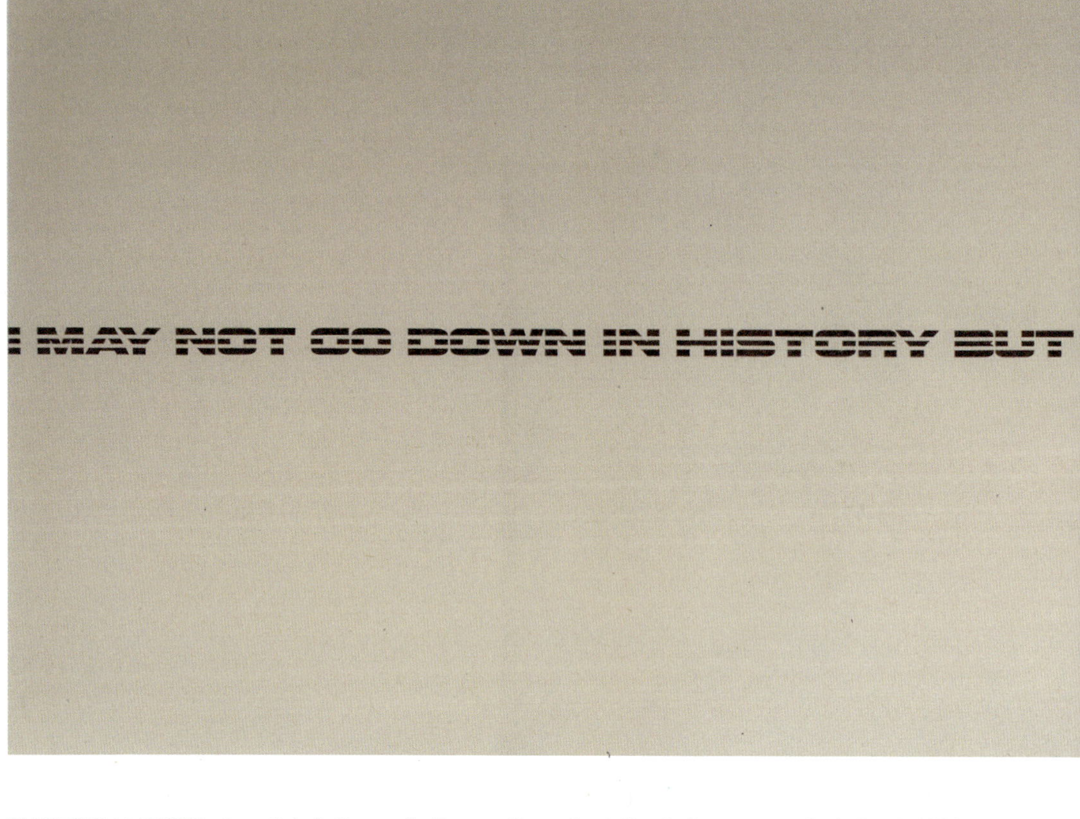

MARLENE McCARTY: *Let it Ride (I May not Go Down in History but I May Go Down on your Little Sister)*, 1991

JOHN DeANDREA: *Self-Portrait with Sculpture*, 1980

AY GO DOWN ON YOUR LITTLE SISTER

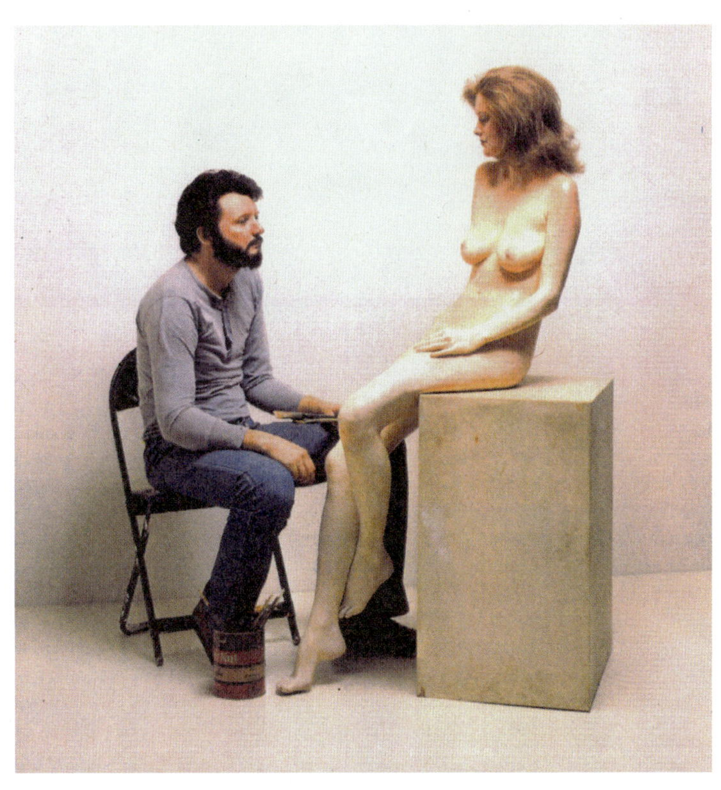

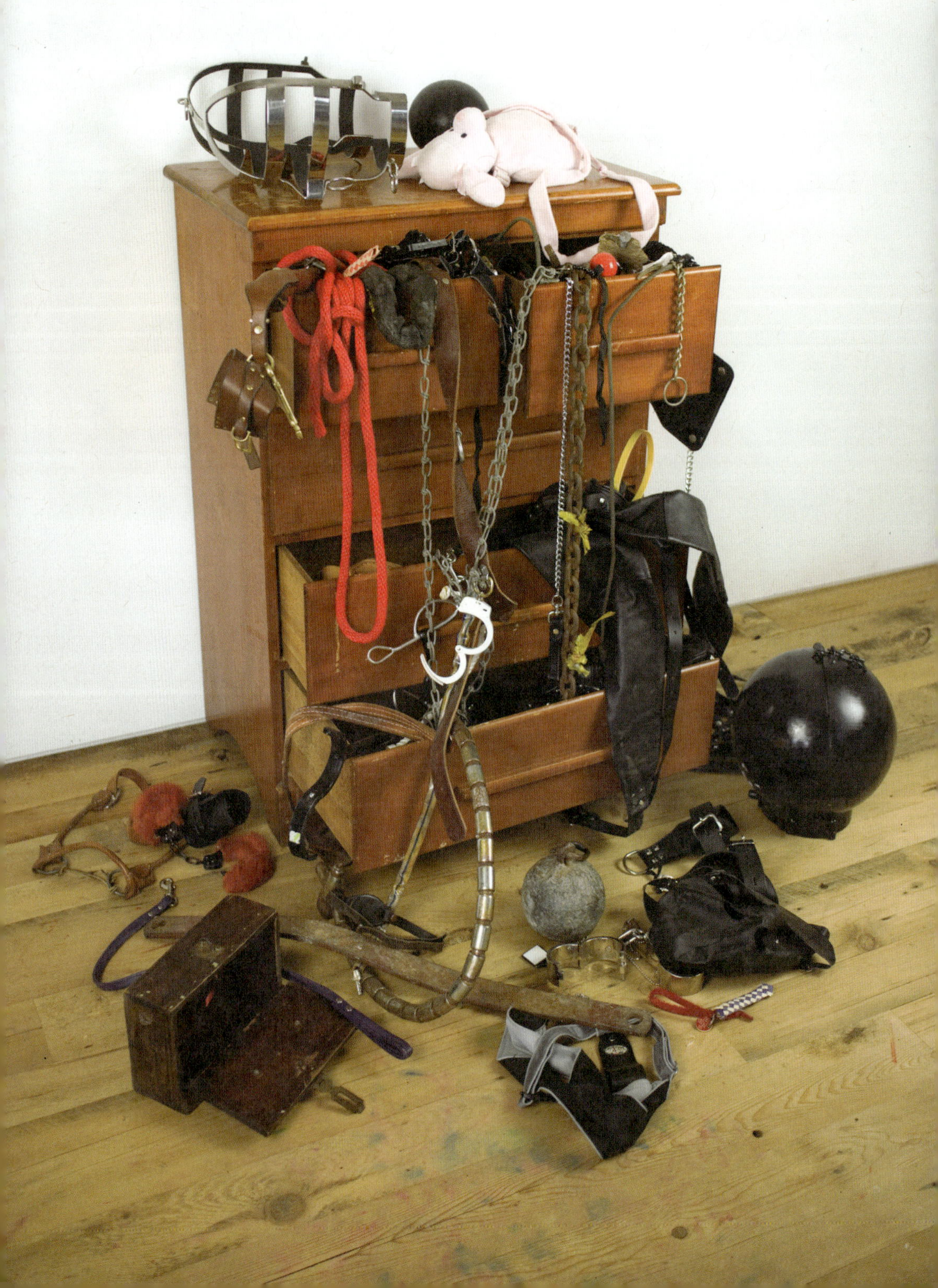

DAN COLEN: *Disappearing Act*, 2013

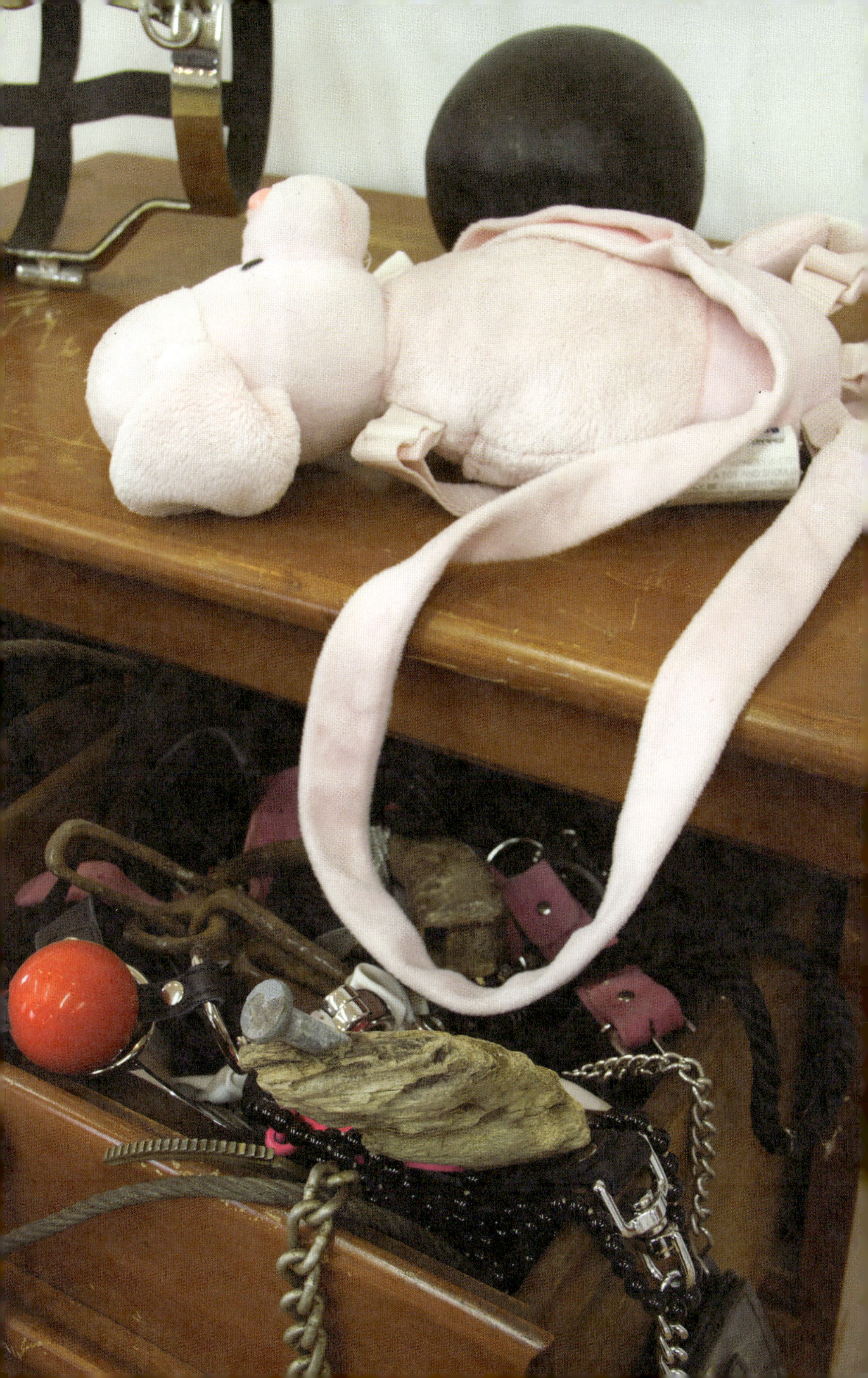

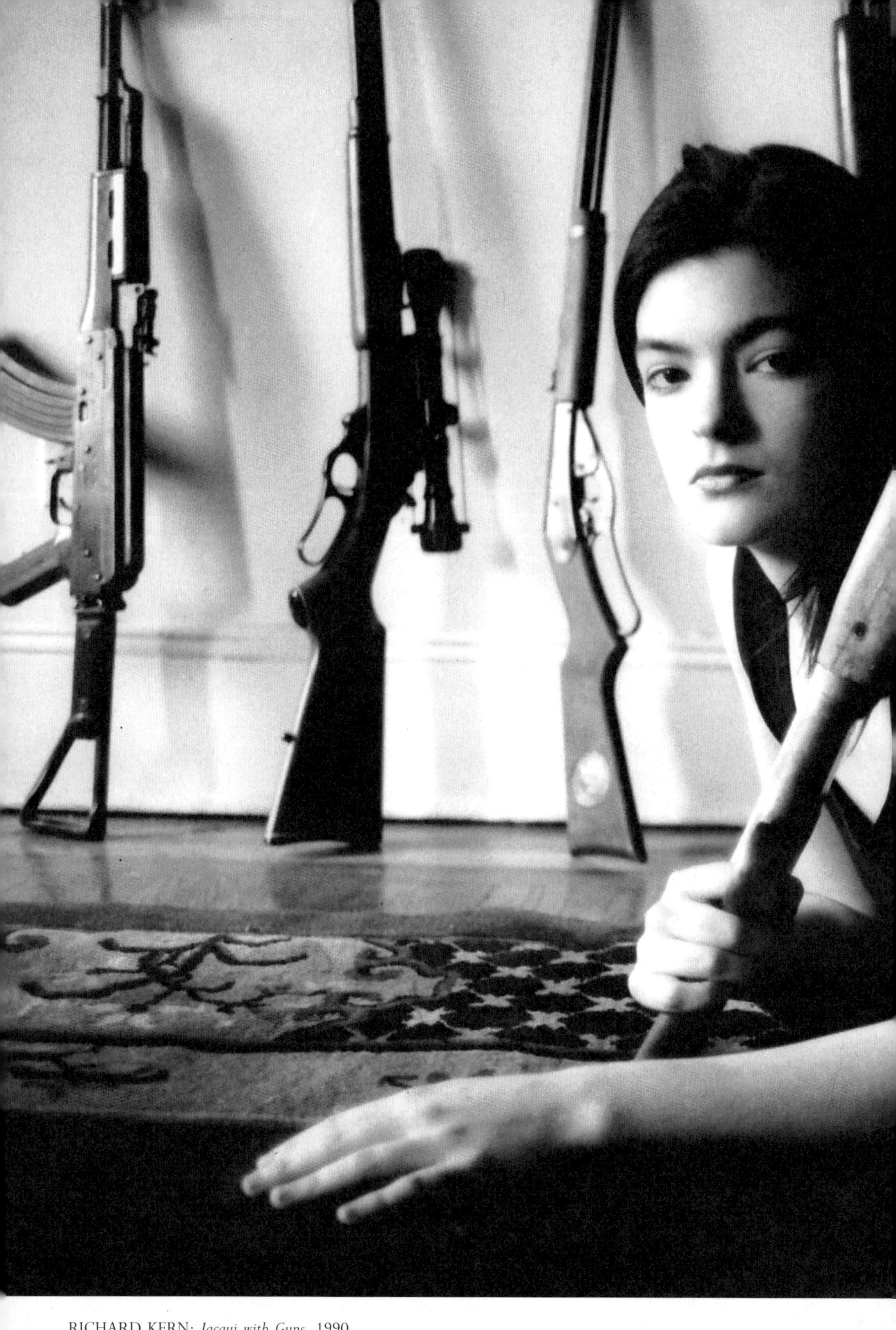

RICHARD KERN: *Jacqui with Guns*, 1990

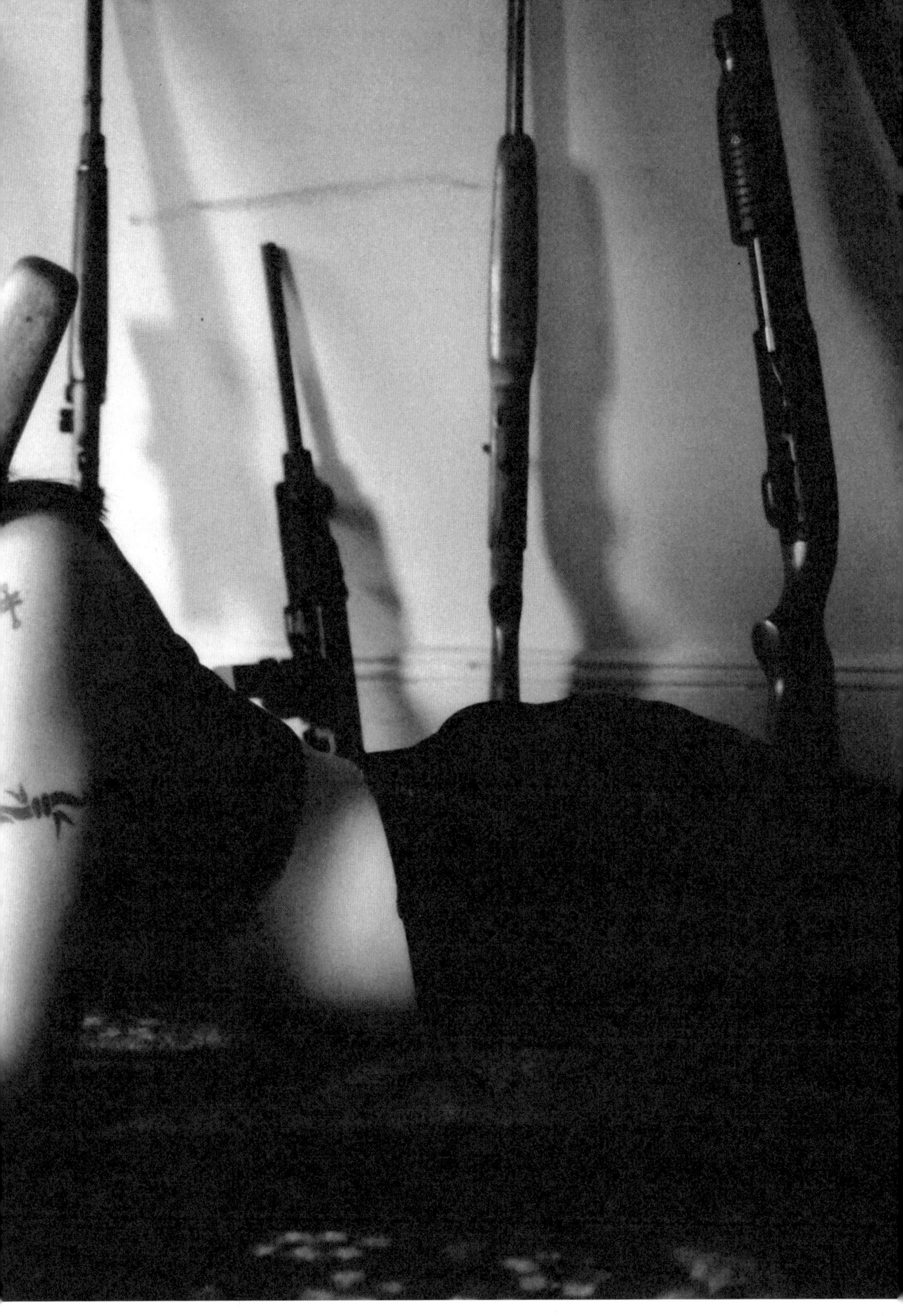

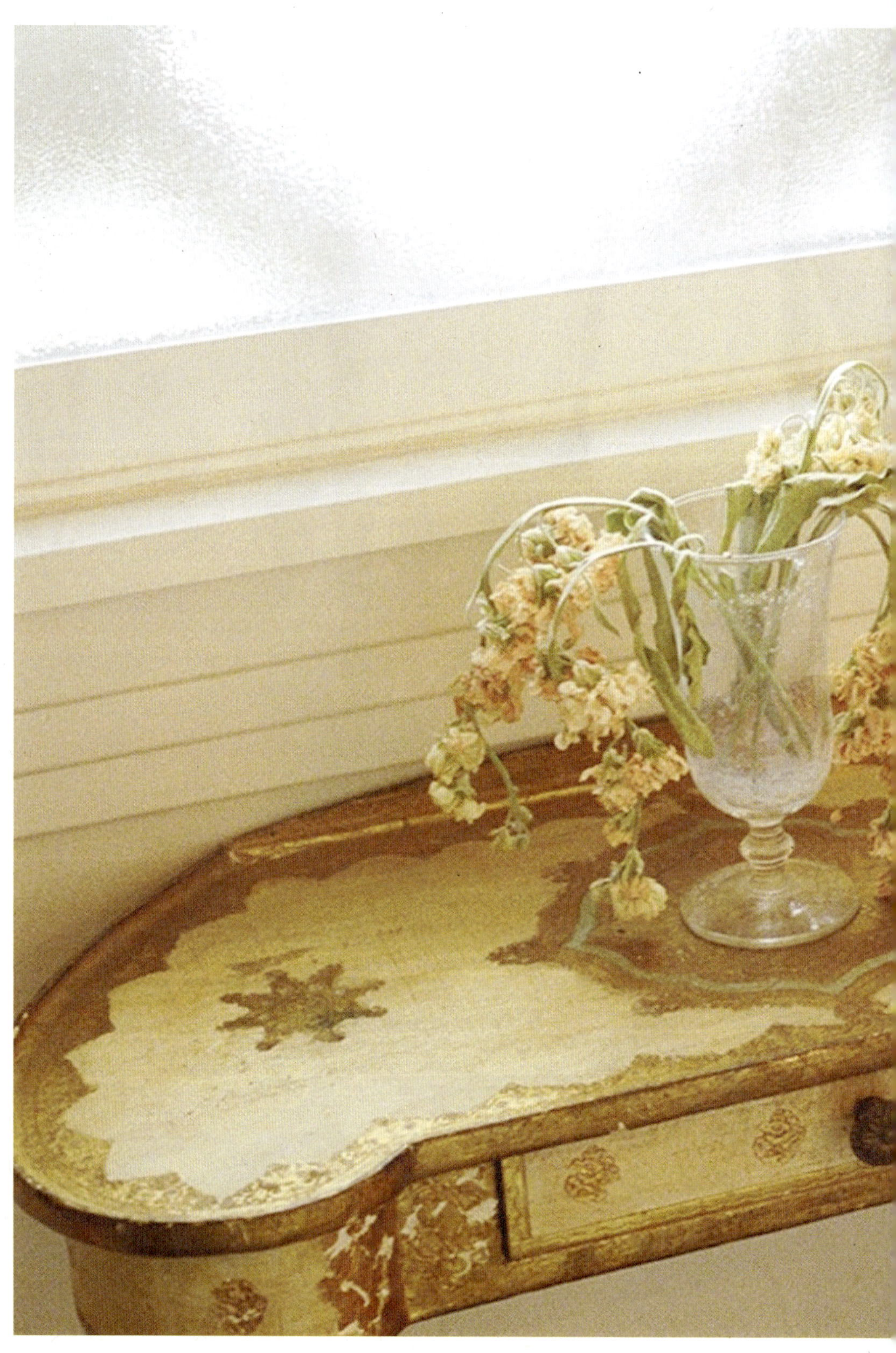

NATE WALTON: *Untitled*, 2014

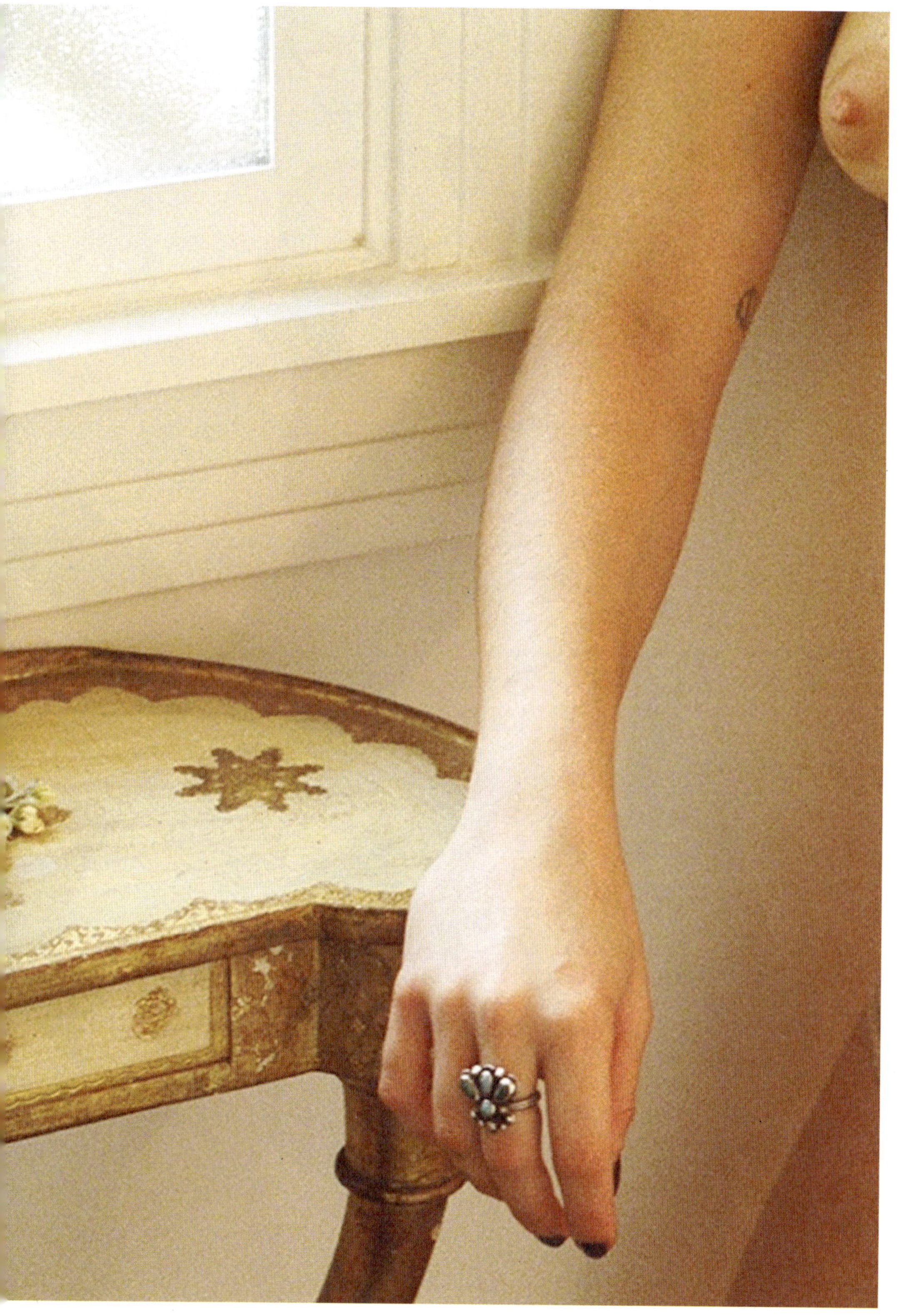

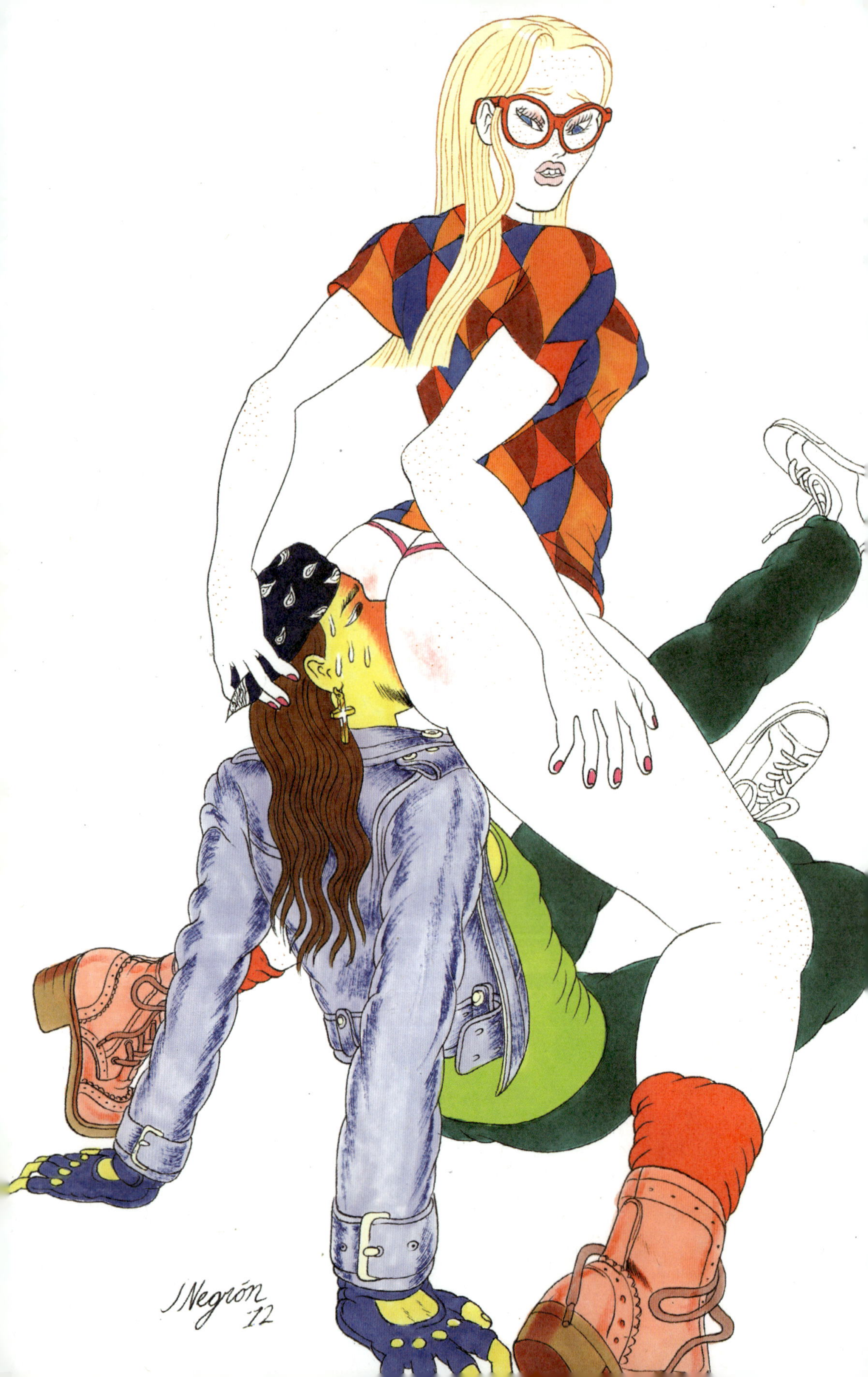

J Negrón '12

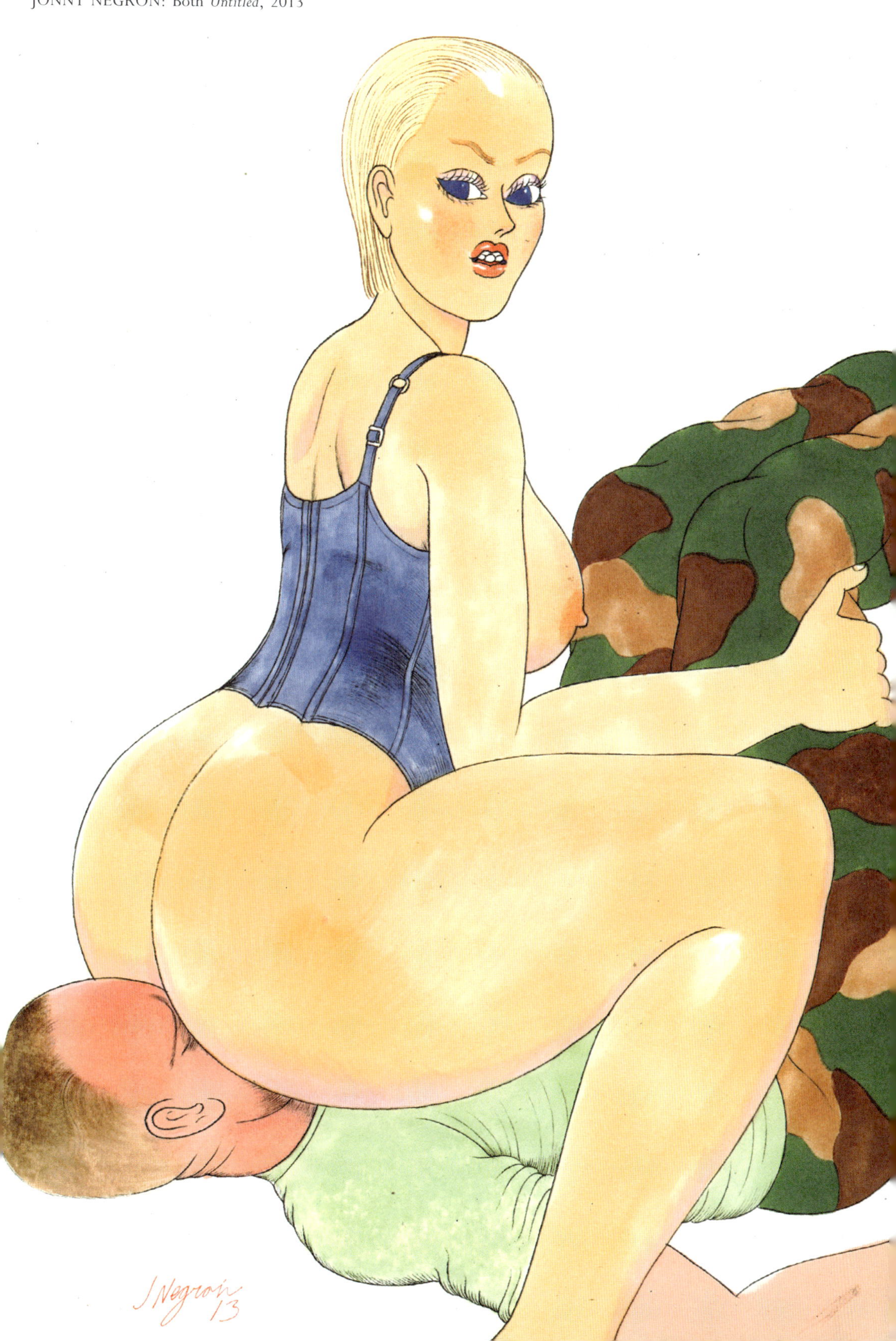
JONNY NEGRON: Both *Untitled*, 2013

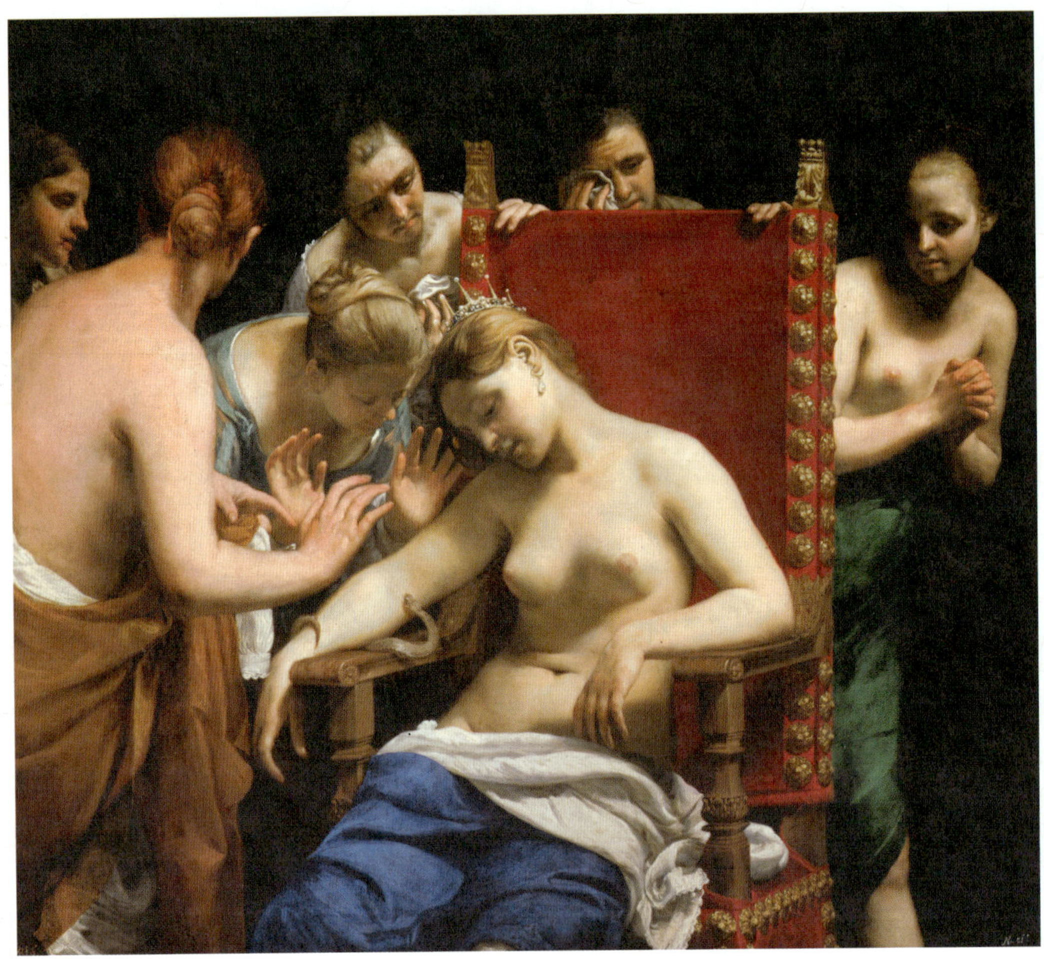

GUIDO CAGNACCI: *Cleopatra's suicide*, 1657-58

PAUL OUTERBRIDGE, JR.: *Cyclops*, ca. 1935

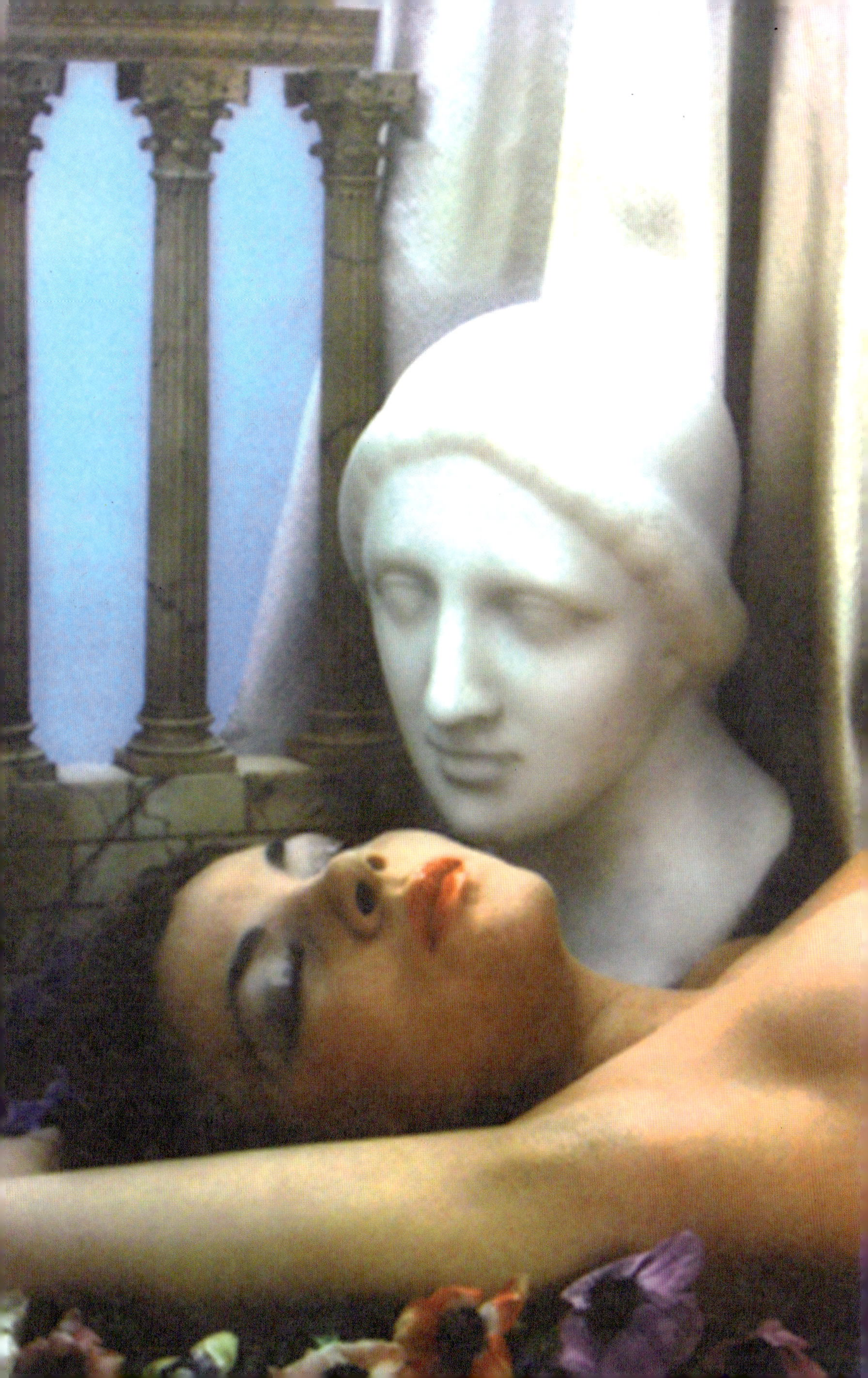

PUSSY
SERVICE

ARSEHOLE
PARTY

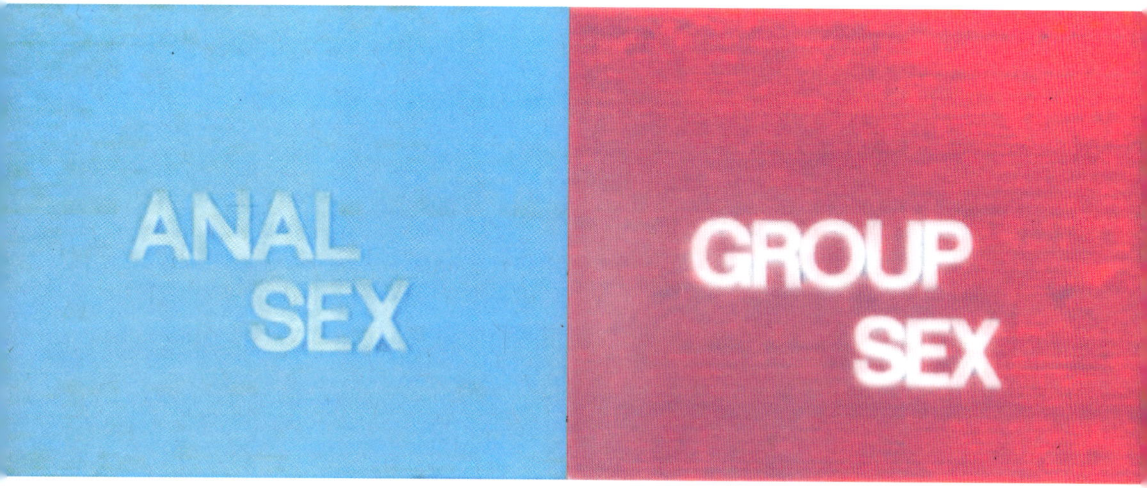

EUGENE COOK: (left) *PS/AP*, 2014; (right) *AS/GS*, 2014.

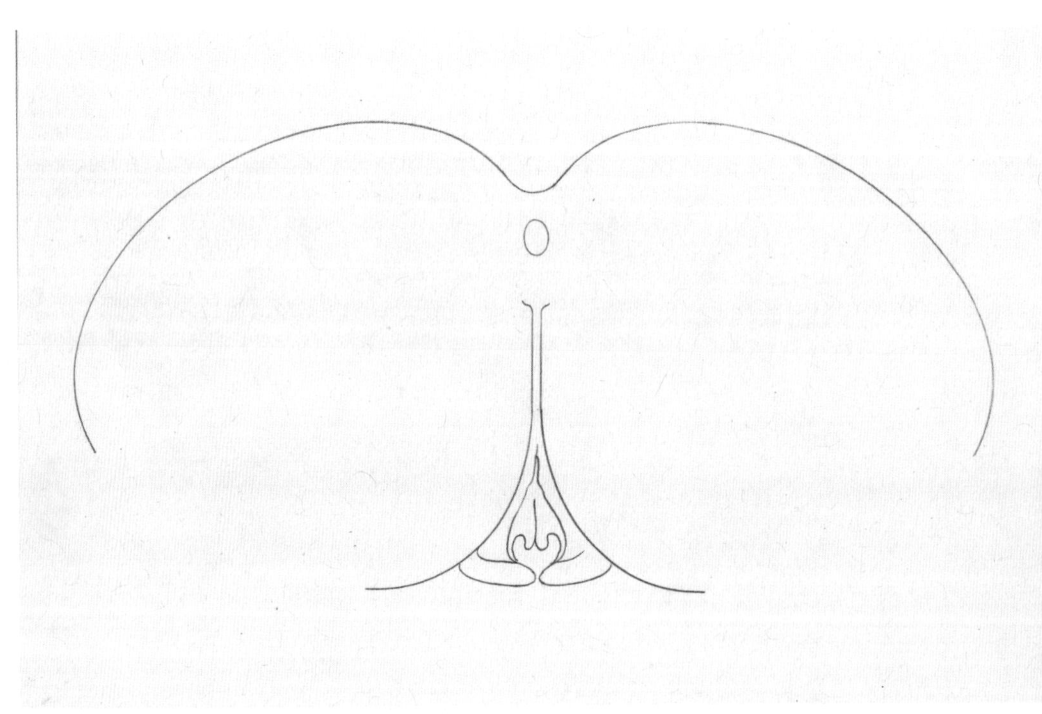

CF: *Untitled*, 2013

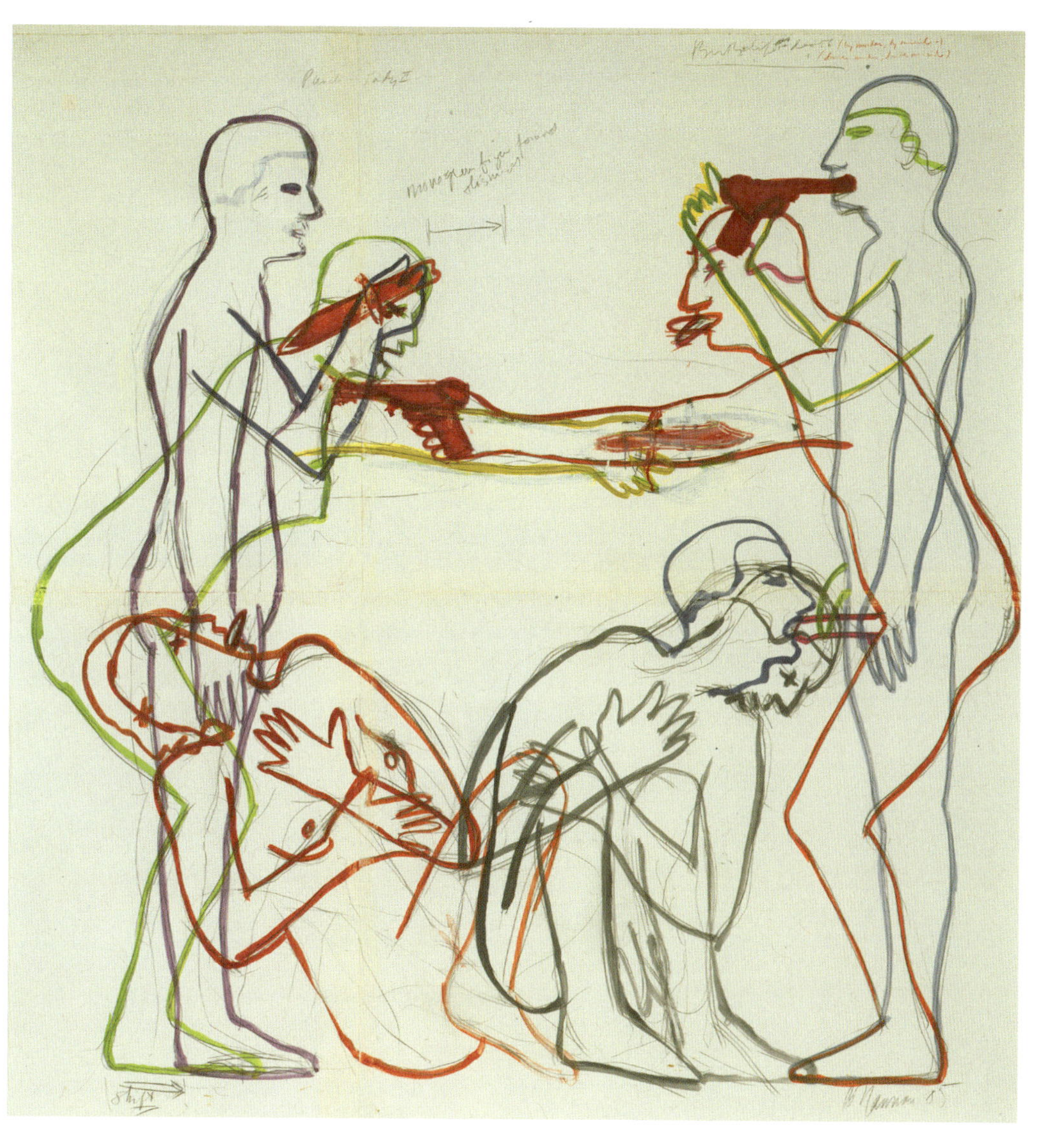

BRUCE NAUMAN: *Punch and Judy II Birth & Life & Sex & Death*, 1985

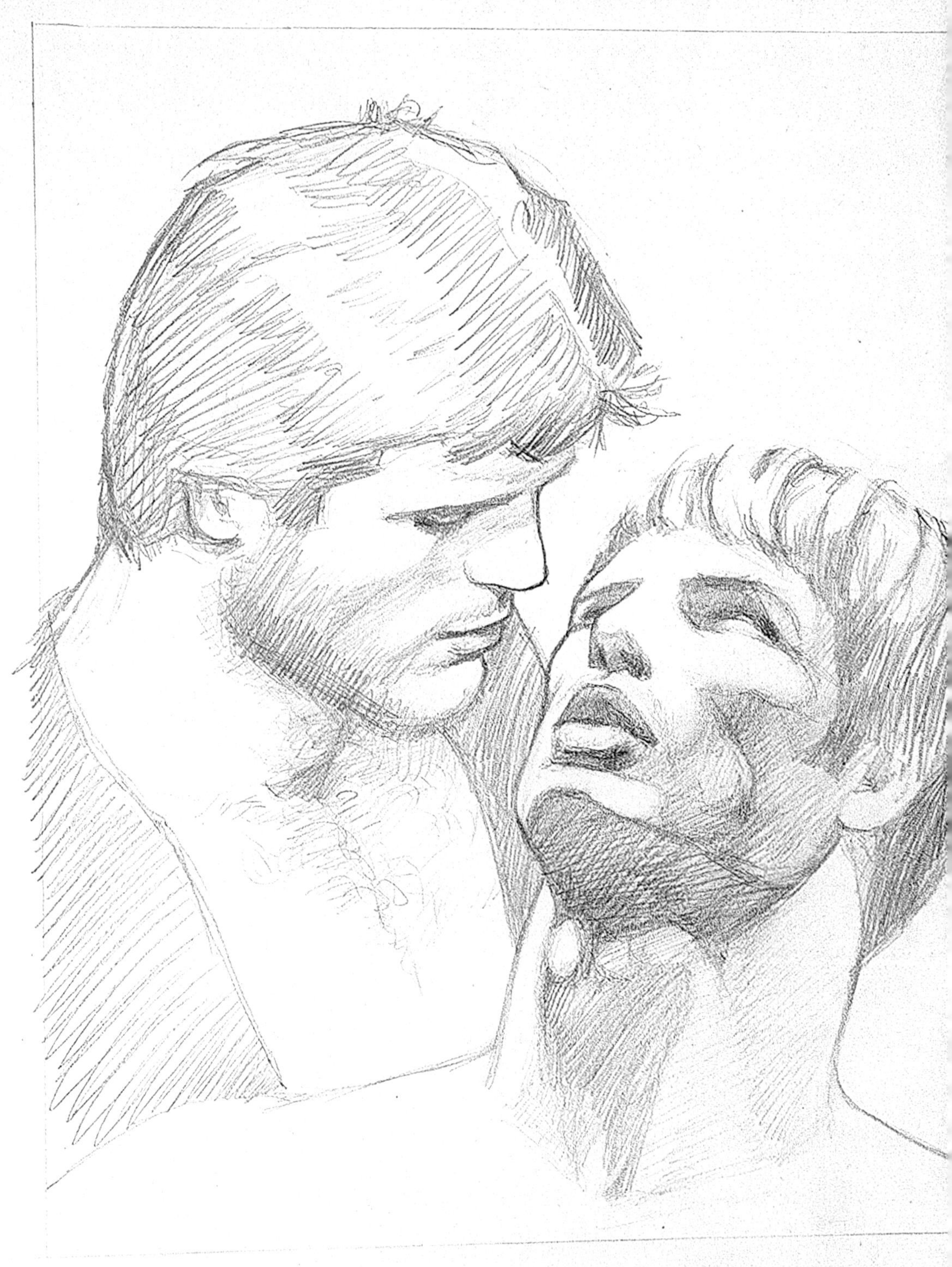

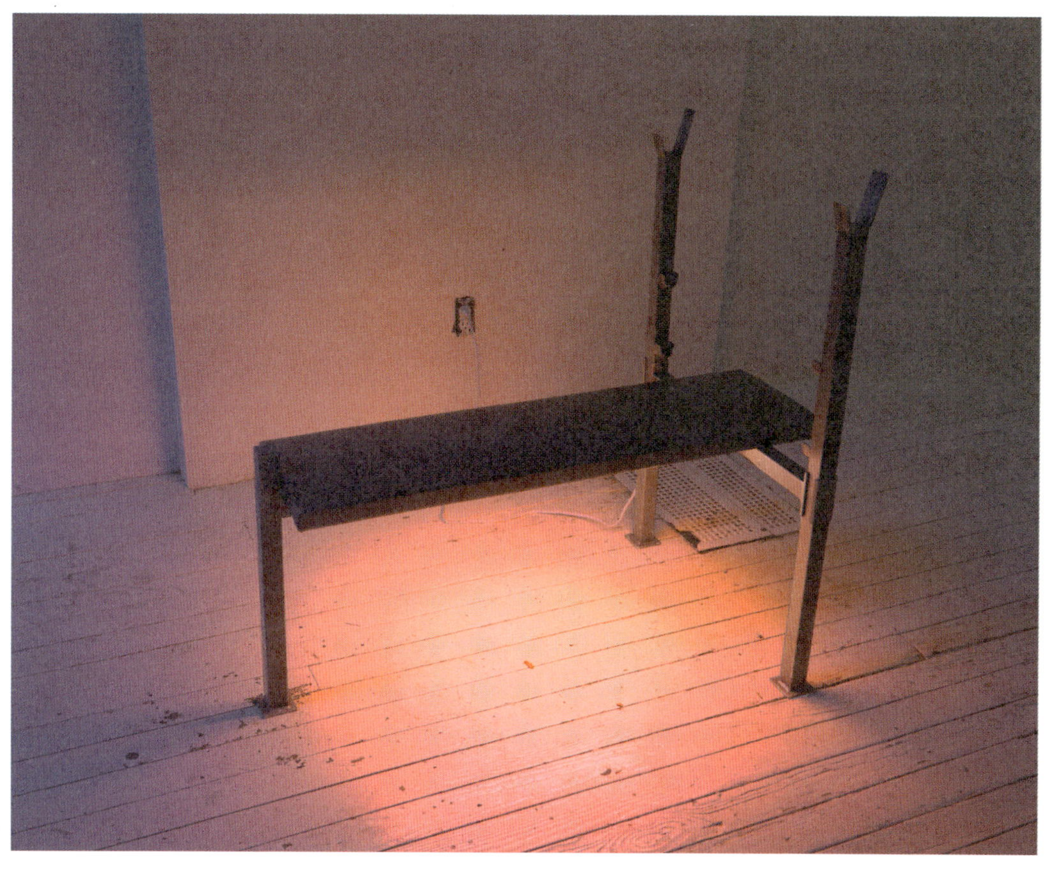

WILL BOONE: *Love Seat*, 2012

TOM OF FINLAND: *Untitled (preliminary drawing)*, 1981

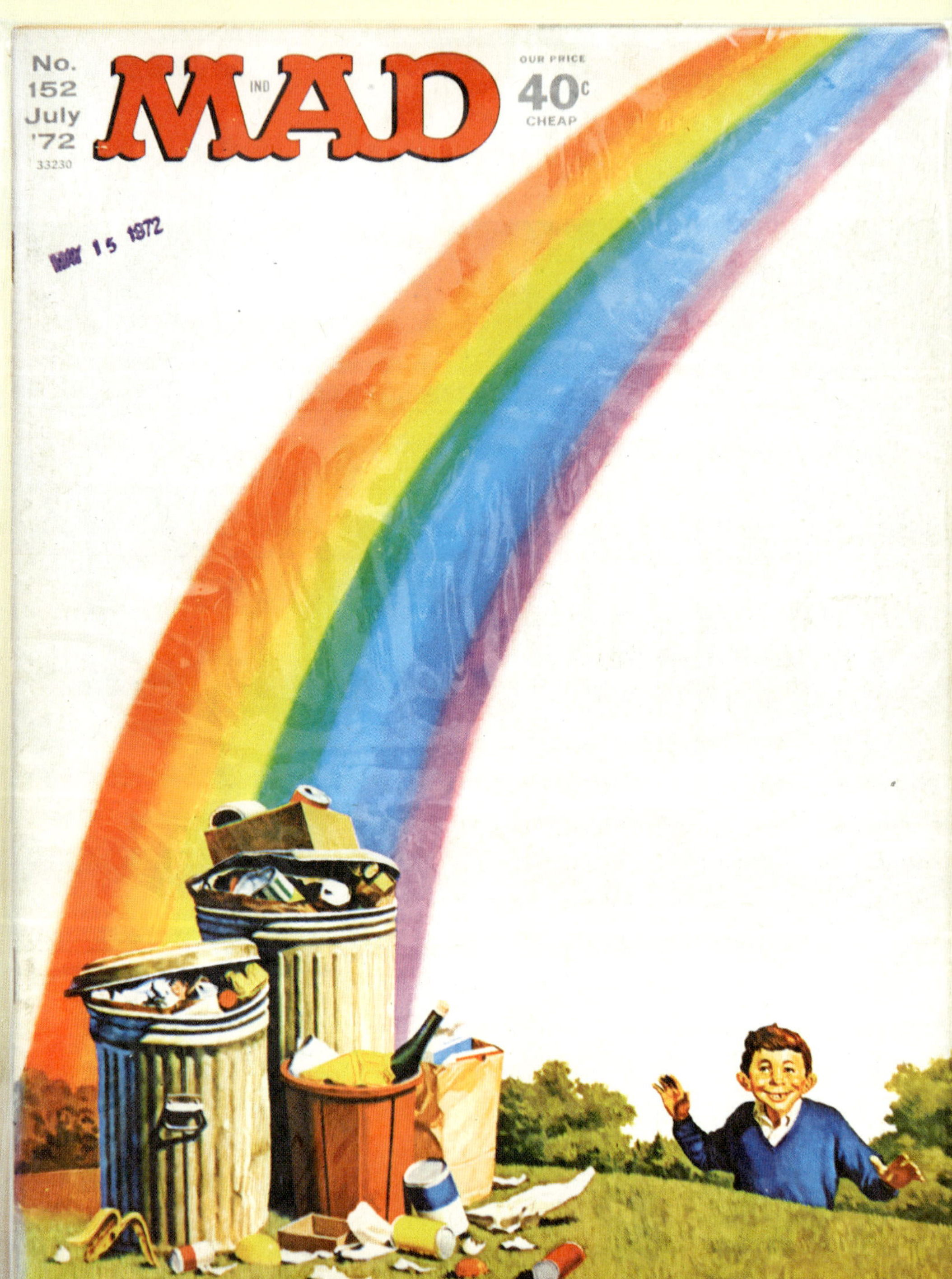

No.
152
July
'72
33230
IND MAD
OUR PRICE
40c
CHEAP
MAY 15 1972

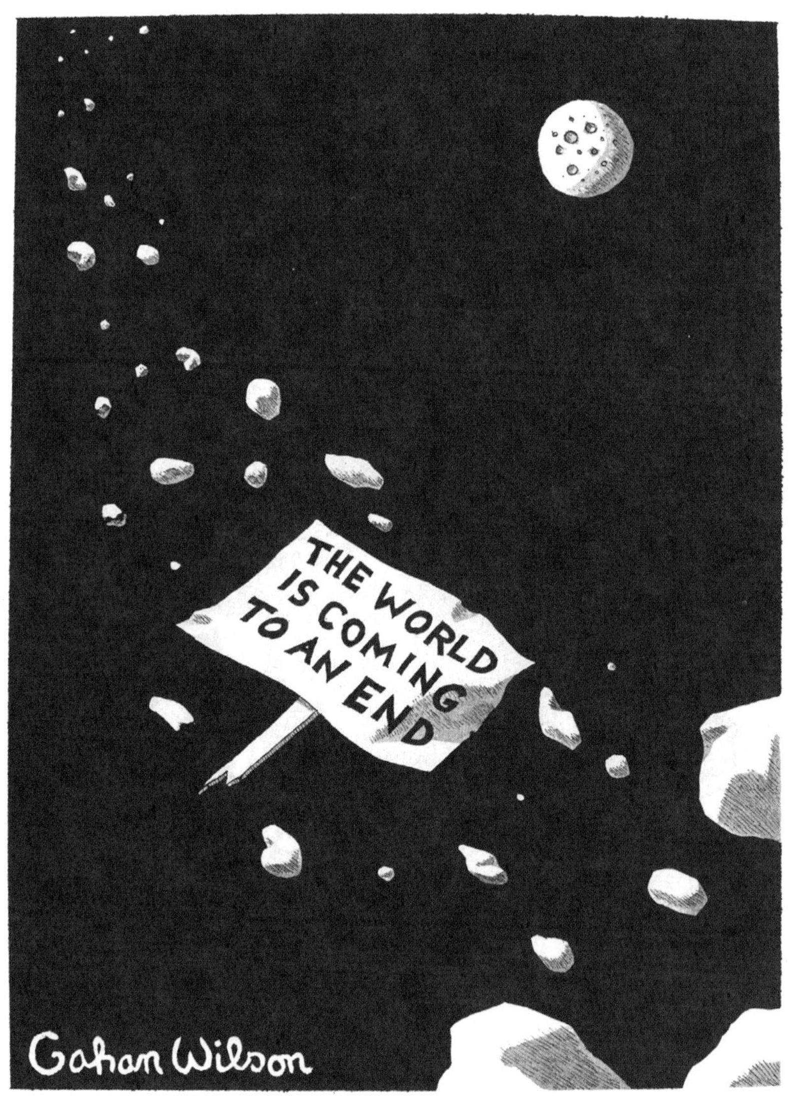

GAHAN WILSON, 1961

MAD Magazine no. 152, July 1972.

Editor's Notes

I USED TO HAVE TROUBLE coming up with an answer when people would ask me what *Apology* is. I've been guilty in the past of referring to it as a magazine even though I know that I don't want it to be a magazine. After 15 years of making them and 30 years of compulsively consuming them[1], that word has come to represent something poisonous to me. Magazines, as I define them today, are overly concerned with the moment; they want to take part in and comment on the noise of right-this-second culture. More and more, they're like the internet. And I don't like the internet.

Okay then, fine, this isn't a magazine. What is it? Even though it contains a lot of literature, it isn't a journal either. I've hinted at this in previous editor's notes, but to be explicit about it, the word "journal" conjures up, for me, an image of a distant ivory tower ringed by a joyless circle jerk of tenured professors and MFA candidates. An unexciting scene.

So when I was asked again recently to define (a.k.a. justify the very existence of) *Apology*, I flippantly said, "It's a very fancy punk zine[2]." It was kind of a joke, but it immediately made sense to me. The best zines, the ones that most seriously influenced me, were deep reflections of their creators' questions about things. Even when they were dirty or dumb, they were earnest. And they didn't make a big priority of being in step with the rest of

the world. If something that was present-tense fit into an issue, okay, great—but timeliness was never a prerequisite. The new, old, odd, profane, and beautiful all mingled; the unifying threads were the sweaty curiosities of the person who put the thing together. I could argue, I think, if you'd really want to hear me do it, that the *New Yorker* of the Harold Ross era has more in common—in terms of ethos— with zines like *Murder Can Be Fun*, *Dishwasher*, and *Rollerderby* than it does with today's version of the actual *New Yorker*.

Plus *Apology* is made by one person, me, in my home, on a cliffhanger budget. It may be in color and the paper may be nice and some of the words may be multisyllabic, but this is still a punk zine.[3] Now I get it. It feels excellent to realize that.

This issue is in large part given over to orgasms. Jamieson Webster and Ben Kafka write about Princess Marie Bonaparte, a patron and analysand of Freud's, a psychoanalyst and writer herself, and a woman who, due to her theories regarding female anatomy, had her clitoris surgically relocated more than once. I talked with the authors about the story last year, at Ben's Greenwich Village apartment, and I decided not long after to accompany it with a lengthy group art portfolio containing work that, mostly without being explicit, brings up associations with sex— often abstract or complicated associations, but still. There are echoes of the various sticky aspects of that basic human drive elsewhere in the issue too, in Tamara

---

1. This figure reflects the elapsed time since I got my first magazine subscriptions, to *MAD* and *Ranger Rick*, at age 8.

2. I said this to an uncle who has very little idea what punk is and no idea what a zine is, so… oops?

3. Almost 40 and still self-identifying as punk: sad or noble?

Faith Berger's and Amie Barrodale's stories, in Will Oldham's poem, and in the work of Leopoldine Core. I think so, at least. The respective authors may disagree with me on that point. Oh, and Daniel Arnold's photo portfolio is designed as it is for two reasons: the layout best serves the photos in terms of giving each one its own unique space, and I like imposing on you, the reader, the masturbatory tactility of having to turn this object around and around in your hands. Really.

There's also death[4] and memory in this issue. If—as many would-be undergrad dorm-room seducers would like you to believe—sex is the denial of death, then it makes sense that all those orgasms follow Paul Maliszewski's moving meditation on mortality and time capsules. Aaron Cometbus's *Suckcesspool*, a board game based on the punk scene in Pensacola, Florida, is a sort of time capsule itself, as is Alexander Chee's memoir of his brief moment in the service of the William F. Buckley family.

Anyway, that's enough of my explaining. Now I have some questions for you:

- How old is too old to dye one's hair green?
- Do I have to live in New York City to make *Apology*? I kind of want to move. Maybe down South.
- Is it weird and/or sad that I always keep a bottle of the classic Polo cologne around, but I don't wear it and instead I just spray it in the air sometimes and sniff and reminisce?
- Is my vegetarianism not really about compassion? Is it actually just a narcissistic reflection of my own fear of dying (since meat = death)?
- Are muscles kind of obscene?
- What do you think about people who do that "mmm, mmm, yum" sound when they're kissing?
- What has been your favorite year of your own life so far, and why?

Please send answers to any and all of the above to jesse@apologymagazine.com. I'll write back. Maybe I'll put some of the replies online.

As always, I offer you my undying gratitude for reading.

J.P.

---

4. I know there was a lot of death stuff in issue two as well. I'm sorry (not really). Don't tell me you don't think about it a lot too.

As I wrote in the second issue of *Apology*, I'm tired of the obligatory magazine contributors page. If you're curious about someone who did something in this issue… it's called Google.

So instead, just now, the night before this issue goes to press, I threw the I Ching for the future of *Apology*. I got hexagram 55, a.k.a. *Fêng* / Abundance (Fullness).

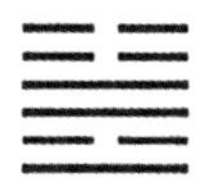 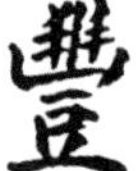

At first, this seems auspicious. The 1950 Wilhelm-Baynes edition of the *Book of Changes* tells us that *Fêng* "represents a time when clarity and progress bring about greatness and prosperity in public life." So far, so good.

But wait. See that broken line sitting at the top of the nuclear trigram *Tui* up there? The tiptop of the entire hexagram? That was a six. Wilhelm and Baynes write, "The six at the top falls into a hopelessly isolated state, for which it only has itself to blame." And they translate the commentary, in part, like this:

> His house is in a state of abundance.
> He screens off his family.
> He peers through the gate
> And no longer perceives anyone.
> For three years he sees nothing.
> Misfortune.

Good thing I don't believe in soothsaying (as of a few seconds ago).
